THE
OXBRIDGE
CONSPIRACY

THE
OXBRIDGE
CONSPIRACY

*How the Ancient Universities Have Kept Their
Stranglehold on the Establishment*

Walter Ellis

MICHAEL JOSEPH

LONDON

To Jamie,
my 'smashing' son, still some years away
from having to make any decisions about university,
and to Sue,
his mother, a new graduate of Goldsmith's College London.
Also to my own mother,
who had to watch me drop out twice and still hopes
I will one day find
a proper job.

MICHAEL JOSEPH LTD

Published by the Penguin Group
27 Wrights Lane, London w8 5TZ
Viking Penguin Inc., 375 Hudson Street, New York, New York 10014, USA
Penguin Books Australia Ltd, Ringwood, Victoria, Australia
Penguin Books Canada Ltd, 10 Alcorn Avenue, Toronto, Ontario, Canada M4V 3B2
Penguin Books (NZ) Ltd, 182–190 Wairau Road, Auckland 10, New Zealand

Penguin Books Ltd, Registered Offices: Harmondsworth, Middlesex, England

First published in Great Britain 1994
Copyright © Walter Ellis 1994

Filmset by Datix International Limited, Bungay, Suffolk
Printed in England by Clays Ltd, St Ives plc
Set in 11/13.5 pt Monophoto Sabon

ISBN 0 7181 3748 5

CONTENTS

ACKNOWLEDGEMENTS

SOME PEOPLE INSPIRED THIS BOOK. Others provided me with help and encouragement. Gina Ferry, the former information officer at Oxford, and Susie Thomas, her opposite number at The Other Place, were endlessly patient and tolerant, though they must have known in their hearts that mine was not a theme either university would cheerfully have embraced. To them, and to their colleagues, many thanks. Masters and dons, more openly dubious about my motives, were also generous with their time and opinions. There are too many of these to mention here, but their courtesy under fire remains a tribute to old-world values. I should like to record my particular gratitude to Michael Hart, senior tutor of Exeter College, Oxford, and a graduate of Cambridge, who regularly counselled me against excess and steered me in several interesting directions. It is not his fault that I hold the opinions I do. Without him, I might well have gone over the top.

In London, Graham Paterson, features editor of *The Times* – himself a Magdalen man – was unflaggingly cheerful about my work in progress. He disapproves more than most of my opinions on Oxbridge but, like the good trouper he is, defends my right to make a fool of myself in public. Matthew d'Ancona, a Fellow of All Souls and assistant editor of *The Times* and still, God rot him, only twenty-six, was equally supportive.

Various publications and authors are quoted throughout, and I have tried to ensure they are all properly acknowledged. If I hope to see further than most, it is because I am standing on a pile of other people's books. Here, too, my debt is considerable.

Finally, Susan Watt, my publisher, and Deborah Rogers, my agent, deserve my heartfelt appreciation. Without them, none of this would have been possible.

PREFACE

FIRST, I MUST MAKE MY CONFESSION. I am not a graduate. Following a confused and shameful academic career, during which time I attended both Queen's University, Belfast and the University of Durham and did not stay long enough at either to complete my studies (being educated to an extent, if not to a degree), I became a journalist. I have worked in Ireland and overseas and now live in London. Transferring to the capital, I quickly came to realize that it was not my lack of a scroll or parchment that was a problem but the fact that I had not been to Oxford or Cambridge. The same would have been true had I been a lawyer, a Conservative, a diplomat, a senior civil servant, an academic, a BBC executive, a City gent, a banker, a publisher, an aspirant to the ranks of the Great and Good, or an alternative comedian.

I am a native of Belfast, from which – in spite of the exalted example of such as C. S. Lewis and Louis MacNeice – only a privileged few achieve the coveted suffix Oxon. or Cantab. Ulster spires do not dream, they accuse, and the bells which summoned me as I revised in desultory fashion for A-levels were more likely to signal the imminent arrival of the police than a breakthrough in my academic prospects. Prior to researching this book, the nearest I ever got to Oxford – apart from a one-day visit to enquire into allegations of date-rape – was the Magdalen College May Ball in 1991. My girlfriend and I had been delayed by roadworks on the M40, and when we finally arrived it was to discover that my Oxonian colleagues were primarily concerned that I might have embarrassed them by wearing the wrong clothes. In fact, to their obvious disappointment, I had hired my antique evening dress from a theatrical costumier and was quite creditably attired. Only my revelation that I had needed the manager of the Randolph Hotel to help me do up my bow-tie saved the day for them, demonstrating yet again the hidden benefits of a 'serious' education.

They had all been to 'good' schools. At my school, a proto-comprehensive in the Protestant heartland of east Belfast, at which fellow pupils were the future rock star Van Morrison and the hostage Brian Keenan, the first boy to attend university at all was called up to the platform during morning assembly and paraded before us as a hero. Of my friends with whom I remained in touch, one rose in the teaching profession, aided by his B.Sc. (Dunelm), to become head of the mathematics department in a local comprehensive and a second is dead, murdered by loyalists while serving as a token Protestant in the Irish National Liberation Army.

Now that I am older and living in England, my everyday situation is radically altered. Most of my friends in journalism are from the two ancient universities, and so are most of *their* friends, in all walks of life. There are constant references to this period in their lives and an unswerving reliance upon it as the foundation of their careers. They keep in close touch with one another and extend every assistance to their younger successors. It is, as we shall see, the same throughout much of British public life. Oxford and Cambridge are by special appointment purveyors of learning to the gentry and manners to the more gifted, socially ambitious children of toil. As to the question, Would I have written this book if I had attended either institution?, the answer is, probably not. Almost certainly, I would have been seduced by the myth. I would have been like those new Labour MPs, recalled by Tony Benn (New College, Oxford), who enter the Palace of Westminster determined to jettison its archaic practices only to end up showing visitors the window ledge where Charles I laid his glove or the chair in which Disraeli reclined after declaring Queen Victoria Empress of India. So does this mean I am wrong and writing purely out of spite? No. It does not. I was not processed and I was not programmed, and I still see clearly, even with a jaundiced eye.

CHAPTER ONE

===

IN EXCELSIS

THIS IS THE STORY OF A PHENOMENON. It tells how the United Kingdom, a country of fifty-seven million people with an unparalleled history of global influence, became dominated by a tiny academic freemasonry and how, in spite of the fact that they generate just 2 per cent of Britain's graduate total, this same élite continues to insinuate itself into every corner of the nation's affairs.

Oxford and Cambridge, which began in the thirteenth century as grubby, ill-disciplined dormitories, presided over by a sometimes tetchy but generally benevolent priesthood, are approaching the millennium as powerhouses of research and citadels of an exclusive, nepotistic culture. They are less overtly arrogant today than they were in the past, less liable to dismiss their rivals out of hand. But they thrive on privilege, as a tropical plant thrives in the heat, and they demand deference as their due. Respect is not enough. First among equals is not enough. In spite of the relentless growth of an egalitarian counter-culture, based more on image than education, bent on seizing the economy's commanding heights, scholars from the twin cities exercise effective suzerainty over Parliament, the Civil Service, the Foreign Office, the law, the Church, banking and the City, commissions of inquiry, quangos, the high arts, publishing and the media. They lead the field in science and technology, if not in practical discovery, and are the recipients of a scale of industrial endowment of which most of their competitors can only dream. They provide us with our most acclaimed writers, our leading philosophers and our critics, being both the givers and the receivers of the glittering prizes. They even decide, by their dominance of satire and comedy, what, and who, should make us laugh. More recently, with the successful launch of international campaigns to make them richer still, they are starring increasingly on the world stage, not only educating the cream of other nations' youth but exporting their native-born graduates to Brussels, Strasbourg, New York and beyond. It has been, without doubt, a bravura performance. What makes it all the more astonishing is that it is conducted by so small a grouping. No more than a quarter of a million Oxbridge graduates are alive at any one time, and many of these are either retired or just beginning their careers. Yet little of importance escapes their grasp. As Britain moves fitfully towards the new century, with 121 rival universities clamouring for recognition and close to a million young people each year registered for degrees, the central questions remain to be answered. Who has benefited from this academic Camelot? Is it us or is it them? The man and woman in the street or the Fellows at high table and their pampered products? For whom has the whole glistering performance been staged?

Historians tells us that the United Kingdom has been in uninterrupted decline since mid-Victorian times. The Great Exhibition of 1851, generally accounted the high point of our international prestige, was in fact a last hurrah for British dynamism. From then on, direction was to be provided less and less by inventors, entrepreneurs and men of action, more and more by a tightly-knit core of well-bred administrators, trained in Latin and Greek or philosophy and mathematics. While other countries in the late nineteenth century borrowed and built upon the qualities that had made the United Kingdom the workshop of the world, Britain's leaders, backed by their administrators and the professions, resorted to military adventurism abroad and gentrification at home. It was a disastrous strategy, and we have paid dearly for it. This century alone, two world wars and the enforced retreat from empire, together with a surge in the industrial and technological strength of our rivals, have combined to leave us economically exhausted and bureaucratically bloated.

Change – a new way of doing things – has long been essential if our natural potential is once more to be realized. Everyone, certainly since the 1960s, has recognized that education holds the key – yet education is precisely what the masses have always been denied. Lacking the necessary skills, in presentation, languages and technology, and with no concept of culture going beyond popular music and the football field, the bulk of our school-leavers have been fit only for the dole queues, and that is where they have ended up. Yob education has led ineluctably to yob culture. Those in charge of our destiny see no need to slice the cake differently. The response of successive governments to the alarming education deficit has not been a return to basics (save in the discredited form advanced by the Cabinet of John Major). Instead, we have seen a succession of patricians on the one hand and self-made men (and one woman) on the other, hamstrung by their own backgrounds into thinking that government must come from above or beyond the ranks of ordinary people. Harold Macmillan, living in the twilight of empire, looked first to America, then to Europe for our salvation, but invested next to nothing in the nuts and bolts of industry. When he handed over the reins to Alec Douglas-Home (famously the fourteenth Earl), it was to a man who confessed he used matchsticks to work out the implications of the Budget. Harold Wilson, Downing Street's next incumbent, allowed his Education Secretary, Shirley Williams, to close the grammar schools and replace them with ill-conceived and underfunded comprehensives, which then floundered in the midst of an ideological morass. Having promised 'the white heat of the technological revolution', this Yorkshire lad turned Oxford don, gave priority to social engineering and compounded his error by imposing ever higher taxes on the few remaining generators of wealth. James Callaghan, the older man for whom Wilson eventually made way, famously spoke of restoring the three Rs – reading, writing and arithmetic – but did nothing about it; his own daughter had gone to Oxford and in due course he accepted a seat in the Lords. Under this former petty officer, schools crumbled. The Winter of Discontent wrapped him in its shroud. Next came Margaret Thatcher, the Iron Lady, determined to restore Britain's fortunes. She pilloried the trade unions. She also presided over a devastating reduction in our manufacturing output, arguing that service industries were the way ahead and that in future we should all work in finance houses, computer firms, or hot bread shops.

Of the above, all but Major and Callaghan went to Oxford – and both of these surrounded themselves with Oxbridge colleagues.

Throughout this comedy of errors, trudging through the mire in green wellingtons with a jaunty, confident air, those outside of government show no signs of weariness, still less of guilt. Continuity within chaos is their motto – the organized management of decline. They have led civilized lives, moving among their own kind with an effortless ease. The British Establishment, for whom economic recession is a mainly abstract experience, whose sense of duty fits hand in glove with massive self-interest, is more than anything else a product of Oxbridge. Its ethos of an all-embracing mono-culture, in which the same arrogant, sardonic, slightly sceptical tone of voice is employed whether the matter in hand be civil war in Bosnia, choosing the winner of the Booker prize or clearing the homeless from the streets of London, scarcely ever changes. What does change is the personnel. Many members of the Oxbridge Establishment were born to the task, as were their fathers before them. An increasing proportion, however, are first or second generation. Old boys of the so-called 'great' schools – Eton, Winchester, Westminster, St Paul's – are already outnumbered by those who attended private institutions of a more modest character, while a minority, mainly from the more prosperous Shires, even made it through the state system. What fuses these separate strands is the crucible of college life, fired by ambition, in which the catalyst is privilege. Not for the island race a pluralist society of all the talents. Not even in the 1990s. The millennium, rushing towards us with intimations of Armageddon, like a time-bomb with a faulty clock, will see the United Kingdom still controlled, as it has been for centuries, by a self-perpetuating oligarchy whose principal claim to reform is that it now opens its doors to a wider social mix of would-be oligarchs.

Many – and not simply those from the quads and courts – will reject this view. Oxford and Cambridge, according to the alternative scenario, are internationally renowned centres of excellence. Visionaries and scientists – intellectuals of every kind – are said to look to them as founts of ancient wisdom, and, in strictly academic terms, they rarely disappoint. At the highest level, on the plain of research and independent thought, there is ample justification for such reverence, even if from time to time it achieves the condition of idolatry. Yet in class-bound, anally retentive Britain, our instinctive response is subtly different. For if the Oxbridge claim is that they encourage undergraduates to think for themselves within an environment uniquely geared to scholarship, the more enduring reality, beyond the book-lined confines of the tutor's study, is that students preparing for their degrees are apprenticed rigorously to the Establishment.

No other interpretation is plausible. The two ancient universities may remain rock-solid in the front ranks of learning, having a preponderance of first-class dons and a high proportion of able students, but their scholastic pre-eminence is far from universal, still less automatic. Other universities have secrets, too, and in quality and volume of research as well as in terms of the teaching they provide are forces to be reckoned with. What they do not provide, critically, is a culture and an expectation. The 'Oxford' and 'Cambridge' view of the world, at once lofty and supremely practical, predicated above all else on superiority and the élitist's right of conquest, is age-old and infinitely subtle. It may not any longer sweep all before it. The grip the pair exerts over the Establishment has relaxed somewhat in recent years, and will lessen further as they shrink relatively in size. The demands of an increasingly cosmopolitan and technocratic society are already forcing employers to draw on broader sources of talent. Yet the duo continue to market themselves as universal suppliers of a *je ne sais quoi* X-factor, based on breeding, and as a result continue to be rewarded with disproportionate wealth, influence and power. Oxford and Cambridge in this context are like a pair of ageing heavyweights facing competition from hungry upstarts. They have to exercise more rigorously now to compensate for the muscular depletion brought on by their advancing years. Unlike boxers, however, they are not bound eventually to go over the hill. They have, after all, a fresh injection of youth every autumn. Instead, rejuvenated but wary, they box clever. They do not yield ground, they shift it. They bend, but they do not break.

Rightly, the process starts from first principles. Newly arrived undergraduates at Christ Church or Trinity Hall, or at Newnham or St Hugh's, are already high achievers. They have performed well in examinations and been marked down by their schools as the potential prefects of the next generation. What they are about to receive – for which they are truly thankful – is no mere academic training, but a residential course in leadership. At Oxbridge, certainly in the humanities, 'giving good interview' is more than ever the conclusive indicator of brilliance, valued above rubies, more 'revealing' than mere A-levels, and is based as much on confidence and wit as on cleverness. Candidates, though required to attain high standards in their written papers, are to a large extent selected on the principle by which Richard Ingrams used to run the satirical magazine *Private Eye*: by 'feel', by intuition, by instinct, by asking if this or that response has the 'ring of truth'. No one should be surprised by this. Camille Paglia, the American post-feminist, has observed that 'the Anglo-Saxon world tends to identify intelligence with verbal facility or aggressive wit', to the detriment of deeper qualities, and this is doubly true of Oxbridge. Applicants whose thoughts do not go off like fireworks are easily overlooked (though not, fortunately, by more modest institutions, which rely less on PR and more on examination results and school reports). History in the 1990s is superbly taught at Birmingham; Imperial College London is unsurpassed in science and engineering; Edinburgh and University College London share a continuing pre-eminence in medicine; the LSE is a world centre for government studies; Warwick, Lancaster and Bradford lead in business administration. The list could be extended further still. Sheffield, Durham, Kent: they all have real strengths. But, in social terms, and in respect of 'getting on', who cares? Once, it would have been equally important which *school* a person went to. There was only a handful of 'great' schools, and these led on naturally – often through closed scholarships – to Oxbridge. Not today. With the surge in private education since the 1960s, Eton, Winchester, Radley and the rest have had to fight for academic supremacy with up-and-coming schools which were previously thought of as 'solid', but essentially second rank. Eltham College, City of London, the Royal Grammar, Newcastle, Nottingham High School, and a range of others: for decades now, these have had achievements among the best in the country, and their expectations have risen accordingly. A number of the better state schools, often in middle-class catchment areas far removed from the inner cities, have understandably attempted to follow suit, sometimes with spectacular success. But as the secondary base has broadened almost out of recognition, higher education continues to be overshadowed by its twin peaks. To the heads and leading figures of our greatest institutions, controlling the professions and the corridors of power, Oxbridge is an ever-fixèd mark, and it is as academies for the nation's traditional and nouvelle élites, geared also to the cultivation of influence world-wide, that they must primarily be viewed.

In making this claim, it would be foolish in the extreme to argue that Oxford and Cambridge are not superb at what they do best. They have the greatest wealth, the highest overall funding, the most glorious and best-appointed facilities and a significant number of the most able academics and students. Research carried out at both universities is in a number of areas among the most highly regarded in the world, reflecting the volume of Nobel prize-winners in residence and the ubiquity of Fellows of the Royal Society. The duo's finest graduates are a credit to the nation – and no wonder. The unique Oxbridge tutorial system, unaffordable elsewhere, yields a degree of personal supervision of undergraduates that tends to bring out the best in young minds, while college life encourages an intimacy to develop between contemporaries and between students and their teachers that is educationally beneficial and socially attractive. Intellectual rigour at the two institutions is, moreover, usually at a high level, encouraged by the sometimes austere exigencies of dons who, since the division of Seconds into 'upper' and 'lower' ranks, no longer smile benignly on a 'gentleman's Third'. Shirkers, and fools, *can* survive an Oxbridge career – and some do – but they have to work at it, and these days such errant behaviour can be more trouble than it is worth.

This much then is beyond dispute. The crucial question that remains is the attitude to Oxbridge of the British people, especially the English. The deference syndrome (not to be confused with respect for learning) by which this country is run, depending on birth, wealth, education and fame, has Oxbridge at its heart. Eton, Winchester, inherited titles and high-profile public status (as with rock stars and billionaire tycoons) are part of the same nexus. Yet, post war, post the 1944 Education Act, post the death of grammar schools, post the Beatles, even post Margaret Thatcher, it is the nation's limpet-like attachment to Oxbridge which most routinely typifies the veneration phenomenon. England reposes a deep faith in its ancient universities. The dons are not responsible for this. But they encourage it. Indeed, they depend on it for their survival as the supreme achievement of our educational system and trade openly in its myths. Who can blame them? They provide the aura; it is society which basks in it and remarks on its wonders.

Builders and planners perpetuate the myth. In London alone, there are thirty-seven roads named after Oxford, as well as Oxford Circus, and no fewer than sixty-five called after Cambridge, plus Cambridge Circus. Manchester is equally well provided. The tally there is Oxford thirty-three, Cambridge twenty-seven. Liverpool even has its own 'Little Oxbridge', a district in which all of the streets are named after colleges, and, on a lesser scale, such collegiate roads and avenues are a commonplace throughout the country. Perhaps it is an academic question, but were they named after their old Alma Maters by nostalgic councillors and officials, or did the names just somehow 'spring to mind'?

Without such deference to them, such automatic cap-doffing, graduates from Oxbridge would be forced to compete for position on a more equal footing with their rivals, particularly at the upper levels of influence and power, and Britain – still struggling to advance from first base in its understanding of meritocracy – would benefit immeasurably in the process.

How long must we wait before there is evidence of change? The answer, for those educated outside the quads and courts, is less than encouraging. British society is much altered from its stereotype. Royalty and the aristocracy have become the stuff of idle gossip. Real wealth is shifting out of the hands of landowners and Lloyd's Names to entrepreneurs, rock stars, leading athletes and market-makers on commission. Official Britain, from the Foreign Office down, no longer presents itself as a granite-faced monolith, reflecting the interests of a single class united by blood and obligation. Instead, politicians, diplomats, lawyers and the rest are sharper, more pragmatic and more truly outward-looking than at any time for five hundred years. Other professions are similarly opening up.

The contention of this volume, however, is that Oxford and Cambridge remain central to the debate. The two no longer have total power. As new generations of Redbrick graduates grow in strength and numbers, they are probably weaker now in absolute terms than at any time since 1945. But the power that remains is considerable and skilfully placed, adroitly adapted to changing conditions: the influence they exercise across the spectrum of our public and professional life is vast. To adapt Churchill's famous speech on Ulster after the war: The whole map of Britain has been changed. People's mode of thought, the whole outlook on affairs, the grouping of parties, all have encountered violent and tremendous changes in the deluge of the world, but as the flood subsides and the waters fall we see the dreaming spires of Oxbridge emerging once again. Their power, in its inequity, is one of the few institutions that has been left unaltered in the cataclysm which has swept Britain.

All that has happened since the Education Act of 1944 and the introduction of universal benefits is that, with characteristic flair, Oxbridge has adapted to the new order. The two great universities already had this country in the palms of their hands. Now, pausing only to check that nothing interesting has slipped irrevocably from their grasp, they are looking beyond. Britain's membership of the European Community, the growing internationalization of banking and manufacturing, increased co-operation in infrastructure, the arts, science and defence, even the growth in influence of the United Nations: these developments have meant the dramatic efflorescence of a global bureaucracy – a kind of nascent One World Establishment – and Oxford and Cambridge, liberal, wise, self-seeking and ruthless, are in on the ground floor.

The ambition that drives home-grown undergraduates is progressively governed less each year by the needs of the traditional professions and more by an appreciation of the rich pickings at the heart of the Global Village, generated by information technology and mass transit. Amid the revolution's roar, one truth remains inviolate: wherever power is to be found, in England it is along the central artery linking Oxford and Cambridge to the capital, that the pulse is strongest. Whether it is the training of future judges and mandarins or of would-be officials of the World Bank or the European Commission, it is this axis that provides the vital link between aspiration and achievement.

Consider first the domestic world that is slowly passing: of 250 British men and women in the 1990 edition of *Who's Who*, chosen at random from among its 28,000 entries, 106 had attended either Oxford or Cambridge. Of those who had not, 25 were service officers (drawn mainly from the military equivalents, Sandhurst, Dartmouth and Cranwell), 11 were defiantly Scottish (Glasgow, Edinburgh, Aberdeen), and the rest were typically landowning members of the aristocracy (too idle, too rich, or too stupid to bother with study), scientists and engineers, sportsmen and businessmen.

The House of Lords, not surprisingly, is in the very van of reaction. An astonishing 510 out of its 1,186 members in 1991 went to one or other of the two ancient universities – 264 to Oxford, 246 to Cambridge – producing a penetration rate for the dynamic duo of 43 per cent. No other university, with the exception of London, even made it into double figures, and in the overall list of peers' Alma Maters, only Eton finished higher, with honourable mention going to the Royal Agricultural College in Cirencester – Britain's premier finishing school for landed toffs. Many peers chose the army (often Sandhurst) over university, and others obviously felt that, after boarding school, further learning was unnecessary. But the significance of the 43 per cent is that barons, earls and the rest are either preternaturally more gifted than the rest of us or else, more convincingly, that they are not obliged to function on anything so plebeian as ability alone.

If anything, the *Who's Who* test underestimates the situation. Jeremy Paxman (St Catharine's College, Cambridge), the suave and deadly presenter of *Newsnight*, on BBC2, interviewed 157 men and women of influence for his book, *Friends in High Places: Who Runs Britain?* (Michael Joseph, 1990). Of the 136 of these whose academic provenance I have been able to trace, a thumping 89 were Oxbridge products, a strike rate of 66 per cent, or two thirds. When one considers that several of the 157 were foreign-born, a number were Scots and no fewer than 18 were high-ranking service officers, the percentage becomes even more impressive. Extracting the Sandhurst sector alone (with which civilian institutions do not, by definition, compete) would take the Varsity element of those with known backgrounds up to 75 per cent – an overwhelming dominance, impossible to justify. So long as the imperial trick worked – Oxbridge ran Britain and Britain ran the world – excuses could be found for such a smug and self-perpetuating oligarchy. Alternatively had our Oxbridge élite changed with the times and led Britain into a beneficial relationship with our European neighbours, founded on mutual respect, then, once again, the existing academic gene pool would have proved its worth. Oxbridge would have proved itself in the market-place. But who could honestly claim that recent British history has shown the Establishment's capacity for wise leadership? No. While Oxbridge has concentrated on maintaining its key role in the governance of Britain and its institutions, as far as possible to the exclusion of others, the compact between the leaders and the led, which allowed inequities to flourish for the sake of the whole, has been broken and society is fracturing.

It is not, of course, the case that Oxbridge is the *cause* of Britain's sorry decline. There are various reasons for the breakdown of trust, most of them far beyond the scope of this book, and consequences which are for others to disentangle. In addition, much of the research carried out in both places is of positive benefit to this country and the world, especially in the fields of science and engineering. Yet there is no disguising the fact that Oxbridge graduates have been in charge of the nation's affairs throughout the last half century and remain largely in place today. The implication is clear. The ruling class looks after itself. Oxford and Cambridge are the marshalling yards for the gravy train. If you are English and without preformed military ambition and wish to be a member of the dominant élite, you know which carriages you have to board. It is true that you can reach desirable destinations via Liverpool or Hull – though it is easier through London, Bristol or York. These, though, are branch lines, with stopping trains that frequently end up in a siding or jammed against the buffers. The Bisto Express, by contrast, runs exclusively from the Isis and the Cam and reaches into all corners of the kingdom and beyond. No other country, not excluding France, with its Ecole Nationale d'Administration and its *grandes écoles*, has so narrow an élitist base. Enarques are at least up front about their calling and concentrate *by definition* on government. They are, moreover, already graduates of other institutions who have gained entry through open competition and are contracted to the government service for at least seven years. The *écoles normales*, of ancient foundation, cater for politics, engineering, mathematics and literature in sites spread throughout the country, while law and the sciences, as well as other subjects at a less-rarefied level, are the province of regular universities, like the

Sorbonne, available to all who have passed the baccalaureate. American Ivy Leaguers come not from two but eight separate institutions (Brown, Columbia, Cornell, Dartmouth, Harvard, Pennsylvania, Princeton and Yale) and, with the possible exception of lawyers from Harvard and Yale, are no more privileged these days than graduates from any other high-grade institute, such as Stanford, MIT, Berkeley, Chicago or Missouri. In Germany, attendance at Heidelberg, Marburg or Bonn arguably retains a certain social cachet within what remains of the aristocracy but means nothing to the hard-faced guardians of the *Wirtschaftswunder*. The same logic holds true for Japan. While the universities of Tokyo and Kyoto enjoy considerable prestige, they are merely first among equals, turning out technocrats as though on a production line. There is literally nowhere else *quite* like Oxbridge.

And yet, and yet . . . here is a strange thing. German education may have given up most of its ancient, home-based privileges, but this does not mean German students do not feel the lack of them. There are now nearly as many Germans as Scots at Oxford and Cambridge, and their numbers are growing every year, alongside the swelling delegations from Italy and France. The Japanese meritocracy would famously kill for an Oxbridge place; the coincidence that Crown Prince Naruhito went to Merton and his wife Princess Masako to Balliol has virtually given a period of residence in Oxford a 'By Royal Appointment' stamp. Large numbers of Americans have meanwhile been coming to the two universities since Victorian days, both as students and teachers. The fact that President Clinton smoked pot (but did not inhale) while a Rhodes Scholar at University College at the end of the Sixties and demonstrated there against the Vietnam War was one of the more entertaining controversies of his 1992 campaign. Today, at least ten of Clinton's closest advisers are fellow Rhodesians, and young Americans anxious to make it to the top in government look as keenly as ever to England's mysterious engine of power. In spite of mischievous suggestions that Oxford actually turned the future President off England and the English, the evidence of their power has added fresh glamour to the dreaming spires.

Asia is also awake to the possibilities. Chinese students, mainly from Hong Kong, are already a commonplace – unlike East Europeans, who are just beginning to appear on college registers. Indians, Singaporeans and Malaysians have been mainstays of Cambridge science courses for a generation. With a cynical genius that cannot be denied, fund-raisers from both universities have in recent years begun to promote their privileged package in a big way overseas, thus helping to make up for the shortfall in funds brought on by Britain's relative economic decline. No one can blame them for this. In a sense, all they are doing is re-creating the idea, considered obvious in the Middle Ages, of the university as an international fellowship, owing only limited allegiance to its country of origin. Scholarship, after all, with its historical basis in moral philosophy, is not supposed to recognize boundaries. At the same time, the universities are clearly making a moral virtue out of economic necessity, blindly following the market, uncertain of the long-term consequences for what it is they are trying to sell. Should the worst come to the worst, Oxbridge reckons, and Redbrick Britain eventually becomes a reality, then the alternative strategy will already be in place – Oxford and Cambridge as World Universities, using the UK as an academic aircraft carrier, with the same loyalty to Blighty as British Airways in one of its periodic fits of 'going American'.

What is beyond doubt is the reputation both universities enjoy abroad, even among our favourite enemies. John Rolley (Lincoln College, Oxford), representative in France of the *Financial Times*, is among those to have profited. 'Many French do not understand the British education system', he told *Oxford Today*. 'How could I be director here without a marketing degree? But there's a terrific amount of glamour attached to Oxford's reputation. People expect you to recite Proust or speak seven languages.' Chanteclair, the pen name of a leading Paris academic, author of *Pour et Finir avec l'Anglais*, takes a rather different, if slightly tongue-in-cheek, view. He holds that the English send their children to public schools to learn sport, arrogance and homosexuality and then to Oxford or Cambridge 'where they perfect the pretentious and disdainful accent which is necessary for their social success'.

In Asia, such 'familial' doubts are less in evidence. Lee Tong Won, a South Korean academic who took a D.Phil. at Oxford in 1958, was left a fortune by his father, a successful property developer, 'to be used for some noble work', and has set his heart on creating a mini-Oxford just outside Seoul. Known, improbably, as the Lee Tong Won College of Technology, its aim is to bring Oxford standards to Korea, and one of its first visitors was Dr Baruch Blumberg, the Nobel Prize-winning Master of Balliol. 'Oxford is famous in Asia', Dr Lee confides. 'When my own father was young, he dreamed of going to Oxford, the best university in the world, to get the best education in the world, and then to bring back something really positive to Korea. But he was too poor, and we were under Japanese domination, so it was impossible. But all through my childhood it was Oxford, Oxford, Oxford!' Dr Lee's son, Lee Jung Hoon, has already followed in his father's footsteps, and his grandson was there for his graduation.

Such may be the Seoul view, but it is not unique. For the moment, it is still possible to see Oxbridge as the stone equivalents of Tennyson's 'immemorial elms' – an embodiment of an England half as old as time without which our culture would be irredeemably impaired. Tempting, but wrong. *Brideshead Revisited* is a fable of decay and renewal in which (in this case) Oxford is presented as a magic kingdom uniquely attuned to the English psyche. The reality is that Oxbridge, for all its charm and undoubted intellectual energy, is, in terms of its effect on British society, a dangerous delusion – a narcoleptic drug from whose influence many under-graduates never truly awaken. Britain has declined non-stop during the last hundred years of Varsity dominance, and while the reasons for this decline are many and various it is certain that it has in no way been arrested by the Oxbridge Establishment. If the products of academe's twin peaks are so clever, the argument must surely go – so gifted, so 'rounded', so amply imbued with the Right Stuff – how is it that the nation whose institutions they control is in such an unholy and disreputable mess? How is it that Britain's brightest and best (so confident of their superiority as to be amazed in one instance that *only* 82 per cent of judges appointed in 1993 were Oxbridge) have guided themselves to the Promised Land, but left the rest of us in the mire? Can it be that we have been deceived? Can it be that *they* are getting good value for *our* money? Yes, indeed. And as they do so, Britain has been sleep-walking into Europe's second division. Oxbridge takes our young aristocrats, our sons and daughters of gentlefolk and our comprehensive school 'achievers' and it fuses their disparate interests, lulling them into a hazy acceptance that this is the best of all possible worlds, to be preserved intact in the memory and sustained, unaltered, for future generations. Most who pass through its college portals emerge with a 2:1 or a 2:2 in their chosen discipline; thousands more achieve starred Firsts in nostalgia.

So how well do they love her? Let us count the ways. The haunting, medieval rooms, seductive in their redolence of past generations; the college servants, the roaring fires reflected in tutors' half-moon spectacles; the mellow, golden stone, the cobbles underfoot; the muscled 'Eights' gliding across the silver Isis or the rippling Cam, punts awash with Chablis and long-legged girls in cotton frocks; the tea shops, the tinkling of bicycle bells and the grander peals from brooding, rose-pink towers; the deer in the park and the paths in flower; the uncertain procession of dons into high table, the fine wines and brandy and earnest conversation over silver salvers about everything and nothing; the Boat Race and Twickers; the loving and the laughter and the rush of independence and the cramming; the essays and the exams and the headlong rush to finals, and, last of all, and sweetest, the May Ball and the champagne and the tragedy of parting and the resolve never to let it fade but to protect each and every one who shared in this, and the creation amid tearful embrace of a new generation of the brotherhood. For they have fed on honeydew and drunk the milk of paradise. Year follows year and age succeeds age, and nothing changes. This is the constancy of the myth.

Other universities evoke nostalgia, too, derived from their graduates' recollection of a time of youthful freedom. The scale, however, does not begin to compare. To Kenneth Clarke, the present Chancellor of the Exchequer, his three years reading law at Gonville and Caius, Cambridge, from 1959–62, were, he told me, 'the most formative time of my life'. He was president of the Union, president of the University Conservative Association, and chairman of what has since become the Federation of Conservative Students.

I had a lot of friends [at Cambridge], a high proportion of whom became Conservative politicians. We were always known as the 'Cambridge Mafia' ... I used to find myself entertaining people to coffee most mornings as I held a kind of central coffee place where my mates dropped in, including a high proportion of politicians. I therefore held a general drifting-in-and-out of people, of which Norman [Lamont] was a particularly frequent participant. I spent most of the nights playing bridge – the only bad habit I've since given up – with Norman Stone, who is now a rather controversial, highly entertaining Professor of History at Oxford. Another of my contemporaries was Colin Renfrew, and just to show how aged we have become and how much we have joined the Establishment, he is now Lord Renfrew, Master of Jesus. He could have been a politician but, no doubt wisely, he preferred to be an archaeologist. Not all of my friends went to the bad and became politicians – one of them was David Frost.

The story of how Clarke and his pals went on from Cambridge to take over the country has been told and retold. The bombardment of gossip relates, however, just as much to the present as to the past. Almost every day brings news from the front. To take examples from recent newspapers presently in front of me, the *Daily Telegraph* informs us that the choir of Christ Church Cathedral is, at the time of writing, about to tour America. Beneath a photograph of himself and two fellow undergraduate choristers, shown against a backdrop of the college grounds, one Charles Mindenhall is quoted as saying: 'Americans always give us a warm welcome. They can't get over the Oxford thing. Some of them think we're all lords.' No doubt they do. In the same week, a letter in *The Times* records a denial by Professor Patrick Collinson, a Fellow of Trinity College, Cambridge, that the Cambridge history faculty is 'at war' over the renewal of Dr John Adamson's fellowship at Peterhouse. 'What Peterhouse chooses to do about a renewable fellowship is a matter for Peterhouse', the professor confides, nevertheless sharing his view with the nation. In the London *Evening Standard*, the interest in Cambridge life is more aesthetic than academic. We are told of a controversy concerning 'a handsome oak-panelled screen' in King's College Chapel removed in the 1960s to make way for Rubens's *Adoration of the Magi*. Some Fellows evidently want the screen restored to its rightful place, and the Dean, the Rev Dr George Pattison, agrees that 'it is not impossible that there has been some private discussion along these lines'. The nation holds its breath. The *Standard* next reveals that during a visit to Oxford by the actor Warren Beatty, the Union Society has upheld the motion that 'homosexuality is a positive force in the community'. Not quite 'King and Country', perhaps – the 1930s motion that split the nation – but still jolly good fun. During the debate, two young men reportedly 'jumped to their feet and gave an Athenian display of affection, to hoots from the audience'. Even the Roux Brothers, Britain's favourite French chefs, have been subjected to Oxbridge's baleful influence. 'Dear Albert', writes Vic Grant, from London NW6, in a letter to the cookery corner of the *Evening Standard*, 'Having come down from Oxford I wish to recreate the atmosphere of formal hall in my London digs, but there is one aspect of breakfast I cannot fathom. Mine is lumpy and chewy and I like it creamy and smooth. What is the secret of porridge?' What indeed? More to the point, why is Vic Grant still lodged mentally in the cloisters?

There are many other instances. John Mortimer's daughter, Emily, we are told, founded a literary magazine at Oxford called *Babel*, while Nat, the son of Lord Rothschild, had earlier helped launch the somewhat racier *Rumpus*. More alarmingly, Booker, prize winner Ben Okri, a Fellow Commoner at Trinity College, Cambridge, was seemingly mistaken for an engineer at high table. 'Over the claret', The *Mail on Sunday* disclosed, 'they were convinced he'd said he was working on "friction" not, "fiction".'

What is most revealing is the assumption that the nation will wish to know these things. It is equally assumed that they will not wish to learn what is happening in the Redbrick world. We do not hear about *faux pas* over brown ale in the chemistry department in Bradford. There are no retainers for student diarists in Leicester. And just about the only time the press consults the records of University College, Cardiff, is to discover if Neil Kinnock's pass degree was really as bad as his detractors claim. It is all of a piece. When John McCarthy, the former hostage, was released by his Shiite captors in 1991, Peter Millar (Magdalen, Oxford), a leading writer on the *Sunday Times*, praised his confidence and composure, which were apparently all the more remarkable considering he had secured 'a second class degree from a second class university' (Hull).

Sadder still than the obsession of the press is the obsession of some Varsity graduates themselves. In February 1994, a classified ad, by no means unique of its type, appeared in the Weekend Section of *The Times*.

> OXFORD GRADUATE, wife sadly died
> aged 34, 3 children boarding, seeks gentle,
> perceptive, possibly shy Establishment girl,
> 25–34.

This is a man who, like Vic Grant, defines himself by his university and expects others to do the same. An Establishment girl is what he wants, and although she must be 'perceptive' it is evident that what she should perceive first is the calibre of the man she is about to encounter.

Surely, this cannot go on. Surely there must be change! Ah, but reform has already taken place. The Cambridge Admissions Forum has disclosed that for the 1993–4 academic year, more first-year places were awarded to pupils from state schools than to those from the private sector. State school applicants had been offered 45.4 per cent of the record 3,068 places available in October, having achieved at least two grade As and a B at A-level, compared with 45.3 per cent from the private sector and 9.3 per cent of "others" (foreign and mature students and products of further education colleges). Cambridge, unlike Oxford, abolished its own entrance examination in 1986, preferring, for the most part, to rely on A-levels and interview, and the result in the case of the 1993 entry was that state schools – mainly grant-maintained grammar schools or Shire comprehensives – had a majority over the private counterparts of precisely 4 (1,393 compared with 1,389). In the previous year, 1992–3, the intake was 46.3 per cent state, 43.6 per cent private, slightly more favourable to the maintained sector. At Oxford, in the same year, state schools (again, mainly from more prosperous areas) increased their share of places for the second successive year, by almost 1 percentage point, to 43.7 per cent. Pupils from independent schools gained 46.6 per cent of places, a decline of 2 points. Overseas students – an increasingly important sector for both universities – made up the balance. Cambridge's 'shocking' preference for the unprivileged did not pass unnoticed. Dr Eric Anderson, the former headmaster of Eton – himself since translated to Oxford as Rector of Lincoln – commented dryly that, as a result of Cambridge's reform, a growing proportion of pupils from the most academic independent schools now preferred Oxford.

Anderson's comment is revealing. It underlines that Oxbridge and advantage are held to be indivisible. Young people opt for the ancient universities because they want more than a good education; they want the imprimatur of those who govern them, and they expect to be recognized for what they are – a united fraternity – to the very end of their days.

Donald Trelford, editor of the *Observer* for eighteen years until relinquishing his post as part of a takeover, recalled in an interview published in the *Sunday Times Magazine* soon after his departure how he had once been staying at the Master's Lodge of Selwyn College, where he had studied as an undergraduate in the late 1950s, when it was suggested to him that his daughter Sally should follow in his footsteps and come to Cambridge. 'We're going to have to take these women, so we might as well have daughters of chaps we know', was the way it was put. Trelford, the great liberal, concurred with enthusiasm and put the idea to Sally almost at once, only to meet with a spirited rebuff.

'Daddy', his daughter informed him, 'that's the most disgraceful thing I ever heard. Just think of all those people who don't have your advantages.'

Trelford replied: 'But darling, *I'm* one of those people' (his parents were of coalmining stock) '. . . when people come to me for a job, Oxford or Cambridge is still a factor.'

Sally stuck to her guns and went to Sussex. But was she wise? At the time of writing, she was deputy editor of a travel magazine in Brighton. And she *could* have been a contender!

So strong is the caste conditioning that it sometimes even produces a paradoxical effect. Self-proclaimed radicals – even traitors like Guy Burgess and Donald Maclean – are easily encompassed within the twin universities' gilded cloisters. They are protected and in-dulged by the more compliant majority and even permitted to mock their comrades in the manner of a jester making sport of his king. Anthony Blunt, architect of the 1930s Cambridge nest of spies, was indulged by his university peers to the very hour of his exposure by Mrs Thatcher in the Commons in 1981 and then, effectively, died of mortification. Burgess, though he did his best to betray a generation, is thought of as a gentleman, not a cad. He was a bit of a wag, perhaps, an 'Apostle' and a 'queer', and clearly not sound on politics but, at heart, he remained 'one of us'. Alan Bennett's award-winning play, *Single Spies*, make this abundantly clear. The audience is told precisely the nature of Burgesses's treachery, yet its sympathies never leave him and, at the end, it is to the strains of Gilbert & Sullivan's 'He is an Englishman' that poor, brave Guy makes his exit. The same twisted logic applies to 'alternative' comedians, dissolute artists, anarchists, even converts to Buddhism. They may sometimes try the patience of their peers but only rarely will they be cast out from among them, and never, ever (God forbid) sent to *Coventry*.

It was ever thus. G. M. Trevelyan, an undergraduate of Trinity College, Cambridge at the turn of the century, who went on to become its Master, writes in his *English Social History* of developments in education in the Tudor period.

A typical 'new man' of the Tudor Age was Nicholas Bacon, father of Francis, and son of the sheereeve to the Abbey of Bury St Edmunds. Nicholas Bacon rose by law and politics to be owner of many of the farms on which his father had served the monks as one of their bailiffs. He founded a free grammar school on those lands, with scholarships thence to Cambridge, and gave other endowments to his old college of Corpus Christi. At Cambridge he had first met his lifelong friends Matthew Parker and William Cecil, the future leaders of Church and State under Elizabeth. The younger and hitherto lesser University was coming rapidly to the front, and her sons played the leading part in the great changes of the period.

Even allowing for the fact that Oxford and Cambridge were the only universities in England at the time – and for centuries to come – this vignette from Trevelyan says it all. We have the go-getting entrepreneur, lately risen from servitude, going to Cambridge, meeting rich and influential friends and, in the fullness of his years, setting up college and university endowments that perpetuate his name. His son, Francis, who no doubt gave 'good interview', subsequently 'goes up' by right (in this case to Trevelyan's own Alma Mater) and spends his working life as a wordsmith, courtier and wit, barely able to stand upright under the weight of his seals of office. There is even – and you can almost hear the great historian licking his chops – the joy of Cambridge putting one over on its eternal rival. It is a paradigm for Bacon's time, and for ours.

The same tale has been repeated on countless occasions since, and even today, with no fewer than 123 universities to choose from (including the constituent colleges of London University, the University of Wales and the former polytechnics), the ruling class of England looks to the same jurassic *Jumelées* as the Tudors to replenish and enrich its blood.

In practical terms, in our own age, Oxbridge encourages intellectual independence within an established corpus of learning while smoothing even the roughest of edges and according self-esteem and style. After three years in college, all but the most irredentist misfits are returned to the outside world as 'civilized' individuals, confident and proud, marked out as members of the élite. There is no need to spell this out. Indeed, to do so is held to be unacceptably gauche. These happy few just *know* that, deep down, they are different now – re-invented – and as the years unfold the unspoken promise is joyously fulfilled. True, there are among the army of the elect many who, like renegade priests do not live up to expectations. Some fail miserably to profit from the myth, and curse the day they ever entered cloisters. Others who have not achieved what they had hoped on graduation cling to their college days as the only worthwhile thing they ever did. Many, of course, lead blameless lives of service, as teachers or country solicitors. There has even been during the recent, prolonged economic recession a tiny percentage of graduates who remained unemployed for six months or more after taking their degrees. Conversely, truly determined Redbrick graduates have surged ahead, even into the Oxbridge bastions of the law and Whitehall. A growing number of the lesser-known but specialist universities, like Bradford, produce extremely employable alumni and provide the finest research facilities for graduates. The 'balanced' argument can be taken further still. It can readily be owned that a preponderance of Oxbridge undergraduates are measurably towards the top end of the ability range – more so than just about anywhere else – and that an Oxbridge man, or woman, will, typically, be intellectually superior to the *average* Redbrick product. Yet this ignores entirely the uncomfortable truth that even the meanest university in the land contains people of unusual ability and potential, many of them with no wish to study anywhere else. More importantly, it ignores the simple mathematical fact that a large majority of Britain's first class degrees are awarded each year to students from 'provincial' institutions, both great and small, on whom few advantages, beyond admission and dedicated teachers, have been conferred. With the number of universities expanding each year, *every* institution has to concentrate on its strengths, and the quality of the best Redbrick awards is such today that a First in law or engineering from, say, Queen Mary and Westfield College London, or in history from Birmingham, or biology from Durham, will often be harder to obtain than its equivalent at Oxbridge and be of a higher standard. So why is it not the case that a proportionate number, 80 per cent perhaps, of the best jobs go to Redbrick people, leaving a handsome 20 per cent to the old pretenders? Why do certain classes of employer deem an Oxbridge 2:1, or even a 2:2, subtly superior to, say, a First from Hull? The answer stares us in the face. Redbrick educations are valued by those who run our affairs in much the same way that traditional grammar schools used to be valued – as providers of middle management and technicians, and as a safety net to catch those few 'ordinary' people who had the talent and drive to overcome their circumstances and contest the top jobs. Lord Robbins, author of the Robbins Report on Higher Education, in 1963, was strongly in favour of expanding the universities but acknowledged privately that the newcomers would be 'second rate'. Others felt the same way. Edward Shils, the American sociologist, observed in an article in *Encounter*, in 1955: 'If a young man, talking to an educated stranger [in England], refers to his university studies, he is asked "Oxford or Cambridge?" And if he says Aberystwyth or Nottingham, there is disappointment on the one side and embarrassment on the other. It has always been that way.' But such antiquated opinions have long since been overtaken by a new reality. The fact that Oxbridge graduates are now too few in number, relatively speaking, to take up what was hitherto their due is one consideration. Redbrick products have not only risen in quality, they have risen immeasurably in sheer volume and can no longer be excluded from the upper echelons of power by prejudice alone. Even so, as far as the Establishment is concerned, the ancient duopoly has done well by it in the past and will always occupy a special place in its affections. Degrees from elsewhere – most obviously from the one-time polytechnics – are seen as worthy at best.

One well-placed Cambridge insider, asked why it was that graduates of her university and of Oxford should continue to dominate the most sought-after employment sectors, was in no doubt of the reason. 'I don't see why 2 per cent shouldn't translate into 90 per cent', she said. 'Employers are looking for the top people of a generation, and these are the people who go to Oxford and Cambridge.'

Outsiders are not shunned. They may even be treated with elaborate politeness. They are simply not included. Apologists for the status quo might, if pressed, point to important exceptions to the rule, as well as to areas which Oxbridge has either failed to penetrate or in which it has no overwhelming advantage. These would include, in terms of disciplines, medicine, business studies and architecture, while the armed services, manufacturing and the welfare state could be advanced as careers in which Oxbridge is, at best, a neutral factor. There are, in addition, several obstinate institutions, most obviously the London School of Economics, Imperial College London, Essex and Manchester, which refuse to be silenced, and others, principally Durham, Bristol, Exeter and York, which, however unfairly, are perceived as Oxbridge surrogates, with a suitable reflected cachet. Scotland, of course, has an academic hierarchy all of its own, and a quite separate tartan mafia, with an ability to infiltrate the corridors of power that speaks volumes for Caledonian pride. Yet the general thesis holds true. Oxford and Cambridge – self-regarding, self-consciously superior – remain twin anchors in British society, holding us firm to *their* traditions and inhibiting progress in new directions. They adapt, they modernize, but they do not change. And always there is the deep well of scholarship, fed by resources both state and private that have few parallels elsewhere, and the inestimable self-belief engendered by eight hundred years of triumph.

Down all the centuries, until our own, most Oxbridge undergraduates came, inevitably, from 'good' families. Sons of the aristocracy and the gentry (and, later, of the prosperous middle classes) 'went up' to Oxford or Cambridge more or less by right of birth, just as they attended Eton, Harrow or Winchester. By 1945, however, it was clear that the admissions policy had to change, and a concession which had always existed – that of the scholarship boy, drawn from the lower orders – was expanded to include the brighter products of the grammar schools. It was a more meritocratic age, ushered in by the communal exertions of the war, and the ancient universities, confronted with Rab Butler's 1944 Education Act, were forced to the conclusion that, if they were to retain their dominance, they must move with the times. By the 1960s, with the new universities, such as Sussex and Keele, enjoying a powerful, and threatening vogue, more and more 'ordinary' people, including an increased proportion of young women, were admitted each year through the hallowed portals. By the end of the decade, indeed, state school pupils actually made up a narrow majority of the intake, and the Old Guard was forced on to the defensive.

It was then that tradition – subtly altered – began to reassert itself. The English genius for social absorption worked its magic, and the new wave of provincial undergraduates, with their flat accents and working class manners, were transformed over three years into passable imitations of their betters, complete with a haughty disdain for less fortunate outsiders. They were given the key to the door, taught appropriate tones and modes of behaviour and, at the end of the process, integrated fully into the network. The old and the new became virtually indistinguishable – at least to the casual eye – and what could have been a revolution ended up as mere reform. From one point of view, this was no bad thing. Revolutions are by their nature unpredictable and dangerous. Reform, by contrast, suggests improvement. If those who attend Oxford and Cambridge are generally supportive of the Establishment, at least that Establishment has become more accessible and more democratic.

A second benefit of the twin universities' broader base is the opportunity provided for people without social advantage to re-shape their lives. A butcher's son from Solihull – or a grocer's daughter from Grantham – having little experience of the wider world, can take the opportunity to construct a brand-new persona and can mix with undergraduates from more rarefied, and useful, backgrounds. Few waste the opportunity. Snobbery or upwards mobility, it makes no difference: whatever their origins, most end up travelling in the same direction.

Reform, by its nature, is not static. Change continues. But reaction, too, can be a dynamic force. By the 1980s, the Labour Party's abolition of the grammar schools and the distinctly patchy performance of the new comprehensives had caused large numbers of middle class parents to place their children in private schools. The Conservatives, naturally, encouraged this development, seeing it as an expression of choice and market forces. They have talked of higher standards and value for money, and one result, perhaps unintended, has been a reassertion of the power of Oxbridge. Those paying thousands of pounds each year for what they used to get free were obviously going to demand a clear academic return on their investment, and for most headteachers, struggling to produce an eye-catching prospectus, there was no better performance indicator than the numbers of their pupils being admitted each year to the old duopoly. Today, whatever the claims of certain disgruntled parents, who allege reverse discrimination, fee-paying schools are once more effectively in the ascendant. Just over 50 per cent of UK-born undergraduate entrants to Oxford and Cambridge in 1993 came from the private sector. The maintained sector, with 93 per cent of total schools, had less than half. Parents who themselves benefited from an old-style state education have rekindled the embers of privilege, and the flames now rage anew.

The rewards of subscription to the theology of Oxbridge are generally high. Recessions create difficulties for individual generations. They do not rewrite the rules. For a majority of graduates from the two universities, there is an early realization of a freemasonry in which jobs and early promotion are practically assured, and a sense, regardless of social origins (though few are genuinely working class), of being part of the nation's finest, destined to take charge of its institutions and hold them in trust for the next generation. With the growth of European and world organizations and companies, opportunities have even been extended for this happy band, and intercontinental influence is fast becoming a reality. The ancient pairing, though containing some of Britain's most acute academic minds and producing a steady stream of outstanding individuals, from a variety of disciplines, is not, at student level, primarily *about* scholarship. It is about the perpetuation of a caste and of a way of life, seeming to embrace the world while drawing it into the confines of the cloister. It is a glittering hypocrisy and an elegant conceit. It is the Oxbridge Conspiracy.

CHAPTER TWO

THE POWER AND THE GLORY

WHEN WE REFER TO AN OXBRIDGE CULTURE, what do we mean? It is not enough to talk of 'ambition' or worldly success, still less of 'effortless superiority'. Nor, as we have seen, can it any longer be assumed that those who go up to the ancient universities have a shared background of wealth and privilege. Many freshers crossing the threshold into cloisters for the first time will certainly have been privately educated, and a majority will be 'well spoken', with parents in the professions. There will even be a smattering of titled aristocrats, from home and abroad. But equally, there will be a large minority whose background is lower middle class, whose arrival at the porter's lodge marks for them a distinct social advance made possible by academic achievement. And for every louche lord, clutching his teddy bear, there will be the son or daughter of a railway clerk or a dinner lady, desperate for self-improvement and a place in the sun. 'It is possible to arrive here from almost any background – difficult, but possible', wrote George Synkaruk, a Cambridge undergraduate, in an issue of *Varsity*, the student newspaper, in November 1993. 'Our common aspirations are a great leveller. Every Cambridge student is here either because they want an excellent education or because they are on the make, or both. Once here, the idea of class becomes largely irrelevant.'

What does unite the Oxbridge mafia is the assumption that they know best what is important and what is not and the knowledge that they will be listened to. Graduates of the two universities, certainly in the humanities, are not subjected during their three or four years of study to a vocational education. The philosophical inquiry that for centuries dominated the curriculum in both places, Oxford in particular, has left behind it a legacy of civilized circumlocution that is profoundly impressive but practically dysfunctional.

Logic, the Philosopher's Stone in Varsity circles, is combined with rhetoric – another much-prized medieval device – to produce a universal discipline that is part discourse, part conversation and part a study in how to behave in public. Intelligence is obviously required if you are to be any good at it, but in the end it is, for all but the genuinely committed, intellectual sleight of hand – a party trick for an élite which sees life as a party. The Oxford or Cambridge graduate is above all else good at talking. He (or, increasingly, she) is supremely plausible. The smooth, measured articulation of logic, applied to almost any field, is what counts most in the cloisters. It confers a deep confidence and self-belief, and this, allied to ruthlessly efficient networking, produces a cadre of high achievers geared to free expression for themselves as individuals, the advancement of their kind and, for the rest, a kind of benevolent repression. Oxbridge people speak in the same tone of voice, often in the same accent. They will disagree with one another at the drop of a hat. They frequently loathe one another. But they remain united by their experience and by the conviction it has given them that they are the natural leaders of society, without whom anarchy would be loosed on an unsuspecting world.

A definition of this kind of self-satisfied preoccupation was given in the *Daily Mail* in January 1994, by, of all people, Simon Bates, a former disc jockey on Radio 1. Bates is both intelligent and articulate – a rare enough combination – and, on air, a consummate professional, albeit in a profoundly superficial field. He parted company with the corporation after many years of loyal service following the arrival in 1993 of a new management, led by John Birt (St Catherine's, Oxford), which he believed saw the nation's premier pop music station as 'broadcasting's equivalent of Essex Man'. The new BBC, says Bates, is a metropolitan world.

It is dominated, naturally, by what the new managers are doing – dining at the fashionable clubs and restaurants of the West End, the Groucho Club and the White Tower, living in Hampstead and Chiswick, going to the football (and good seats, too) on a Saturday or a Sunday, cottages in the country for the odd weekend, chauffeur-driven cars, tickets for the theatre or a fashionable pop concert. This is a dilettante's world – a million miles from reality. It is also a world of patronage, which is partly why the upper echelons of the BBC have now fallen into the hands of people who are so alike, who combine the best of intentions with almost complete blindness to what ordinary life is really like all around them.

Bates was not, of course, writing about Oxbridge, which, in any case, has always been a Varsity preserve. But he *could* have been. Nearly all of the present top management at the BBC comes from the two ancient universities, and the kind of élitism of which he complains – combining self-regard with generalized good intentions – though not confined to Oxbridge, remains its hallmark.

One has only to listen to the comments of graduates to get a flavour of the way in which group identity is exploited. Baroness Mallalieu QC, who read history and law at Newnham in the 1960s and is now a Labour 'working peer' (riding to hounds with the Bicester Hunt), was the first woman president of the Cambridge Union. 'It opened up all sorts of doors. With respect to my legal career, it was at the Union I met Sir Elwyn Jones (then Labour's Attorney-General), who arranged two superb pupillages for me. It also raised opportunities to write articles and appear on television and radio. Things that I became a regular on, like *Any Questions* – they were all a result of that period of Cambridge.'

Even when the result is not entirely gratifying, the fact of having been at Varsity can be a vital factor in creating an image. 'One thing I still find slightly irritating is how people's attitudes change because they discover I went to Cambridge', says the actress Judith Brydon (née Phillips). 'At interviews for acting jobs, for instance, people either tend to make a great deal about it – who I knew when I was there – or they look at you and say, "You're too intelligent for this part". It's something that I think actresses who went to Oxford or Cambridge run into more than most, possibly because there's a difference in attitude towards men who act – who can be considered as intelligent – and how most women working in theatre are still regarded.'

Whether or not there is a gender difference in how Oxbridge products are perceived (and in a lingering bimbo culture the possibility is not to be excluded), the fact is that outsiders tend to be deeply impressed by a Varsity background and regard graduates from the Isis and the Cam as somehow different from the rest of us. If this were true and Britain was as a result a vibrant nation, building on its traditions and powering into the new century with confidence and brio, the inequities discussed here would be of secondary, and mainly social, importance. As it is, modern Oxbridge, in spite of the significant contribution it makes to science and engineering (of which more later), and the recurrent genius of its more distinguished dons, is like a constitutional monarchy, in which the sovereign reigns but does not rule. Oxbridge confers prestige, but it doesn't do the job that needs doing. It teaches its sons and daughters how to seize power and cleave to positions of influence. It does not encourage them to break new ground or overturn conventions. Rather, it seeks to instil a respect for authority and established sources of power. It teaches undergraduates how to talk and think 'correctly' – as though mere words were themselves a substitute for action or moral force – and it grants its students the unbridled confidence to wade through blood and argument (usually with others of their kind) in pursuit of whichever goal they have selected. Its ethos, in short, is competitive, but deeply conservative – concerned to place the individual first, the Establishment second and society a poor third.

Supporters of the Oxbridge system will argue that it is no place of universities – and certainly not those founded on the purest consideration of knowledge – to instruct their undergraduate members in how to govern society, but rather to ensure that they are properly conditioned to take on their inheritance. Very well. In that case, criticism can focus just as easily on the demonstrable fact that Britain under Oxbridge is a failed experiment. The élite continues to do very well, thank you, paying themselves handsomely in terms of cash and mutual esteem. The rest have either been granted supporting roles in the management of society or else neglected entirely, with consequences that are building up almost daily on our streets.

We are talking of graduates here – those who have done their three or four years and moved on. Dons, bound tightly to their colleges and departments, are, for the most part, markedly less selfish than those they teach. They give as much weight to academic tradition and the needs of a scholastic community as to personal considerations, and in this way keep college life close to its monastic origins. At the same time it is they, often unwittingly, who encourage an egocentric, Oxbridge view of the world.

John Tusa, former head of the BBC World Service and himself a Cambridge man, twice stressed this reactionary tendency in his letter of resignation as President of Wolfson College after just six months in the job. Tusa is a broadcaster and analyst, whose entire career has been spent in words and their use in the presentation of ideas. Yet he is also a 'doer', who prefers programmes of action to agendas and procedures. When events at Wolfson, a graduate college, began, in his opinion, to get out of hand soon after he had been invited to take over as head of house, he was deeply disturbed – so much so that he threw in the towel out of sheer frustration. There were several factors at work, including the virtually unheard-of suspension of the Senior Tutor (arising out of matters that are no part of this narrative) and difficulties over the setting up of Wolfson's promised centre for the Cambridge Global Security Programme (GSP). Tusa was irritated by his colleagues' inability to confront what he saw as the key features of the suspension issue. 'I found the attitude of too many of the Council to resolving the matter dilatory, hesitant and more concerned to address the minutiae of procedure than the urgent matters of principle and behaviour involved.' This is pure, unreconstructed Oxbridge. It could have been lifted almost intact from the pages of C. P. Snow's *The Affair*. But Tusa then goes on to the matter of the security centre. He had pressed for the early establishment of a college institute that would attract world leaders and academics engaged in the business of reducing world tensions and minimizing outbreaks of war. Instead, all he got was talk.

I have never said that the arguments in its favour were conclusive beyond a doubt, but I have a strong conviction that it is consistent with what Wolfson claims to be – and would strengthen what Wolfson says it is aiming to do. It would strengthen and give focus to its academic profile ... what I found was ... that the opposition to the GSP was fuelled by those who, while claiming a readiness to welcome the outside world, were and are resistant to, even alarmed by, its intrusion into the College.

Tusa's conclusion is bleak: 'Sadly, behind the rhetoric, there is a deep fear of a real involvement with the outside world.'

It would be wrong, obviously, to pretend that Oxford and Cambridge are pathologically inward-looking and unable to engage with the dynamics of a world in turmoil. Their tradition, dating back many centuries, is of international scholarship, and again and again these days (if partly for reasons of financing) they stress their ties with Europe, America and, increasingly, the Pacific Ring. The Wolfson case could well reflect the frustration of one man, himself Cambridge-educated, used to executive decision-making, who was unable to have things all his own way. There is a lesson here even so. College life, on which Oxbridge turns, *is* cloistered – colleges literally turn their backs on the world – and there *is* a premise of donnish dominion that can easily become a tyranny. For all their genius, neither of the ancient universities has a monopoly of wisdom, and their way of looking at things, though hallowed by age, is not always best practice.

Angus Macintyre, a Senior Fellow in modern history at Magdalen College, Oxford, widely recognized to be one of the finest teachers the university has produced in recent decades, is a passionate supporter of the Oxbridge experience and the part played in it by the tutorial system. 'One of the glories of Oxford', he says, 'is that we turn our people into real historians, using original sources and research.' It might come as a surprise to London, Manchester and Birmingham – all highly rated for their prowess in history – that they suffer under some inherent disadvantage in the field, but Dr Macintyre is quietly confident of his position. Other aspects of Oxford are to him equally vital. 'Graduate degrees are hugely important to us – more and more as the years go by. They bring us lots of international connections, and these connections are an important part of the power of Oxbridge. Networking is another factor. It reflects the intensity of the experience: the mix of college life, university societies and the whole Oxford experience. It actually *is* real. My pupils keep in touch. They become pals.'

Michael Hart, Senior Tutor in modern history at nearby Exeter College, accepts that the Oxbridge culture has not traditionally been an enterprise culture or an executive culture, but an administrative culture. 'The British are good at talking', he says. But the situation, apparently, is changing. 'A new Oxbridge culture is alive in the banking and brokerage sector – a financial enterprise culture that is claiming more and more of our graduates.' Wealth and worldly success of the type associated with the financial services sector are vital to the contemporary Oxbridge image, and Hart believes that this is one reason more high flyers go to Oxford and Cambridge than to other universities. 'Our rejects go to the Red-bricks. One of my students, who failed PPE Mods twice, went on to get a First at Liverpool. When things go wrong for our people here, we have no problems getting them placed.'

At Cambridge, where steps have been taken in recent years to compel engineers and scientists to forge closer links with industry, the problem is that dons – as distinct from ambitious undergraduates – still remain rooted in abstract thought. Dr Eric Howell, recently retired director of the Wolfson Cambridge Industrial Unit, set up to encourage a more entrepreneurial approach, says that many of the researchers he was in contact with at Cambridge, though starting to get the picture, still lacked dynamism in the commercialization of research. 'Imperial College [London] regards Oxford and Cambridge as amateurs in this game', he confessed. 'The thing is, though – and I say this conscious of the interpretation that might be placed on it – Imperial doesn't have our endowments and has to fight for every penny.' Howell, in spite of an obvious reverence for the quality of Cambridge research ('We seem to have Nobel prizes and FRSs coming along every five minutes'), cannot help admiring what other universities have managed on more limited resources, as at Warwick and Salford. 'They listen better to society. Durham, for example – another collegiate institution – is more ready to understand Britain's problems and put its shoulder to the wheel. In the long run, the ancient universities have to understand society, and its needs, if they are to be appreciated.'

Howell achieved much during his years at the industrial unit, but accepts there is a long way still to go. 'It's a question of attitude', he says. He also, one suspects, feels a little let down by the student sector. 'There is no doubt that the undergraduates here are often frighteningly intelligent. But they are less vocational than they used to be. Industry's demands for science graduates has declined drastic-ally over the last ten years, and today many young scientists disappear into the City and accountancy. The figures really are quite alarming.'

*

So what are they like, these 'frighteningly intelligent' young people? It is lunchtime in January in The Eagle public house in Cambridge, just opposite King's. A small group of college applicants, up for interview, is gathered for lunch. They are 18- and 19-year-olds, the boys in suits, the girls in smart dresses. As they pick over their ploughperson's lunches and sip at their beers, they compare notes on how things are going. Jamie, from St Paul's Boys' School, one of the most successful private schools in the country, had applied last year to do modern languages at Caius, but didn't get in. This time he is trying for Corpus, and if he doesn't make it he thinks he'll go to Edinburgh instead. 'If they're looking for potential rather than achievement', he says, referring to Cambridge's alleged preference for state school pupils, 'then that's all right by me.' Susannah, an extremely loud girl, from St Paul's Girls', laughs and jokes her way through lunch. Perhaps she's just nervous. She is hoping to read law, and she tells of a tutor asking her, If you find a snail in your bottle of beer, whose fault is it? They all laugh. Another boy, very quiet, from Belfast, reveals that he hopes to study French. He is confident of being accepted, he says, obviously a swot. Jamie says that he is better at Italian than French because he has spent a year working in an Italian estate agent's. He has a friend who wants to go to Birmingham. 'I just can't understand her', he says. Susannah snorts, plainly unaware of the self-serving nature of today's student regime. 'It's just *got* to be Cambridge. I'm *really* lazy, and I want my laundry done for me.' Jamie, though himself plainly anxious for acceptance, affects not to understand. 'I've met so many people who think like this' (he indicates blinkers with cupped hands to his eyes) 'Cambridge! Cambridge! It's all they think about.' As he speaks, a newcomer to the group arrives and sits down. He has applied to Emmanuel to read economics. 'I went back to the JCR after the interview', he tells them, 'but it was full of sodding engineers talking about widgets.' It turns out that he has been interviewed by a 'wanker' called Rankin. 'A year ago, I'd have pissed myself silly at a name like that.' Susannah giggles. Not easily impressed, the late arrival at this applicants' ball is even more dismissive of his female fellow applicants than he was of his tutor. 'They're just *so* ugly', he discloses, breathily, raising his glass.

In Bradford, they play by different rules. Bradford has one of the highest vocational job-take-ups in the country. John Moores University, in Liverpool, similarly ploughs its own furrow, teaching its students how to use computers and read balance sheets, and liaising with the manufacturing sector, including nearby Pilkington Glass, to provide tailor-made graduates for industry. At Imperial College, applied research and theoretical training go hand in hand, as at Manchester and its high technology counterpart, UMIST (the University of Manchester Institute of Technology). Other universities turn out 'doers'. Campus students learn languages or computers or chemistry or law and then go out and practise their skills in the market-place. They have few pretensions, and whether they succeed or fail depends on their talent and how hard they try. Only occasionally does one hear of disputes or disturbances in the Red-brick sector, where, ironically, a straight majority of professors in many disciplines are themselves Oxbridge products. There are genuine concerns in campuses up and down the country, usually about money. But they rarely attract headlines, and only a tiny minority of the academics involved have public, as distinct from professional, reputations. In Hull, Southampton and Preston, they keep their heads down and they get things done. The skills they offer are practical and down to earth.

At Oxford and Cambridge, added value is provided, both academically and socially. Of that, there is no question. But the addition that counts most is an incestuous clubbability and a feeling of self-satisfaction, together with the unshakeable belief that argument, administration and government are best left to those who have the aptitude for it and know what's best for the rest of us. Young people apply to the ancient universities because they are ambitious and see it as the fast track to success and soft living. That is why neither university attracts nearly as many applicants as, say, Manchester or Nottingham and why one-third of those who apply are successful against one in six for those seeking admission elsewhere. Most A-level students do not apply to Oxbridge either because they do not think they are good enough or because they do not wish to be part of the Varsity's unique, rarefied world. Self-selection at the admissions stage means that the divisions that Oxford and Cambridge will confirm and intensify are at work years before that first arrival at the porter's lodge. The British system, tolerant of eccentricity at the top, neurotic about the need to preserve overall social stability, isolates its future leaders as early as possible and nurtures them in the peculiar skills and responses essential to maintaining a deeply stratified society. Those already at the top, the Great and the Good, are sympathetic, even affectionate, towards their eventual successors, recognizing in them the same confident swagger, the same cockiness that was theirs twenty or thirty years before. They feel sure that when their stewardship of affairs finally fades, they can safely entrust the future to these their natural heirs. They know that even if most of what is left of British industry is owned by foreigners, even if three million of their fellow citizens are unemployed and even if masses of the elderly can barely survive on their pensions, England, *their* England, will survive into another generation.

It is a large claim to make for just a few thousand people coming on-stream each year from two medium-sized institutions, each some sixty miles from London and a similar distance from each other. Set against the claim Oxbridge graduates stake for themselves in Britain and the world, it is small enough.

The traditional, 'safe' areas of dominance are politics, the Civil Service, the Foreign Office, the Church, academia itself and the law. The City, in all its guises, both ancient and modern, comes next, followed in no particular order by publishing, cultural bureaucracy, the media and the upper echelons of industry and commerce. As times alter, so does the graduate profile. What does not change is the attempt, thus far successful, by the ancient universities to keep their fingers firmly on the pulse of British and world affairs, so that any new areas of interest which are on the move, such as the European Community, the United Nations, global investment and accountancy and communications, are properly 'covered'. There is no paranoia involved in recognizing this. Oxbridge is used to being on top, and it intends to stay that way. From the perspective of privilege, that is all there is to it. What is revealing is the extent to which the pair are scaling down their involvements in some activities and building them up in others.

In later chapters, we shall examine in detail the character of the dual domination in key sectors. The point to be borne in mind is that the conspirators are shifting their ground. Modern society is too variegated, too complicated, too *big*, for Oxbridge any longer to govern it at every turn. For a start, there are not enough graduates to go round. The two universities would have to swell to at least twice their present size in order to maintain their traditional spheres of influence unchecked *and* expand significantly into new territory. Within limits, they are trying. The two accept larger numbers of undergraduates every year, and new building-work to house them all seems endless. But they have learned lessons, too. Of necessity, there has been a trade-off, with the controlling interest in core professions slipping gradually from, say, 90 per cent to 55 or 60 per cent while strategic stakes are built up elsewhere, especially abroad and in the 'sunrise' sector. The result, by early next century, should be a more balanced portfolio, easier to manage and defend, every bit as insidious. As has often been shown in business, the shareholder with 51 per cent of a company's stock can take the same executive decisions as one with 100 per cent, and so long as Oxbridge graduates control a majority of the levers of power in the areas of their choosing, and have a voice that carries in the rest, they will be well satisfied. They are not, after all, a Balkan militia, bent on vocational cleansing. Rather, they are a talented and arrogant minority, self-fulfilling prophets who make handsome livings as individuals within a network of academic replicants and enjoy to the full the exercise of power. If those who cannot join them – or do not wish to – hope to keep up, they must learn first of all to beat them at their own game.

Politics is where it starts and where it finishes. Douglas Hogg (Christ Church), minister of state at the Foreign Office, son of Lord Hailsham (Christ Church), husband of the Prime Minister's economic adviser, Sarah Hogg (Lady Margaret Hall), son-in-law of Lord Boyd-Carpenter (Balliol), begins his career recapitulation with 'pres. Oxford Union, 1965'. Close on a hundred members of the Commons could do the same – and probably do. The Conservative Party is steeped in Oxbridge. The Tories' key players include a number of mavericks from elsewhere and nowhere, but they are used merely to fill gaps or, as with Norman Tebbit during the Thatcher years, to provide the kind of ideological muscle that cuts through voter resistance and builds support in unlikely quarters. Outsiders wax and wane with party fortunes. At the core of

Conservatism, older values remain, and with them their Varsity connections. There are at the time of writing seventeen Oxbridge graduates in the Cabinet of John Major, eight from Oxford, nine from Cambridge. At the same time, fellow Oxonians and Cantabrigians make up 46 per cent of Tory MPs overall, most, though not all, of them in 'safe' seats. Should Major lose the next election, it is likely that a high proportion of Conservatives rejected by the voters will be Thatcherite right-wingers from New Age industrial towns, where disappointment in the Government will be felt most keenly, while the bulk of those hanging on will be traditionalists from the shires. Thus, the Oxbridge proportion will almost certainly increase.

On the Labour side, the Shadow Cabinet contains just three graduates of Oxbridge, including Tony Blair, plus John Prescott, an alumnus of Ruskin College, with a further forty-eight (including four Ruskinites) in the parliamentary party, fourteen of them first-timers. The proportion overall is on the increase for the first time in years, and should just three duopolists be promoted between now and the election, the result potentially could be a Labour Government with up to 25 per cent of its front bench, including the occupant of 10 Downing Street, from the ancient universities. Any alliance or pact with the Liberal Democrats, however unlikely, could only further augment this tendency.

Politicians are supposed to be the masters, but we all think we know who is really in charge in the great departments of state. It is Sir Humphrey, and it will come as no surprise to learn that he is above all else an Oxbridge product. Permanent secretaries and their deputies are nearly all from one or The other, presided over by the formidable Cabinet Secretary, Sir Robin Butler, who, after Harrow, scored a double First in 'Mods and Greats' at University College, Oxford. Sir Robin has spoken several times of the need to cast the net wider than Oxbridge, arguing that he wants 'the best people from everywhere', and indeed, with the publication in November 1993 of a wide-ranging review of recruitment policy, there are signs at last of changes to come. In future, the review states, the top 620 Whitehall jobs will no longer be the exclusive preserve of the graduate 'fast stream', but will be open to outsiders holding specialist skills. What difference this makes on the ground remains to be seen. In 1991/2, despite the fact that degree-holders from the ancient duopoly made up less than 7 per cent of the UK graduate total, 49 per cent of successful candidates for the Civil Service Administrative grades were Oxbridge – well up on the previous year. Anthony Sampson, author of *The Anatomy of Britain*, himself a graduate of Christ Church, recalled once being told by a lordly Whitehall denizen that he and his colleagues, when selecting recruits to the upper levels of the service, made a special point of seeing as many Redbrick candidates as possible before plumping for the applicants from Oxbridge. 'They spoke the same language, you see', was the only explanation.

Judges and leading counsel are massively, almost morbidly, Oxbridge. Lord Lane, edged out in 1992 as Lord Chief Justice after a series of Appeal Court blunders, was a Fellow of Trinity College, Cambridge; his successor, Sir Peter Taylor, won an exhibition to Pembroke College, Cambridge. The eleven law lords and thirty Appeal Court judges are Varsity educated almost to a man – so much so that when Lord Woolf, a graduate of University College London, suggested in 1993 that the Government had got it wrong on penal policy, every single newspaper report on the subject drew attention to his out-of-kilter academic provenance. Some circuit judges – and even the occasional High Court interloper – did not tread the primrose path. The fact remains that, as in the Civil Service, the higher they go the rarer they become. In spite of the emergence in recent years of a healthy Redbrick contingent, whose members are already beginning to find preferment, leading barristers, especially QCs, remain preponderantly Oxbridge, while the Bar Association is traditionally governed by products of the Spires and Backs.

It would be rare indeed for a British ambassador not to be Oxford or Cambridge – for nearly all top diplomats are of the company. Sir John Coles, the Permanent Under-Secretary at the Foreign and Commonwealth Office and head of the Diplomatic Service, is a graduate of Magdalen College, Oxford. The university origins of our eight most senior ambassadors (Washington, the European Community, the United Nations, Moscow, Bonn, Paris, Tokyo and Rome) is divided as follows: Cambridge five, Oxford three, the rest nil. The one surprise is the slight underrepresentation of Oxford, but, as with newspaper editorships, time and chance will no doubt restore the traditional balance. The view taken is that if you are going to represent your country, you should know one wine from another and which knife and fork to use. Only an Oxbridge education, it is felt at the FCO, guarantees this, helping to refresh the parts other universities cannot reach. In 1993, no fewer than sixteen of the twenty-two graduates admitted to the Administrative, fast stream of the service were Oxbridge, a hit rate of 73 per cent. Other graduates did better in the less prestigious Executive stream – sixteen out of seventeen – but in most cases must reckon on spending their careers in the long shadow of the Chosen.

HM armed forces are a traditional exception to the Oxbridge rule. As has already been observed, they have their own élite colleges – Sandhurst, Dartmouth and Cranwell – where the social input is similar. The army and the navy, in particular, have an officer caste which looks back to its days in training with the same fondness as an Oxford or Cambridge graduate reflects on life in college. Yet even here, changes are afoot. Today, more and more young officers are coming through to the services via university, and the ancient duo, with their proud record of flocking to the colours in time of war, are in the forefront of the trend. Mike Campbell-Lamerton, the bursar of Balliol and a former Guards colonel, has noted a significant rise in the number of army scholarships in recent years, but points out that the top brass have always looked to Oxbridge for at least part of their intake. General Sir Michael Rose, Britain's dashing head of UN forces in Bosnia in 1994, is a graduate of St Edmund's Hall, Oxford. Admiral Peter Abbott, deputy supreme allied commander, Atlantic, is an MA from Queens' College, Cambridge. Air Vice-Marshal Michael Douglas, formerly director-general of strategic electronic systems at the Ministry of Defence, now a systems consultant, first flew with the Cambridge air squadron while studying engineering at Trinity Hall.

The police, too, are beginning to take an interest in the Spires and Backs. At least three chief constables are already Oxbridge, and the highest-ranking of them all, Commissioner Paul Condon, is a graduate of St Peter's College, Oxford.

Publishing, arguably, is changing – faster indeed than one might have imagined. An increasingly cut-throat business, more the culture of commerce than the commerce of culture, it has long ceased to be a hobby for 'gentlemen' and become a target profession for New Britain. Yet, even today, traces remain of an older past. A majority of those who considered this manuscript prior to publication came from one or other of the ancient institutions (one well-known house rejecting it on the grounds that 'it would give too much offence to too many people in this country'). Outsiders are not exactly frowned upon in the administration of the book world; they are, however, a minority. Bristol or York will do at a pinch, or a First from UCL – but superiority comes easier at Balliol.

Banks and the City repeat the pattern. According to *Graduate Varsity*, the out-of-term publication for Cambridge postgraduates, 48 per cent of graduate recruits to the City of London financial services sector – the largest in the world – have in recent years been Oxbridge, while 28 per cent of graduates securing first-time jobs in top company management (i.e. firms in the FTSE 100) similarly have Oxon. or Cantab. after their degrees. From the governor and directors of the Bank of England, through the clearing banks, merchant banks, brokerage firms and consultancies right through to the board rooms and fast tracks of blue-chip industry, three years beneath the Spires or next to the Backs remains one of the most sought-after components of a serious C.V. The same applies to accountancy, as lucrative these days as the law. Some 7 per cent of Oxbridge graduates in the 1980s became accountants – a remarkable figure – and the result, as the tradition has taken root, has been the creation of an area of Varsity penetration formerly underexploited.

An important exception to this repetitive litany of old college ties is manufacturing itself. Here, in the world of making things, in which invention, hard work and initiative, rather than 'background', are imperative, the Oxbridge connection slides mysteriously away. A number of chief executives are certainly Oxbridge. Many, though, studied elsewhere, and some did not attend university at all. Few middle managers are Oxbridge and only a tiny minority of 'sharp end' operators and innovators. The moving parts of British industry are not fashioned for the most part in the cloisters but in the provinces, in Bradford, Newcastle and Manchester, and, even yet, in the University of Life. Here, more rugged types, reminiscent of British inventors and entrepreneurs of past centuries, still survive, even if under constant pressure from banks and overseas competitors. It is the same with new businesses. Factory start-ups are mostly by self-made men (and sometimes women), either with no third-level education or with technical degrees from unfashionable universities like Hull, Loughborough and Stirling. Management buyouts are similarly the preserve of pushy executives with big ideas – ideas only rarely fashioned on the Isis or the Cam.

What, though, about the workers? Surely their spokesmen are free of such subfusc élitism. Well, yes . . . up to a point. John Monks, general secretary of the TUC, is a graduate of Nottingham, and impeccably Redbrick in tooth and claw, while several of the best-known union figures, like Gavin Laird, leader of the AEEU, and Arthur Scargill, of the NUM, held no truck with academe beyond the age of 15. But Alan Jinkinson, general secretary of Unison, the public services union – the largest in the country – studied at Keble, while John Edmunds, leader of the number three-ranked GMB, took a First in history at Oriel and is now a Visiting Fellow at Nuffield. Norman Willis, the boss at Congress House for nine years until giving way to Monks, is an alumnus of both Ruskin and Oriel, and was at one point an Oriel Fellow. The TUC's assistant general secretary, and its prime mover on the European scene, is David Lea, of Christ's College, Cambridge. Willis's predecessor, Len Murray – later Lord Murray of Epping Forest – was a New College man, and later a Fellow of both that college and Nuffield. George Woodcock, general secretary before Murray (prior to the interregnum of ex-miner 'Lord' Vic Feather) was another New College product, who in his declining years was elected to the Standing Committee of the Oxford Union. Harold Macmillan, an Oxonian Medici, once described Woodcock as 'an intellectualist and therefore tricky, though agreeable'. It does not sound like contempt, more like an acknowledgement that, at heart, he was 'one of us'.

Royal Commissions, government inquiries and the posher quangos are famously an Oxbridge stronghold. Practically all of the public investigations into scandals and alleged scandals of recent years, as well as into disasters and aspects of public policy, have been placed in the hands of Varsity chaps. Lord Denning, Lord Scarman, Lord Franks, Lord Salmon: the list of noble and learned friends from good colleges goes on and on. Even the momentous

Scott inquiry into the Arms to Iraq affair, often cited as having been conducted by an 'outsider' (born in colonial India, raised in South Africa), was in fact in the hands of a Cambridge Blue: Sir Richard Scott. As in the plusher corridors of Whitehall, it is not so much that the Great and Good are deliberately selected from college lists to chair national inquiries or adjudge standards, it is simply that, somehow, at the heel of the hunt, it is those old, familiar faces who most readily spring to mind. That said, outsiders do sometimes make it through the minefield, and many others are called upon to *assist*. Wholly to exclude the higher achievers of London and the provinces from the business of regulation and inquiry would evidently be bad form. It might make the system appear, well, élitist. A complete list of the Great and Good, a veritable repertory company of wisdom and virtue as seen from Whitehall, is held by the Cabinet Office (Sir Robin Butler, prop.), whose staff work hard to ensure adherence to the number one criterion: members, save that they be extremely wealthy and successful businessmen, from whatever background, should be able to recognize high table at a hundred paces and have kept their noses clean since graduation.

Science and technology, in their various academic incarnations, are far from being dominated, let alone cowed, by Oxbridge. Nor is medicine. Such eminence as the pair *do* enjoy in both fields is well earned, built almost exclusively on hard work, pioneering research and external funding. *The Times* in its controversial 'Good University Guide' for 1993 ranked Cambridge, Oxford and Imperial College London joint first in science, while in medicine Cambridge, Oxford and London (overall) were tied at the top, followed closely by Edinburgh and Glasgow. Only in engineering, a very practical science, are the thermodynamic duo edged out of the top slot. Imperial reigns supreme here, while just behind the second-placed Spires and Backs comes UMIST. It is when we get to the talking shops of science that Oxbridge truly comes into its own. Dr Antony Hughes, director of the Laboratories, Science and Engineering Research Council, took both an MA and a D.Phil. from Jesus College, Oxford, and several of his colleagues have equivalent pedigrees. The British Association for the Advancement of Science, with its headquarters in Fortress House, Savile Row, London W1, exists, according to its charter, 'to promote understanding and development of science and technology and to illuminate and enhance their contribution to cultural, economic and social life'. Oh dear. So who, in 1993, could possibly be in charge? Ah yes. Dr Anne McLaren, a geneticist, educated at Oxford, now at Cambridge, had just replaced Sir David Weatherall, Nuffield Professor of Clinical Medicine at Oxford, and a Fellow of Magdalen, as president. The six vice-presidents included Professor Colin Blakemore, Wayneflete Professor of Physiology at Oxford (another Magdalen Fellow), Sir Walter Bodmer FRS, a former professor of genetics at Oxford *and* Cambridge, and Sir Claus Moser, recently retired as Warden of Wadham. The chairman was Professor Jeff Thompson, Professor of Education at the University of Bath, but a double graduate of St John's, Cambridge, and Balliol. The association is lively and forward-looking, and its annual general meeting is an important and widely reported showcase for British science. Nevertheless, when it comes to putting on a public face, the preferred expression is one that is used to an Oxbridge outlook.

God's house, the Bible tells us, has many mansions, but does not, so far as is known, contain a special place for Oxbridge colleges. Logically, and scripturally, there is no room for élitism in Christianity, which in theory at least remains unfashionably socialist. The fact is, it exists and is woven deep into the fabric of the Church. It might be thought significant that Dr George Carey, the Archbishop of Canterbury, is not Oxbridge, having obtained his first and subsequent degrees at London, but he is the John Major of Anglicanism, and, like his political counterpart, he is surrounded by the Brotherhood. Bishops, deans and other senior clergy of the Church of England are recruited practically to a man (no women thus far) from the ranks of the Oxbridge elect. From the Archbishop of York and the bishops of London and Durham to the humblest suffragan, Oxbridge is invariably the common factor. Not only do they study there, they frequently go on to become dons, administrators and chaplains, clustering in college life like bees in a hive. Very few of the higher clergy are state school and Redbrick. Moving from cloister to cloister almost from cradle to grave, theirs is the doctrine of grace made flesh and has been so for centuries.

Nor is there much difference in the Church of Rome, which in its English incarnation is either colonial Irish or Oxbridge. The higher up the papist hierarchy you go, the fewer of the former you get and the more of the latter, until you reach the intimately Oxonian Cardinal Hume.

Turning from the sublime to the ridiculous, even the more sophisticated, socially adept comedians are Oxbridge, from the legendary era of Alan Bennett, Michael Frayn, John Cleese, Jonathan Miller, Eric Idle and Peter Cook, all the way to Rowan Atkinson, Mel Smith, Griff Rhys Jones, Angus Deayton, Stephen Fry, Hugh Laurie, Rob Newman and David Baddiel. Fry, who is 6 feet 4 inches tall, sees size as a complicating issue here. High altitude comedians like himself, Cleese and Cook, tend, he says, to be cold-hearted, sarcastic, public school-educated and go to Cambridge; short-order comics, like Dudley Moore and Terry Jones, are more likely to be generous, emotional products of grammar schools . . . and go to Oxford. People of middle height are presumably middle-brow, Middle England and extruded from the comprehensive mixing machine straight into Redbrick sausage factories. Step forward, Jasper Carrot.

The written word, in its broader and deeper form, has long been a favoured Oxbridge preserve. Think of every prize-winning writer in this country in the last ten years (Amis *père et fils*, Anita Brookner, Ben Okri, James Fenton, A. S. Byatt, etc., etc.): all but a handful have been graduates of the Spires and Backs. This bifurcated élite has dominated the world of literature and the high arts in Britain for hundreds of years, and in the present century, with cultural bureaucracy ever more powerful, the tendency is, if anything, increasing. Where long ago it was enough for a writer to be inventive, linguistically skilled and determined, today he, or she, will invariably have a degree from one or other of the ancient universities and be part of a network extending beyond creativity into criticism, teaching and administration of the arts. It would be no exaggeration to say that novels, poetry, biography and drama are in the main produced by Oxbridge people and reviewed by Oxbridge people. Plays written by Oxbridge writers are staged by Oxbridge directors. The grants each receive come from quangos stuffed to the gunwales with Oxbridge placemen. Provincials from beyond the Pale are permitted to read and watch, and to contribute their three ha'pence-worth of thinking along with their credit cards.

44

As practitioners, they have little influence – except as rebels or 'naives' – over the direction in which their chosen art form is going. Exceptions to the rule, like Malcolm Bradbury, are aware that this is what they are – exceptions – and aim mainly at ploughing their own furrow while cocking a snook at the majority. They do not expect that their tendency will take over at the top. They may not even wish it to.

Sport has its own fascination for Oxbridge watchers. Possession of a 'Blue', or even a half- or quarter-Blue (for less 'serious' sports), is more prized than many a degree and, like the presidency of the Union Society, is seen as evidence of leadership and healthy competitiveness. The reality is that standards are no more than average, and only rarely do the chariots catch fire. The Boat Race has for years been an anachronism, matching two teams neither of which is in the top rank and which are often beaten in open tournaments. Yet *le tout Londres* halts for the duration of their annual contest on the Thames and the impression is conveyed – albeit with less and less conviction – that what is frequently a dull aquatic procession is one of the events of the Season.

Oxbridge cricket and rugby are similarly revered, as though they possessed a special magic, outside consideration of 'winning' and 'losing', that transforms them from the ordinary. It is impossible to justify the first-class status of the Varsity sides in cricket (especially when recognition of any kind is denied to other universities), and the annual pre-Christmas pilgrimage to Twickenham to watch the light and dark blue XVs scrumming down, while the champagne corks pop like flashbulbs, is a further, frayed anachronism, the more so for being followed enthusiastically by thousands who never attended either institution. Such people appear actually to believe that what they are seeing is the game at its best – or at least its most Corinthian. It is what is going on in their minds, rather than what is happening on the field, that is unusual. For those with real expertise, the most athletic achievement associated with sport at Oxford and Cambridge in recent years has been the leap of imagination required to consider it as anything more than adequate.

The quasi-academic construct of British society may be outrageous, but it also has its entertaining side. The chairman of the British Cement Association, Sir George Moseley, is a Wadham man; the

Rev. Brian Halfpenny, chaplain-in-chief to the RAF, took the Queen's shilling after St John's, Oxford; even the Chief Scout, William Morrison, an authority on Scottish juvenile crime, spent three formative years at Pembroke College, Cambridge. There is no disrespect intended here. It is not that these are not honourable men. They are *all* honourable men. Rather, it is that the passage each worked was less crowded, less cluttered, less *grimy* than those occupied by the rest of us.

If Britain did not have its twin forcing houses for the Establishment, it would not be necessary to invent them. That is the point. Other countries, more successful than we, have managed very well this century without such narrowly based élites. What *will* be necessary, if we are ever to change and move ahead, is that we should have something else to put in their place – and that something, logically, must continue to be rooted in higher education, but with the emphasis vitally reordered so that good people everywhere are given a fair chance to compete. First, though, let us look more closely at the enemies of progress. Let us look at where they came from, how they got where they are today and where they predict, with such confidence and pride, they will be found tomorrow.

CHAPTER THREE

TWIN PEAKS

I'm afraid the fellows in Putney rather wish they had
The social ease and manners of a 'varsity undergrad,
For tho' they're awfully decent and up to a lark as a rule
You want to have the 'varsity touch after a public school.

(JOHN BETJEMAN, 'THE VARSITY STUDENTS' RAG')

THE OXBRIDGE EXPERIENCE IS AN ANCIENT ONE, built stone upon stone, myth upon myth over the centuries. Yet, like a Gothic cathedral, constructed in many styles by many builders, it presents a united and harmonious front. There is no escaping it. If you are drawn to it, no matter what your starting point, you will remain in its shadow for ever.

Normally intelligent observers of society tend to lose their objectivity when they write about Oxford and Cambridge. Realization that, say, Redbrick universities frequently attract higher research grants, that the best business studies graduates come from Bradford, that Imperial College is tops in engineering, or even that London University's first eight frequently trounces both ancient rivals on the river, does nothing to dent the conviction that Oxbridge is in a league of its own. Other institutions may well, it is felt, have their good points, even, God knows, *virtues*, but they are not to be spoken of in the same breath as the Spires and Backs. When *Oxford Magazine* published an article, in May 1993, protesting against the innate sexism of university appointments, the press chose to see the issue purely in Oxbridge terms. No one was interviewed from the 'provinces'; the similarity of the discrimination elsewhere was deemed beneath public notice. It is difficult to avoid the conclusion that disputes are only worth the name, and entertaining, when they involve personnel from you-know-where. Altercations in Sheffield or Keele are considered about as interesting as watching paint dry.

The converse of this discrimination, centring on the social

invisibility of most tertiary education, is that one is allowed to make light of Oxbridge, but not disparage it. Being nasty to either of the dynamic duo is akin within the governing class to being beastly about Camelot. Gossip is OK. In fact, it is distinctly encouraged, particularly if it is pithy. We can laugh as much as we like at the 'antics' of undergraduates and the intellectual pinhead-dancing of the dons. They're just *so* clever! But that is all. Serious criticism is rare, and among alumni just about non-existent. Varsity graduates are surrounded by a penumbra of nostalgia, mixed with superiority, like space rockets glowing white-hot as they re-enter the atmosphere. The rest of us keep our mouths shut for fear of scorn or of being accused – that most English of jibes – of having chips on our shoulders.

Effortless inferiority and impotent rage are what Oxbridge traditionally evokes in outsiders. Those who did not gain admission to the ancient universities are – with important exceptions – valued by the Establishment at a discounted rate, and are held, at bottom, to lack class. This is the point. It is class, not learning, which is at the heart of the Oxbridge debate. Not just, or even mainly, inherited class – the sort reposed in what remains of the aristocracy and the gentry – but aspirant class and class values. To understand what class offers in its revised sense, we must turn briefly to the nature of British society.

Concentration on the past, and on hierarchies of the past, is a sure sign of a nation in decline. England today looks back endlessly to its rich cavalcade of history, conscious of the fact that all but the vestiges of glory are long departed. Just as disturbingly, foreigners have begun to do the same, regarding Britain either as a convenient platform for the European market or as a theme park, often charming, that is gradually being taken over by yobs and acts as 'a terrible lesson to us all'. Despite its occasional bouts of economic vigour, suggesting a cancer patient in remission, England is like ancient Egypt as perceived by the Greeks, or Rome by the Goths as they swept in and put it to the torch. Outsiders, newly vigorous themselves, or at least still looking forward with confidence, must wonder how it was that Britain was able to run a third of the world just half a century ago. Oxbridge, they will have heard, is a vital part of the answer. What they may not have heard is that it is even more deeply implicated in the subsequent decline. For generations, the twin universities trained the nation's élite to become *administrators*, not doers. All Britain needed to run the empire and pile up wealth, it was believed, was a strong army and navy and well-spoken task forces of politicians, teachers and civil servants. Oxbridge provided the thinkers and administrators; the services did the rest. The fact that this louche and lofty view of the world had not corresponded to reality since at least the 1930s took decades to sink in, and Oxford and Cambridge continued for years to turn out a class of person by the ton whose chief role was to run existing institutions, at home and abroad, without reference to change. Several factors helped rescue the venerable pair from the consequences of their folly. The world of communications grew at a phenomenal rate from the 1970s onwards, and with it came an insatiable appetite for plausible men (and women) good at giving interview and sounding as if they knew what they were talking about. Simultaneously, lawyers, managers and accountants became the revitalized, upgraded clerical class of the new materialism, and at the highest level were recruited preponderantly from Oxbridge. Finally, Britain's belated membership of the European Community and a powerful surge in the scope of multinational corporations, quangos and agencies like the United Nations opened new doors to eager young graduates, many of them from Oxbridge. Bureaucracy was suddenly big again and had an attractive, and lucrative, international dimension.

To those who believe in equality of opportunity, the special position accorded in British life to Oxford and Cambridge can appear almost deliberately perverse. How, they ask, can two institutions, yielding just 2 per cent of British graduates, be so dominant in so many fields? Worse, in a way, how does Britain get away with convincing the wider world that they should choose the bulk of any British personnel they need from so narrow and privileged a base? Such a view, however, ignores the duo's perceived central function and the imprimatur they are given by the governing élite. What unites Oxbridge graduates is not their cleverness – though most are of above average ability – nor even the quality of the teaching they receive, but their unwritten contract with the Establishment. To be blunt, Oxbridge graduates have Expectations, and these

Expectations are matched, indeed instilled, by their predecessors, whose principal duties to the state are held to be the propagation of their kind, the maintenance of 'civilized values' and protecting the even tenor of public life.

The fact is that the debate that has been going on since the Second World War about Britain's future, centring on our loss of empire and search for a role, has been conducted in the main by graduates of Oxford and Cambridge, with occasional interventions from the London School of Economics. The decision to join the European Community was taken by Oxbridge graduates, and opposed by Oxbridge graduates. Decisions on schools and curricula, the welfare state, legal reforms and economic revival are almost exclusively an Oxbridge preserve, with commissions of inquiry, press commentaries and television interviews similarly biased towards the twin citadels. Perhaps it would have been little different if we had been in the hands these last fifty years of a governing class drawn from every stratum of the nation. Perhaps a cabal based on Manchester, Southampton and Hull would have struck the same attitudes and taken the same key decisions. The point is, we shall never know – not, at least, until the Redbrick revolution, now beginning to gather pace, finally storms the barricades and takes over the engines of power. For now, the old order persists and will not willingly slacken its grip, and we need to ask ourselves: is the innate conservatism of a tightly drawn academic élite what Britain needs in the last, brittle years of this century? The middle classes – more tortured in England than anywhere else – still look upon an Oxbridge education as the Philosopher's Stone, turning their pallid pasts into golden prospects. In this United Kingdom, separation is still defined by accent and education as much as by profession, income and interests. The gradations of the bourgeoisie are infinite, and most of us spend much of our time parading, or concealing, our provenance in the hope that the world will take us at our own, inflated estimation. Middle-class life embraces millions of people, from High Court judges and Surrey stockbrokers with daughters at Roedean to bank clerks in Oldham, wearing Brut and offering Niersteiner with the Sunday roast. The upper middle classes like to regard Oxbridge as their domain. In fact, it has always been as much a beacon to those below, aspiring to rise.

Getting in is the passport to getting on, and school is where thousands of small tragedies begin. Which schools still matter? An Eton career represents an enormous boost to the social and worldly success of those whose parents can afford it. The same is true of Winchester, Radley, Harrow, Westminster, Charterhouse, Shrewsbury, Marlborough and a handful of other 'great' public schools. At the opposite end of the scale are the inner city comprehensives, turning out the 'trash' that will eventually work in the car factories, join the colours, sweep the streets, or form the dole queues. Grammar schools, which would formerly have rescued the most talented inner city children and offered them at least the chance of a university education, are for the most part gone, and their successors, damned by political correctness, can neither inculcate learning nor even imbue the basic sense of discipline that holds society together. The decline of the British working class began in the classrooms of the 1960s. It was Labour which did for the grammar schools, but it is Conservative politicians, most of whom went to public schools and Oxbridge, who have presided over the subsequent neglect and who continue to sustain the worst comprehensives. Some state schools, particularly those in prosperous 'shire' counties, do, of course, continue to provide an excellent, free education. A handful are among the best schools in the country. The problem is, most Britons live in cities. Today, the urban middle classes, afraid of state education, unable to afford the time-honoured alternative of boarding, have mostly gone 'private', mortaging themselves into old age in a bid to lift their children's chins above the rising tide of decay. Squeers, thou shouldst be living at this hour.

Conrad Black, the Canadian tycoon and owner of Telegraph Newspapers, ventured once that the difference between the American and the British approach to business was that when an American made a million (or, these days, 5 million), he was determined to turn it into 10, whereas the Brit wanted to turn it into a country house and membership of Boodles. The upper classes, such as they are, rarely work at all. They 'manage' their estates. The soft core of the middle classes, eschewing manufacturing, fill the professions, striking a fine balance between venality and integrity, struggling each day to create the conditions in which they can retire as 'gentlemen'. What unites these proud fellows is you-know-what.

They did not all go to the two ancient universities. But the majority did, and the rest feel their inferiority for the rest of their lives.

Stuck, socially and economically immobile, are the 'workers' – once variegated and proud, now increasingly uniform. No group has been more betrayed by this generation's destruction of the patrician conscience and *noblesse oblige* than the masses of people who were born, effectively, to serve. Factories are closing, a majority of comprehensives are more like remand centres, housing estates are violent and filthy, with drink and drugs and pornography and television for many the principal activities. In the 1990s, the mob is once again stirring in the streets of England; the underclass is rising like a blocked drain. If there *is* a class war in this country, it will be fought on the decaying streets of our cities, towns and villages, with the dispossessed taking revenge on the homes, vehicles and persons of the rich. The gulf between the top 25 per cent and the bottom 25 per cent is enormous and getting wider. So is the mutual resentment. Disraeli's Two Nations are by now so well established that only the police, and what little remains of British reticence, prevents class conflict from being a nightly occurrence.

Education, once thought of as the means of escape for ordinary people from the drudgery of working-class life, has failed them abysmally. Some, it is true, do succeed against all the odds in getting their GCSEs, A-levels and degrees. Most of those in this category attend the civic universities or former polytechnics and then move on, if they can find jobs worthy of their talents, to modest but useful careers. Fewer than one in a thousand workers would even *think* of applying to Oxbridge, and of those who make it through the fabled portals one in ten, perhaps, is not utterly recast in the process. Joining the Brotherhood, the small print of their unwritten contract informs them, means that origins are wiped away. It is the second baptism. Your parents are forgiven you; go and sin no more.

The central truth of what I have said is widely understood. Only a fool would think that Britain, since the war, has got it right and today stands tall among the nations of the world. Yet the general perspicuity that informs social criticism in this country rarely ex-tends to the Oxbridge dominance. Few outside the editorial ranks of the *Sunday Times* will risk having a public 'go' at the twin seats of privilege. Those who do, invite instant rebuke as well as insidious, long-term opprobrium. Positivism, perforce, is wise when writing about the quads and courts. We shall take the risk, and start with Oxford. One of the most blatant, if best-written and informative, examples of Varsity hagiography is *Oxford*, by Jan Morris, first published by Faber & Faber in 1965 and since taken over by the Oxford University Press as if it were an example of holy writ. Morris, an Oxonian from the days when she was James Morris, an Everest expeditionary, has been in love with her Alma Mater all her life, and in more recent times has produced the semi-official *Oxford Book of Oxford*, with which, thankfully, we need not detain ourselves.

Morris spares us not even the most intimate detail of her most enduring amour.

The *presence* of this institution remains inviolate, however its details change or its institutions vary. Ancient fretted cluttered buildings; plonking tennis balls and laughter off the river; the smells of wood, printer's ink and beeswax; the great dome of the Radcliffe Camera, like a huge old egg beside the Bodleian; green grass everywhere, and noticeboards fluttering with a thousand announcements; a feeling of easy-going irony, like a wink behind an admonition; a tacit assurance that here you may do, look and especially think how you like; a sense of generosity, tolerance and humour impregnating the very stones of the place, the very paragraphs of [its] incomprehensible Statutes: like it or not, all these really do survive, and raise this University and its patron city into the upper ranks of human artifacts, up there with the works of art, the codes of law and the philosophies. Sometimes as I walk through Oxford, cursing at her traffic, marvelling at her obscurity, and wondering when on earth they are going to bring her up to date, this old magic momentarily dazes me, and I lean against some gold-grey stone beneath the ragwort, and think how lucky I am to be grumbling there at all.

What does this bring to mind? Hang about. Of course. It reminds me of my own parody of Oxbridge thinking, spelled out in Chapter I. It turns out that my imagined idyll was no parody at all, but straightforward graduate orthodoxy. Morris may have attempted, in other areas of her literary endeavour, to approach the 'upper ranks of human artifacts'; in consideration of her undergraduate years, she achieves only sustained bathos.

Outsiders wishing to experience the stately rhythms of Oxford but lacking the wherewithal, or the inclination, for Morris dancing, can do so, of course, through visits to the city's many colleges and public buildings. At least they can when these are open, which, as the institutions gradually privatize themselves, is less and less often each year, and in some places scarcely at all. Thousands of visitors make the effort each day in open-topped tour buses, pointing their video cameras at the obvious sights and sounds along the Appian Way from Worcester to Wadham.

Oxford is not, in fact, the oldest university in Europe. That claim is disputed between Paris and Bologna. English clerics in the Norman and early Plantagenet periods went to the Sorbonne for their education, and transferred to the small town on the Isis in the late 1160s only following the protracted quarrel between Henry II of England and Philip II of France. Trevelyan describes the early days as 'riotous, lawless and licentious'. The typical student, he says, was 'miserably poor; he often learnt very little for want of books and tutoring, and left without taking a degree'. It sounds like the 1960s. Some of these olde Oxonians, apparently, were as young as 14, but took easily to the tavern and the brothel. They even had a tendency to roam the countryside in robber bands. Order came with the foundation of the colleges, first University and Merton, in 1264, then, soon after, Balliol and St Edmund's Hall. In the fifteenth century, Magdalen and Lincoln were constructed, followed by Brasenose, Corpus Christi, Trinity and St John's. Others arose in the succeeding centuries, with the high point coming in 1546 with the foundation, and refoundation, of Christ Church, by Cardinal Wolsey and Henry VIII. The colleges, halls of residence as well as teaching institutions, were intimately bound up with the Catholic faith, but had a worldly dimension as well, and on both counts were as ornate as their founders could afford. They also, from the start, had strong and distinct personalities and owed allegiance to the university proper only out of sufferance, in the knowledge that they could either hang together or hang separately.

Visitors disinclined to active observation may prefer to make their first contact with the university by way of 'The Oxford Story', a unique funicular history of the university, constructed in a former warehouse in Broad Street, directly opposite Balliol, adjoining the old city wall. The Story, chronicling eight hundred years of influence, achievement and self-importance, was set up partly on the initiative of a group of dons in 1984 and is 20 per cent owned by the university, several of whose senior figures, including the President of Magdalen, sit on its board. In 1992, it attracted no fewer than half a million undergraduates *manqué*, many of them from abroad, and it would seem that the spell it weaves on the human psyche is universally effective.

It is when the desks begin to move that visitors realize they are in for a treat. Up to then, they have been sitting in a mock lecture hall, done up with oak panelling and old sepia photographs of dons and students in their gowns, watching a video montage of Oxford's glory. Now, each is seated at a genuine Victorian desk, one of a series which follow one another like benign fairground cars up a steep spiral incline from the ground floor almost to the roof. Translations of the spoken text are available into the usual languages, including Japanese (big Oxford buffs, the Japanese – from Nippon to Oxon is but a step). The original, for adults at least, is most commonly by Magnus Magnusson, the avuncular presenter of *Mastermind*, Britain's longest-running television quizshow – appealing to people who think they know a thing or two and enjoy showing off in the privacy of their own homes. Alternatives are available from Sir Alec Guinness, the lugubrious interpreter of John le Carré, and, for the children, the 'entertainer' Timmy Mallet. But it is Magnusson, with his persuasive Scottish burr, so redolent of Morningside's proudest families, that is somehow most appropriate. The Icelandic-born TV presenter, who took a degree from Jesus College in the early 1950s, begins our tour by telling us that Oxford is home to 'the ablest young people in the world'. The 'home of lost causes', he continues, its scholars have 'changed the world' and left an 'Oxford mark on history'. As our train of thought, drawn by the locomotive of learning, begins its creaking ascent in the thirteenth century – when Oxford struggled as a kind of theological flophouse – it passes various tableaux of the one-time Great and Good, including John Wycliffe, Master of Balliol, who, in a most un-Oxford way, tried to teach Christian thinking to the common people in a language they could understand. Early students, the commentary informs us, were taught to learn – 'and to lead'. Their forcing house, within which they were apprenticed to established greybeards, was destined to become 'one of the greatest intellectual workshops of the world'. By the fourteenth century, 'Oxford scholars governed Europe', and come the time of Elizabeth I, the Virgin Queen looked to Oxford to provide leaders of her government. 'Oxford obliged', says Magnus, approvingly, 'and was rewarded with wealth and privilege.' Not a lot has changed since.

And so on and so on, down the centuries. Very enjoyable it is, too. We are fed all manner of snippets. Christ Church became the headquarters for Charles I after the Battle of Edgehill, and the university was to remain loyal to the King throughout the Civil War, to its discomfiture thereafter. John Wesley, in the eighteenth century, was a fellow of Lincoln College for twenty-five years, but, my goodness, 'detested Oxford life'. Could it be something to do with the fact that they tried to run him out of town? By the time the founder of what became Methodism was in residence, the ascetic ruminations of John Wycliffe and Roger Bacon, with their overtones of monastic purity, had given way to the braying of upper-class wine louts, whose social rank was indicated by gold tassels in their hair. Magnusson, a liberal Lutheran by sentiment, is faintly censorious here, yet still essentially tolerant, and responds to the decadence of eighteenth-century Oxford mainly by moving on swiftly to the Victorian age. Ah yes. Much better. Now it begins to sound familiar. A total of twenty-two British prime ministers, as well as a number of overseas leaders, including Bill Clinton, came, he informs us, from Oxford, including almost all heads of government from the nineteenth century. Gladstone, the definitive Liberal, turns out to have been emotionally enslaved to his old university and established the Science Museum in London as a tribute to its work. Women, it is noted, were not admitted to the drooping spires until late in Oxford's history and were unable to sit for degrees until the 1920s. Since then, apparently, they have taken to the place like ducks to water, yielding such varied notables as Mrs Gandhi, Mary Goldring and, yes, Esther Rantzen. Every student, Magnus concludes (as he is talking to strangers he does not use the more usual 'undergraduate') is 'touched and changed' by Oxford. Indeed, such is the appeal of the place that The Oxford Story – a kind of Tardis for the timeless – has even created its own 'freemen', led by Colin Dexter, the Cambridge-educated creator of Inspector Morse. Presumably, these worthies are not required to pay up at the mock porter's lodge upon entry and can come again and again to pay vicarious homage to the old grey stones.

A few dons are reliably reported not to approve of this tabloid interpretation of their history – which is 'twinned' with Dover's 'White Cliffs Experience' and 'The Canterbury Tales' – but Father James McConica, as reactionary a fellow of All Souls as one could hope to meet this side of Purgatory, was impressed. 'It is what I call honey-coloured Oxford', he told the *Sunday Telegraph*'s Nicholas Farrell (Gonville and Caius, Cambridge), after an exploratory Away-Day excursion, 'but it was not trivialization.' Anthony Smith, President of Magdalen, takes a unashamedly commercial approach to the exhibition he has helped Oxford make of itself. 'Tourists come to consume Oxford, not to understand it', he has said, and so long, presumably, as the turnstiles keep clanging, he will be happy. Even more august support comes from the Oxford Chancellor, Lord Jenkins of Hillhead, OM, who unveiled the plaque on opening day, 1988. 'A key to unlock the door of Oxford University', he called it. Jenkins, however, turns out to have something of a personal interest: the bespectacled undergraduate facing an 'essay crisis', which makes up the introductory tableau, is no less a personage than the young Roy, fresh up from the Valleys. The whole extravaganza is kept on the rails by Chris Dee, its personable marketing manager, who has plans for the expansion of its section dealing with the twentieth century, possibly into the next building. He has good cause to be cheerful. His waxworks of academe is a huge success, and a tribute to the magic of the Oxford marque. What price 'The Hull Story', narrated by Roy Hattersley, or 'The Red Bricks of Birmingham', commentary by Jasper Carrot? No. On second thoughts, perhaps not.

Cambridge has as yet no equivalent to the fast-track technology of its ancient rival and continues to rely on 'live' bus tours and native guides to expound its glories to the city's 2 million annual visitors. 'The Cambridge Chronicle' cannot, however, be far off. It could take the form of a punt journey along the Backs – a kind of tunnel of love for lovers of learning – with the highlights of the university's long history unfolding at each bend of the Cam. Stephen Fry and Hugh Laurie would be the obvious narrators. In their inspired company, we should no doubt soon be convinced that a place at King's or Newnham or Peterhouse, or even little Lucy Cavendish (founded 1965), was a prize worth fighting for, and that those privileged enough to have earned their BA (Cantab.) are among civilization's finest products.

Cambridge in fact (whisper it soft) began life a little later than its great rival. Riots in Oxford in 1209, occasioned by bad blood between students and townspeople, led a number of academics and their charges to up-sticks and transfer to Cambridge. The fact that they moved to the Fens rather than, say, Winchester or York, supports the view that learning of a kind had already been established there, most notably around the monastic hospital of St John, which later gave birth to the college of the same name. At any rate, by 1225, with students receiving regular instruction from regent masters, a chancellor had been appointed, and eight years later the Pope granted legal privileges which gave the experiment university status. Halls of residence, like those in Oxford, were quickly established, starting, probably, with Peterhouse, in 1284, then Clare Hall (now Clare College), Gonville Hall (later refounded as Gonville and Caius), Trinity Hall and Michaelhouse and King's Hall (the last two subsequently merged into Trinity College, one of the grandest and richest foundations in the country). King's College, with its sublime chapel, followed in the fifteenth century, requiring the demolition of much of the ancient town, and then St John's, whose 'New Court' across the river, a pioneering example of the Gothic revival, is reached by the Bridge of Sighs. Construction continued at a feverish pace throughout the next hundred years, and has continued sporadically ever since. As in Oxford, the tension between scholars and locals in the early years was considerable, frequently degenerating into outright warfare. One affray, in 1381, was so bad, involving the kind of behaviour associated today with football hooligans and Yardies, that the Bishop of Norwich felt obliged to send troops to the town 'where he attacked the rebels, killed some and imprisoned others' (Charles Henry Cooper, *The Annals of Cambridge*, 1842). Order was also required within college. At

Peterhouse, according to the early Statutes, the ideal was that scholars

shall act in such sort in their disputations, that none shall dispute with impetuosity and clamour, but in a civil and honest manner; that none shall interrupt another while declaiming, either in argument or reply, but listen to him with diligence; that all contumelious, quarrelsome, and indecorous words, which, as is frequently the case, only generate hatred and discord, shall be interdicted among them. But if the contrary be attempted by any one, he shall be gently reprehended by the . . . deans.

Well, it was either that or a visit from the Bishop of Norwich.

By the end of the fifteenth century, G. M. Trevelyan tells us, Cambridge had established itself as a serious rival to Oxford, and already a majority of English bishops were Fensmen. Learning, starting with the Trivium in Latin, rhetoric and logic, had expanded to include the Quadrivium, leading to an MA in arithmetic, geometry, astronomy and music – all major Cambridge interests to this day. Trevelyan points out, however, as though it were a matter of little consequence, that 'neither Cambridge nor Oxford added much to scholarship or thought until the coming of the New Learning in the first years of the Tudor kings'. A century of indolence, then. Nothing new there. If learning was a long time coming, arrogance was not. An early Cambridge 'rag', recorded in 1597, involved a cruel satire of the locals by scholars, who 'conceiving themselves somewhat wronged by the townsmen betook them for revenge to their wits'. The mayor and other councillors, and their wives, were invited to attend a drama at Clare Hall, but upon taking their seats found themselves subjected to satire, abuse and rude gestures by the students, which they 'were fain to attend till dismissed at the end of the comedy'. Today, such behaviour is, of course, the special responsibility of the Footlights Society and Newman and Baddiel.

The exigencies of the Reformation and, later, of the Civil War left a lasting mark on Cambridge. The Oxford Martyrs were in fact Cambridge bishops, in the wrong place at the wrong time, while the university's subsequent royalism was to cost it dear at the hands of Cromwell, notwithstanding the fact that he was himself a Cambridge man. Three college heads were rendered headless, and their skulls displayed in London. On the credit side, the great Isaac

Newton was in residence at Trinity, displaying his effortlessly superior *gravitas*, and Milton, a puritan of catholic taste, was drafting *Paradise Lost*, the greatest epic poem in the language, at Christ's. No such compensations were available to students in the eighteenth century. By then, the decadence that also affected Oxford was in full flood, and between 1725 and 1773 not a single lecture was given by any Regius Professor of Modern History. Trevelyan, in his *English Social History*, goes on to relate how one holder of the chair that he himself was to inherit with such distinction died in 1768 from a fall while riding home drunk from his vicarage.

A bad show, but all part of the Great Tradition. Another tradition, that of staffing government administration, was to emerge in the nineteenth century, when both Oxford and Cambridge, freed by the Test Act of 1871 from the Church's monopoly of teaching and membership, began to send large numbers of their graduates into the home and imperial civil services. Trevelyan, born just five years after the Test Act and a brilliant undergraduate at Cambridge's Trinity College in the closing years of the century, makes no bones about his approval of this development. 'It was a compliment', he wrote, 'paid to the reputation of the Oxford and Cambridge system of examination for degrees, and it had the effect of making closer than ever the connection of University men with public life.'

Quite so. And so the myth does grow by what it feeds on.

The 'Cambridge Chronicle' is not yet with us, and, until the technology has been perfected, a real-life punt, with a reliable guidebook in the hands of the reclining puntee, remains the best means of viewing the university's several splendours. Initiative, however, is not entirely absent from the scene. Coleridge Community College, a pioneering local school, has devised a board game, 'Cambridge by Degrees', which allows players to move around the city streets on bicycles, study for A-levels and win places, seemingly without interview, at the principal university colleges. Aimed mainly at tourists but, one suspects, with far wider potential, the venture excited considerable interest in the local business community. Thirty companies, or branches of larger concerns, including Barclays Bank and McDonald's, were in the end allowed to contribute stake money to Coleridge in return for the purchase of a square, complete with logo, on the circular board. Steve Goss, the school's business manager – a post that is itself a sign of the times – was brimful of confidence: 'The game', he said, basing its appeal in the enormous pulling power of the university, 'is the first potential mega-earner we have had.'

For an insider's view of this power, we turn again to Lord Jenkins and his definitive monograph, *An Oxford View of Cambridge*, delivered as the Rede Lecture in Cambridge in May 1988. The biographer of Asquith, liberal statesman, political reformer and one-time President of the European Commission, is in mellow mood.

Exploring the history of Oxford and Cambridge . . . I have been struck by the symbiotic nature of the relationship between the two universities. Over eight centuries they have greatly influenced and cross-fertilized each other. They have been more pacers than rivals. At times one has gone ahead (indeed it could I suppose be argued that in the Middle Ages Oxford was more consistently so) but the other has then caught up or overtaken, frequently building on a development initiated in the first one. The result has been a history of a relationship a great deal more fluctuating and interesting than the average course of the sporting event for which we are best known to the world.

Jenkins, by temperament, if not always in his judgements, is clearly of the Jan Morris school of Varsity studies. He talks of 'muscular intellectual competition' having begun at Cambridge a good fifty years before cricket and rowing and goes on to praise what Sir Charles Dilke, a Victorian alumnus of Trinity Hall, called 'good, calm, clear Cambridge English'. Later still, he calls the roll of British prime ministers who honed their skills at Oxbridge. Of the fourteen eighteenth-century premiers, he tells us, seven were at Oxford, five at Cambridge and two at neither. The nineteenth century yielded nine Oxonians, six Cantabrigians and three from neither. This century, Oxford's count is eight, to Cambridge's three, and 'nowhere or elsewhere' six (now seven, with John Major). 'Nowhere or elsewhere' is an appropriate phrase, suggesting a certain synonymity between the two. Lord Jenkins is dyed in the wool. In the past hundred years, we are informed, relentlessly, there have been thirteen Oxford Lord Chancellors and just four from Cambridge, while in the 90-year history of the viceroyalty the score was Oxonians fifteen, Cantabrigians five.

Despite his natural adherence to the paean principle of Oxbridge studies, Jenkins is far too honest a critic to let either university – especially his own – get away completely free of stricture. Thus, in reporting that Balliol and All Souls ran the empire virtually unaided, he adds, devastatingly: 'It is a little difficult not to comment that the main direction in which they ran it was into the ground.' He confesses, too, that Oxford, though a 'crucial guardian' of 'humanistic learning', is, at its worst, 'glib and flippant' – a university based on talking, rather than listening, 'which has kept Britain well supplied with those good at the chattering occupations, such as defending the criminal classes, conducting television panels, and governing the country'. And having praised the 'great interlocking dynasties of Cambridge families' which set up their encampments west of the Cam towards the end of last century, and the many 'brilliant' men who 'added their lustre' to the Cavendish Laboratory in the inter-war years of our own age, Jenkins then concedes that by the 1950s 'the flame of intellectual enquiry ... had substantially migrated, for reasons outside our control, to the banks of the Charles River and the purlieus of Harvard Yard'. And where is that same flame today? Again, Jenkins is unsparing (though it must hurt). 'Still in the United States, I think, but more disseminated in accordance with the westward tilt in the balance of the country, and with Berkeley and Stanford able to claim at least a piece of the true cross.'

So much for truth, justice and the American way. Finally, in the contemplation of money and the growth of private funding – never far from his mind – we have Jenkins's vision of the future, and with it the resolution of the syllogism he has hinted at but never quite expressed.

A return to private money is likely to mean a return to that duopoly of quality [i.e. Oxbridge]. We, to put it bluntly, have richer alumni, greater treasures, more glamour and therefore greater money-pulling capacity. I do not think we should refrain from exploiting these assets. An equality of second-rateness, a Britain without any university of world class because the government is too short-sighted to pay for it, and the universities at the margin too supine or too squeamish to overcome that short-sightedness by exploiting their own fame, is in nobody's interest.'

So there we have it. Others – God help them – are stuck fast in the margins. Their cause is hopeless. The great social democrat weeps tears of commiseration for the rest, tears of joy for history's darlings. When Lord Jenkins looks to the future, he begins with the past.

Another key insider, this time from the Fens, is Lord Annan, born on Christmas Day, 1916, educated at Stowe and King's, Cambridge, a historian destined to become Provost of his old college, then of UCL and Vice-Chancellor of the University of London. In *Our Age*, his study, in more than 600 pages, of British life this century, as seen from Oxbridge, Noël Annan does not once question the ascendancy of his own, deeply privileged academic class. It might be thought that a man who spent fifteen years in the running of London University and was also for five years a member of the academic planning board of the University of Essex would be immune from the notion of duopolistic supremacy, but that would be to stretch a point.

Our Age opens with a discussion of the Oxford conspirators the author knew as a young man – 'The Children of the Sun' he calls them – who, in the definition of their leader, Maurice Bowra, came from the upper or middle classes, grew up in public school and went to Oxford or Cambridge. On page two, a verse by John Sparrow, a long-standing Warden of All Souls, is reproduced in praise of Bowra, who we are told was 'the most famous Oxford don and wit of his day'. Neither Sparrow nor Bowra, be it realized, left much memorable behind them. Sparrow was a minor academic and a capricious college manager. Bowra, a renowned classicist and one-time Vice-Chancellor, who could terrorize friends and enemies alike. In his rhyme, Sparrow pictures Bowra at the head of his fellow wits greeting God at the Last Judgement.

He'll seize the sceptre and annex the throne,
    Claim the Almighty's thunder for his own,
Trump the last Trump and the Last Post postpone
Then shall we supplicate at Heaven's high bar:
    'Be merciful.' You made us what we are,
Our jokes, our joys, our hopes, our hatred too,
The outrageous things we do, or want to do –
    How much of all of them we owe to you!

What a card! It may be satire, but the conceit rings through, clear as a bell. Oxford men are made in heaven and have the ear of the Lord. One cannot help feeling that with this kind of arrogance, one Sparrow at least may have fallen without registering on God's calculator.

Yet Annan appears a most agreeable fellow and is a shrewd judge of the mores of his time. Oxbridgeans often are. Listen to him on the differences between Oxford and the Other Place in the inter-war years.

No Cambridge college could compete with the Christ Church mafia under its *capo*, that quintessentially Establishment figure, J. C. Masterman. Oxford's tentacles stretched through the ministries into the secret intelligence and security services. Oxford was always news; the disputes of its dons and the frolics of its undergraduates regaled in the London press. Cambridge's bleak motto was: *nil admirari*; and its tone of voice was impersonal, less playful, witty and mondain, the dry biscuit served with the Oxford madeira. Many of the ablest students at Cambridge studied mathematics or science, and the most striking names were to be found in the laboratories – in the Cavendish under Rutherford where the atom was split or among Adrian's physiologists, or again after the war in the Cavendish where Crick and Watson discovered the structure of DNA. It was in the laboratories rather than in the humanities 'that the earliest marxists were to be found. Bernal and Haldane, and such sympathizers as Gowland Hopkins and Waddington, preached the gospel that scientists, guided by scientific principles, should replace politicians and run public affairs.

Plus ça change, one might say, even down to the point where the scientists are being urged to get their fingers out and *do* something. Alas, lack of change is hardly progress, and the continuing rivalries of Oxford and Cambridge, the frivolous gawping of the press and the inability of Oxbridge scientists to do enough that is practical, and marketable – or to achieve a lasting place in the shaping of the nation – have been maintained, almost intact, to this day.

Annan is aware that his generation (by which he means anyone in authority since the First World War) has presided over a period of virtually unbroken economic decline in this country. He adduces all manner of reasons for this sad fact, including, centrally, the need of Englishmen to be accepted as gentlemen, unconnected with labour, but only obliquely suggests that it might have anything to do with Oxbridge. This is, from his point of view, understandable, and it would indeed be absurd to pile up all of Britain's woes at the feet of just two universities, however august. Equally, it seems odd that they should not, explicitly, be brought into the reckoning. Annan provides the evidence, but skates over the obvious conclusion. For example, while quoting Newman's disdainful description of the then new University of London as a series of 'bazaars or pantechnicons, in which wares of all kinds are heaped together for sale in stalls independent of each other', he offers no critique. The future cardinal admitted, apparently, that without the 'mechanical arts' life could not go on, but believed they were inappropriate areas of study for the élite. Annan further recalls how long it took Cambridge to establish a faculty of engineering (they are only now getting round to business studies) and how, as recently as 1986, Geoffrey Elton, the then Regius Professor of History at Cambridge (that job again!), rejected as 'ignorant parrot talk' the notion that the universities could be blamed for the country's economic performance. In a chapter that seeks to pin down the causes of Britain's economic misery, Annan refers again and again to Civil Servants, diplomats, politicians and experts, nearly all of them from the Spires and Backs, but *still* does not see the common thread. Later in the book, in a chapter entitled 'The Dons Learn Bitter Realities', he records how between 1900 and 1940 an Oxbridge First was 'a permanent hallmark for life', and how a lesser award could be ameliorated by a Blue, or by making a mark in the Union or editing *Isis* or *Granta*. There then followed, he writes, 'the golden age of the don', when academics came down from Oxford in particular to become 'indispensable backroom boys' in Whitehall, advisers to politicians and the prize guests of London's salon society. Annan proceeds to condemn the behaviour of protesting students in the 1960s and '70s, especially those at the LSE, Essex and the North London Polytechnic. Only one university escapes his lash: Oxford – which 'had no hesitation in expelling thirteen students who defied an instruction and broke into the Indian Institute'. Eventually, Annan breaks cover.

It had been right to expand higher education. What had been wrong was to imagine that all students could be given a Rolls-Royce higher education. No country could afford it. No country could afford within a generation to double the number of university institutions, create 32 polytechnics, upgrade the colleges and finance this expansion *on the principle of parity of esteem* . . . No country could afford centres of excellence (the equivalent of Harvard and Berkeley, the *Grandes Ecoles* and Max Planck Institutes) and declare that all other universities were to be given equal status . . .

Annan makes no mention of Oxford or Cambridge in his argument. He does not need to. Their presence is draped over his prose like a bishop's cope across his shoulders.

Jeremy Paxman, while supporting the need for widespread change in our system of higher education, devotes much of his own chapter on university life in *Friends in High Places: Who Runs Britain?* to a description of Oxbridge, and in particular of life at All Souls. In the old days, he informs us, 'the achievement of All Souls was to be simultaneously the most cloistered and the most worldly of colleges', with a dining-table at which scarcely a significant area of British public life was unrepresented. Today, by contrast, although it is 'bristling with the ambitious and the competitive' and includes two cabinet ministers among its fellows, it 'now seems much less grand'. Well, perhaps. Tell that to the steady stream of established figures who queue up to attend its Chichele dinners, from the Lord Chief Justice and Lord Goodman to the Education Secretary, John Cleese and the Archbishop of Canterbury. Paxman, whose abrasive television manner famously once caused him to be blackballed from the Garrick Club, also concedes that 'Oxford and Cambridge continue to fashion the ruling élite', but then goes on to observe that their dominant position 'cannot last'. Is this hope or judgement? He quotes one graduate as telling him: 'If you go to Oxford or Cambridge, you're given a different map of the world. It has a different projection. Instead of looking up at the institutions of power, you look down upon them, and you can see the way into them, the links between them.'

Many otherwise liberal, even radical, commentators have no problem with this Olympian cartography. The historian and political writer. Peter Hennessy, in close contact with the everyday business of UK administration, sees the two universities' grasp on the Civil Service (his specialist field) as 'meritocratic' and tells us, in his prodigious analysis, *Whitehall* (Secker & Warburg, 1989), that he enjoyed, 'even relished', his time at St John's College, Cambridge, in the late 1960s. Who could doubt it for a moment? Although currently Professor of History at Queen Mary and Westfield College – one of the core members of the old London federation hoping to form an élite rival to Oxbridge – Hennessy remains a frequent visitor to the Fens and often writes for *Cam*, the alumni magazine and house journal of the Cambridge network. He knows the answers, one suspects, yet remains part of the problem.

Those of us who are mere spectators at the feast are almost bound to take a contrary view. Elites will sometimes discuss modifications of their power; they can hardly be expected to campaign for their own abolition. Asking Oxbridge dons, and their legions of triumphant students, to give up part of what they see as their birthright would be like asking the Mafia to support a crackdown on organized crime. They won't hear of it. Instead, they say it is up to rival institutions to improve their standards and enhance their prestige – if they can.

The argument, at face value, is difficult to refute, and the implicit challenge has been taken up by a number of universities over the last thirty years. What the challengers lack, however – apart, perhaps, from London's top six, Edinburgh, Manchester, Bristol, Durham, Essex and York – is the will that they should succeed. England *wants* Oxbridge. It *needs* Oxbridge. Even when the central nexus of politicians, administrators, soldiers, educators, artistic directors, businessmen and commentators who make up the Establishment accords respect to other institutions, it has no desire that they should acquire equivalent standing.

In the next two chapters we shall turn to what those who passed through Oxford and Cambridge have to say about their experience. In the biographical literature of England this century (to look no further), chapters on the two universities are a commonplace. Indeed, it is a commonplace to say so. Pick up three out of any four volumes of memoirs of the Great and the Good, and there it will be, simply labelled, with the dates of going up and coming down. The experience of attending either institution is pivotal. Not all who have been undergraduates endorse the experience. Some feel that too much is made of three short years at the end of their youth. They may not have done much to get in or much to get on. They may consider that it was of no lasting importance. But they are wrong. The fact of their Oxbridge years is like a hallmark in fine silver. It ages them; it defines them; it values them. Whether they like it or not, it is a large part of what made them. Yet, ironically, what much Varsity literature also reveals is the seeming insignificance of the experience *at the time.* The three or four years an undergraduate spent at Oxford may have been pleasurable, even stimulating. In the majority of cases, it was certainly something to look back on with fondness. But it was only afterwards, once the images of hired gowns and mortar boards had been consigned to fading photographs and the network had built up in front of them like a London Underground map, that the true magic began to work. Some were surprised by this. Others knew it when they applied. Or if they didn't, their parents did. They knew that these were no mere finishing schools for the Establishment, but crucibles, where raw ore was transformed into shining steel.

What is perhaps most interesting, and revealing, about this prolix literature of recollection is its almost uniform lack of emphasis on academic matters. Oxbridge alumni are not in the main joined by nostalgia for past tutorials or lectures. Nor do they make much mention of essays or dissertations or their dynamic resolution of intellectual doubts. Instead, what comes unbidden into their minds is the good society of their friends and their stuttering attempts to climb to the top of whichever greasy pole they had grasped, whether it be the Union, a political club, or sport. Oxford and Cambridge might imagine that they are perceived first and foremost as centres of higher learning. Few outside the narrow world of academe would agree with them. To their former undergraduates, in particular, the pursuit of degrees appears to have been an unwelcome distraction from the important business of having a good time and building up contacts. Only occasionally is work mentioned, and then often with derision. Exams come across as tiresome intrusions. An Oxbridge education, it seems, is too important to be left to the dons.

The evidence between hard covers is not, unfortunately, comprehensive. The personal histories of graduates who were successful but who did not go on to become household names – inevitably the bulk of each year's product – are obviously thin on the ground. Their attitudes, and the value of their Varsity years, must be separately gauged. Most biographies, and autobiographies, are, moreover, written many years after their subjects 'came down', at a time when their careers are perhaps drawing to a close. Thus, the bulk of Oxbridge recollections currently available do not cover recent years, and evidence of contemporary, or near-contemporary, developments must again be sought elsewhere. Even so, the literature that does exist is extensive and illustrates well the prevailing ethos in much of our century. It is as good a guide as we have got, and what it shows above all else is the impressive permanence of Oxbridge thinking. Constancy within change is supposed to be a central feature of life at both institutions, and only by claiming that there has been a revolution since, say, 1975, that has utterly transformed eight hundred years of tradition, and effectively 'trashed' it, creating a new Year Zero, can the current university authorities deny the representative nature of the record.

One other caveat should be entered. Most of the available books quoted in the two chapters following cover the lives and careers of those who pursued the humanities and went on to make their names as wordspinners. Scientists, engineers and doctors – genuine 'performers' in a world constructed largely of mirrors – are significantly more reticent, perhaps less boastful, than historians, lawyers, politicians and the rest. They may also be less interested in their public personae. Such exceptions as there are are invaluable, but in the main the 'doers' must declare their hand in other ways. The 'talkers' are only too willing to speak for themselves.

CHAPTER FOUR

LOST CAUSES?

When the High Lama asked him whether Shangri-La was not unique in his experience, and if the Western World could offer anything in the least like it, he answered with a smile: 'Well, yes – to be quite frank, it reminds me very slightly of Oxford.'

(JAMES HILTON, *Lost Horizon*, 1933)

THE UNIVERSITY OF OXFORD IS LIKE THE ELDER of identical twins born into a great and titled family. Though the fraternal love it feels for Cambridge is real and enduring, the rivalry is necessarily intense and the laws of primogeniture are constantly invoked.

Oxford feels that its responsibility for running the country is greater than that of Cambridge, which it sees as preoccupied with intellectual abstractions. Accordingly, its graduates down the years have tended to dominate government, administration and the professions, and the links with London are strong. A clear majority of Oxonians, even today, come from the south-east, and remain there after taking their degrees. Those who came down (to 'go up') from the Midlands or the north were in the past seen largely as district commissioners of the dominant culture, rather in the way that Highlands aristocrats, with their Oxford accents, kept Scotland safe for the Crown. Gradually, but with increasing speed, this Home Counties tyranny has been relaxed, so that recruitment drives by the colleges now concentrate much of their energy in former *terra incognita*. Even so, the impact of seven hundred years of metropolitan awareness is not going to disappear overnight, and the effect of Oxford's sales drive beyond the Watford Gap is more an attempt to spread its influence over a broader geographical area than a recognition that other values matter too.

The obsession with London – for which we can read power, influence, money and bright lights – is, of course, inimical to true scholarship and convincing evidence of the fact that Oxford is really two universities occupying the same space. *Universitas Oxoniensis* is a deeply serious institution, with its roots sunk in the past but reaching always upwards towards the frontiers of knowledge. Anyone seeking to question the role, or capacity, of this venerable body of knowledge is inviting rebuke, for Oxford research is justly famed. There are many good universities in the modern world, and standards everywhere are rising – a fact which too many employers and institutions in England conveniently forget. Yet in terms of overall scholarship and scientific and technological achievement, Oxford has few equals anywhere, and, at the highest level, only a tiny handful of true rivals, including Cambridge, in this country. This much is clear. But it is not the end of the story. It is, in fact, a quite separate story. For then there is Oxford Mark Two – Varsity – the place where the emerging Establishment, not all of it especially brilliant, frolics for three years in unique and glorious surroundings and where those with ambition and an eye for the main chance invest heavily in the networking that will help set them up for the rest of their lives.

This is the Oxford the world knows and looks to most keenly – the place extolled, with unaccustomed bathos, by John Fowles as 'Mother Oxford, Venus-Minerva, triple-haunted, hundred-tongued'. Even the Students Union – a body less devoted to Oxoniana than its better-known rivals for undergraduate affection – is unambiguous about its importance.

Although work is, without doubt, a necessary part of life at Oxford, even the most demanding of tutors would think it unnatural if you didn't have some interests outside the weekly essay. And one of the obvious advantages of this particular University lies in the fact that, whilst you are undoubtedly working with some of the most educated and respected minds in the world, you are also presented with the opportunity to play with probably the liveliest and most intelligent people you'll ever get to have good time with.

(The Oxford Handbook, OUSU, 1993)

The author of this self-satisfied tribute, which stops just short of saying how 'useful' such college contacts could prove, might have added that his fellow students, as well as being 'the most lively and intelligent people' you could ever hope to meet, are also among the

luckiest, the most privileged and the most likely to succeed. But he
didn't. That much is taken as read. It is part of Oxford's furniture.
As the late Kenneth Tynan once observed: 'More time is more
cleverly, eloquently and productively wasted at Oxford than anywhere else.'

The literature of Oxford this century, covering the magical,
quadrangular world of undergraduate life, is, of course, almost a
genre in itself, stretching from *Zuleika Dobson* and *Brideshead
Revisited* right up to Inspector Morse. But the biographical output,
dealing with real experience, is even more prolific. Were there to be
an Oxford Book of Oxford Chapters, it would be suffciently large
as to justify availability in either Full, Shorter or Concise editions.
No Great Man who has ever dreamed beneath the Spires of his
brilliant career would conceive of a book of memoirs that did not
deal in depth with his undergraduate days. The same will no doubt
be true of the women; for most of these we must, alas, wait a little
longer.

Yet it is with a woman, very much of our own time, that we start.
Benazir Bhutto, the two-times Prime Minister of Pakistan, has lived
her entire life in the shadow of her father, Zulfiquar Ali Bhutto,
deposed by the military as his country's leader in 1977 and hanged
in desperate circumstances two years later. Bhutto *père*, like a lot of
Asia's ruling class (Indira and Rajiv Gandhi and the Crown Prince
and Princess of Japan among them), was an Oxford product and
held his old university in almost reverential awe. It was inevitable,
therefore, that as he rose to the top in Pakistan, he should want his
children to enjoy the same benefits.

Oxford, Oxford, Oxford, he'd drummed into all of us. Oxford was one of
the best and most respected universities in the world. Oxford was steeped
in English history. English literature, the Church, the monarchy, Parliament
all had some connection with Oxford. American education was very good,
he allowed, but was conducted in a more relaxed manner. Oxford would
give us all a new horizon and a sense of discipline. He'd entered all four of
us at birth. As the oldest, I was the only one who had the luxury of
completing my Oxford education before the coup turned our lives upside-
down. Mir left Oxford shortly after the beginning of his second year to

fight for my father's life in England, while Sanam never got there at all. My years in my father's beloved Alma Mater meant a great deal to him.

(*Daughter of the East*, Hamish Hamilton, 1988)

They certainly did. In a letter to his daughter, written soon after her arrival at Lady Margaret Hall in the autumn of 1973, Bhutto senior – whose relationship with Oxford obviously carried clout as well as conviction – seems almost in tears at the sheer, mystical appositeness of it all.

I see your presence like mine in flesh and blood, over every cobble of the streets of Oxford, over every step you take on the frozen stone ladders [*sic*], through every portal of learning you enter. Your being at Oxford is a dream come true. We pray and hope that this dream, turned into reality, will grow into a magnificent career in the service of your people.

A simple progression: today Oxford, tomorrow the world. Benazir, whose second term as Prime Minister of her country was considerably assisted by the appointment of Farooq Leghari, a fellow Oxonian, as President, enjoyed life to the full as an undergraduate, free from the misogynist constraints of Islamic society. She did enough academically to be admitted to postgraduate studies in international law and diplomacy after taking her degree in PPE, but is perhaps best remembered for her time in the Oxford Union. She claims to have joined mainly to keep her father happy, but quickly discovered that this was the real point of her university education. The Union, she writes, was 'one of the most important and pleasant focal points of my life'. She worked hard at it, listening to speakers ranging from Germaine Greer and Arthur Scargill to Lord Stockton and Edward Heath. She loved everything about it: the formality, the dressing up, the feasting, the fine words, the candle-lit dinners. Here, clearly, was a prime minister in waiting.

In December 1976, after a determined Union career, during which she served on the Standing Committee and as treasurer, she was elected president – one of only a handful of women to have been so at that time. Her father had been on tenterhooks. 'In an election one side has to win and the other has to lose', he wrote to her, sagely, before the poll. 'You have to do your best, but the result must be accepted in good grace.' Cabling her from Rawalpindi a month later, he was beside himself with glee.

OVERJOYED AT YOUR ELECTION AS PRESIDENT OF THE OXFORD UNION. YOU HAVE DONE SPLENDIDLY. OUR HEARTWARMING CONGRATULA-TIONS ON YOUR GREAT SUCCESS, PAPA.

Her term as president was busy, centring on two motions, 'That capitalism will triumph', opposed, without obvious prescience, by Tariq Ali (a predecessor in her chair) and 'That the West can no longer live at the expense of the Third World'. When she presided over the 'fun' debate, on the proposition that 'This House would rather rock than roll', she was carried out of the hall on the shoulders of her peers to the tune of 'Jesus Christ Superstar' – presumably without the approval of the mullahs.

Vision, at Oxford, goes with the territory. Eighteen years before, on the eve of the 'Swinging Sixties', someone else, destined for stardom of a different and more enduring kind, arrived at Oxford. Stephen Hawking, a precociously brilliant physicist from St Albans, came up to University College, the original foundation, in October 1959, having recorded some of the highest marks ever achieved in his examination papers the previous January. His biographers are in no doubt that he was in for a treat.

It has often been said that there is a certain light in Oxford, a wonderful interplay between sunlight and sandstone which, like the comparably beautiful cities of Italy and Germany, has inspired the work of poets and painters down the centuries . . . on summer days, with the sunlight strong against the stonework and the river dotted with punts, their navigators sweeping a pole into the sparkling water and those on the grassy banks lifting a glass of champagne to their lips, it can, if you let it, seem like an earthly paradise in freeze-frame.

(Michael White and John Gribben, *A Life in Science*, Viking, 1992)

Hawking almost did let it. He was not yet fully engrossed in the dense mathematical interplay between light and time, constructing what may eventually yield his all-embracing theory of Everything. He will have been aware, though, that, on earth, especially at

Oxford, time comes dropping slow, and an idea that seems suddenly to have blossomed may in fact have started on its journey centuries before. The student intake in Hawking's freshman year was still largely male and from the country's private schools, with a majority from the top ten, led by Eton, Harrow, Winchester, Rugby and Westminster.

The number of students from middle-class and working-class backgrounds was beginning to increase, but in many respects the class system took on a greater refinement and a sharper profile at Oxford University. There were definite lines of demarcation. The friendships and relationships capable of crossing those invisible boundaries were still amazingly few. The twain rarely met.

In one camp were the élite, the children of the aristocracy and heirs to 'old money', the Sebastian Flytes of this world; they made up a substantial proportion of students at Christ Church and, to a lesser extent, Balliol. The privileged spent their often considerable allowances largely on entertaining their chums from school who had gone up with them or friends who had chosen to go to 'the other place', Cambridge. They looked upon those from minor private schools such as St Albans as a lesser breed, lumping them in with the lowest of the low – ex-grammar school boys . . . the 'Northern chemists' and the 'grammar school oiks' made do on their scholarships and grants, forfeiting quails' eggs and champagne for pork pies and beer.

Surprisingly, perhaps, Hawking, who had yet to develop the first outward symptoms of the motor neurone disease that was later to confine him to a wheelchair, speaking with the aid of a computer, did little work during his first year at Oxford. He found the set work 'boring' and, apart from occasional lectures and a weekly tutorial, was left largely to his own devices. As he himself recalled in his privately produced pamphlet, 'A Short History':

The prevailing attitude at Oxford at that time was very anti-work. You were supposed either to be brilliant without effort or to accept your limitations and get a fourth-class degree. To work hard to get a better class of degree was regarded as the mark of a grey man, the worst epithet in the Oxford vocabulary.

He even took up rowing to stave off boredom, coxing a boat in the all-college Torpids 'bumping' races, and succumbed increasingly to the pleasures of women and drink. He was branded as 'difficult' and lazy, and by his own calculations studied just one hour a day for most of his Oxford career. Only as 'Schools' (Finals) approached did he at last change gear and begin seriously – but not too seriously – to apply himself. It was enough. He scraped a First, requiring a viva for his upgrade, and with it ensured his extraordinary rendezvous with destiny. Next stop, Cambridge, the universe and Everything.

Dropping down a gear or two, Auberon Waugh, son of Evelyn, arrived at Christ Church ('the House'), to read PPE, in October, 1959, having lost several of his inner organs to a rogue machine-gun while serving with the Horse Guards in Cyprus. Like Randolph Churchill, he was to remain splenetic while lacking a spleen, but, unlike the irascible Randolph, Bron was to display his bile mainly in print, and in private remains a most affable and considerate fellow.

It was something of a mixed blessing to be the son of Oxford's most famous twentieth-century chronicler. But there were other problems, too – the same problems, in fact, noted by his distinguished contemporary, Hawking, though seen from the reverse perspective. To his chagrin, Waugh (Downside and the Guards) was confronted for the first time with the prospect of members of the lower orders as his 'equals'.

I was appalled by how few public schoolboys there were, appalled by the number of earnest, working-class youths whose humourless faces betokened young men on the make: they would never have time to frolic, take risks or make fools of themselves.

(*Will This Do?*, Random Century, 1991)

The difference between these 'state scholars' and the more traditional inhabitants of the quads was, as Waugh saw it, mainly one of temperament.

The state scholars saw Oxford as their means of escape from wretched circumstances such as we could only imagine. We must all agree with the puritans in our midst that it is closer to the true function of a university to train technicians and mass-produce technical qualifications than it is to harbour the idle young for a few years of frivolity before they settle down to the exigencies of earning their livelihoods . . . it honestly never occurred to me that there was anything to be gained by applying myself to a degree course in politics, philosophy and economics. I had chosen this subject in a foolish moment at Downside, on the grounds that it sounded vaguely clever and modern.

Waugh regretted that he had not chosen to read English (which he would not have needed to study in any serious sense), but he had been talked out of it by his father, who said it was 'a girl's subject, unsuited to the dignity of a male'. The result of his error was that he was doomed to examine the nature of formal logic and economics, and made no progress in either. His conclusion is typical: formal logic, 'like so many other things studied at university, must surely be a colossal waste of time'. As for economics, dealing, he felt, in tautologies and untruths, it, too, was 'a waste of time'.

Contemporaries of the budding controversialist and critic, like Peter Jay, David Dimbleby, Paul Foot, Richard Ingrams, Dominic Harrod and Ferdinand Mount, all stuck the course and duly graduated. Waugh did not. In an 'alcoholic haze' and knowing little of his subject-matter, he failed his prelims not once but twice, and was rusticated. He blamed the 'swarthy' Lord Gowrie, a Balliol intruder, who had stolen his girlfriend from St Hugh's and made him miserable.

Nine years earlier, it had been the turn of the ultimate meritocrat, Michael Heseltine, to come up to Oxford for the first time. He did so in the company of another future Conservative MP, Julian Critchley, who, though clever, was deemed to lack 'bottom' and thus never made it to ministerial rank. Critchley recalls their stuttering progress in vivid detail.

Both of us chose Pembroke for its ease of entry. In those days (1951) it was the sole college not to require the passing of an entrance exam. Matriculation, derived from the results of the Higher School Certificate when taken with a dialect-free accent and the wearing, in my case at least, of my father's suit, was deemed to be an adequate qualification. Some stress was placed upon the interview, which would have provided few difficulties for either of us. A more egalitarian age would have demanded 'straight As', a qualification which might well have excluded the young Michael Heseltine or Julian Critchley.

(Julian Critchley, *Heseltine*, André Deutsch, 1987)

Pembroke was, according to Critchley, 'an obscure college, anchored in the lee of Christ Church, famous for the brief residence of Dr Johnson ... a pretty place, placid and undemanding, whose undergraduates were on the worthy side, with a taste for wearing college ties and sporting scarves'. It was, he remarks, 'too provincial a park' for Heseltine.

The university was to be the marketplace for his ambition. Oxford was to be the antechamber of his career in politics, a career which had as its goal No. 10 Downing Street. A good degree was relatively unimportant. Michael even then knew that he would 'go into business', which would permit him to make the necessary fortune. What was important was to be elected president of the Union, that traditional stepping-stone to political success. The presidency was unobtainable save through politics. It was plainly necessary to join a political party whose vote would be deliverable throughout the progress of election to committees, to office and then to the presidency itself. Which one would we join?

Which indeed? No prizes here at least.

Critchley, evidently a kind of general factotum to the monstrously egotistical Heseltine, quotes a mutual friend, Ian Josephs, who had witnessed a scene in hall on the first night of term. 'They did not speak', he writes, 'but Josephs' attention was drawn by Heseltine striking his spoon three times against his glass. "I am practising", he explained, "to become president of the Union".'

By the Trinity term of 1953, Heseltine and his faithful amanuensis had moved out of college ('Pembroke was unvisited') into rooms in St John's Street, the most fashionable part of town. The idea that college life is all-important for a good Oxford career was certainly untrue in their case. Heseltine believed it more beneficial to know the right people and, in his quest for Union office, had teamed up with the fabulously well-connected Sarah Rothschild. With Sarah at his side, he began employing speech writers, including the future Sir Peter Tapsell MP, and quickly developed his famous 'blue rinse' style of oratory that was to dazzle successive party conferences. His only problem was the imminence of Schools for which he was singularly unprepared, regarding them as an unwelcome interruption of his triumphant progress to the presidency. Typically, the 'machine' swung into gear. Essays were loaned and impromptu tutorials were organized. Heseltine emerged with a Second, closed his books and moved on at once to more important matters.

Yet the burgeoning politician was, as always, racing against the clock. He had left his bid for the presidency too late to be achieved within the conventional three years of undergraduate life and was obliged to plead with Pembroke to grant him an additional term. Obligingly, they did so, thinking no doubt that he might one day prove useful to them, and the following autumn young Michael, already rehearsing for life as a Godfather, was installed in the president's chair.

He was in distinguished company. Also active in Union circles during these years were Robin Day, Tony Benn, Jeremy Thorpe, Kenneth Tynan, Shirley Catlin (later Williams) and Peter Parker. Thus were the politics, and the media, of a generation moulded.

While Critchley's major concern is necessarily his depiction of the youthful Tarzan, he is equally good on the subject of 1950s Oxford. It was a time when many of the people who now run Britain's affairs were being nurtured for greatness. As well as the Union bosses mentioned above, Heseltine's student acquaintances included the future politicians Patrick Mayhew, Gerald Kaufman and Bryan Magee; Jeremy Isaacs, who was to become chairman of Channel 4; Patrick Dromgoole, now a leading theatre producer; and the novelist David Hughes. Ian Josephs was to be his first business partner in the property business; the second was Clive Labovitch, an acquaintance from Brasenose, part of a wealthy Leeds family which now controls the building firm Brenta Construction.

The undergraduate way of life was not exacting, at least on the academic side. Critchley remembers copying out chunks of learned tomes 'to keep the dons at bay', and describes attending tutorials 'more from courtesy than from love of learning'. Sex, as ever, was a problem. There were few women at the university, and many of these, it seems, were tediously preoccupied with study. Girls had to be imported from London on the Friday evening 'fornication flyer' or else procured from the nurses' homes surrounding the Radcliffe Infirmary and the Oxford General Hospital.

Overall, the image of Oxford in the 1950s presented by Critchley is of a university whose undergraduates were in the main almost perversely divorced from learning, for whom politics and good times were all that counted and who were destined to go out and take the world by the throat. If there existed brilliant young minds in healthy bodies, wrestling with essays on complex issues of history and philosophy, and tutorials resounding to the fierce exchange of radical opinions, they are not recorded. Certainly, they do not appear to have been key ingredients of a successful Oxford career.

While Michael Heseltine's grasp on greatness was insecure, and laboured – a quality which has dogged his footsteps ever since – that of Robin Day was as vice-like as his subsequent political interrogations on television. He did not go up to St Edmund's Hall until 1947, when he was nearly 24, after four and a half years in the army, and quickly put his added maturity to good use. His experiences during his three university years demonstrate the potency of Oxford's name better than almost anything else.

I had my first taste of journalism as an undergraduate. I was a 'stringer' (local free-lance reporter) in Oxford for the American magazine *Time*. I had met Miss Honor Balfour, *Time*'s expert on British politics, when she was writing a feature about Oxford. The magazine happened to need a stringer in the University, and I was sent various assignments. *Time* had an insatiable interest in Oxford happenings, from undergraduate pranks to the eccentricities of dons whose prestige as egg-heads seemed to be greater over there than over here.

(*Day by Day*, William Kimber, 1975)

He recalls sending one story to *Time* that ran verbatim for a column and a half (imagine such interest in undergraduate windbaggery at Liverpool or Bath). It was a report of a hot-tempered Oxford Union debate, over which he had presided, between Randolph Churchill and Professor Cyril Joad, on the subject of American power in the world, and Day was paid the princely sum of 15 guineas for his trouble.

Day's 'desultory studies of the Law' were interrupted in 1949 when he was chosen, along with the future broadcaster and politician Geoffrey Johnson Smith, to represent the Union on a three-month tour of America. During an arduous round of some fifty universities and colleges, including Yale, Columbia and Chicago, the young Englishmen, with their plummy voices, were invited to lunch by Mrs Eleanor Roosevelt no less and to a meeting with General Eisenhower, then in training for the presidency. It was a long, if entertaining, haul, and by the time they returned to England 'Schools' were looming. Day once again wished he had chosen another subject – perhaps PPE – instead of law. 'I could not work up much interest in academic legal studies', he tells us, in time-honoured Oxford style. Naturally enough, he passed. Indeed, he did better than he expected and, in *Grand Inquisitor* (Weidenfeld & Nicolson, 1989), his next stab at autobiography, he even records that his Second had 'a touch of the Alpha'. Whatever its real merit, it served its purpose, and twelve months later the man destined to have ministers quaking in their boots on television paid out the requisite sum required to convert his humble BA (Oxon.) to a Master's.

In 1989, further honours came his way. Sir Robin, as he had become, was invited to return in glory to Teddy Hall as an honorary Fellow. He was also photographed, in his gown, in 1987, queuing to vote in the chancellorship elections. Even after thirty years in television, he was still, in his heart, an Oxonian.

Not so the future Lady Thatcher. As Margaret Roberts, homesick for her home town of Grantham and painfully removed from the influence of her father, her arrival at Somerville in the autumn of 1943, to study chemistry, was filled with anxiety. It was not how prime ministers were supposed to begin. Not only was she a woman, she was provincial and she was studying a science subject when, by all precedent, she ought to have attempted PPE, law, or Greats. Worse – if possible – she hadn't even won a scholarship. Indeed, she was lucky to have got in at all. Her biographer, Hugo Young (himself far-sighted enough to read jurisprudence at Balliol), takes up the tale.

Her offer of a place at Somerville came only at the last minute. She had had to mug up Latin, and had failed to reach Somerville's priority list for entrance. Only when someone dropped out was she hoisted off the waiting list and offered the chance to fulfil the ambition of many self-taught parents: to send their child to the peak of the educational system which they themselves had been obliged to quit in the foothills.

(Hugo Young, *One of Us*, Macmillan, 1991)

Young – like most *Guardian* writers an ardent defender of the Oxbridge ethos – observes that Margaret took her studies seriously, without ever really being noticed.

It was a time when hard work was both obligatory and fashionable. No shades of *Brideshead* here. Lectures and labs were in heavy demand. According to Sidney Bailey, a contemporary of Miss Roberts, who has taught in Oxford ever since he graduated, the fear of being sent down for poor work or failed exams was more pressing then than it has been since. Margaret, predictably, never ran any risk of that. She is remembered, by Bailey, and many others who dredge their recollection for any sightings of a then pretty unmemorable girl, as a hard-working, efficient, well-organized performer in the labs, though not as a particularly brilliant practitioner of academic chemistry.

So the future Mrs Denis Thatcher, Lady Thatcher and Baroness Thatcher was a bit of a swot. Few, surely, can be surprised. But she was also a Tory-in-waiting, and it was her membership of OUCA, the Oxford University Conservative Association, that was to trans- form her prospects and propel her to prominence. Unlike Heseltine and innumerable other Tories, Margaret Roberts was not drawn to the Union. Nor was she at that time, even if she could have afforded it, a keen socialite, lubricating her way to the top with champagne. For her, it was sheer graft and determination that did the trick. Ten years earlier, Edward Heath had pursued a similar course. Two diligent grammar-school toilers, Young observes, 'were transmuted into dedicated Conservative politicians, and, strengthened by the indestructible benefits of the Oxford experience, took every chance of fulfilling their high political ambitions'. They were hard-working. But they were lucky, too. 'The university gave them a reputation in the party and acquainted them with the right people to know.'

Many years later, Thatcher and Heath were to be exposed anew to the power of Oxford. Thatcher, respectful but never a servant of her university, was deeply shocked when a proposal to grant her an honorary doctorate in 1985 was rejected by dons, mainly from the sciences, who opposed her education cuts and wished to teach her a lesson. She was cut to the quick by the slight and has never since visited her Alma Mater. The humiliation – for that is what it was – is one of the defining points of her premiership, and one of the several from which her decline can be calculated. Heath did not have so traumatic a ride, but was wounded nevertheless when he lost out to Roy Jenkins in his bid to be Chancellor of Oxford in 1987. He, after all, had been Prime Minister for four years and had taken Britain into the European Community. Jenkins, by contrast, had not made it to Downing Street and had gone to Brussels as President of the European Commission only as a consolation prize. A later offer to Heath to be president of the Balliol Society was accepted, and Sir Edward has remained close to his old college even in the midst of an extremely busy life. He was hurt, even so, not to have won the university's supreme accolade and today is a rare visitor to his student haunts.

Rather less conscientious in his studies, and ambitions, beneath the spires than Thatcher and Heath was John Mortimer, who matriculated, more by accident than design, during the bleak early months of the Second World War.

'I think we might run to Oxford,' my father had said, 'provided you fall in and read the law.' I still felt that my time was likely to be short and my future, as the news of the war grew more depressing, uncertain. In the meantime I fell in and read law with no real faith in ever surviving to practise it. Again I wondered about my father's choice. Why Oxford? He'd been at Cambridge and Brasenose was a college he'd only heard mentioned, in an apparently disparaging way, by someone in his Chambers many years before. But as he offered me Oxford like the sausages and scrambled eggs of the condemned man's breakfast, I felt it churlish to refuse.

(*Clinging to the Wreckage*, Weidenfeld & Nicolson, 1982)

Mortimer – barrister, novelist and creator of *Rumpole of the Bailey* (and screenwriter of the celebrated television adaptation of *Brideshead Revisited*) – went up in 1941, when the age-old certainties of the British way of life were undergoing their severest test. As the Harrow-educated son of a distinguished jurist, it was hardly surprising that he should run the Oxbridge gauntlet, but he appears to have been embarrassed by the prospect. No doubt he recognized that three privileged years in the cloisters presented an awkward contrast to the desperate efforts by British forces to dislodge the Nazis from their stranglehold on Europe.

No matter. Needs must. Mortimer, a dedicated socialist, trod the primrose path with all the trepidation and guilt of a miners' leader being introduced into the House of Lords.

Whenever I hear now of the appalling efforts, suffering and anxiety of those who are trying to get their children into the older universities, I think of my entrance examination with a pang of guilt. I went to Brasenose and was led up some stairs by a college servant. After a long, solitary wait, a bald-headed man wearing carpet slippers and carrying an encyclopaedia of gastronomy came in. He handed me a passage from Lucretius, told me to translate it and shuffled away. I sat for a while puzzled by the complicated stanzas describing the nature of atoms, and then another door opened and I found myself staring at a pair of familiar scuffed suede shoes. Looking higher I saw knife-edged grey flannels, white teeth and well-brilliantined dark curls.

'Good God. Oliver! [Oliver Pensotti, a friend from Harrow] What're you doing here?'

'The same as you, but rather more efficiently.'

'I'm doing a sort of entrance test. It's not very easy.'

'Is it a test of our knowledge of Latin or our ingenuity? I have chosen to look at it as a test of ingenuity.'

'Look, there isn't time for that. What do you mean?'

'The question isn't what I mean. It's what I did.' And, bubbling with mysterious laughter, Pensotti held up a small Latin dictionary he had been out to buy at Blackwells. With its aid we wrote out a translation and went to find our examiner. He was having lunch, reading a recipe from the book propped up on a stand in front of him whilst he feasted on – what was it, dried egg or Spam salad? He took our work without a word and later we discovered that we had passed into Oxford.

Mortimer was not impressed by wartime Oxford, which he depicts as a surreal place, inhabited almost entirely by exotic incompetents.

The famous characters still behaved as though they lingered in the pages of *Decline and Fall*. They were famous for being nothing except Oxford characters; once they left their natural habitat in Magdalen or The House [Christ Church] they grew faint and dim and ended up down back corridors in Bush House, or as announcers on Radio Monte Carlo. They had double-barrelled names like Edward Faith-Peterson and Tommy Motte-Smith. By day they lay naked in their rooms, listening to Puccini or to Verdi's *Requiem*. By night they would issue into the black-out, camel-hair coats slung across their shoulders, bow-ties from Hall Bros settled under their lightly powdered chins, to take the exotic dinner (maximum spending allowed under the Ministry of Food regulations five bob) at the smartest restaurants.

Can it really have been *quite* like this? Perhaps it was. England is a mysterious place. But for Mortimer there were to be more familiar distractions as well.

I suppose Oxford's greatest gift is friendship, for which there is all the time in the world. After Oxford there are love affairs, marriages, working relationships, manipulations, lifelong enemies, but even then, in rationed, blacked-out Oxford, there were limitless hours for talking, drinking, staying up all night, going for walks with a friend. Winter [a classicist friend and conscientious objector, later to perform heroically in a Pacifist Service Unit] and I were emerging from the chrysalis of schoolboy homo-sexuality. At first the girls we loved were tennis-playing virgins posed, like Proust's androgynous heroine, forever unobtainable against a background of trees in the park, and carrying rackets and string bags full of Slazengers. There is nothing like sexual frustration to give warmth to friendship, which flourishes in prisons, armies, on Arctic expeditions and did well in wartime Oxford. Winter and I became inseparable and when, as time went on, I began to do things without him I felt twinges of guilt about my infidelity.

Heseltine and Critchley would have understood the sexual *Angst*. Their only surprise might have been that things should have altered so little in the ten years between Mortimer's time and theirs.

Academically, the future barrister and *belle-lettriste* adopted much the same relaxed attitude to his studies as Heseltine – though for rather different reasons. If the principal purpose of Oxford is intended to be the pursuit of knowledge and the rigorous examina-tion of ideas, it was, to say the least, unexacting in its demands in the 1940s and '50s. Mortimer, always an anti-lawyer anyway, says he learned most of his key facts from books with titles like *Tort in a Nutshell* and *All You Need to Know about Libel and Slander* (this was before York Notes) and threw his genuine creative impulses into poetry, drink and anguished sexual fumblings. The war, meanwhile, in which his contemporaries on all sides were busily engaged, was approaching its climax. Our hero was in due course given a 'wartime degree', without ceremony of any kind, and caught the train to London and real life.

Among the other wartime entrants to Oxford (a group whose memoirs now fill whole shelves of Blackwell's and Dillon's) was the comic novelist and poet, Kingsley Amis. Amis, a middle-class boy from south London, who called his parents 'Dadda' and 'Mater', won an exhibition in English from the City of London School to St John's College in 1941, but read mainly alcohol, jazz and communism before being called up a year later to help 'see the Hun put in his place'.

When he resumed his studies, in 1945, he was allocated a 'handsome set of rooms' in St John's New Quad, only to discover a contraceptive machine, left by wartime civil servants, affixed to a nearby lavatory wall.

There came a night when two others and I kicked this device off its mounting – it takes three to do that – and chained it to the bars of a window of Somerville, the women's college just up the Woodstock Road. None of us could have explained why we went to this considerable trouble. Boredom conceivably.

(*Memoirs*, Hutchinson, 1991)

Philip Larkin, the poet, who was to remain a close friend of Amis for many years, had already graduated, but the vacuum, keenly felt, was soon filled by the discovery of John Wain, a junior fellow and 'a budding academic without the crap'. The two, although jealous of their respective literary prowess, appear to have enjoyed each other's company, but Amis was still an undergraduate and, after two years of sloth, needed to apply himself in his final year if he was ever to take his degree.

I attended lectures, most assiduously those of the repulsive but necessary (J. R.) Tolkien ... also visited a succession of tutors offering instruction in the same part of the syllabus, the almost-universally disliked area that included philology, the structure and history of the language, and the literature of the period roughly up to the death of Chaucer in 1400. Just writing those last few phrases, the bare thought of when Chaucer died or that he lived at all, has brought me a strong whiff of the depression the thing itself regularly brought me. To go through all of it, even a bit of it, would kill me.

So much, the Old Devil would have us believe, for Oxonian scholarship. It is worth noting, however, that Amis, for all his idleness, still managed a First – partly, he says, by guessing the likely questions correctly – and went on to take a B.Litt. ('with lectures on the Oxford principle of fending prospective candidates off by the prospect of intrinsic boredom combined with entire practical uselessness'). Odder still, as he matured Amis even developed something of a taste for philology and Chaucer. Clearly, he would argue, however implausibly, it just required being away from Oxford to bring it out in him.

Four years before Amis came on the scene, while Hitler was still gearing up for war, Frank Giles, destined to be the lordly successor to Harry Evans as editor of the *Sunday Times*, found himself in a quandary when confronted with his Oxford entrance. He had been a high flier at Wellington and had already secured an open history scholarship from Brasenose. Writing in his memoirs (*Sundry Times*, John Murray, 1986), he recounts the esoteric nature of his agony. 'My mother knew little about Oxford, but at least she knew Christ Church had a social cachet, whereas she had only vaguely, if ever, heard of Brasenose.' What to do? Should young Frank take the Brasenose option, accept a lesser 'exhibition' from the House, or wait another twelve months for a Christ Church upgrade? Problems, problems. And the unemployed thought *they* had it hard!

In the end, prompted by his history teacher at Wellington, Giles opted for Brasenose, going up, as though in a lift at Harrods, in October 1937. His great-aunt was pleased and made clear that she did not regard the prospect as anything but agreeable.

'I know nothing about that Coll. [Brasenose]', she wrote, in her flowing, nineteenth-century script, but 'Uncle Tom [her late husband] always said they were very strong and could hit out well . . . my dear Boy, I hope you will have a very happy time there and think Oxford the happiest place in the world.'

Giles did not disappoint the old girl.

Brasenose did hit out well, in the sense that it was full of cricketers, oarsmen, rugby players, some of them owing their admission to their athletic prowess or promise. They tended intermittently to get drunk and make a great deal of noise in the quads ... I made friends and went around with a group of people who were not primarily, often not at all, games players, but who liked music, wine, good talk ... We even formed ourselves into a loosely constructed club called the Lotophagi (Lotus-eaters who, according to Tennyson, dwelt in 'a land in which it seemed always afternoon'). I don't believe the club ever met but it bound us together, or so we priggishly imagined, by indissoluble links of fastidious taste and appreciation.

Such elevation! Oscar, thou shouldst have been living at this hour. But at least Frank, though clearly something of a Wilde man on the quiet, was far from idle. He would never have hit it off with Heseltine or Mortimer.

In the midst of all this freedom and pleasure-making at Oxford, I worked hard at my history and became convinced (the dons did not demur) that only bad luck or some unforeseen cataclysm could prevent me from getting a first. This combination of work, fun and friendship gave reality to my great-aunt's second observation about Oxford being the happiest place in the world. So it was and so, in my memory, it has remained. I had panelled rooms giving, on one side, on to one of the most pleasant if not the most distinguished seventeenth-century quads in Oxford, and on the other to the Radcliffe Square, an urban landscape which has, in my view, a claim to be the third most beautiful public place in Europe after the Campidoglio in Rome and Place Stanislaus in Nancy. My style of living was modest, nothing like the sound-of-broken-glass school of Oxford reminiscence or fiction. But it was all I wanted, or could have dreamt of. All I desired was that it should go on, preferably for ever.

Sadly, war intruded on this Oxford idyll – but not too strenuously for the developing aesthete. Giles's guardian, Major-General Sir Denis Barnard, had recently been appointed governor of Bermuda and, with the opening of hostilities in Europe, drafted the would-be lotus-eater as his ADC. So, once more, a choice had to be made: Oxford or Bermuda? 'The coin, so to speak, came down with Bermuda uppermost.' Oxford's loss was Bermuda's gain.

Among the last Oxford undergraduates to complete their studies before the university was put on a wartime footing was its future Chancellor, Lord Jenkins of Hillhead, then plain Roy Jenkins, son of the Labour MP for Pontypool. An early biographer, writing in the wake of his subject's resignation from the Labour Party and the formation of the SDP, deals swiftly with the notion that by winning a place at Balliol Jenkins was in some way a class traitor.

Only the most puritanical Welsh fundamentalist could criticize a clever boy of his background for looking ambitiously to Oxford. In any case, the determination that he should try was much more strongly his father's than his own: since his own days at Ruskin – 'then only a ship moored alongside the university' – Arthur had nursed a romanticized idealization of the dreaming spires ... no one thought in 1938 that such upward mobility from father to son was a betrayal of socialism; on the contrary, it was part of the march of labour that the opportunities of Oxford should be open to sons of trade unionists. Arthur was intensely proud of his son.
(John Campbell, *Roy Jenkins*, Weidenfeld & Nicolson, 1983)

Jenkins himself, a disarmingly entertaining man who now doles out Oxford's glittering prizes and is as well known for his love of claret as for the clarity of his politics, evidently shared his father's view. Campbell says simply that Oxford was 'the gateway to wider horizons, in which he would leave Pontypool far behind'. A page later, he repeats the message: 'Jenkins's life only really began to flower when he got to Oxford.'

And what a place it was. Campbell (a graduate of Auld Reekie) is hopelessly intoxicated.

Oxford has been the nursery and forcing house of aspiring politicians of every generation going back at least to Gladstone's day in the 1820s. Whatever the academic claims of Cambridge, it is overwhelmingly from Oxford that the governing élite of the country has reproduced itself. The rise of the Labour Party introduced the tradition only briefly. The pioneers, naturally, had not been to university at all. The London School of

Economics made a stab at becoming Labour's university between the wars. But by the time Labour fully came into its inheritance after 1945, its younger leaders were increasingly Oxford men, and very often dons, like Hugh Gaitskell, Douglas Jay, Patrick Gordon Walker, Richard Crossman and Harold Wilson.

Campbell goes on to extol the virtues in particular of Balliol, which he affirms to be thrice-blessed, by brains, a democratic admissions policy and a strong ethos of public service. No sooner had his subject arrived at Oxford, he confides approvingly, than he had slipped smoothly into the Balliol mould and taken on the Balliol impress (well, you would in a mould), inevitably defined as 'an air of aloof superiority and an inability to suffer fools'.

One might well accept the first quality (there can be few more aloof men than My Lord Jenkins in full flow), but, as to the second, arguably he has been suffering fools for most of his adult life, and more than a few of them have come from Oxford!

At the academic coalface, Jenkins, like most of our 'brightest and best', turned out to be a nutty slacker. For his first two years, Campbell writes, he was too preoccupied with the Union and the Labour Club to do much serious work, and only when warned by his tutor that he ran a real risk of failing his exams did he buckle down and open up the set texts. Naturally, he got a First. All that remained for Pontypool's proudest product was a suitable wife, Jennifer (Girton, Cambridge) and a suitable venue for the marriage – the Savoy Chapel. In Jenkins's case, you could take the boy out of the Valleys, but you could also take the Valleys out of the boy.

A future colleague of Jenkins, Denis Healey, was that rarity at Oxford (at least until recent times), a genuine student. Healey is formidably clever and seems to have inhabited a different world – a kind of parallel Oxford – during his four years at Balliol, from 1936 to 1940. He was reading Mods and Greats (classics), which took four years instead of the usual three, but found time as well in his first two years to read practically all the English poets of the sixteenth and seventeenth centuries, while cultivating an interest in jazz and opposing appeasement.

Yet even Healey would not claim that it was the teaching he received that made him the man he is.

The main function of Balliol at that time was to enable us undergraduates to educate one another. Purely academic work took second place to our other interests. There were three terms each year, each of only eight weeks. I used to spend the mornings going to lectures, until I found that I could learn much faster and better by reading than by listening. Afternoons and evenings were free, apart from tutorials two or three times a week after tea.

(*The Time of My Life*, Michael Joseph, 1989)

More a communal kitchen, then, than table d'hôte. And when the university *did* serve up an occasional feast of philosophical inquiry it was not always to the young Healey's taste.

In my opinion you should study philosophy not to learn rules of good behaviour but in order to understand a little about how the human mind and the nature of language influence your understanding of reality. In that sense it is useful to everyone, and especially to politicians. Unfortunately, the fashion at Oxford in my time was for logical positivism and linguistic philosophy, which I regarded as intellectual nosepicking.

Determined to learn, Healey certainly got his finger out. The main imprint made upon him, he recalls, came from other undergraduates and from academics in disciplines outside his own, including the scientist Solly Zuckerman and the Master of Balliol, Sandy Lindsay. He attended endless numbers of talks and debates, pursued his hobby of painting in the Oxfordshire countryside and built up contacts with a body of men, many of them at Balliol itself, who were to go on to dominate British politics, Tory and Labour, throughout the 1960s and '70s.

At home, during his final year, Healey was preparing an essay on philosophy, 'racking my brains over Kant's views about the transcendental synthetic unity of apperception', when his mother burst into his room with a dread announcement. 'Put away your books', she said. 'War has been declared.' Healey had been expecting it and it made his final two terms at Oxford a 'bizarre' experience. Even so, prior to joining up, he still managed to steel himself sufficiently to his studies to be awarded his First. There can be little doubt that he deserved it.

For Alan Taylor, late of Bootham's Quaker school in York and an unsurpassed future historian of war, the Oxford of the 1920s was a fearsome place entirely dominated by the upper classes. At his college, Oriel, there was only one old Etonian – 'a man called Cartright who lived in aristocratic seclusion, attended by a valet and taking his meals in solitary state' – but the college was run by former Charterhouse men, encouraged by Provost Phelps, himself an Old Carthusian.

Its products were agreeable young men, obsessed with Association football and with not a thought in their heads, at least none of the thoughts that were in mine. They had never heard of Marx and I had never heard of the things that interested them. At Bootham I had been able to discuss politics. At Oriel, Asquith, let alone Ramsay MacDonald, were regarded as dangerous revolutionaries.

(*A Personal History*, Hamish Hamilton, 1983)

Taylor, a deeply serious scholar, though extremely funny in his private life and recollections, was bewildered by Oxford, which he had 'foolishly assumed was a place devoted to the higher learning'. It was, he discovered, nothing of the sort.

Few of my contemporaries were devoted to learning. They regarded Oxford as a place that would give them the necessary social stamp for well-paid jobs in the Civil Service. Work was a tiresome interference with more interesting things such as Association football and the drinking of beer. Here again I kept out of the way and even conformed. I spent my days reading in the Camera or the library of the Union, where no one knew me and I was safe from interruptions. Needing some exercise in the afternoons I took up rowing which I came to enjoy greatly. I rose to stroking a boat in the spring races and made four bumps. The rowing men then accepted me even if as an oddity. Rowing was a sort of Danegeld with me, with compensations from the physical achievement.

Each morning in these Brideshead days (Sebastian Flyte and Aloysius were just across King Edward Street), Taylor would be awakened by his scout, who would rake out the ashes from the antiquated grate and light the coal fire. Next, a jug of hot water would be brought, with which the future historian shaved prior to his bath, two quads away, and the arrival of his breakfast, on a tray. Taylor's one complaint, still keenly felt after an interval of some sixty years, was that lunch at Oxford was invariably cold, comprising cheese, beer and a hunk of bread, again delivered to his rooms. 'This was no use to me', he recalled bitterly. 'I am tempted to say that not eating a real lunch was the deepest mark Oxford left on me, and this accident reinforced my solitary inclinations.'

Hard cheese. But not the whole story, surely? Oxford's greatness (at least outside Merton) is supposed to consist not in good food but in ideas and the teaching of ideas. Was the young Taylor not at least impressed by the calibre of his tutors and the dedication with which they transmitted their knowledge?

Well . . . yes. Sort of.

I had two tutors: G. N. Clark and Stanley Cohn. Clark already had a high reputation and I expected great things from him. Again I was disappointed. Personally we were on very good terms, so much so that we became close friends and I was often at his house. But he was bored by tutoring and I do not blame him. He listened to my essays in a detached way and then complained how dreary the business was. I was supposed to cover all modern history with him. When we reached the Glorious Revolution of 1688, Clark said: 'You know all the rest from the books you read at school' and taught me no more. Thus of the recent history to which I have devoted my life I learnt at Oxford precisely nothing.

Cohn was different. He was to teach Taylor a great deal, 'though on a subject remote from my interests'. He gave his pupil an understanding of the Middle Ages 'in their own terms and not as a happy preparation for the perfect constitution as operated by Stanley Baldwin'. Unhappily for this urbane, clever man, he was never able to achieve his life's ambition of getting out of Oxford. When he died, shortly after the war, he left 'not a word to show the brilliance he had once possessed'.

Someone else to have left little trace of his alleged brilliance behind him was the long-serving Labour MP Tom Driberg, a contemporary of Taylor, who was sent down, 'completely disgraced', from Christ Church in 1927 after falling asleep when confronted with the enormity of his ignorance during Schools.

Driberg, who cultivated his old college all his life, accepting an honorary MA and bequeathing it his 'papers', was both a socialist and a swell, but most of all a bugger. At Christ Church, where he boasted of doing almost no work at all, he led a life of enviable ease.

He cut an attractive figure, even in his Oxford bags: tall and darkly handsome. He had shed his schoolboy glasses. His withdrawn, rather diffident, apparently aloof manner – a consequence of having spent so much of his childhood on his own – now seemed to give him an air of mystery. The hint of wickedness behind that saturnine countenance merely heightened its allure. Christ Church had plenty of undergraduates who would undoubtedly have been delighted to sport their oak with Tom; yet he seems not to have gone to bed with any fellow students during his three years at Oxford. While Evelyn Waugh mooned over young Richard Pares, and John Betjeman swooned over Hugh Gaitskell ('Hugh, may I stroke your bottom?' 'Oh, I suppose so, if you *must*'), Tom sought sex where he had always found it, in the shadows. He haunted public lavatories; he ambled along the canal towpath at twilight. A favourite memory was of 'romantic walks' with a milk roundsman 'who seemed to smell deliciously of milk'. There was a brief fling with a don, but this was – in the first instance at least – a case of mistaken identity: when they met in a gents' lavatory in Bear Lane the man 'looked far from donnish'.

(Francis Wheen, *Tom Driberg*, Chatto & Windus, 1990)

Turning to the opening years of the century, one account stands out, of an Oxford career based, at least in part, on hard work and dedication. Harold Macmillan (later Lord Stockton), the Donald Wolfit of British politics, appears to have been a much more serious – and certainly much duller – man when he was 'up' at Oxford than he became in later life. He was so priggish, in fact, that one wonders if he was not really in 'deep cover', playing the role of an earnest undergraduate in case the memory of it should be of subsequent value to his career. At any rate, in the Indian summer of empire, just before the slaughter of the Great War, the nascent Supermac comes across as a self-stropper of the first order.

He had first visited Oxford in the company of his parents at the age of 9. His father, Maurice, and his formidable American mother, Nellie (why are so many quintessential 'Englishmen' – Churchill, Hailsham, Astor – half-American?), had sent their younger son to Summerfields school, on the city's outskirts, to prepare him for Eton, and in the holidays would take him on excursions round the colleges.

'Few boys between nine and twelve', declared its future Chancellor, 'can have known so well at least the exterior of the University.' Seen from a distance, to young Harold its denizens 'seemed to be so old; so odd, with such white hair, and such myopic eyes. It was by the spectacle of these no doubt wise and learned, but queer looking, men that I was deeply impressed.'

(Alistair Horne, *Macmillan, 1894–1956*, Macmillan, 1988)

By the time he made it to Balliol in 1912, following in the distinguished footsteps of his brother Dan, Macmillan was helplessly in thrall. Alistair Horne enthusiastically conveys the scene.

Suddenly, for the first time in his life, the sun seemed to burst through the clouds in a blaze of golden glory. His rooms in the front quad were lofty, cold and inconvenient – 'but my own'. To him Oxford represented, at last, escape from 'a home where the discipline was severe and a mother's love almost too restraining', he remarked, with moderation, in his memoirs. 'It was an intoxicating feeling to be on one's own, in a society of countless friends, old and new.' He also soon discovered the delights of alcohol, unknown at home.

Horne continues:

Looking back with nostalgia on those early Oxford days, he remembered Talleyrand's remark that anyone who had not known France before the Revolution had never known 'la douceur de vivre'. The Oxford of *Zuleika Dobson* was indeed a sparkling place. 'There is nothing in England,' claimed Max Beerbohm in 1911, 'to be matched with what lurks in the vapours of these meadows, and in the shadows of these spires – that mysterious, ineludible spirit of Oxford! The very sight of the word printed, or sound of it spoken, is fraught for me with the most actual magic.' At the heart of it lay Balliol, still iridescent in the wake of the great Jowett, whose undergraduates were frequently thought to appear superior, self-satisfied and intellectually arrogant, with what Asquith described as 'a tranquil consciousness of effortless superiority'. It was a rather incestuous little world, where 'the sun rose over Wadham and set over Worcester', where friendships and conversation (especially on religious matters) were conducted in a hot-house atmosphere verging on the precious.

Horne's attitude to his subject's responses is, it must be owned, entirely laudatory, complete with paeans of Oxonian praise. He himself studied at Jesus, Cambridge, during the early years of the Second World War, later going on to establish a history fellowship in his own name at St Antony's, Oxford, where he now teaches. One senses, almost, that he would like to have been at Balliol with his Childe Harold and that for him, too – scholar though he is – the Union, with its old-fashioned debates on Charles I, would have been a 'good rag'.

For Macmillan, however, by now a fervent Anglo-Catholic, it was not all fun and games. Relations between the sexes, for a start, were stiffer than a matron's corset, and 'fornication flyers' would have seemed as remote as space travel. Sex at Oxford was either a solitary affair or conducted with other men, or else – as with Macmillan . . . was sublimated into religion. The university's polite, highly structured society, about to be blown apart by war, was in reality an affectation. Writing in his old age, with the scandal of John Profumo (Brasenose) safely behind him, Macmillan is astonished.

How different the mood of the day was, how little there was to argue about, because everybody agreed on general principles of morality, unlike now . . . for instance, as well-brought-up girls were virgins; so one of the great arguments was on religion. Perhaps they were rather scholastic arguments – possibly in rather a narrow context – and the Protestantism of the public school life I was brought up in all seemed rather arid . . . our arguments were curiously unrelated to life, partly romantic.

What Tom Driberg would have got up to in this particular set can only be imagined.

Macmillan was forced to leave Oxford early, 'sent down by the Kaiser', but had already made 'many good and lasting friends' before he headed off to the trenches, including many he would meet again in politics and diplomacy. In 1965 (in an article for *The Times*), he was to reflect on what of value he had learned there. He recalled the words with which his professor of moral philosophy, J. A. Smith, had opened a lecture in 1914:

Nothing that you will learn in the course of your studies will be of the slightest possible use to you in after life – save only this – that if you work hard and diligently you should be able to detect when a man is talking rot, and that, in my view, is the main, if not the sole, purpose of education.

A robust view, if not a complete one. Whether Macmillan, who died as Earl of Stockton, concerned about Mrs Thatcher selling the family silver, ever truly profited from it is for history to judge. What is certain is that, like Lord Jenkins, he returned to his Alma mater as Chancellor trailing clouds of glory.

CHAPTER FIVE

THE OTHER PLACE

At Oxford [the undergraduates] walked as though the street belonged to them. At Cambridge they walked as though they didn't care to whom it belonged.

(SHANE LESLIE, *The Film of Memory*, 1938)

CAMBRIDGE IS SUPPOSED TO BE AN ALTOGETHER more serious place than Oxford. The young Wordsworth, not best known for his love of life's sunlit uplands, was driven off, without graduating, by its 'mathematical gloom'. Noël Annan, in his magisterial study, *Our Age*, writes that 'to move from Oxford to Cambridge is like moving from a gallery displaying the paintings of Veronese and Rubens to one in which are hung the austere simplicities of Piero della Francesca'. The great Erasmus, in residence at Queens' College from 1511 to 1514, observed despairingly: 'In this place are colleges in which there's so much religion and so marked a sobriety in living that you'd despise every form of religious regime in comparison, if you saw it.' When Oliver Cromwell, warts and all, went up to Sidney Sussex in 1616, he discovered not merely that Master and Fellows were obliged to 'abhor' popery – a requirement posing few difficulties for the future Butcher of Drogheda – but that undergraduates were forbidden 'long or curled locks, great Ruffes, velvet pantables etc.' and were to avoid bear-baiting, bull-baiting, bowling, taverns and games of chance. In short, they were to get on with their work or face the consequences. Even the young Oliver, surely England's most unbending statesman, found these prescriptions a touch on the demanding side, and by the time he left – like the author of 'Daffodils', without a degree – was better remembered for his 'boisterous' pursuit of sport than for his learning. It was enough. In 1960, after three centuries of undignified to-ing and fro-ing following its posthumous sever-ance from his body, the Lord Protector's head was given a final resting place in the chapel of Sidney Sussex, his old college.

The traditionally greater emphasis on science is partly responsible for Cambridge's no-nonsense approach. Astrophysicists from the Fens may occasionally opine on *The Sky At Night*, with the gravely monocular Patrick Moore. They tend, however, not to appear on the *Jimmy Young Show*, nor do they 'talk back' with any frequency to Clive Anderson on Channel 4, even if he is a fellow Cantabrigian. The House of Commons and café society are for Cambridge's reclusive scientific strain equally frivolous and obscure – exactly as they were for Newton or Darwin – and they prefer to publish 'papers' and 'observations' than personal memoirs or diaries. A 'good' day for them is one passed at their desks or bent over their laboratory benches building up the reputations needed for a Nobel prize or a fellowship of the Royal Society. Splitting the atom, evolving the theory of natural selection, or discovering the building blocks of life through the mysteries of the double helix: fundamentals are what Cambridge believes itself to be about, and the tradition continues to this day. This mood has its echoes in the humanities, too. Annan tells us that the Cambridge historian John Bury regarded history as 'a science, no less and no more', while I. A. Richards, the controversial English don, would illustrate Shelley's 'Ode to the West Wind' by drawing electrical circuits on the blackboard. The Bloomsbury Group is not best remembered for its levity: Clive Bell, infinitely precious, wanted 'not to mean anything, but to *be*'. For long the doyen of literary critics, F. R. Leavis was almost insufferably solemn – as dry as a breadstick, though infinitely more wholesome. John Maynard Keynes, economics' answer to the Bourbons, not only did not suffer fools gladly, he was positively offensive to those who sought solace in laughter from his arcane dissection of society. Today, there is less portentousness about the place than there is in Oxford. Undergraduates apply themselves more and cause less fuss. The Cambridge Union Society is more sober, in both senses of the word, than its celebrated rival, and more measured. It knows how to let off steam without, for the most part, going daft. Masters and dons give more of their attention to attracting the brightest and the best, from whatever background, and then require the lucky few to justify their selection.

According to John Vaizey, writing in the anthology *My*

Cambridge (Robson Books, 1987), Cambridge's main contribution to the tone of intellectual life has been a ruthless, forthright intellectual honesty, with the Puritan revolution as its exemplar. 'Not for them any soft Carolinian [i.e. Oxford] ways. I think that this intellectual ruthlessness has appalling effects on the manners and emotions, but excellent results on the intellectual morals of the Cambridge young ... I would have been a nicer but a wobblier man if I had gone elsewhere. It is the wobblies who get on.'

Demonstrably, there is a holier-than-thou aspect to Cambridge élitism. Not only do Fenspersons claim privilege, they drape it in almost jesuitical habit, as though the fact that they do not, in volume terms, *quite* approach the worldly influence of Oxonians is, of itself, something to celebrate. G. M. Trevelyan, the great Cambridge historian, would applaud such a sentiment. 'I often think', he wrote, 'that young men who are in danger of being flashy should go to Cambridge, and those who are in danger of being dull should go to Oxford: too often the opposite principle is adopted.' Oh dear.

The essence of Cantabrigian high seriousness is well illustrated in a letter from H. S. Foxwell, a turn-of-the-century economist from St John's, to a colleague, J. N. Keynes, who had been mentioned as a possible professor of political economy at Oxford. No doubt with tongue slightly in cheek, yet with an underlying seriousness, he wrote:

Pray don't go. Think of the effect your move may have on your son [the future Nobel prize-winner, Maynard Keynes]. He may grow up flippantly epigrammatical and end by becoming the proprietor of a Gutter Gazette, or the hero of a popular party; instead of emulating his father's noble example, becoming an accurate, clear-headed Cambridge man spending his life in the valuable and unpretentious service of his kind, dying beloved of his friends, venerated by the wise and unknown to the masses, as true merit and worth mostly are.

Keynes stayed.

Against such unconscionable unctuousness has to be set the fact that Cambridge, in our own time, has produced John Cleese, Eleanor Bron, Eric Idle, Clive James, Griff Rhys Jones, Emma Thompson, Jonathan Miller, Peter Cook, Stephen Fry, Hugh Laurie and Michael Frayn – to name but many. If the prevalent atmosphere around the university's 'combination rooms' is one of *gravitas*, it certainly lifts sufficiently from time to time to reveal a generous measure of frivolity – a frivolity, moreover, with an ancient resonance. Writing in 1592, Robert Greene, a minor poet, recalled happily: 'For being at the Universitie of Cambridge, I light among wags as lewd as my selfe, with whom I consumed the flower of my youth.' Aha! So it *was* possible to have fun at Cambridge, even if the atmosphere did sometimes suggest a plot by Ibsen. Just as well, too, one might think. E. M. Forster, the Bloomsbury novelist, whose works have turned to gold since his death and whose least-known novel, *The Longest Journey*, is set in Cambridge, was aware of the coexistence of these opposites and described it as an attempt, however unconscious, at synthesis. 'Body and spirit, reason and emotion, work and play, architecture and scenery, laughter and seriousness, life and art; these pairs which are elsewhere contrasted were fused together [at Cambridge] into one.'

Realism or fancy? One suspects the latter, laced with vanity. Yet the fact remains that in the eternal two-horse race of Varsity prestige, Cambridge can never be discounted. Politics is very much a case in point. Oxford, perennially tilted towards the metropolis, is self-consciously the forcing ground of House of Commons front benches, and is well ahead of its East Anglian counterpart in its gallery of prime ministerial alumni. Allegedly, this is because Oxford keeps its ear to the ground while Cambridge keeps its head in the clouds. But look at the situation today. The Cabinet of John Major (University of Life) has Cambridge at its heart. Kenneth Clarke, Douglas Hurd, Michael Howard, Lord Mackay, John Patten, Norman Fowler, Peter Lilley, Michael Portillo, John Gummer *et al.* each has dipped his punt pole in the Cam. There have been many others, too – including the luckless Norman Lamont – and to this day they dine regularly with each other, hunting office as a pack. Whether they are more *serious* than a selection of past and present Oxford colleagues – Margaret Thatcher, Michael Heseltine, Nigel Lawson, Geoffrey Howe, David Mellor, William Waldegrave, Tony Newton, Peter Brooke – is a moot point, and would no doubt stimulate keen debate at the respective Union societies, but they could not by any stretch of the imagination be described as less concerned with the affairs of this world.

What *is* probably true is that Cambridge, still blinded by the brilliance of Newton, is more self-contained, more cut off, than Oxford. The degree of confidence, bordering on arrogance, is just as great, if more subtle and understated. Cantabrigians, at least while undergraduates, do not seem to need the immediate approbation of anyone beyond their peers. They prefer to do their time in college, without regular exeats to London, and then sit back and let the world come to them. And it does. Not in single files, but in battalions. As we shall see, the path to their door this century has been worn as smooth as Sartre's pebble in *La Nausée*.

Stephen Fry, one of the most entertaining, if reclusive, Cambridge products of recent years (bright enough to win a one-off revival of *University Challenge* virtually unaided), is on record as saying that his existence at Queens' College in the late 1970s was 'one of unparalleled bliss'. Alas, unlike his friend, Kenneth Branagh, he does not yet feel he has lived long enough to justify placing his life between hard covers. What he has done instead, pro tem, is to star in the film *Peter's Friends*, directed by Branagh, a production based on his own student days (and their fictional aftermath) when, alongside Hugh Laurie, Martin Bergman and Emma Thompson, he was a mega-star of the Footlights Society. They were an ill-assorted bunch. Laurie, somewhat surprisingly, was a bit of a real-life hearty at Magdalene, even rowing for Cambridge in the Boat Race, and Thompson had thrown herself enthusiastically into acting almost from day one. Not so our Stephen, even if he was recruited as an extra in *Chariots of Fire*. His sexuality and career still undetermined, he worked a bit, played chess a bit and mused, no doubt wryly, on the absurdities of life.

The Liar, his 1991 bestselling novel (William Heinemann), a picaresque fantasy in which a Cambridge undergraduate lives several lives at once, none of them totally real, is, needless to say, even less directly biographical in its intent than *Peter's Friends*. Indeed, the inside-cover disclaimer is unusually precise. 'Not one word of the following is true', it says. Fair enough. What the book does convey, surely, is something of Fry's attitude towards the academic world, and in particular the relationship, part intimate, part cynical, that exists between a Cambridge tutor and his more gifted students.

In the following extract, Adrian Healey, an undergraduate prepared to go to almost any lengths to avoid work, comes face to face with Professor Trefusis, his senior tutor, who, unknown to him, has uncovered his most recent skulduggery.

'You have a fine brain. A really excellent brain, Mr Healey.'

'Thank you.'

'A fine brain, but a dreadful mind. I have a fine brain *and* a fine mind. Like Russell. Leavis, a good mind, practically no brain at all. Shall we continue like this, I wonder?'

'Like what?'

'This fortnightly exhibition of stolen goods. It all seems rather pointless. I don't find the pose of careless youth charming and engaging any more than you find the pose of careworn age fascinating and eccentric, I should imagine. Perhaps I should let you play the year away. I have no doubt you will do very well in your final tests. Honesty, diligence and industry are wholly superfluous qualities in one such as you, as you have clearly grasped.'

'Well, it's just that I've been so . . .'

Trefusis pulled the handkerchief from his face and looked at Adrian.

'But of course you have! Frantically busy. Fran-tic-ally.'

Trefusis helped himself to another cigarette from a packet that lay on top of a tower of books next to the sofa and tapped it against his thumbnail.

'My first meeting with you only confirmed what I first suspected. You are a fraud, a charlatan and a shyster. My favourite kind of person, in fact.'

How faithful the above is to Fry's actual university career can be judged from an interview he gave in October 1993 to *Varsity*, the Cambridge student paper.

I was actually on probation [for theft] when I arrived in Cambridge. So, having sown my wild oats in a way that many of my contemporaries hadn't, there was actually more to enjoy. As the only Scholar of my year in English, people assumed that I was going to be very serious. When they discovered that I was more interested in acting than in my work, they tended to leave me alone. I went to about three lectures in my entire three years. I turned up to supervisions and told them that I was vaguely thinking about doing an essay. They realized that I did not have to be nannied.

For Clive James, later to entertain millions with his television footage of kamikaze game shows (and rather fewer with his learned notices in the *London Review of Books*), Cambridge was not so much shrouded in mystery when he arrived, in October 1963, as obscured by mist. He seems to have found his way from the railway station to Pembroke College mainly by braille, and was then allocated a set of rooms 'large enough to accommodate Benny Goodman, and his big band along with him', in Old Court.

As I stood beside my suitcase in the middle of the sitting room, a handsome young man in a silk brocade dressing-gown appeared suddenly beside me with a silence made possible by monogrammed leather slippers. 'Abramovitz', he said, holding out a pampered hand.

(Clive James, *May Week Was in June*, Jonathan Cape, 1990)

Brideshead, it transpired, could *still* be revisited, even if it was to the accompaniment of the Beatles and the Swinging Blue Jeans. The affectations of an Oxbridge education are seemingly eternal.

At least five years younger than I, Abramovitz carried on as if he were fifty years older. He was reading law and naturally assumed that the only reason I was reading English for a second undergraduate degree was in order to give myself time for plenty of extracurricular activities. He advised me to step around to the Societies Fair in the Corn Exchange before I decided finally on trying out for the Footlights. He himself believed the Union to be the only thing that counted if one had one's eye on high government office. I asked him if he was going to be Prime Minister. 'No, Disraeli was the last of our boys they'll ever let in there. Chancellor of the Exchequer: that's the spot.'

Abramovitz was no fool (though where he and his brocaded dressing gown are now remains a mystery). James proceeded to the Societies Fair and, after a cursory look at the other stands, made straight for the Footlights. Eric Idle, destined for celebrity in *Monty Python's Flying Circus*, was seated behind a trestle table, wearing a tan cashmere jacket. 'How do I join?' James wanted to know. 'You don't', came the bored reply, spoken through a barely controlled yawn. 'You audition.' James did, and was accepted. It was the vital second step in his career (the first being admission to Pembroke), and he never seriously looked back. From now on, though he pursued personal literary interests more seriously than most, he was in Cambridge principally 'for the ride'. He had, for example, better things to do than to look again at John Donne, a particular favourite of his supervisor of studies. As he puts it himself, he had 'done Donne' and he was not yet ready for a reprise.

I got increasingly nervous about turning up for my weekly supervision. As usual, I lied my way out of trouble, inventing various ailments. Shoving a piece of cotton wool behind my lower lip and pretending to have an abscess was perhaps the silliest trick [James was 24]. Even my better wheezes were schoolboy stuff and the man in charge wasn't fooled. He could have had me rusticated. It sounded like being castrated with a rusty knife and it hurt even worse, because it meant being thrown back into the harsh world where you had to earn a living. Instead, very generously, he passed me further down the line, to those junior dons who were still, as he put it, 'in the first fury of their supervisions'.

Taking his finals after three years of à la carte study, James was in trouble again. He answered a question on Book IV of *Gulliver's Travels* seemingly with fluency and style, only to notice, too late, that there were three other questions as well. He was shocked.

Ballsing up the Swift paper set the tone for my whole effort in the examinations. The novel paper went only just better. With some ingenuity I answered the questions on the Russian novel by making references to nobody except Jane Austen, but there is a limit to how much you can say about D. H. Lawrence when you have read only *Pride and Prejudice*. As for the English moralists, I was still ignorant as to who they might be, let alone about what they had said.

James may sound as though literature – and, with it, a university education – was not for him, but after graduating, with a surprise 2:1, he quickly recovered his poise. 'Nowadays', he observes, modestly, 'I devour whole literatures in sequential order, making notes and writing essays all the way.' This is good to know. The rusty knife, its edge as dull as an Antipodean epic poem, looks as though it may not be needed after all.

Another foreigner, this time from America, was Sylvia Plath, who arrived at Newnham College in the autumn of 1955 brimful of confidence that she could absorb European culture, confirm her budding reputation as a poet and find an English husband, all at the same time. She was a Fulbright fellow, who had graduated *summa cum laude* from Smith College, New England, but, like James, was convinced that a 'proper' degree was necessary to complete her education. To that end, she made her way to sleepy post-war Britain on the SS *United States*, flirting, it is said, with various men on route and enjoying sex with the ones who most took her fancy.

'If only I get accepted at Cambridge!' she had written to her mother the previous spring. 'My whole life would explode in a rainbow.' This is girlish infatuation of a Lawrentian order, and Plath's biographer, Linda Wagner-Martin, is in no doubt that her subject loved the place.

She raved about its formal gardens, King's Chapel and the Bridge of Sighs. Surrounded by the archaic walled colleges and lovely stone buildings, Sylvia felt tranquil and happy when she arrived. An academic world was her world; people here would understand and approve her aims, and would nourish her in attaining them. She bought furnishings for her third floor single room – a black pottery tea set, a large earthenware fruit plate, sofa pillows and some prints – and she got to know Irene Morris, her tutor, and housemother and housemates (largely Commonwealth women, but among them several other Americans).

(*Sylvia Plath*, Chatto & Windus, 1988)

Men at Cambridge outnumbered women ten to one in 1955, and Plath, attractive and outgoing as well as intelligent, soon got noticed. As Wagner-Martin puts it: 'In Cambridge, one of the arts was to appear non-competitive, although everyone was fiercely so.' She wore bright lipstick to set off her long, blonde hair. She wrote poems and pieces for *Varsity* and, daringly, she even modelled for a two-page feature on student fashion. What she did not do – and never did – was subscribe to the notion that a woman's concern for her appearance precluded academic judgement.

Within weeks, she had established herself as a key undergraduate 'personality'. Yet in the midst of her precocious social success, she was already troubled by the depression that would eventually lead to her suicide. Tutors and fellow students rallied round. There was no shortage of sympathy for the personable young American, who, evidently, was anxious to show that *A Yank at Oxford*, Bing Crosby's execrable *film blanc* from the 1940s, had got it wrong about the US and academe. After a promising start, they failed. The seeds of her despair were lodged in fertile soil.

Men were always a major part of her problem. Writing a 'Cambridge Letter' in *Isis* in May 1956 (Oxford has always felt it necessary to keep its people advised on events in the rival camp), Plath observes that the most difficult feat for a Cambridge male was to accept a woman not merely as feeling, not merely as thinking, but as managing a complex, vital interweaving of both.

Men here are inclined to treat women in one of two ways: either (1) as pretty beagling frivolous things (or devastating bohemian things) worthy of May Balls and suggestive looks over bottles of Chablis by candlelight, or, more rarely, (2) as esoteric opponents on an intellectual tennis court where the man, by law of kind, always wins.

She obviously enjoyed these contests, and, as a proto-feminist, engaged in them whenever possible. Most of all, however – at least until the rangy figure of Ted Hughes swept into her life – she studied. She was not English, after all. She attended eleven hours of lectures a week (a feat rare among native undergraduates), given by such luminaries as Leavis, David Daiches and Basil Willey, and read intensively everything in literature she could lay her hands on, from Aristotle to Lawrence. This was her territory, and she could cope. Cambridge's cold, wet winters were something else. 'I wear about five sweaters and wool pants and knee socks and *still* I can't keep my teeth from chattering', she wrote in a letter home. 'I was simply not made for this kind of weather.' She began to suffer from colds, flu and bouts of the most acute depression, yet remained determined to 'conquer' Cambridge just as she had earlier 'conquered' New York.

Hughes had already graduated from Pembroke, where as a swaggering Welshman he had always presented himself as an outsider. He added spice to the challenge. He was the one man in the world, she said, who was her match, and she threw herself body and soul into winning him. Too much alas. For though she did indeed marry the rhymster who, as Poet Laureate, now writes verses for the Queen Mother, she managed only a Second at Newnham and, frustrated both by her failure and the constrictions of marriage, decided to return home to America. Six years later, back in England and with her real fame still ahead of her, she was dead.

More cavalier still, and certainly more *Jamesian*, were the behaviour and attitudes of the young Nicholas Tomalin, a prize-winning journalist, killed by a stray rocket in the Yom Kippur war, who went up to Cambridge in 1950, five years before Plath.

Nick had intended to become a doctor, but failed to do well enough in scientific subjects to get a scholarship to Cambridge [*clearly the only acceptable option*]. Wilfred Cowley [*his housemaster at Bryanston*] had fortunately drummed into him enough knowledge of English literature for him to be able to read that instead when two years later he went up to his father's old Cambridge college, Trinity Hall. He threw himself into undergraduate life with tireless enjoyment. Ten years later, his undergraduate career was still a Cambridge legend.

(*Nicolas Tomalin Reporting*,
introduced by Ron Hall, André Deutsch, 1975)

Hall points out that the two most coveted student jobs at that time were the presidency of the Union and the editorship of *Granta*, judged to be the smartest and cleverest of the undergraduate journals. 'To get one such job set the seal of fame on a Cambridge career. To get both was like winning the Cup-and-League double. Nick set his sights on both.'

He got them. In spite of 'St Vitus tendencies' as a debater, he participated actively in the Union and rose through its ranks until elected president in his third year. He also acquired the editor's chair at *Granta*, seizing it from Mark Boxer, who had been rusticated (this being 1953) for publishing a rude poem, and went on to 'expose' his predecessor for accepting six bottles of champagne in return for promoting drinking chocolate. Tomalin did not get a First. He was too busy for that. But he left Cambridge in a burst of fireworks and set off at once to take Fleet Street by storm.

Towards the end of the 1940s, when Francis Crick and James Watson were at Cambridge carrying out the research that, with the help of their London colleague, Maurice Wilkins, would eventually yield the secrets of DNA and secure for the three the 1962 Nobel prize for medicine, the university authorities appeared unappreciative of the rare quality of their scientific community. There was genius aplenty in the famous Cavendish laboratory, where, earlier, Cockcroft and Walton had first smashed the atom, but college and university administrators seemed to think that the 'boffins' could rub along somehow, with little or no practical help, and did virtually nothing to ease their passage or obtain for them vital facilities. Sir Lawrence Bragg, a Nobel laureate and formulator of Bragg's Law on X-ray diffraction, was a gallant exception. The head of the Cavendish, he did what he could to secure resources, stimulate research and keep his army of bright young pioneers stuck to their tasks. (Years afterwards, in his old age, he continued in catalytic vein and gave valuable encouragement to Martin Ryle and J. A. Ratcliffe in their experiments in radio astronomy which were to yield important breakthroughs in the discovery of quasars and pulsars in the distant universe.) What Bragg could not do – or perhaps did not think important – was ensure that Crick and Watson had somewhere adequate to live and enough cash to keep themselves and their families from starving. Thus, the celebrated double helix, the molecule of heredity, one of the most potent symbols of twentieth-century science, was uncovered among squalor by men whose life-styles were the very antithesis of glamour. Watson in particular, an American, whose academic background was post-war Chicago, describes how, with no Cambridge college willing to take him in as a Fellow, he was forced to exist in digs like prison camps, with just $1,000 to live off for an entire year, and of how, later, he was saved from vagrancy only by the generosity of departmental friends.

My landlady ... threw me out after less than a month's residence. My main crime was not removing my shoes when I entered the house after 9.00 p.m., the hour at which her husband went to sleep. Also I occasionally forgot the injunction not to flush the toilet at similar hours and, even worse, I went out after 10.00 p.m. Nothing in Cambridge was then open, and my motives were suspect. John [now *Sir* John, former President of St John's College, Oxford] and Elizabeth Kendrew rescued me with the offer, at almost no rent, of a tiny room in their house off Tennis Court Road. It was unbelievably damp and heated only by an aged electric heater. Though it looked like an open invitation to tuberculosis, living with friends was infinitely preferable to any other digs I might find.

(James Watson, *The Double Helix*, Weidenfeld & Nicolson, 1968)

In Tennis Court Road, within sight of the university administration offices and the Fitzwilliam Museum, Watson lived as best he could a hand-to-mouth existence, falling ill in the end from the dubious cuisine available in late-night cafés and restaurants. Jesus College – then best known for its prowess on the river – had, belatedly, offered him a research fellowship, but only if he studied for a Ph.D. (which he already possessed). No research student could live in the college at that time, and, to Watson, 'the only predictable consequences of being a Jesus man were bills for a Ph.D. that I would never acquire'.

It was then that Clare College, more open to invention in those days than some of its rivals and more welcoming to foreigners, stepped in to save the day with the offer of a residential fellowship. The one stumbling block was that there would not be a room available to him until the following year – but he did have dining rights and the college authorities wished him well. Watson was grateful. He was less happy with the food.

After matriculation I went into hall for several meals until I discovered that I was unlikely to meet anyone during the ten-to-twelve minute interval needed to slop down the brown soup, stringy meat and heavy pudding provided on most evenings. Even during my second Cambridge year, when I moved into rooms on the R staircase of Clare's Memorial Court, my boycott of college food continued. Breakfast at the Whim [a local café] could occur much later than if I went to hall. For 3/6d the Whim gave a half-warm site to read *The Times* while flat-capped Trinity types turned the pages of the *Telegraph* or the *News Chronicle*. Finding suitable evening food on the town was trickier. Eating at the Arts or the Bath Hotel was reserved for special occasions, so when Odile [his girlfriend, later his wife] or Elizabeth Kendrew did not invite me to supper I took in the poison put out by the local Indian and Cypriot establishments.

Crick, though English and relatively inured to the discomforts of daily life in the Fens, was no less dissatisfied with his day-to-day existence. A graduate of University College London, who had migrated to Cambridge 'to find his level', he had dining rights for one meal a week at Caius, but, partly by his own choice, was not yet a Fellow. In Watson's opinion, 'clearly he did not want to be burdened by the unnecessary sight of undergraduate tutees'. Nor did he enjoy college conviviality, believing, apparently, 'that most High Table life was dominated by pedantic, middle-aged men incapable of either amusing or educating him in anything worthwhile'. The American's opening to the second chapter of *The Double Helix* is a classic of disingenuous realism masquerading as understatement. 'Before my arrival in Cambridge', he writes, 'Francis only occasionally thought about deoxyribonucleic acid (DNA) and its role in heredity.' (Of how many of us might this not be said?) The coming together of the unorthodox Anglo-American duo was catalytic, but fortuitous, and had little to do with Cambridge, which was a berth rather than a birthplace, and an uncomfortable one at that. Even Bragg did not for a long time approve of their work. He tolerated them, while believing almost until the end that they were intellectual delinquents. He wanted Crick to get on with his assigned work on haemoglobins and Watson to concentrate on his thesis. Without the pioneering work of Wilkins, a brilliant biophysicist from King's College, London, and that of Wilkins's intensely difficult colleague, the late Rosalind Franklin, the two men's work would not, moreover, have had a recognized starting point. The true laboratories of this most romantic of scientific constructs were not in the Cavendish, for all its proud history, but in the minds of two anarchic, irrepressibly ambitious young men. Watson's description of how he nursed his stomach pains in midwinter, then retreated to Clare to try to get some sleep, is in this context both vivid and revealing:

Back in my rooms I lit the coal fire, knowing there was no chance that the sight of my breath would disappear before I was ready for bed. With my fingers too cold to write legibly I huddled next to the fireplace, dreaming about how several DNA chains could fold together in a pretty and hopefully scientific way. Soon, however, I abandoned thinking at the molecular level and turned to the much easier job of reading biochemical papers on the interrelations of DNA, RNA and protein synthesis.

Such is genius: nine-tenths condensation, one-tenth inspiration.

Of all the things for which Cambridge this century is remembered, the most notorious is without question its 1930s network of communist spies. Anthony Blunt, 'Kim' Philby, Burgess and Maclean, the more shadowy fifth and sixth men, the suspected umpteenth men: these are figures central to England's present-day understanding of itself. They are emblems of imperial decline and of an effete snobbery. Had they had not been 'Cambridge men', and consequent movers in high society, their treachery would probably have been uncovered years before it actually was and their contemporaries might have been spared not only the pain of betrayal and opprobrium but an embarrassment that lasted for years and threatened the nation's very self-confidence.

This is not the place for a detailed consideration of what it was that motivated the Cambridge ring. New political ideals, of the left and the right, were much in vogue, and there was debilitating unemployment and social unrest throughout the country. As Marxists, either covert or open, these intellectual class deviants did not feel themselves confined by what they would have termed bourgeois ideology. Theirs was a higher duty – perhaps even a higher aesthetic – and at a time when Stalin was slaughtering his people, they, the sons of privilege and recipients of imperial bounty, were concerned only with abstract questions of 'truth'. What is beyond dispute is the sheer depth of Oxbridge involvement. Nearly two-thirds of prominent British communists and party sympathizers during the 1920s had studied at the two ancient universities, and of these a clear majority was academically and philosophically rooted in the Fens.

Blunt was the ringleader, but so removed from the action that he might have been, as in Joyce's conception of God, 'the great artificer, paring his fingernails'. He had pursued a glittering career at Marlborough, and when he arrived at Trinity College in 1926, it was with a reputation as a brilliant mathematician that, fatally, he was not to sustain. Philby, three years Blunt's junior, was the son of a Trinity College alumnus who, after a promising start, had turned his back on British colonial administration and ended up a Muslim, living in Jeddah. As a child, Guy Burgess had lost his father, a promising naval commander, to an unexpected illness and spent much of his early life surrounded by women. Later, he was sent to Eton, where, perhaps in revolt, he became an ardent homosexual. Donald Maclean's father was a former Liberal Party Cabinet minister, and Donald was educated at Gresham's, Holt, in Norfolk – the same school which produced W. H. Auden. An extraordinary group, combining jesuitical posturing with high-octane sexuality, they first came together in the 'Apostles', a university-wide secret society that stretched back to Tennyson and beyond.

Others, including, most obviously, Maurice Dobb, a Fellow of Pembroke College, had already done much to establish communism as a fashionable Cambridge pursuit, but it was Blunt, emotionally constipated, perceiving art as an enema, who crafted the web that was to trap so many. He had wanted to be another Russell or Wittgenstein, who would re-energize the world of mathematics, but, alas, as his 2:1 in his first tripos exams showed, he lacked the capacity. Still, in the mix 'n' match world of Cambridge, this was to be no permanent obstacle to success, and it was subsequently as an aesthete and art historian that he was publicly to make his mark. Hard pounding, though. A damn close run thing.

When it came to flamboyance, Blunt ... discovered that he would need more elaborate props than the toy balls and hoops he had used at Marlborough to make an impression. Cecil Beaton, for example, had arrived in Cambridge wearing an evening jacket, red shoes, black and white trousers and a huge blue cravat, and had already been sent down. The elegant Steven Runciman, however, remained as Trinity College's resident aesthete, cutting elegant poses with a parakeet perched on his heavily ringed fingers and his hair cropped in an Italianate fringe.

(John Costello, *Mask of Treachery*, Collins, 1988.)

Blunt, a closet queen, considered social status to be at least as important as learning. As his close friend Louis MacNeice was to remark, study 'was what the grammar school boys did ... those distorted little creatures with black teeth who held their forks by the middle and were set on making a career'. MacNeice, the son of a North of Ireland rector, held grandly that persons of his sort,

from public schools, went to university 'either for sport and drinking
. . . or for the aesthetic life and cocktails'.

Costello is no defender of such opinions. He seems, without
saying so, to see through them to their worm-eaten core.

Public-school boys and the attitudes of the privileged class dominated
Cambridge. Instead of schoolboy 'fags', there were regiments of college
servants called 'gyps' and 'bedders', who deferred to the whims of young
gentlemen by drawing an undergraduate's washing water, making his bed,
fetching coal and waiting on him at mealtimes. Young gentlemen were
made to feel in every way that they were the future prefects and proconsuls
of the British Empire.

This was Blunt's world. Marxism for him was merely an intellectual kaleidoscope, in which there was no contradiction in serving
Stalin one minute and the royal family the next, alternately spymas-
ter for the Lubianka and Surveyor of the Queen's Pictures. If it was
a juggling act that was ultimately doomed, his smart friends, nearly
all from the same background, saw to it that the end was a long
time coming.

Burgess, the most sympathetic, and the most dissolute, of the
ring's inner circle, had been extremely able academically while at
Eton but had failed to be elected to Pop, the élite sixth form group,
analogous to the Apostles, because of his undisguised sexual proclivi-
ties. At Cambridge, such inclinations were not a barrier.

Guy Burgess enjoyed every minute of his Cambridge career. There were so
many attractive young men to try to seduce; there were intelligent friends
to gossip with and about; there were excellent libraries and the superb Pitt
Club, modelled on a London Gentleman's club, to relax in.

(Barrie Penrose and Simon Freeman,
Conspiracy of Silence, Grafton Books, 1986)

Quite obviously – and his response is almost an Oxbridge commonplace – Burgess did not regard his years reading history at
Trinity as turning primarily on study or research. Rather, he saw
college life as an agreeable interlude between youth and maturity
through which he would pass *en route* to his rendezvous with
destiny. It was not a time, certainly, for deep seriousness. Penrose

and Freeman, quoting one of Burgess's contemporaries, Robert Birley, provide a vivid memory of the young traitor-elect in the summer of 1931.

Of course, Guy wasn't in when I arrived [Birley recalls], so I entered his rooms in New Court and waited. There were many books on his shelves, and I'm always drawn to other people's taste in reading. As I expected, his taste was fairly wide and interesting. I noticed a number of Marxist tracts and textbooks, but that's not what shocked and depressed me. I realized that something must have gone terribly wrong when I came across an extraordinary array of explicit and extremely unpleasant pornographic literature. He bustled in finally, full of cheerful apologies for being late as usual, and we talked happily enough over the tea-cups.

Maclean, reading modern languages at the adjoining Trinity Hall, became one of Burgess's conquests sometime in 1933, around the time his seducer became an active member of the university communist circle. The future diplomat – whose passage to Moscow of vast quantities of top-grade nuclear secrets was to cloud Anglo-American relations for more than a decade – liked to think of himself as multi-faceted. In a *Granta* profile, published in his last year, he described himself, somewhat unendearingly, as having three sides to his character. There was 'Cecil', who wore blue velvet trousers and had a *real* passion for flowers, 'Jack', the rugger-bugger, who fancied 'damn-fine waitresses at the George', and 'Fred', some kind of intellectual ponce, worried about the distinction between the 'material and the dialectic'. It is hard to know which of these one would least like to know. Together, they made up the sort of personality Burgess would have regarded as a 'tease'.

To his credit, Maclean hid little about himself and openly admitted to being a communist. How his political allegiance was ignored at the height of the Cold War is a mystery that has Establishment values at its heart. To quote Andrew Boyle, in *The Climate of Treason* (Hutchinson, 1979): 'Their political opinions, no matter how extreme, would not detract from their standing, always provided that the normal civilized rules and conventions were observed.'

Throughout this elaborately theatrical milieu, barely connected with such mundane matters as essays or seminar groups, Philby moves as though some kind of superior bank manager, charming, gregarious, massively heterosexual, but substantially less brainy than his three associates – and therefore, naturally, destined to go to the top. His penchant was for concealment, and at this he was a genius. Ending up as MI6's leading man in Washington while in reality a senior officer in the KGB is arguably the greatest espionage achievement of all time.

Academically, the four were to meet with mixed fortunes, and it was as well for Burgess in particular that exam results are only sporadically the true measure of Oxbridge talent. Blunt scraped his First but, humiliatingly, had to switch from maths to languages to ensure it; Maclean, ever the swot, achieved his First without such sleight of hand; Philby, changing in midstream from history to economics, picked up a Second; poor Burgess, sputtering like a Roman candle let off in the rain, collapsed with a nervous break-down at examination time and left with just an *aegrotat*, a consola-tion pass degree equivalent to a 'gentleman's Fourth'.

Cambridge's reputation for treachery is not wholly deserved. More Cantabrigians probably died each morning before breakfast at Dunkirk than were ever caught up in Blunt's espionage ring. Oxford, moreover, in spite of Sir Humphrey's anguished denial in *Yes, Prime Minister* of the suggestion that he might be a spy – 'But I couldn't possibly be a spy, I was at *Oxford!*' – had several suspects of its own. What Cambridge had, though, to make it qualitatively as well as quantitively different, was the Apostles. In the Bible, the original apostles were, of course, those chosen by Jesus to hear his revealed truth and take it to the four corners of the known world. Their namesakes in the Fens, at least in the 1930s, were, by contrast, a batch of well-born, politically confused snobs, for whom evangelism, other than by stealth, would have been anathema and, far worse than that, *vulgar*. Socialists, they might have been; their cause was *never* common.

Ten years earlier, it had been the turn of Malcolm Muggeridge to enter Cambridge's hallowed portals. Fresh from a secondary school in Croydon, the future scourge of 'modern' values already felt inferior to grammar school boys, let alone Etonians, Wykhamists and the rest, and his discovery at Selwyn College of the lunatic *detail* of the English social hierarchy was to affect him for the remainder of his long and eventful life. Student colleagues had, he says, a language of their own, which he scarcely understood, games they played which he could neither play nor interest himself in, and ways and attitudes which they took for granted but which were foreign to him. He records how sodomy was 'more or less normal behaviour', practised by young men who dressed in velvet, painted their rooms in strange colours, hung Aubrey Beardsley prints on their walls and read *Les Fleurs du Mal* (it sounds like the 1960s). In his splendidly readable, if not wholly reliable, memoirs, Muggeridge writes of how he and his fellow freshmen, many of them 'gentry', were addressed by the Dean and told that, as a result of their Cambridge entry, none of them was likely ever to be in want or to lack for the essential requirements of a bourgeois way of life. Muggeridge, at the time a convinced Stalinist, found this certainty bizarre, but no more so than the fact that he was reading chemistry, physics and zoology for the Natural Sciences tripos. He had no interest in science and knew nothing of it and was pursuing this (to him) arcane trio purely because his school had been unable to prepare a place for him in any other discipline. As he admits, with a characteristic candour that never quite achieves the condition of humility, he managed somehow to scrape a pass degree but thereafter did not open a book on, or think about, any of his three subjects ever again.

He did not even like Grantchester and its echoes of Rupert Brooke ('How somehow second-rate it was!'), and could not wait for the Revolution that would end the whole charade and usher in the age of the common man. One can well imagine him composing the following paragraph, reading the words aloud to himself in that inimitable voice of his, somehow combining Robert Runcie, the former Archbishop of Canterbury, Lord Deedes and the Queen Mother.

Cambridge, to me, was a place of infinite tedium; of afternoon walks in a damp, misty countryside; of idle days, and foolish vanities, and spurious enthusiasms. Even now, when I go there, as my train steams into the station or my car reaches the outskirts, a sense of physical and mental inertia afflicts me. It was my father who tingled with excitement at the thought of my being at Cambridge; not me . . . It was my father who used expressions like 'my Alma Mater', or 'sporting my oak'; when he came to visit me at Cambridge he was thrilled by my rooms, the Union, dinner in hall, boating on the river; everything . . . For me, the years at Cambridge were the most futile and dismal of my whole life. I look back on the self I then was with the utmost distaste – the showing off when I came to Croydon in the vacations; the getting into debt (which my father always paid with little complaining, though he could ill afford it) through buying clothes and other unnecessary things out of vanity; the fatuous imitation of a sort of person I could never be, nor ever wanted to be.

(*Chronicles of Wasted Time: The Green Stick*, Collins, 1972)

It is obvious, even to the eager eye of the present writer, that this is extremist stuff – memory as refracted through the distorted prism of St Mugg. According to Ian Hunter, author of *Malcolm Muggeridge: A Life*, published by Collins in 1981, the old fraud actually enjoyed his college days to the full and only much later chose to see them as hollow and unrewarding. It is a fact, moreover, that he took full advantage of the networks to which he was introduced at Cambridge. Here was the forcing ground of that extraordinary voice and accent, wholly inimical to his Croydon origins. Here he was given the vital precondition for several early jobs, including the lectureship in Cairo that led to his joining the staff of the *Manchester Guardian*. Here, too, he established lifelong friendships with the theologian Alec Vidler and the polemicist Hugh Kingsmill. More crucially still, here he met his future wife, Kitty, sister of his Cambridge roommate, Leonard Dobbs, and through her was introduced to her aunt, Beatrice Webb, and the Fabians, leaders of the left's intellectual aristocracy. The Blessed Malcolm may not (retrospectively) have appreciated much that he was getting from his Cambridge education; he got it just the same.

The Bloomsbury Group, whose members assumed their better-known identity only much later when they moved from Cambridge to literary London, were, after the Spies, the most famous Apostles this century. Leonard Woolf, Lytton Strachey, Thoby Stephen, Saxon Sydney-Turner and the rest went up to Trinity College in 1899, to be joined, three years later, by Maynard Keynes, an undergraduate at King's. According to Woolf, they were 'very serious young men', and there seems no reason to doubt him. Sydney-Turner, though destined to end up a rather dull Treasury official, labouring in an area in which Keynes was to be a revolutionary, was the one who first brought them together. He was obsessively well informed, even in his freshman year. He kept a list of all the operas he had seen and who had sung each role and was a fount of general knowledge as well as an avid solver of crossword puzzles. He would, without doubt, have been a natural on *University Challenge* or *Mastermind*, but was secretary-organizer of the group rather than its inspiration. Meeting for the first time in Clive Bell's rooms and calling themselves the Midnight Society, this high-minded fellowship soon demonstrated that they were not to be taken lightly – least of all by themselves. Leon Edel, their group biographer, tells us of their activities:

They read a great deal, wrote a great deal, formed societies, charged into the Great Court in the rainy days declaiming Swinburne; they also quoted Henry James, enchanted with the efflorescence of the Master's mandarin style, his verbal slyness and wit, little grasping his psychological sagacity. Chroniclers have made much of Lytton's and Leonard's (and Saxon's) being elected . . . to the Apostles. This was very important to them at the time and afterward in cementing and preserving friendships. Clive was not elected, but it is to be noted that he wasted no time lingering at Cambridge. He went out eagerly into the world. Leonard stayed on long enough to take examinations qualifying him for the Civil Service. Lytton would gladly have remained at Trinity all his life, had he been able to become a don.

(Leon Edel, *Bloomsbury: A House of Lions*, Hogarth Press, 1979)

It is all so recognizable. Plainly, the Oxbridge patterns that have remained to this day were set long since. Some of these Cambridge Chosen entered the public service; others wished to remain in their student idyll for ever but were forced out into the world; a tiny few achieved true greatness. What they created in undergraduate combination was slight indeed. Mainly, they affected a kind of abstract amoralism, in which the teachings of George Moore, author of *Principia Ethica*, were bowdlerized in an attempt to justify a selfish, but supposedly superior, way of life, centred, in part at least, on sexual intimacy. 'By far the most valuable things', Moore had written, 'are . . . the pleasures of human intercourse and the enjoyment of beautiful objects . . . it is they . . . that form the rational, ultimate end of social progress.' The Apostolic Succession at King's couldn't agree more, and got stuck into aesthetics, and human intercourse, with a vengeance. Edel asks himself what in the end Cambridge meant to his young heroes – 'much more aware of life and feeling than many of their peers' – 'and quotes Leonard Woolf, writing in old age, in reply.

I have never again been quite so happy or quite so miserable as I was in the five years at Cambridge from 1899 to 1904. One lived in a state of continual excitement and strong and deep feeling. We were intellectuals, intellectuals with three genuine and, I think, profound passions: a passion for friendship, a passion for literature and music (it is significant that the plastic arts came a good deal later), a passion for what we called the truth.

Woolf, a lapsed and embittered Jew, recalled his Cambridge years as a time of hate, contempt, misery and violence, but also one of love, friendship, admiration and ecstasy. Not so Strachey. He had spent a miserable year at Liverpool University before coming up to King's, and his joy at leaving the north-west and its mercantilism far behind was wholly unalloyed.

For Lytton, Cambridge from the first was a romp, a lark, a phallic universe. 'Ho! Ho! Ho!' he exclaimed, and he told his doting mother, 'How proud I was as I swept through the streets arrayed for the first time in cap and gown.'

Strachey's exhilaration was shared by Bell. So was his sense of the status college life immediately conferred.

Clive also put on his hat and gown; but it was raining, and he carried an umbrella. 'Anyone can see you're a freshman, sir', the head porter at Trinity said, and he explained that it wasn't customary to carry an umbrella with cap and gown – presumably these were protection enough against fluvial Cambridge. Clive remembered this because he liked to dress properly for all his roles. It would always be important whether the tie was black or white.

Edel, at one time Citizens Professor of English at the University of Hawaii – a post about as far removed from Bloomsbury as it would be possible to imagine – believes that his lofty pursuers after truth did well to band together when they did.

Leonard and Lytton both testified that the Apostles was the deepest experience of their youth: on Keynes too the society had a lasting influence. It meant that they had all become, as it were, 'insiders'; it brought them into an ideal community, a secret élite. The Society had a mission: 'to enlighten the world on things intellectual and spiritual.' But it was also a kind of superior fraternity, providing a religion of the mind, an enduring sense of fellowship. They were Apostles in a special sense of that word and G. E. Moore was their Christ. He gave them their religion.

Such sentiments would not be expressed today. Time has not been kind to Bloomsbury. They gave a boost to the avant-garde at a time when English artistic life was admittedly dull, and Strachey's 1918 work, *Eminent Victorians*, caused something of a furore with its colourful iconoclasm. But that was it. With the distinguished exceptions of Keynes and Virginia Woolf – never more than semi-attached anyway – its orotund disciples are reduced to mere footnotes in history, and the group's repellent sense of self-importance, bred at Cambridge, is almost a definition of intellectual deception.

One sad little postscript will serve to close this chapter. Bernard Levin, the highly respected columnist and author, went not to Oxford or Cambridge, but to the London School of Economics, which in 1946, as now, was an intellectual powerhouse fully the equal of any such institution in the world. But was Levin happy? Was it an ambition fulfilled? No, on both counts.

I had dreamed of Cambridge as the university I would go to; I had never seen it, but I had read *The Longest Journey*, and been fired by Forster's love of it, and the way he showed his characters growing and blossoming under its benign, unhurried influence, into complete human beings. I, too, would go to Cambridge and talk the night away, discussing whether the cow was really in the meadow, whether the meadow itself was really there.

(Bernard Levin, *Enthusiasms*, Jonathan Cape, 1983)

So what happened? It was a 'violent, youthful infatuation with politics' that decided him, perversely, on Houghton Street. Absurd as it now seems, the future columnist, famous for his etoliated prose, actually wanted to be an MP. The aberration, thankfully, was to prove short-lived, but the consequences lingered on. Though Levin certainly relished the opportunity to sit at the feet of such giants as Harold Laski, Morris Ginsberg, Lionel Robbins, Michael Oakeshott, K. B. Smellie and Karl Popper, he was soon to repent being in London, embarrassed both by his misplaced sense of vocation and by the notion that the LSE was the place to go to realize it. Thirty-seven years on, in the middle of a brave and celebrated career, his sense of loss remained little short of acute.

It is strange, at least I find it so, to reflect that my life, crowded, apart from my career, with disappointment and failure, contains only one absolutely unassuagable yearning for a second chance, only one vain regret that I cannot shake off: my desire to have been a student at Cambridge. It became one of my favourite cities later, and when I visit it now, and wander into those courts with their grass shining in the sun, as bright as a sword, I never leave it without having to fight back the tears. What makes it worse is that if I had been a little older, even by a single year, I would have had the best of both worlds, for the LSE was evacuated to Cambridge during the war, and housed in Clare College; the year I went up, 1946, was LSE's first year back in London. Oxford I have never learned to love as much.

Poor Levin. After all these years, he is still fretting. His nostalgia is out of joint, dislocated, misappropriated. He has been robbed of his memories. He must wait for the day when the Japanese bring out their latest electronic novelty, 'Virtual Cambridge'. Then, with his tele-goggles on and dressed in his undergraduate gown, he can at last join the Footlights from his armchair, edit *Granta*, speak at the Union and sip champagne with an elegant beauty while the Backs ripple gently in the heat haze from the river. Dream on, Bernard. Dream on.

CHAPTER SIX

STRANGERS AND BROTHERS

LIFE AT AN OXBRIDGE COLLEGE IS AN INTRICATE WEAVE of hierarchies, history and interests. At the top, nominally, are the heads of house, often chosen for their worldly fame beyond the university. Next come the Fellows, senior and junior, dividing into administrators and pure academics, then the lesser dons, just starting on their careers, followed by the graduate researchers and, finally, the great mass of undergraduates. Together, they form tightly knit communities, masking a complex of rivalries within a unified front. What holds them together so effectively is a shared affection for the whole and a genuine respect for the purpose that caused the college to be established in the first place.

Whatever one's views of the efficacy or otherwise of Oxford and Cambridge, it is difficult not to be seduced by their mellow congruity of life and scholarship. Here, in the words of Matthew Arnold, are colleges 'whispering the last enchantments of the Middle Ages'. Step through the gate-lodge and one is transported to a different world, in which Fellows enjoy a dominion, both spiritual and temporal, that is rarely replicated beyond. The quasi-religious nature of college government, springing from seminarian roots, is immediately apparent, not just in the chapels and the ubiquity of Latin inscriptions, or in the persons of dean and chaplain, but in the feeling of an enclosed order in which the rules are laid down without reference to secular society. Here, the proctors and 'bulldogs' enforce the law, while the fellowship is a kind of court under the moral guardianship of the Master. When 'Lord Hinksey', as Oxford's Chancellor in *Twilight of the Gods*, an Inspector Morse mystery, complains to the police that the attempted murder of a doctoral candidate during an Encaenia is surely a matter for the proctors to clear up, he was scarcely exaggerating the atmosphere of a place apart. Indeed,

Morse more or less agrees with him 'It's an Oxford crime; it needs an Oxford man to solve it', he tells his long-suffering, but gauche, Superintendent. Both ancient universities are made up, essentially, of their colleges, with laboratories and lecture halls as necessary addendums, and each community likes to feel it has its own, unique identity, separate from the rest, governed by its own rules.

Undergraduates scarcely differ from their teachers in this regard. There is more social mixing between colleges today than in the past, and the demands of science and engineering in particular have meant the growth of strong departmental ties as well. Yet the fact that colleges dine together, pray together and compete against one another on the sporting field and, most of all, the fact that resident tutors conduct much of the teaching, means that the first loyalty is invariably to Trinity or King's or Balliol or Newnham rather than to the more amorphous notion of the university.

There is an obvious advantage to this approach. It breeds commitment. But it is also a starting point for the feeling of aggressive exclusiveness that characterizes Oxford and Cambridge and a fertile source of the networking from which the two derive so much of their strength in the market-place. Membership of a college is for life. Getting a degree, or not, doesn't come into it. As Clive James puts it: 'To be thrown out was to be kept in. Oxbridge had you even when it let you go.' Gaudies at Oxford and Feasts at Cambridge bring former students back at regular intervals to dine once more in hall and to exchange gossip with others of their kind. Each college is seen as 'family' by its alumni, and this is why there is such a strong tradition, even today, of children following their parents into the same community, and, if possible, even the same set of rooms.

The corollary is the undeniable incestuousness and backbiting that build up over the years between dons who have spent too many years cloistered in each other's company. Sir Nevill Mott, winner of the 1977 Nobel Prize for Physics and Cavendish Professor of Physics at Cambridge from 1954 to 1971, tells in his autobiography, *A Life in Science*, how he was driven to distraction as Master of Gonville and Caius College by the infighting of dissident Fellows. The previous Master, Sir James Chadwick, had resigned over their antics, and Mott eventually followed his example, unable to concentrate on his real work against the dyspeptic background chatter.

'Will those bastards never stop it?' a friend wanted to know. Mott was more philosophical. 'C. P. Snow', he recalls, 'did not know the half of it.' The recent, acrimonious resignation of John Tusa as President of Wolfson College, Cambridge (detailed in Chapter 2) suggests a continuing basis for such scepticism, but it would be wrong to assume that masters and dons are forever at each other's throats. So long as the traditional niceties are observed – usually the crux in these matters – a kind of harmony, built around crusty charm, English reserve and intellectual endeavour, is the more representative result.

Heads of house come in all shapes and sizes: from regal one-time Cabinet ministers, like Lord St John of Fawsley, of Emmanuel, or Lord Windlesham, of Brasenose, through skilled administrators and diplomats, like Juliet Campbell, of Girton, and Derek Wood, of St Hugh's, but are preponderantly academics. To this extent, they are often a big disappointment to the media, which likes to portray them as political mastodons and to speculate on their successors as soon as a vacancy falls due.

When Balliol's mastership came up for grabs in 1993, in anticipation of the retirement a year later of the then incumbent, Baruch Blumberg, Fleet Street ran with the idea that Neil Kinnock, former leader of the Labour Party, was one of the contenders, then mocked him when he didn't get the job. In fact – though he might well have proved a first-class Master – he was never considered. He was not an Oxford man and is largely without academic pretensions. The man actually chosen was Colin Lucas, an historian of the French Revolution, probably best known for *The Structure of the Terror*, an epic study of the effects of political violence in the Midi during the rise of Napoleon. Lucas is a practised teacher and administrator and until recently was Dean of Social Studies at the University of Chicago. But though he enjoys considerable academic prestige and respect, he is not exactly a household name, and such friends as he has in high places – François Mitterrand among them – tend not to be from these islands.

Nor was Blumberg, despite his Nobel prize in medicine, a figure to set British pulses racing. Courtly, almost touchingly old-fashioned in his civility, this American cancer specialist, responsible for major breakthroughs in the treatment of Hepatitis B, is a front-rank academic who found himself obliged to offer daily opinions on such mundane matters as the state of undergraduate accommodation and the colour of the carpet in the senior common room. It is as if a brain surgeon in a bankrupt hospital had to spend his evenings moonlighting as a brush salesman.

Blumberg was elected to the Master's Lodge for three reasons: he was a Balliol man, with a genuine love of the college; he was an American; and he was a Nobel laureate. To the Fellows, this combination represented impressive pulling power. He had spent decades exploring the genetics of cancer, to the benefit of millions of people around the world. Now, he was expected to apply himself with equal vigour to the politics of the greased palm and the extracted promise. As the first scientist to be elected Master, 'apart maybe from an alchemist in the fifteenth century', he had hoped to pursue his medical interests while back in Oxford (where he had both studied and taught). He found instead that the real Master of Balliol was the College Appeal.

The problem is that Balliol, though ancient (founded by John de Balliol around 1263, and kept alive in its infancy by the attentions of his exotically named widow, Devorguilla), is not especially rich. It is not anything like as well endowed as, say, Christ Church, Merton, or Magdalen, yet with extremely high standards to uphold and with students and postgraduate members forever running out of cash, finds itself in the position of filling a bottomless well of obligation from a dripping tap of funds. Blumberg was far from idle in the face of these demands. 'I am by nature an activist', he remarked, over a modest ham salad in the Master's Lodge. 'Scientists can't just sit around. You need new experiments and new ideas. Basically, science is optimistic, and this rubs off on administration. You have to believe you can solve problems, and after five years in the job I think I got a sense of where we're at.'

What was never in doubt was the American's commitment to the task. He *adores* Balliol. Not only did he study there and later return as a visiting professor, but his daughter Jane followed in his footsteps and was awarded a D.Phil. in 1990 for her thesis on the early novels of Mary Shelley. Under his direction, a full-time appeals staff was set up, with a development officer and a secretary, and a business expansion scheme was launched, in conjunction with

Magdalen, in which investors combine college patriotism with at least the possibility of satisfactory returns. Just as significant – certainly in terms of potential funding – a joint exhibition, in co-operation with Merton, was staged in Tokyo in 1993 to celebrate the coincidence that Crown Prince Naruhito spent two years at Merton (investigating eighteenth-century Thames navigation) while his bride, Princess Masako, studied international relations at Balliol. University College may claim President Clinton as Oxford's most powerful living alumnus, but Balliol is working hard on the Japanese connection and is confident of substantial royalties to come.

After five years as Master, Baruch Blumberg said he was some-times uneasy about the way Oxford is able to provide its students with easy access to old members and the corridors of power. 'It's not that our young members are not very bright. They are. Science is really outstanding at Oxford. But I know some very bright people elsewhere and I have a high respect for other institutions that isn't always shared. There is a tendency in British life towards élitism. German students who come here love it. People pay attention to them. They get to meet with their professors ... Oxford and Cambridge are like Guards regiments. This notion that you have élites in universities is highly developed and recognized here – a bit like Japan, with Tokyo and Kyoto.'

The low-key pragmatism of the contest to succeed Blumberg is a far cry from the days of Benjamin Jowett, Master from 1870 to 1893, whose lofty ambition, almost realized, was to re-create the empire in accordance with his own principles and who educated an entire generation of Balliol men to go out and do his bidding. It was after Jowett that the celebrated phrase, 'Life is one Balliol man after another', was coined by Lord Samuel, and it remained true for generations to come. The Victorian was an impossible blend of faults and virtues, combining cleverness, vanity and prudery to a degree that would be wholly unacceptable today. 'Never explain, never apologize', was the maxim he enjoined on the Viceroy of India, and for years the empire appeared to be run along these lines. Jowett's saving grace was the depth of his intellect and the passion for order behind his reforming zeal. He thought he had the answer to every-thing, and he had the confidence to say so. He was, however, wrong.

> First come I, my name is Jowett
> There's no knowledge but I know it
> I am the Master of the College
> What I don't know isn't knowledge.

That was the jingle. Those were the days. A century after Jowett's death, the job-description for the Balliol mastership is much altered, being more concerned with wealth creation than the wealth of Empire. The revised, politically correct jingle might thus run:

> First among equals, my name is Lucas
> I'm not very famous but at least my book is.
> I am the fund-raiser, forever appealing,
> Less ruling the roost than wheeler-dealing.

Martin Conway, a modern history Fellow at the college, is convinced that the head of house is vital in such ventures. 'Being Master of Balliol has name-recognition. At a time of intense financial pressure and political change, we need Masters as a symbol and as people who can animate and energize the college.' What special quality Colin Lucas, with his Napoleonic nose buried deep in the French countryside, can bring to this hallowed, if diminished, role in English society remains to be seen. History would suggest that his response to the world around him is what counts, not some pre-packaged five-year plan. Yet in the age of the manager, and of the actuary, even the élite bow before the dictates of accountancy. Balliol, a favoured institution in an unfair world, must deign to fight for its place in the sun.

Professor Alec Broers, head of the Department of Engineering at Cambridge, has a lot in common with Baruch Blumberg. They are both celebrated for the practical and detailed nature of their scientific scholarship and came to England as postgraduates with ideas of what a university should be already formulated elsewhere. The difference is that, as Principal of Churchill College, Broers heads an institution that is still establishing its traditions, and thus he has a chance to make a major impact on its future. An engaging Australian, from Melbourne, he spent twenty years in America working as a top-flight researcher for IBM and was appointed to his present role, running the largest faculty in the university, only after serving his time as a hands-on professor of international standing. That said, he has taken to college life like a duck to water.

Churchill, he says, is the tops in Cambridge for engineering. 'We take the brightest in the country. We turn away people with three As. But we also have to get them functioning properly, so that they can use their brains. We end up at Cambridge with some very strange people – socially maladjusted. And at Churchill we try to shake them out.'

Despite the image he has just painted of a remedial institution, Broers insists that Churchill is a very happy place.

When I came here in 1990, I was amazed by the lack of pretence. It was a community, and an extremely successful one at that. We've got a pleasant, open environment. We like to be modern and friendly and get on and have a good time. I like to see the college boats doing well on the river and I try hard to get my engineers to join the debating society so that there is some chance they can become the future advocates of science. But we're academically rigorous at the same time. Upper-class people complain to us that we discriminate against public schools. But that's not so. We don't. We favour academic accomplishment, and at the moment that happens to mean a state school intake of around 70 per cent.

Broers views Churchill in the same way that Churchill himself did – as an institution primarily for the training of scientists and engineers, which encourages its students to work closely with industry in the development of ideas. 'We try to raise money, but we've got no real networks going. I'm not like St John Stevas. To be honest, I haven't got the time.'

The college was designed in the 1960s by Richard Sheppard as Cambridge's first major attempt at post-war modernism. Some like it, others do not. Visually, it is like a reduced version of the National Theatre combined with a multi-storey car park and various small blocks of flats, and when the wind blows in from the east in winter it is hard not to wish that its architect had paid greater regard to the value of enclosed spaces and trees.

There are comforts, though, even in Siberia, even out of term. After discussing his role as chief executive, the Principal puts on his academic gown and leads the way from his sitting-room, downstairs and along a corridor, to the Fellows' dining-room. An old friend, John Clarke, Professor of Physics at Berkeley, is over to help elect the university's first holder of the chair of superconductivity, and the informal dinner they are attending is a spontaneous display of scientific firepower. Clarke is himself a Cambridge man and says the only place he would consider working in England is his old university. 'Much better than Oxford', he adds, sniffily. Professor Archie Howie, head of the Cavendish, looking and sounding like a benign minister of the Church of Scotland, is also at the dinner table. He tells of how he has had to sort out the claims of an optimistic Northern businessman who claims to have discovered a revolutionary heat-proof plastic. 'He hadn't discovered anything amazing at all', he alleges. 'The man is a mountebank.'

The Cavendish, probably the most famous laboratory in the world, in which the atom was first split and DNA was discovered, appears to be in good hands under Howie. He himself is a solid state physicist, but, with the relaxed candour of the best scientists, he feels that the radio astronomy department, harbouring, among others, Stephen Hawking, is presently the star turn. It is rubbish, he insists, to write off radio astronomy as useless. 'It has helped create radio dishes so precise that they can locate distant vehicles to within six feet. I don't think the police would call that useless.'

But is it true that Oxbridge still has the edge in science among the British universities? The professor smiles mischievously. 'Oh yes. They're tremendously dominant. To be truthful, our professors are better than most of the Redbrick equivalents. So are most of our departments. If you look at Nottingham, for example, they're supposed to be our rivals in semiconductor physics. The Science Research Council says they are working hard and producing excellent results. But the *whole* of the Cavendish is like that.'

Clarke, huge and affable, reveals that he only got into Cambridge as an undergraduate on the strength of his hurdling. The thought amuses him. Broers then announces that *he* got in on a *choral* scholarship. Suddenly, the notion that only young people with three As are good enough to get into Cambridge seems turned on its head. The Principal discusses what it was like when he was reading for his BA at Caius. 'In those days, Cambridge was very snobbish about other university degrees. They scarcely recognized them.

Doctors from elsewhere, other than Oxford, were listed simply as "Mister".' He remembers how he had to combine his growing interest in electronics with his choral studies. It can't have been easy. His tutor in music was Martin Neary, now organist and master of the choristers at Westminster Abbey, and young Alec had to sing twenty-one hours a *week* in his first year.

After dinner, an offering with more than a hint of *nouvelle cuisine* about it, other luminaries move to and fro, helping themselves to coffee and liqueurs. A top administrator from MIT discusses the grim business of fund-raising with a British colleague. Someone else says that when Tusa left Wolfson, half the other masters in Cambridge were ready to come out in sympathy. But there is no chance, after all, to meet John Gurdon, the geneticist, whose work on cloning helped inspire *Jurassic Park*. Apparently, he had to leave early and skipped coffee. A pity. But who is that over there, handing out the coffee-cups? It is Professor Bob Edwards, who with his colleague, the late Patrick Steptoe, pioneered the world's first test-tube baby. There is no getting away from it: this is an impressive gathering. Cambridge at its best.

It forces the question, what on earth was John Casey, the high-octane Cambridge media don, on about when he wrote that for Britain to try to produce more scientists was just another example of 'panacea politics'? Casey, a Fellow in English at Caius, is opposed to science – in much the same spirit, ironically, that Evelyn Waugh thought English was a subject for 'girls' – and is not afraid to make money saying so. 'Scientists', he wrote in the London *Standard*, 'are no wiser than other people. People who live and work in the universities, hearing that "Scientists tell us . . ." something or other may be tempted to substitute "Professor Jones thinks . . ." – Professor Jones being a scientific colleague, a child-like naif, good with his hands and with a mind too fine for any idea to violate.' And Dr Casey's solution? He recommends 'useless subjects', like pure mathematics, philosophy, theology and classics 'for their inherent interest' and mind-expanding qualities. Presumably, he wrote his piece with a quill pen and sent it to London by stagecoach. He has certainly got the boffins on the run.

Such discourse – a mixture of the facile and the deeply serious – is part of the stuff of intellectual exchange. But there is room, too, for pure comic diversion, and, if we turn to Magdalen College, Oxford, we can see that something very odd indeed is happening. The head porter has gone mad. He is dressed in a three-piece suit, with full academic gown, and is behaving as though he were the senior tutor. Like some real-life Skullion, escaped from the script of *Porterhouse Blue*, he looks to be part of a successful coup, and one wonders who on earth – possibly the chef – has murdered the President and taken over the college. But then reality breaks in. The 'senior tutor' raises his walking-stick and calls out to the lodge: 'Shut the main gate! There's people there just walking in and out. And *you!*' (pointing to a helpless undergraduate, who cringes in fear). 'What are you doing with that bicycle? Get it out of 'ere. Don't you know you're not allowed to bring a bicycle into the quad?'

Thus is the natural order restored. For Michael Strutt, head porter of Magdalen, it is the end of another morning's filming *Shadowlands*, the story of the autumn love affair between C. S. Lewis, prolific author and Oxford don, and his American bride, Joy Gresham. Across the quad, in the chapel, the stars, Sir Anthony Hopkins and Debra Winger, stand around, chatting with the director, Sir Richard (now Lord) Attenborough, while the supporting cast and ranks of undergraduate 'extras' drift slowly across the lawns, complaining of the heat.

'Marvellous', says Mr Strutt, running a finger inside his stiff white collar. 'Lovely fun. Sir Richard's a perfectionist. The work that's going in this is tremendous. If it doesn't win a Oscar for him, I don't know what will.' He strides off, chortling, towards where a crowd of onlookers was threatening a break-in. 'Sorry, ladies and gents. The college is closed.'

Film-making is a notoriously egotistical business, and for one of Oxford's grandest colleges to throw in its lot with the prima donnas of the silver screen might be thought potentially explosive. In fact, everyone, except the publicists, is perfectly relaxed, and the conversion of Magdalen's venerable cloister garth into a 'location' seems to have gone ahead without a hitch.

Lewis, a don at Magdalen for thirty years, was something of a curmudgeon when it came to the world beyond academe, and the idea that his precious relationship with Joy should end up on video, watched by millions, would have appalled him. His wife's death from cancer, in 1960, at first shattered the crusty academic. Later, he was to reconcile himself to it and even came to believe that, in essence, she was with him still and that they would be reunited in heaven. The film, a surprise commercial success, was greatly boosted by its Oxford setting. Magdalen, in Lewis's view, was 'beautiful beyond compare', and Attenborough's version of the annual May Morning ceremony on the top of Magdalen tower, for which cameras were hoisted aloft to catch each golden tremor of the dawn and each angelic, English face among the choir, remains in the memory much as do the Cambridge glories of *Chariots of Fire*.

In the 1990s, Magdalen, behind its glorious façade, is inevitably more mundane. Anthony Smith, the President, is a former television producer and one-time director of the British Film Institute, who turns out books on the media at a phenomenal rate. He is also an old friend of Attenborough and extracted from him a handsome five-figure sum for the 'hire' of his college during the filming of *Shadowlands*. He does not apologize for Oxford's dominance of so much of public life, preferring to stress the excellence of the education provided and the high calibre of students and teachers. More to the point, he expresses surprise that 'only' 85 per cent of Appeal Court judges are Oxbridge. 'I should have thought it would have been somewhat higher.'

It is said that Smith has been in contact with the Prince of Wales concerning the education of Prince William, but, if so, he is keeping quiet about it. He talks instead of the splendours of Magdalen's Science Park, constructed on a site three miles south on the way to Henley in the late 1980s just as jobs and investment in Britain were plummeting. The Park, intended as a link between Oxford science and sunrise industries – and as a money-spinner for the college – is a joint venture with the Prudential Assurance Group, governed by the Magdalen Development Company, but one suspects that the men from the Pru are better able to absorb its protracted start-up costs than is Magdalen, hemmed in as it is at present by ambitious plans to increase student accommodation.

By the spring of 1994, the park proper was a little more than two-thirds full. There was still no profit to speak of, but thirty-three companies had rented premises, including Sharp Laboratories of Europe (a subsidiary of the Japanese giant), seventeen computer and software companies and several medical and pharmaceutical concerns. Rand Information Systems, another major player, though it has moved out of its original location in the innovation unit, has restarted in larger premises nearby and is maintaining its Oxford connection.

Smith is not obviously enthused with the idea of a domestic contribution to the venture. 'One isn't even talking to large British companies', he says simply. Rather, Magdalen is intended as a magnet for Asian Rim and US investment, attracted by Oxonian genius. Is such a viewpoint cynical and unpatriotic or just a measured reflection of economic reality? Either way, times have changed and native enterprise is once more off the floor. A pioneering group of small British firms is now safely onboard, at the start-up stage, and it is unlikely others will be turned away. Who knows? The park may yet turn out to be a sterling success.

Again and again in interview, President Smith stresses the global nature of Oxford.

Oxford and Cambridge are international universities, like Harvard and Yale, Tokyo, the *grandes écoles* and the German research institutes. We are involved in training the élite of the world. The next emperor and empress of Japan, Bill Clinton, Bob Hawke, the leaders of India and Japan ... For a small, island society, this is no bad thing. If you think of the total number reigned over or ruled by Oxford people, it's very considerable. The US Secretary of Defence, Les Aspen, has the biggest budget in the world. There is a Supreme Court judge, several senators and congressmen – all Magdalen. It is the same at other colleges. These are Oxford's 'trophies', and given Britain's lack of success in the twentieth century, it's good to know that we're still good at something.

At this point, the telephone rings. It is 5 February 1993. The President picks up the receiver and listens intently. 'Yes!' he says. 'We've got it.' The 'it' turns out to be the editorship of *The Economist*. Bill Emmott, a Magdalen man, has just been confirmed in the job (in a race against two other Oxford candidates), and for Smith another trophy has been acquired for the mantelpiece.

A compulsive talker, he agrees that Oxford is very much associated in the public mind with privilege. As a working-class boy, however, the thought does not bother him in the slightest. 'One father wrote to me the other day', he recalls, 'congratulating me on taking his son.

It completed a hundred years of the family at Magdalen. Another family goes back uninterrupted to the eighteenth century – but we didn't know that. [No, indeed.] There is a family atmosphere, and why should we seek to combat that?

It can be hypocrisy to try to measure 'potential'. You can't be certain that someone who has been less well taught would actually benefit from an Oxford education. Oxford and Cambridge don't exist in a just and equitable society. We certainly attempt to correct the balance, but often we reproduce the privilege. We absorb more and more people into an atmosphere of privilege. Coming here helps people without background to make successful careers in privileged sectors of the professions.

Angus Macintyre, a Senior Fellow in modern history and one of Magdalen's most experienced teachers, takes a rather different view. He believes there is less difference in standards now between Oxbridge and its rivals, particularly in London and Scotland. He also differs with his President on the methodology of selection. 'I think my main criterion with candidates is, how will he or she develop under our rough tutelage. I'm not interested in the tough goose who's been very well taught and can go through the hoops. What I want to know is, what is this person like now and what might he or she grow into?'

The two men do agree, however, on the value of the tutorial system. 'Tutorials are a huge factor in our success', says Macintyre:

but they are under massive pressure financially. The old one-to-one tutorials were rigorous and tough, but even one-to-two allows close monitoring and close personal contact. We tend to know our pupils more intimately. Its loss would be serious. I would accept moderation, but I would want passionately to retain the chance of grappling one-to-one, especially in the third year.

At Trinity Hall, one of the most attractive Cambridge colleges, tucked in alongside Clare and Caius between Trinity and King's, Jonathan Steinberg, its American-born Vice-Master, is looking ahead to his thirtieth year of teaching. He loves his job. As Director of Studies for History, he assigns students to teachers and helps shape the reading list and pattern of courses. As Vice-Master, he is the college's deputy chief executive, with responsibility for administration and budgets. Finally, as a Fellow, he has students of his own to teach and an obligation to conduct his own research.

He emphasizes his foreign roots:

I don't share the values of this society. Neither of my children went here. English people think vertically. I think horizontally. There is an English preoccupation with the vertical social order which I do not share. Cambridge is something of an exception to the rule. It is a more normal place than England is generally – more sensible. But it remains distinct. In the US, Harvard and Yale are similar perhaps to Oxbridge. The difference is, they don't have anything like the same dominant role. In Germany in the eighteenth century, there were fifty universities. In England, there were only two – and there still are only two.

Trinity Hall, says Steinberg, is very informal, very democratic. 'Most of my students call me by my first name.' And are they privileged? 'Of course they're privileged. We certainly get the people with three As – but are they the best people? I wonder.'

Even if they are not, Steinberg still does his best for them: I know everyone. I have met the Queen and Prince Charles. I know Cabinet ministers and I can pick up the phone to under-secretaries. I don't have to click my fingers to make things happen. I can place my best people in jobs, no problem, but the rest do OK as well. This is entirely to do with English snobbery. Cambridge graduates feel they have an enormous advantage. Employers feel that, too. In my view, the professional middle classes are buying élite educations all along the line. We've got kids from the state school system – but they're often kids from families with normal professional parents who happen to live in areas with good state schools. They have the same social background as most of the others from the private sector.

Surrounded by books, seated in his rooms overlooking one of the most beautiful gardens in England, Steinberg has by now warmed utterly to his theme. 'I say to my students that the most important thing they ever did was getting in here in the first place. Once you're in, you're made for life. We take very good care of them.

Counselling, tutoring, accommodation, facilities: whatever they need, they've got it. Only one in a hundred fails. It was the same for me at Harvard. It transformed my life-chances. That's what Cambridge does. Never forget it.'

There is a knock at the door. Christopher Clark, a young lecturer in modern European history from St Catharine's, comes in to discuss a problem he is having with one of his research students. Clark endorses the Steinberg thesis (which he has obviously heard before) and offers some observations of his own:

What is offered here is a truly exceptional product. France, with its *écoles normales*, produces a different kind of élite, tightly tied to the professions. Germany, on the other hand, is much less élitist. They have many large, impersonal universities. Italy is worse. Pisa is about the best, based on the French model. But here, it's a good general grounding, reinforced by good teaching. We take the top 3 per cent of the country and we teach them how to use their brains.

A discussion follows on the relative merits of Oxford and Cambridge. Steinberg is worried about the current state of supervisions (tutorials) at Cambridge. 'The system is not always appropriate. All this experimenting with twos and threes. It has become a nervous and strained institution.' And Oxford? 'There, college teaching is obsessive. We are prepared to farm people out. We don't have the same concept of discipleship. Cambridge is far more rational, less romantic, more scientific. We offer a spread of the talents.'

'That's right', says Clark. 'Oxford colleges will not allow undergraduates to take papers they do not offer themselves. Oxford tutors are regarded as "charismatic" – a bit like it is here at Caius.'

Outside, in the college courts, the flowers are in bloom, growing in gorgeous profusion in the herbaceous border alongside the Tudor library. In the Fellows' Garden, there are several magnificent chestnut trees, long-term replacements for which are already being planned, and it is easy to see why Henry James should have written, in 1905: 'If I were called upon . . . to mention the prettiest corner of the world, I should draw out a thoughtful sigh and point the way to the garden of Trinity Hall.'

All Souls, in Oxford, is equally beautiful but a world apart in the mood it presents to the world. If it were a London hotel, it would not be the Savoy or the Dorchester, but Brown's. Its discreet High Street location in Oxford is a distinguished address, where the residents do not wish to be disturbed. Just as film actors and rock stars retire to Brown's, in Dover Street, in the knowledge that they can enjoy the best without being stared at by the natives, so the Fellows of All Souls rejoice in the reputation of their college as a retreat house for the mind.

The epitome in England of intellectuality for its own sake, All Souls is in addition a place where, as the cliché has it, the very stones do speak. Unfortunately, they do so mainly in Latin, thus discouraging casual enquiry. Inscriptions set into the mellow, golden walls give the names, dates and college achievements of Fellows down the centuries, a process which confirms not so much their stature as their obscurity. Who remembers them now, these grey-beards from antiquity? Unquestionably formidable in their day, loaded with honours and braid, they are as remote as, but infinitely less pitiable than, the fallen, say, of the Indian Mutiny commemorated in scrollwork tablets in Kanpur.

Yet history – real history, the stuff of remembered achievement – *has* frequently walked All Souls' draughty passages. If many outsiders see it as elitist and unproductive, spurning teaching and requiring little of its Fellows beyond cleverness and table manners, the college down the ages has produced giants as diverse as Christopher Wren, Gladstone and Lawrence of Arabia. Today, Lord Hailsham is a distinguished Fellow, Charles Monteith, legendary former chairman of Faber & Faber, is Emeritus Fellow and William Waldegrave, Chancellor of the Duchy of Lancaster, is a quondam (sometime) Fellow who regards his time at All Souls as having been 'immensely useful to him' both as Civil Servant and politician. John Redwood, the ambitious Welsh Secretary, is a current Fellow and attends college whenever he can, to rub shoulders and break bread with others of influence. All Souls seeks, however, to be more than a registry of the Great and Good. Beneath and beyond the bombast, the college is, at heart, its Prize Fellows – those young postgraduates whose academic brilliance and mental dexterity have earned them temporary respite from the full rigours of the world. Getting into All Souls by the prize route is more than ever a badge of distinction. At present, there are sixty-seven Fellows in all categories, including just four women, all of them, while in residence, looked after by college servants and with access to free telephones, secretarial support and the glories of the wine cellar.

In addition to providing our universities with a steady supply of rarefied senior staff, All Souls has become an institution which feeds the quality press, banking, even management consultancy, as well as the more traditional areas of politics, economics and the law. Just as important, it impresses the hell out of people.

Matthew d'Ancona, 26 years old, from Catford, south-east London, was elected a Fellow in 1989 after obtaining the best First in history in his year as a student at Magdalen. He originally considered becoming a don and worked for fifteen 'delightful' months on aspects of medieval confession, with a view to taking a D.Phil., before deciding that his best penance for being such a conspicuous success was a year working for the human rights organization, Index on Censorship. Today, as a 'special writer' on *The Times*, he no longer keeps a permanent suite of rooms but remains a Fellow, attending formal dinners and spending frequent weekends in college. 'The fun', according to him, 'lies in having this dual existence. People often think of All Souls as some kind of ivory tower. But it has strong links with the secular world. When I was elected, Justin Walters, "my twin" [successful fellow candidate], had already started a career in management consultancy. At dinner, you are as likely to find yourself next to a diplomat or an actor as a don.'

Distinguished guests abound at All Souls feasts, and dessert, followed by port and malmsey, is taken by candle-light in the Codrington Library, an exotic construction, Gothic on the outside, classical inside, overlooking Hawksmoor's famous North Quad.

During one particularly sumptuous dinner, I was able to exchange words with Sir Isaiah Berlin and Lord Weidenfeld, discuss the future of Hong Kong with an ex-governor, debate the character of judicial appointments with the former Lord Chancellor and join in a heated discussion about the dearth of female Fellows.

All Souls, or, to give it its full title, the College of All the Souls of the Faithful Departed at Oxford, founded in 1438 to commemorate the dead of the Hundred Years War, is a research commonwealth of impeccable credentials. Prize Fellows, chosen from Oxford's brightest and best, are elected following a process which even the embattled Judge Clarence Thomas would have found unacceptably rigorous. Fellows must first of all be graduates of distinction. A First among such as these is a satyr to Hyperion. Next, they must sit an examination which tests not merely their specialist subject but the broad range of their knowledge, including languages. The last paper, for which three hours are allowed, examines the response to a single word, such as 'death', 'corruption' or 'green', and is considered vital. This is where candidates let their hair down and show off. 'The pompous thrive', one hail fellow (well met) confessed.

Flexibility is also required. Midway through the translation paper, candidates must submit themselves to a short *viva* with the Warden and Senior Fellows, drawn up in ranks in the dining hall. Here, they are interrogated by experts on their specialisms and drawn out by others into bizarre and contentious areas. A short list is compiled, and those still in contention next appear before the entire fellowship of the college to be interrogated on their written papers. Later still, they attend a formal dinner at which they are allegedly appraised for their ability to use cutlery correctly, identify fine wines and pass the port to the left under duress.

Such conceited rites of passage are easy to dismiss – and what the outside world is supposed to make of the ritual 'hunting of the mallard', a midnight trek across the battlements in pursuit of the college's ornithological symbol (next due in 2001), is anyone's guess. What is immeasurably less easy is to be a candidate and emerge successful at the other end. The elections which complete the process establish a genuinely collegiate verdict. There is no appeal. You are either in or you are out.

No one disputes that the benefits of playing the game and exploiting one's fellowship are considerable. William Waldegrave, a Fellow from 1971 to 1986, is quite unabashed in his praise. 'All Souls', he told me, 'contrary to the reputation which it unfairly won in the 1960s, is in fact one of the most "modern" institutions in Oxford:

The concept of a very high-powered group of professional Fellows, multi-disciplinary, including a number of people selected by the same procedure who have chosen to leave academic life for other careers, is exactly what was reinvented in the United States at Princeton, Stanford and elsewhere. It was immensely useful to me, both when I was a young Civil Servant [in the Cabinet Office] and a newly elected Member of Parliament, to be kept in touch with really vigorous professional academic thought. The college also provides an ideal home for some very brilliant dons who are not natural teachers; the same sort of role is fulfilled by, for example, the Research Fellows at Trinity College, Cambridge, or St John's, Cambridge. The imitations, like Nuffield or Wolfson, I am sure, do useful jobs, but none of them provides the same sense of community because at All Souls our academic Fellows and our non-academic Fellows are all there on the basis of intellectual equality.

Waldegrave's reference to 'unfair' criticism in the 1960s refers to comments in the report of the Franks Commission into Oxford University published in 1966. Up until then, All Souls had only Prize Fellows and Distinguished Fellows, plus a batch of professors, and the gap in the middle was yawning. The subsequent introduction of research and visiting fellowships proved a valuable reform and provided a kind of chronological continuity between youth and old age.

Jonathan Clark, a controversial historian, who washed up at All Souls after a stormy career at Cambridge and is soon to move on again, approves the creation of Senior Research Fellows while in general feeling that reform had probably gone far enough. 'We may seem Olympian and aloof from the outside', he told me, 'but from inside I can assure you there is an egalitarian atmosphere.' He supports the election of women but is equally concerned that there should be a spread of appointments across the traditional disciplines, including the theoretical sciences. An active university lecturer, Clark is proud of All Souls and of the way in which it has managed its resources. The college used to be a major landowner, but has now sold most of its holdings and, advised by Fellows such as Sir Jeremy Morse, chairman of Lloyds Bank, used the money to purchase equities. The change was effective. All Souls today is rich without being profligate, and Clark attributes the sustained sound management to a deep sense of collegiate involvement in all major decisions. 'We take a meritocratic view of the world. We have the opportunities, the candour and the resources to be meritocratic to a degree greater than anywhere else. If you can't be happy here, you can't be happy anywhere.'

Scholarship on the Isis and the Cam is clearly not endangered. Less certain is the attitude of the undergraduates who benefit from the Oxbridge experience.

Duncan Rourke, who went up to Trinity Hall in 1992 to read medicine, came from King Edward VI School, Lichfield, a classic shire comprehensive. 'It was an established thing that the cleverest people should go to Oxbridge. In my case, it just happened. Cambridge attracts ambitious people. We are the sort who would do well wherever we went. I can see my friends doing well. A number of them will be famous.'

Kate Rissik and Seama Mandal, fellow medics from adjoining Gonville and Caius, held similar opinions. Kate went to Walthamstow Hall, a private girls' school near Sevenoaks, where there was an 'expectation' that the high achievers should go to Oxbridge. Seama, a product of Newcastle Grammar, another private school, was 'encouraged' to apply. Her sister had been at Caius before her and graduated to Bar School in London. 'A number of our friends are here', said Kate, 'because this is where they belong.' She hadn't known what to expect when she arrived. She thought she would be intimidated. But it wasn't that way at all. It was simply a matter of getting involved. Seama said she had expected a higher proportion of public school people – 'I mean, *boarding* school people' – and had pictured life at Caius as being a bit like an extension of St Paul's. 'But they're really OK.'

Duncan took a year off before coming up and had toured Pakistan with a group of public schoolboys. 'They were incredibly different from me. But there's not the same dichotomy here. Hooray Henrys are in a minority.' At the same time, he was aware of pressures to conform. He took up rowing and was a member of the crew in the slowest men's boat of 1993. 'A lot of kudos came from that', he recalled. Kate was intrigued by the Union Society. She went out with a man who wants to do well there and has already turned out election papers and manifestos. But Duncan was not yet convinced. 'I know some people who are in the Union because they feel it is what they should be doing at this stage in their career, and I'm not sure how I feel about that.'

Glencora Senior, from St Paul's Girls' School, West London – *the* school for Oxbridge entrants in recent years – went up to Newnham College, an all-women foundation, to read economics, in 1993. 'A lot of my friends were trying. It wasn't such a strange thing to be applying to Cambridge as it might have been at other schools.' She toured the various Oxford and Cambridge colleges and used the college prospectuses a lot, and in the end plumped for Newnham because she felt it would be supportive to female undergraduates. 'In the faculty, there is only one female lecturer. It means you don't have any role models. Here, my director of studies is Dr Jane Humphreys, and the atmosphere, even if it is a bit claustrophobic at times, is relaxed and free of the usual pressures.'

Cranbrook Grammar School, Tunbridge Wells, a coeducational grant-maintained school, was the starting point for Karin Giannone, reading French and Italian.

We had a strong Oxbridge tradition. It was very competitive. Chosen candidates were taken into rooms and encouraged and given special tuition. I ended up with two As and a B. Two of us in my year [1993] got to Oxford and two to Cambridge. Two others were offered places but didn't make the grades. I really liked Durham, but the general pressure was to come here for the name and the degree.

Karin was not ecstatic about Newnham, but felt reasonably content. She had joined the college soccer team and was hoping to make the university side ('a half-Blue, I think'), and most of the previous weekend had been taken up with auditioning for various student plays. So might she make Footlights? 'I don't think so. You need a lot of confidence for that – and I'm not sure I'm funny enough anyway.'

At Christ Church, Oxford's most fabled college, there was no such reticence. Here, too, the general experience of undergraduates was that they were fulfilling an expectation. The difference was that they seemed to *relish* the experience. 'I have no objection to the Oxford domination of society', said Sarah Dunn, who arrived at the the House in 1991, to read law, from, first, Cheltenham Ladies College, then Kent College, Penbury, and finally, Sevenoaks School, where she was a sixth form boarder:

You get here on ability. Other courses elsewhere are at a lower level of ability and impose lesser demands. The Oxford law degree is tougher than anywhere else. There is a philosophical approach, which is a very good training for judges, who help make the law. Most barristers I know say that going here is an advantage – and most of them went to Oxbridge. I see nothing wrong in Oxford and Cambridge people getting the best jobs when they are obviously the best people.

Martha Lovell, a Scholar at Christ Church (complete with three-quarter-length gown and the right to walk in the Fellows' Garden) is one of the strongest advocates of traditional Oxford encountered in this book. She came up from Durham School in 1991 to read Mods and Greats, but switched to ancient history when she realized the demanding nature of her subject. She disapproved of the college's policy of targeting state schools for untapped talent. 'These new people', she argued – 'all they want to do is work. They play with their computers. Spotty boys and swotty girls. Scientists! They don't take part in the community.'

Martha's other concern was social climbing. 'There is so much of it about. Tweedy affectations, people reinventing themselves. The scene at Oxford is very divided. Here, my friends and I go around in gowns and attend Evensong and behave as we want. At St Hugh's, it's a low-grade jeans culture. We go to a certain kind of party. We go beagling. We drink champagne. One doesn't always feel happy about this, but we have established our own social groups, and we keep to them.'

Her one active dislike was the Bullingdon Club, a vestigial aristocratic drinking club, with animal connections. 'It is vastly expensive. It is hearty, destructive, arrogant and obnoxious. Its members, who are frequently thick, can spend £800 on their white tie and tails and don't care who they offend.'

Martha is, needless to say, a beautiful and elegant girl who likes to shock. When Lady Howe turned up with the members of her Cathedrals Commission for discussions with the Dean (Christ Church, famously, incorporates Oxford Cathedral), the men in Martha's set turned up in white tie and she wore fur. 'The Dean was *so* embarrassed. It was not quite the meritocratic image he was trying to present.' For Martha, ironically a Quaker's daughter, descended from the Clark's Shoes family, Brideshead was but a magnum away and the bubbles were still popping in her head. But her boyfriend was a genuine Old Etonian and there seemed little chance she would end up a social worker back in her native north-east. 'I'd like to look after the dolls' houses in the V&A', she trilled.

A world away from such rarefied pleasures, Chris Measures was the 1994 communications officer with the Cambridge University Students Union. He is a history graduate and an alumnus of Fitzwilliam College and was on sabbatical for a year advising, among other things, on the Target Schools scheme.

'I wouldn't say that the world owes me a living just because I went to Cambridge', he said:

But Cambridge does give you a unique opportunity to develop as a person. There are two hundred societies and thirty-one colleges, and because the town is so small the university tends to dominate our lives in a way that wouldn't be true elsewhere. If there *is* a Cambridge syndrome, of the negative, snobbish type, it tends to apply to people who have come up from a top public school. They don't really know the world and their progression is from school to Cambridge to the City.

I think I'm very lucky to be here. It makes me want to give things back. I've had all these opportunities and I'd be stupid not to have taken advantage of them, but I realize there are three or four people who could have taken my place here and I'm conscious of the fact that I mustn't waste what I've been given.

Very un-Martha-ish, of course. But where had Chris come from? The Kimbolton School in Cambridgeshire, the same private school, founded in 1600, attended by the Prime Minister's son. And how much does he see of his non-Cambridge friends? 'They think I've joined some sort of race apart. They think I've changed – that I'm somehow different. To be honest, I see very little of them.' And what would he do when his year was up? 'I'm hoping to get into advertising. That's the reason – well, one of them anyway – for doing what I'm doing now. It's good experience.'

Two undergraduates epitomizing the left-right, state versus private split at Oxford are Ian Corby, an ex-Charterhouse boy, reading PPE, and Jasmin Buttar, an historian, of Asian origin, who won her place to Somerville from a London comprehensive. Both came up in 1991 and were due to complete their finals in the summer of 1994.

Both were intent on making a political career – Ian with the Conservatives, Jasmin with Labour. To that end, Ian was a member of the national executive of the Young Conservatives while Jasmin was a member of the National Youth Forum of the Labour Party.

Ian maintained that public schoolboys at Oxford were 'persecuted' by the media. 'To a great extent, you're revealed as an Oxbridge person as soon as you open your mouth. It's the whole ethos here – analytical, precise, factual. People resent it.' Jasmin saw things slightly differently: 'In the admissions procedure, it's dog eat dog. When people get here, they know that they've made it and it colours their whole experience.' Ian was cynically aware of the practical advantage of coming to Oxford, and made no bones about it. 'It's crucial in politics. Wasn't it Ed Pearce in *the Guardian* who said that the trouble with the Labour Party today was that there weren't enough PPE-ists on the front bench? Same thing with law. If you could show me from some study that most of the best lawyers weren't from Oxbridge, then I'd be worried. That's why I came to Oxford and that's why I came to Balliol. I think they would be taking a chance if they chose people from anywhere else.'

At this, Jasmin affected a certain outrage. 'I think that someone graduating from Hull should have the same opportunity as us to rise to the highest ranks.'

Ian: 'The truth is, the important and crucial moment for all of us is when we get into Oxford.'

Jasmin: 'But you change as life goes by. No one should be discriminated against for their rest of their life just because of the accident of three years of education.'

So why had Jasmin not gone to Hull? Silence. Then: 'I suppose Oxbridge people help each other up the ladder.'

One thing is sure. If Ian Corby and Jasmin Buttar end up on opposite sides of the House of Commons, quite possibly on their respective front benches, they will still join each other to exchange gossip over tea on the terrace. 'We may be enemies', said Ian, 'but we'll always be friends.'

Beneficiaries of the college network see only its virtues. All organizations, they point out, depend on relationships, and relationships are built on familiarity and trust. The problem with this argument is that Oxbridge networking is not founded solely, or

even mainly, on personal friendship or acquaintance but on membership of the club. Thus, a Balliol, or King's, graduate from the Class
of '66 will do his best to secure work or preferment for his
successors a generation on, regardless of the fact that he has never
met them. If this were to happen on ethnic grounds, so that the
Foreign Office, for example, was staffed largely by Scots, or Sikhs,
there would be a massive outcry. Not so with Oxbridge. Here, the
prejudice, though deeply ingrained, is rendered acceptable by the
canard, Catch 22-style, that those who benefit are, by definition,
the best people in the country. Just by getting in, they expect to get
on, and it is as an unconscious freemasonry that they subsequently
advance in society. Colleges are where the nexus is formed and
sustained. From college to the university itself and then on into the
world: this is the pattern. The rules are not to be found in any
ledger or guide, but they are there for all to read in the stones of the
cloisters and in the faces of the portraits surrounding the tables in
'hall'. You are in. You have joined the club, and the privileges are
considerable. This is why young people go to Oxford and Cambridge. It is what Oxbridge is all about.

CHAPTER SEVEN

GETTING IN

Gentlemen . . .

THE OLD POOLS MAXIM, 'If you're not in, you can't win', could have been designed for Oxbridge. Every year, in schools throughout the United Kingdom, 17- and 18-year-olds preparing to sit their A-level examinations have to consider the Oxbridge option. Most ignore the ancient pairing entirely, as though it was intended for beings of a different order, or perhaps a different class. They believe, rightly or wrongly, that Oxford and Cambridge are beyond their grasp, and they choose instead from a growing wealth of alternatives, from London, Bristol, Durham and York, through Manchester, Birmingham and the other Redbricks to the former polytechnics and, of course, Scotland.

Arguably, this is how it should be. Choice, the battle-cry of modern Conservatism, is integral to the whole concept of academic freedom. The problem is that like is not being compared with like. Volumes could be written on the relative virtues of, say, Nottingham and Liverpool universities. They are both fine and competitive institutions, with high reputations in several areas of advanced research. The same is true of Manchester, Cardiff, Reading and at least a dozen others, while the Scottish universities – particularly Edinburgh and Glasgow – have an international renown. But this is to miss the point. It is not just that the system deems the majority of school-leavers with A-levels to be unworthy of Oxbridge. Many young people *agree* with the assessment. They do not even apply. Like me when I was 17, they cannot believe that they have got what it takes to join an encrusted intellectual élite. Thus, while several of the big civic universities can boast six or more applicants for every place awarded, especially in the arts, just two or three join the race for a typical set of rooms at Oxford and Cambridge.

Apologists for the cloisters believe that this self-selection process is important and sensible. What is the point, they ask, of a young man or woman who expects a B and two Cs at A-level applying for a place at Oxbridge? Three As, or two As and a B, are what is required, and why jeopardize a place at Hull for a romantic dream that cannot hope to be realized?

What this argument, seemingly sound, leaves out is twofold. First, the reason a significant number of young people do not gain three As (excepting, of course, those without the necessary mental infrastructure) is very often that they have been poorly taught and come from disadvantaged home backgrounds. The potential may be there; the wonder is that they have sat A-levels at all, let alone aimed at top marks. Many who would benefit from three years at Oxbridge, are rejected, in effect, because of their origins. This problem is being addressed by both institutions, especially Cambridge. It will be many years, however, before the products of inner-city comprehensives can hope to achieve more than the occasional 'freak' admission. Private schools and shire comprehensives remain the overwhelmingly usual route to Oxbridge, and only a tiny proportion of successful applicants could genuinely be called working class. Second, and conversely, it is a little-known fact that most of the other universities, in certain disciplines, make demands of applicants that are no less exacting that those of Oxbridge. While it is true that, overall, a small minority of first-year students in Britain have no more to offer on paper than two grade Cs (or in rare instances two Es), a respectable category of those going up to Redbrick colleges each autumn have assembled an academic cocktail every bit as heady as those presented to the admissions tutors of Magdalen or Trinity Hall. The difference is that, rightly or wrongly, these low-profile high flyers do not feel that Oxbridge is for them. They do not want to wear subfusc; they do not choose to live in cloisters or in court; they do not wish to offer their essays each Tuesday to the same crusty dons and to accept dry sherry as an act of secular communion uniting fine minds in a barren land.

Neither side in this argument has a monopoly of wisdom. There are virtues in each approach. As we shall see, the two ancient universities, Cambridge especially, are widening their net and trying to draw in the best undergraduates from all backgrounds. Oxford, while persisting for the moment with an option under which candidates can choose to sit the University Entrance Examination in the November prior to A-levels, is in practice placing more and more reliance on external results. Whichever the route, academic achievement has to be combined with successful interviews and personal assessments. Cambridge has gone further, first introducing the new Sixth Term Examination Paper (STEP), to be sat in no more than two subjects immediately after A-levels, then, for the most part, restricting it to borderline cases or to those seeking admission in an unfamiliar field. Personal assessment is as vital at Cambridge as at Oxford, but tutors try to encourage candidates not to over-prepare for interviews and, as far as possible, to remain themselves. Adrian Poole, Admissions Tutor at Trinity, points out that some schools underestimate the ability to discriminate between the merely trained and the genuinely talented. 'There is a belief in many parts of the maintained sector', he says, 'that candidates can be "trained up" for interviews just as they used to be for the entrance exam. Candidates can sometimes do themselves a disservice by having been trained in interview techniques. It doesn't work with academics.'

The point, years ago, of abandoning the old 'seventh term' – the practice under which would-be entrants were coached for Oxbridge papers post-A-level – was to create conditions of greater equality in which state schools could compete on improved terms with those who had spent seven years as boarders. But other arguments, relating to the system as it now stands, remain to be resolved. The Oxbridge tutorial system (known as 'supervisions' at Cambridge) suits those who enjoy advocacy in the guise of drawing-room conversation – a phenomenon in which public school boys have a built-in advantage. It enables individuals who perform well on their own, with just books for company, to explore their subjects in a relaxed fashion and then to test their theories against proven experts in the field in a civilized version of one-to-one combat. The weekly ritual of essays and tutorials (combined where appropriate with experiments and demonstrations) gives young people of a certain cast of mind the ideal opportunity to show off their talents while affording them daily opportunities for self-improvement through intimate contact with friends and college society. Redbrick education, which places much greater emphasis on classes, lectures and seminars, with substantially less contact between staff and students, is more impersonal, and constructs self-reliance through social abrasion. Acquiring the necessary knowledge and skills for a First in chemistry while living in a back street, say, in Salford, rarely meeting your instructors other than in the circumstances of a public forum, breeds character and resilience. It also keeps students' feet firmly on the ground, so that they do not feel elevated from the rest of society. Town and gown means a lot in 'The High' or Sidney Street. In Preston or Cardiff, little distinction is drawn – socially, at least – and students, obliged to move in the same circles as their peers, and share the same streets, are much the better for it.

The empirical evidence for Oxbridge admissions bears out time-worn prejudice all too well. It may no longer be routine that the cleverer scions of great households should be sent to the 'family' college to read mathematics or 'Greats' (though dynasties continue, in some cases, right up to the present day) while the stupider ones are guided towards a 'gentleman's Fourth' in estate management or forestry. But there is no doubt that class, in its revised, modern form, still counts. *Varsity*, the Cambridge student newspaper, reported on 1 October 1993 that just 10 schools, all of them private, had provided 6 per cent of the 1993–94 intake. A total of 233 freshers had come from these 10 élite schools, compared with 101 from the equivalent 10 in the state sector. None of the state schools was a 1960s comprehensive. All were long-established, all attracted most of their pupils from 'professional' homes, with only a leavening from the working class. 'The differences between the performance of the independent and state schools', *Varsity* reports, 'are more clearly seen when their entrance figures are expressed as percentages of each school's sixth form. The top state school, Royal Grammar School, High Wycombe, is sending 8.4 per cent of its final year pupils to Cambridge; Westminster's total of 44 represents nearly a third of leavers. The highest percentage among state schools is the 11.3 per cent of upper sixth formers sent to Cambridge by the Colchester County High School.'

The statistics, displaying a bias not away from, but *towards*, the

TABLE 7.1   THE TOP TEN INDEPENDENT SCHOOLS 1993

	School	No. of Cambridge freshers
1	Westminster (mixed)	44 (1)
2	St Paul's Boys School	34 (3)
3	St Paul's Girls School	26 (5)
4	Royal Grammar School, Newcastle	20 (44)
5 =	King Edward's, Birmingham (boys)	19 (7)
5 =	Bradford Grammar School (boys)	19 (13)
7 =	Manchester Grammar School (boys)	18 (8)
7 =	Haberdashers' Aske's (boys)	18 (10)
7 =	King's School, Canterbury (mixed)	18 (48)
10	Eton (boys)	17 (6)
TOTAL		233

(No. in brackets: position in *The Times* survey of top schools, based on Universities Central Council on Admissions points)

great public schools, and, much more modestly, in favour of 'shire' schools within the state system, speak volumes for privilege.

It is worth noting not only that the top independent schools secured as many places as they did – 233 to 101, with a similar number to Oxford – but that all of the top state schools are themselves far-removed from the common run of schools which most pupils in Britain are obliged to attend. Just two of the state schools actually bill themselves as comprehensives. The rest are grant-maintained or grammar schools, applying selection, and all take pride in their ability to provide specialist preparation for Oxbridge.

Students do not end up at Cambridge by accident. Dr Philip Ford, chairman of the university admissions forum, has said that fee-paying pupils were still expected to do better as they were 'more likely to get the personal attention able applicants need'. Chris Measures, as 1994 Students Union communications officer, with responsibility for the Target Achievement Programme (TAP), made a related point in *Varsity*: 'A tradition of Oxbridge applications is a

TABLE 7.2   STATE SCHOOL INTAKE 1993

School	No. of Cambridge Freshers
1 Royal Grammar School, High Wycombe (boys)	16 (11)
2 Methodist College, Belfast (mixed)	13 (n/a)
3 Latymer School, Edmonton (mixed)	12 (5)
4 = Colchester County High School (girls)	10 (1)
4 = Chelmsford County High School (girls)	10(8)
6 = St Olave's, Orpington (boys)	9 (7)
6 = Dr Challoner's Grammar School, Amersham (boys)	9 (37)
8 = Harrogate Grammar School (mixed)	8 (80)
8 = Cherwell School, Oxford (mixed)	8 (13)
10 Several schools	6 (n/a)
TOTAL	101

(No. in brackets: position in *Sunday Times* table of state schools A-level results, based on percentage of A/B passes)

big advantage to schools ... they know the procedure and what to expect.' A Westminster School old girl, quoted in the same article, confirmed this. She and her schoolfriends had been rigorously selected in the first place. There were excellent pupil-teacher ratios, there was a meticulous approach in preparing candidates for the Oxbridge admissions procedure and, finally, those put forward were provided with regular two-hour preparation classes, practice interviews and a week's special tuition at the beginning of their final year. Who could possibly be surprised that Westminster does so well?

What is beyond dispute is that private schools seeking Cambridge admissions continue to outperform state schools to such an extent that the correlation between money and success is everywhere apparent. As Deborah Thom, Admissions Tutor at Cambridge's Robinson College, puts it: 'We support broadening of access because we think the university should be more representative of the population as a whole. There should be more women, more people from "working-class" backgrounds, from ethnic and religious minorities. We think talent is more evenly spread among the population than those parts we're currently reaching.' The fact that so many of the successful state sector applicants are themselves from shire counties that have held on to a limited number of grammar schools only reinforces Thom's point. In the 1993–4 academic year, 45.4 per cent of Cambridge places were taken up by state school pupils, against 45.3 per cent from the private sector. (In the previous year, 1992–3, the intake was 46.3 per cent state, 43.6 per cent private – suggesting, if anything, a marginal improvement in the private schools tendency.) Not only does this rough equivalence mask the fact that only 7 per cent of all schools in the UK are private, it also fails to take account of the 'shires' factor. The sorry truth is, when the annual statistics game has been played and won, that only a tiny number of Cambridge undergraduates come from what most people would regard as working-class backgrounds – and all talk about target schools and democratization has to be set against that single fact. Sir David Williams, Cambridge's Vice-Chancellor, says that he and his colleagues are attempting to broaden access not by positive discrimination, but by telling schools what is available. 'When I was Senior Tutor and Admissions Tutor in my old college, Emmanuel, in the late '70s, it used to be difficult even to make contact with inner-London and other inner-city comprehensives. That is no longer true. But we still need diplomacy and sensitivity in this matter. We have something special here, and I would regret it if the trend was to reduce or eliminate Cambridge's unique status.'

Most of those who go to Oxbridge are clever – and measurably so. They are also preponderantly middle or upper-middle class, from professional backgrounds, and have, in the main, attended the finest schools in the country. Cause and effect, according to Susie Thomas, the Cambridge press officer, are obvious. 'We know that the boys and girls who come here are the brightest in the country. I would frankly worry if the Civil Service didn't look to Oxford and Cambridge. They're the brightest of their generation.'

'Absolutely', says Geoffrey Skelsey, a senior adviser to the Vice-Chancellor:

If the nation feels it is a good idea to place barriers in the way of people who are the best of their generation at both school and university, then heaven help us. We choose our people carefully and then we give them the best teaching available. The college system is likely to develop skills that you would not develop if you're living in grotty digs at the end of the worst end of a provincial town or inner city. And there's another factor, too. Other universities don't encourage networks and alumni associations. We do. There is a sense of corporate spirit here which is very enviable. The experience marks most people for the rest of their days.

Similar certitudes prevail at Oxford. There, according to figures released in March 1993, 46.6 per cent of freshers were from independent schools, compared with 43.7 per cent from the state sector, only fractionally down on the previous year. The arithmetic is unassailable, yet, astonishingly, the fact that state school pupils now receive positive encouragement to apply has become a source of *Angst* to fee-paying parents. Tenth-generation Old Etonians and embittered viscounts, whose sons have been attending the same college since Cromwell's time, have joined with ambitious, upwardly mobile professionals – many of them first-time Volvo-owners – to protest that their progeny are not being accepted into the cloisters as a matter of right. Background is what matters to such as these. What is the point, they argue, of being better than the rest if the top universities in the country then proceed to treat one's offspring as no better than anyone else? In 1993, Maureen Lipman, the actress, caused a bit of a stir when she complained in public about the fact that her daughter had been turned down by Oxford. 'OK', she conceded (forever playing the Jewish mother), 'my own child is an acquired taste. But . . . something weird is going on. None of the nine from her school got in, and some, with 10 As, weren't even called for interview.' Phew! Ten As and still no place at the inn. Would young Einstein have stood a chance?

The retiring headmaster of Eton, Dr Eric Anderson (since appointed Rector of Lincoln College, Oxford), joined the great debate on Oxbridge and privilege in April 1992, in a report to the Old Etonian Association. No doubt he felt strongly on the subject, for his own daughter, Kate, was among the victims, and he had written to every Oxford and Cambridge head of house seeking clarification of what was to him an alarming trend. 'Some factors now militate against Etonians', he warned the OEs, tremulously. 'When it comes to filling the last few places each year, a number of those [college heads] who wrote to me admitted that, other things being equal, their colleges might well choose candidates from state rather than independent schools.' *Quelle horreur!* Will new generations of Etonians now look to Lincoln for a change of attitude? Ian Beer, a former headmaster of Harrow and member of the Independent Schools Joint Council, agreed with Anderson that the abandoning of the seventh term was not helpful to his pupils. 'The young person who returned to school in September having already passed A-levels spent the next three months developing study habits which not only did the individual good, but influenced the entire community in which he was studying.' Another independent head, Keith Dawson, of Haberdashers' Aske's, recalled in *Cam* that at his three previous (state) schools, Abingdon, Scarborough and Henley – 'none [of which] could be described as infected by the inner-city malaise' – he had found 'a mixture of indifference, antagonism and fear towards the older universities' which seemed to him unfair and which he had sought to redress. Dawson argued strongly for the return of the old seventh term on the same basis as Beer, but insists that the main beneficiaries would be candidates from the maintained sector. Again, he was obviously thinking of the shire academies of which he has direct experience. Inner-city schools simply do not have the resources, or, in most cases, the necessary parental support, for such a luxury. The seventh term sounds good, but is divisive. For most pupils at most schools, it is simply not a viable option. Even STEP, which serves to increase academic tensions by doubling examination pressure on school-leavers in key subjects, is increasingly recognized at Cambridge to be unfair and is applied only in specific, usually technical, areas in certain colleges.

Not everyone is as sympathetic to the state sector as Dawson. Roderick Smart, a public school teacher, writing in *The Spectator* in August 1993, made it clear that he for one wanted an Oxbridge system that favoured his boys. And now that he is not getting it in the abundance required, he is reduced to an odd mixture of vulgar abuse and envy.

Who wants to go to 'Oxbridge'? The teaching is either dreadful or perfunctory. Dons are poorly paid and nourished by an unappetizing diet of social resentment and arcane theory. There is an obsession with trivial neuroses about sexual harrassment and suicide. Yet everyone who is clever and has any sense wants to go to Oxbridge as an architectural and social experience. Admission or rejection determines the shape of a life. Especially since, unlike France and America, we have no *grandes écoles* or graduate schools where the going gets intellectually tough and an ideology might be picked up. Our band of brothers is formed earlier.

One gets the picture. Smart by name, smart by nature. But it turns out that Smart is also smarting that some of his bright lads – at a *public* school, for God's sake! – are not receiving their due reward from the twin peaks. The Oxbridge admissions system, he complains, 'is officially cool towards the public schoolboy and often unofficially hostile'. He has tried every device, every stratagem, but, somehow, the tried and proper quotas are not being met. Smart lashes out.

Oxbridge on admissions now bears all the hallmarks of an élite system embarrassed about itself, even though it was élitism which always produced the best candidates. Guilt and confusion about class lead to embarrassing and patronizing ploys. Videos are dispatched to state schools in order to dispel the impression of élitism and to encourage applicants.

So far, so bad. But Smart now turns Stupid. Conceding that the independent sector is still doing disproportionately well, he laments the fact that direct grant schools are now being treated as the equals of the Great Public Schools, like Eton, Winchester and Harrow. 'Manchester Grammar School and Eton are now in the same boat so far as the admissions regime is concerned.'

Perish the thought. Why Smart should want his chaps educated in such a poisonous atmosphere cannot readily be explained. Perhaps he just wants to ensure that they 'get on'. At any rate, he is mightily peeved. Oxbridge's tutors are next lambasted for the fact that public schoolboys 'are strikingly less successful at getting good degrees at Oxbridge than their contemporaries from other schools'. This sounds odd. Are the boys in the bum-freezers a bit dense then? Surely not. But the conundrum is soon resolved.

Perhaps they see through the pretence, are less grateful to the system, conclude that the game is not worth the candle and get on with living. Independence of mind may be more valuable to them than a craven first. After all, they have already enjoyed the luxury of being well taught and can recognize when nonsense is being spoken. Meanwhile, in the courts and the quads, the admissions tutors will soon have to decide whether the next step is to discriminate against candidates from grant-maintained schools. They would be better off reflecting on how poverty of ambition cannot be cured by social engineering.

One is instantly reminded of what Harold Macmillan's old professor told him before the Great War: that the sole purpose of an Oxford education was to be able to detect when a chap was talking rot. Oxbridge, in this interpretation, is not about learning; it is about taking one's place in a society of like minds, in which fools are not suffered gladly. Another *Spectator* contributor, Hester McIntyre, who tried and failed to gain admission to read history at Oxford in 1993, takes a rather different view of the object of the exercise but is equally at odds with the procedure. She trooped along to her unnamed first-choice college in early January for what turned out to be 'three days of psychological torture'. Her interview, she says, did not 'constitute reality'. Logically, this suggests that it did not take place, but I think what she means is that it did not go quite as she had hoped.

The first session was relatively relaxed, although the two dons had cunningly placed me opposite a window so that the sun shone directly into my eyes. What is more surprising is that they admitted having done so knowingly, making it impossible for me to move. The two men then sat at opposite ends of the room so that answering each of them in turn was like watching a game of tennis.

From then on, apparently, things got worse. They asked her to identify economic trends from a graph showing wages in terms of consumables by building craftsmen from 1264 to 1954. She could not oblige. Next, they wanted to know why a map of the distribution of lunatics in Britain in 1902 should be particularly dense in Surrey. She had no reply at all to offer when they asked why she had not already studied economics, but when she attempted to raise with them her 'other interests', they only laughed. Afterwards, she discussed her ordeal with fellow applicants.

I was not alone in suppressing my inclination to speak more frankly. Aspiring lawyers were asked perverse, and perverted, questions about sado-masochism and the law, and their embarrassment was even greater than mine. Some may have spoken too frankly, particularly when several music candidates fell for one interviewer's ploy of getting them drunk at a party he organized in an undergraduate's room. One attractive young woman was wholly disconcerted to be required to answer her questions while seated in a rocking chair, exposing more of her legs than her intellect.

Miss McIntyre did not win a place that year (though she said she would apply again next time), but if her account of what took place at her, and others', interviews is typical of what goes on at Oxford, then clearly something is wrong. The fact is, however, that most interviews are considerably more prosaic and to the point. They can be rigorous, even eccentric, but only rarely brutal. Upper middle-class parents whose privately educated offspring do not make it to Oxbridge believe that the new generation of tutors are out to 'get' non-state candidates when, in fact, all that is happening is that those who have already been privileged are being asked to demonstrate that they deserve another three years of the same.

At Christ Church, traditionally a bastion of privilege but now in the van of change, state school applicants in the '90s achieve around 50 per cent of places, slightly higher than for Oxford as a whole, and even though there was a slight falling off in 1993–4 following the departure of the radically inclined Val Elson as Admissions Officer, the situation remains good. Dr Michael Vaughan-Lee, Admissions Tutor, says that the bottom line is that the good independent schools still do well, but contemporary Dotheboys Halls do not. Two out of the five biggest suppliers to Christ Church in 1993 were state schools, almost certainly shire- or grant-maintained, but, in spite of all the efforts made by dons and undergraduates through the Access Scheme and the TAP scheme, many schools continue not even to apply. Standards at the House are, it must be said, high. 'When we make two As and a B the condition for entry', says Vaughan-Lee, 'it doesn't mean that just anyone with two As and a B would get in:

We make our judgements on the basis of an individual assessment, and if we want a person we will accept him even if he drops a grade in one subject. Some universities, when they can't give candidates the individual scrutiny we give, just use a rule of thumb and let the A-level results make the decisions for them. That is not the position here. Most of our people will in fact have three As, or even four, but there is just one offer for each place, and each offer is personal.

. . . And Players

Other universities cannot match this individual approach, and there is no doubt that careful selection of candidates, allied to tutorial teaching and matchless resources, make an education at Oxford or Cambridge both challenging and worthwhile. At the same time, it is a fact that a growing number of young people, when contemplating a university education, do not even consider the Oxbridge option, preferring to apply to 'provincial' institutions in which academic standards are not intertwined with social aspirations and students are freer to grow up as individuals, not as 'types'. Figures for 1994–5 compiled by the *Sunday Times* show that, in terms of the ratio of applications to available places, Nottingham is currently the most popular university in England, followed by Bristol, Warwick, York and Birmingham, while the ancient duo, on this interpretation at least, are in the bottom ten. The situation in the mid-1990s seems to be that an increasing volume of gifted candidates are happiest with more modest institutions, enjoying high reputations in particular fields, in towns and cities of middle England which they feel relate to their own lives and experience. They want to be able to study amid high-grade researchers in up-to-date facilities, but they also want a life around them that is not entirely circumscribed by their faculty or students' union. The Universities Central Council on Admissions (UCCA), which processes applications throughout the UK, has observed this trend in recent years and, on the basis of applications overall (i.e. without reference to the number of places), now lists Leeds, Manchester and Birmingham as Britain's most popular student destinations, with Nottingham a respectable fourth, followed by Sheffield, Manchester Metropolitan, Sheffield Hallam, Liverpool John Moores, Nottingham Trent and the University of

Ulster. Leeds, the top performer, had received a massive 51,245 applications by February 1994 for just 4,600 available first-year places – a ratio of 11.3 – and was appealing to the Higher Education Funding Council to increase the number it could admit. Oxford, by contrast, had received just 20,876 applications for some 3,100 places (a ratio of 7.0), while at Cambridge, with a similar number of vacancies, a mere 11,237 were received (a ratio of 3.7). Self-selection obviously complicates the situation here. Many young people, judging themselves unlikely to achieve three As, prefer to apply to institutions they think will genuinely consider them rather than to a duo they fear would send back only polite rejections. How many – especially in the case of Cambridge – rule themselves out in this way is impossible to say. But it must be many thousands. Some will have gone to schools with no Oxbridge tradition and less-than-exalted standards of teaching. Others will simply not be bright enough. What remains is a majority, lots of them extremely able, who positively *choose* to go elsewhere – and it is these whose choice is still not given the recognition it deserves in the wider world.

Michael Pitt, Schools and Colleges Liaison Officer at Nottingham, points out that several of his university's faculties recruit candidates with A-level grades as good as anything sought by Oxbridge. To take one example, many applicants for degree courses in English among the 1994 entry, though only *obliged* to have an A, a B and a C, actually ended up with three As. The same heightened performance was noted by the history department, while in law and medicine, both wildly oversubscribed, two As and a B were practically *de rigueur*. Entry standards in the sciences are, however, noticeably lower than at either of the ancient rivals. Two Bs and a C were the norm here, with a low of just two Cs and D for agricultural and food sciences, probably (and shortsightedly) one of the least glamorous courses in the country.

Nottingham, despite the existence of the castle and the legend of Robin Hood, is not one of the most prepossessing cities in England. It is, on the other hand, unintimidating and prosperous, and the university campus, with no fewer than eleven top-rated departments, is well laid out and attractive, close to the city centre, Wollaton Park, the River Trent and the M1. Most of those who wish to live in are offered rooms in the various on-site halls of residence, each with a resident tutor. Others prefer to stay in digs. The point is that the university, while a focus for students' lives, is not set rigorously apart from the city in which it is set, so that undergraduates experience what it is like to live in an open, functioning community rather than interconnected sets of cloisters. Town versus gown has been a theme at Oxford and Cambridge down the ages. At Nottingham, as at most other universities in Britain, the links with the world outside are fundamental and strong.

At Leeds, standards are as high in some areas as they are at Nottingham. Applicants for the basic civil engineering course are not required to offer As, but they must achieve at least three Bs in relevant subjects plus one other A-level at grade C. Leeds produces more engineering graduates than any other university in the country and demands the highest standards in specialist areas. 'A' grades are in fact a commonplace among undergraduates in the faculty, just as they are in the hugely popular, and thus oversubscribed, courses in communications and broadcasting. The university is proud of its contribution to regional industry and points to its unique courses in textiles and colour chemistry and dyeing, but it is under no illusions that Leeds, in social terms, is now the 'smart' place to be. 'It will take centuries to get rid of the Oxbridge thing', says spokesperson Frances Ledgard. 'We have as good results as anyone, and industry knows this very well. Employers certainly know it. The problem is, not everyone is interested. But they should watch out. I know students here who wouldn't even have *considered* Oxbridge.'

Scottish universities, as has already been remarked, have never laboured under the view that Oxford and Cambridge are academe's ultimate goal. North of the Border, the most obvious rivalry is between Edinburgh, founded in 1583, somewhat aloof, up-market and steeped in tradition, and Glasgow, even older, founded in 1451, but with many of its undergraduates drawn from the city and living at home with their parents. Edinburgh probably enjoys a greater international reputation, particularly in medicine and law, and attracts more than 40 per cent of its students from England, as well as a substantial number from overseas. 'I don't think the Scots are terribly impressed by Oxbridge', says Ann McKelvie, the Deputy Director for Admissions. 'We are certainly not overawed. We have been confirmed as the top research university in Scotland, and that means that many of our applicants are of extremely high calibre.' She points out that, due in part to a change in the UCAS rules, Edinburgh had 32,000 applications in 1994 for just 3,100 places – a 30 per cent rise on the previous year, yielding an unsurpassed ratio of candidates to places of 10:1. In medicine and law, candidates were being asked to come up with an A and two Bs (or three As and two Bs in Scottish 'Highers'), but in practice tended to do better. In law, too, the A and two Bs requirement was regularly exceeded, with a number of would-be lawyers offering three As, the same as at Oxbridge.

But if Aul' Reekie is proud of its position at the top of the Scottish pile, it has to be said that its new Principal, the theologian and philosopher Professor Stewart Sutherland, after taking his first degree at Aberdeen, continued his studies at Corpus Christi, Cambridge, where in 1989 he was elected an Honorary Fellow. Such deference to the Sassenach élite is rare, but not unique. Stewart's predecessor at Edinburgh, Sir David Smith, an eminent agricultural biologist, was not only educated at Queen's College, Oxford, where he took an MA and a D.Phil., but was also for three years a Fellow and Tutor for Admissions at Wadham. By contrast, Sir William Fraser, Principal of Glasgow University, a former permanent secretary at the Scottish Office, was educated exclusively at the same university he now heads and professionally has rarely ventured further south than the Tweed.

Scotland's intellectual independence has a proud history. Robert Anderson, an historian and educationalist, now teaching at Edinburgh, believes that Scotland was never so overshadowed by Oxford and Cambridge as the English 'civics' and provided its own counterweights to their influence when the demand for university education expanded. Universities like Aberdeen and Glasgow (and also Queen's University, in Belfast) provided, he says, a dominance in training the professional and business leaders of their regions in Victorian times never quite attained in England.

With a tenth of England's population [Scotland] had four university centres, at Aberdeen, Edinburgh, Glasgow and St Andrews. The universities had reached a peak of fame during the Enlightenment, when Oxford and Cambridge languished, and lived on this intellectual capital well into the nineteenth century. The long-established cultural and political interchange with England gave the Scottish universities a strong influence on metropolitan intellectual, literary and scientific life, and they served as a model for foundations like University College London.

The reasons for their success were the obverse of the reasons why Oxford and Cambridge stagnated. While providing a liberal education for the leisured classes, the Scottish universities did not neglect professional training. The faculties of law and divinity served the areas of Scottish life which had retained their autonomy since the Union, while the very successful medical schools exported graduates to the rest of the British Isles.

(R. D. Anderson, *Universities and Elites in Britain since 1800*,
Economic and History Society, 1992)

In England, such self-assuredness took longer to develop. Even in the capital, with a hundred and fifty years of experience, deference to the original models on the Isis and the Cam persists to this day. An example – by no means extreme – of the ambivalence towards Oxbridge in England is reflected in the staffing and organization of Queen Mary and Westfield College London, which, in spite of its location in the heart of the East End, is considered one of the core colleges of the London federation. The Principal of QMW is Professor Graham Zellick, a leading jurist, who took an MA and a Ph.D. at Cambridge and, after a period at Stanford Law School, returned to a distinguished teaching career in London. In the foreword to his college's 1994 prospectus, Zellick warns candidates not to expect 'acres of rolling green fields, or the tranquillity and grandeur of mediaeval quadrangles and dreaming spires'. Instead, he promises a 'friendly and serious community of students and scholars, drawn from every part of the world, confident of the quality of what we are all doing in teaching and research, as well as a much-improved campus with some outstanding facilities'. So far, so good. But the professor, who won his place at Caius from a north London state school, makes no bones of his admiration for the ancient exemplars. 'Of course there is an Oxbridge dominance', he tells me:

It really isn't very surprising. Oxford and Cambridge are the places to which the most able and the most ambitious aspire. It is the supreme accolade for a state school boy. At my own school, five or six were chosen each year to sit for Oxbridge, and we were told they were places of great distinction. They have a great deal of breeding behind them, and you might even say they ought to be doing better than they are.

This is not to say that there aren't people of great distinction coming out of the other universities. There are. But some professions – for example, the law – attract a rather traditional kind of person, which is where Oxbridge scores. One schoolfriend of mine turned down a place at Caius and went to Birmingham. I haven't a clue what happened to him. It's a bit like women in engineering. You can't break the barriers down.

But while Zellick clearly benefited from Cambridge, his supreme recollection of university life was of its 'ordinariness'. He was 'up' with Prince Charles, David Mellor, Richard Ryder, the Government chief whip, and Roger Evans, the Tory MP for Monmouth, whom he recalls as 'a very pompous little chap'. Many of his fellow undergraduates were public school. 'But there were northern accents, too. It wasn't like being translated into something extraordinary.'

Contrasting Cambridge with Queen Mary's, Zellick says that his present college is 'fiercely élitist, but only in the American, meritocratic sense'. And his staff? 'Many of them are Oxbridge, or took Ph.D.s or D.Phil.s there. A number were dons. Oxbridge graduates are genuine scholars and teachers. It says something about Oxbridge that they stand for something pure in life.'

The professor is not, however, totally captivated by Old Firm values. 'Teaching at Oxbridge is in some ways inferior', he says:

It can be unutterably boring and repetitive. It can also be remarkably and indefensibly inefficient. There is nothing to beat the cut and thrust of a seminar. The tutorial and supervisions system only works because most of the undergraduates are bloody bright in the first place and have had good previous educations. It is preposterous for Oxbridge to claim credit for that. I would say, conservatively, that 100 per cent of our students could cope with Oxbridge. We have a greater range of ability at entrance, but we take good care of them. If you transferred our students to Cambridge to do the same subjects, they would do rather better. They would get more Firsts than they do here. But that is because QMW has external examiners, like most universities, while Oxbridge assessments are much more internal.

There are no two ways about it: Zellick is ambivalent. To win a place at one or other is 'the supreme accolade'. But an Oxbridge education is at the same time 'unutterably boring' and 'demonstrably inefficient'. What are we to make of it? The professor concludes by pointing out that people are too easily 'mesmerized' by Oxbridge. 'It needs to be remembered that most of its graduates do not lead glittering lives. Many are humble schoolteachers or middle-grade Civil Servants or solicitors.' Perhaps we should be grateful.

Ralph Walker, a leading Tutorial Fellow in philosophy at Magdalen, Oxford's second most grandiose college, finds it 'hardly surprising or discreditable' that Oxbridge should have a special position in English life:

It must be the character of the job we do that attracts so many able candidates. I'm pretty inclined to believe that Oxford does a reasonable job for its undergraduates, otherwise I wouldn't have stayed here so long, and I've been here twenty-two years. I was largely self-educated at McGill [one of North America's leading universities]. There, no one had people to turn to to help them overcome problems. My father was on the academic staff, so I knew the dons, but most didn't. Two-thirds of the students didn't take degrees and we had up to 1,800 people at lectures.

Walker, an authority on Kant, agrees it would be possible to lower entry standards and teach in larger groups. 'But then there would be less supervision, the way there is now in France and Germany.'

At Queen Mary and Westfield, John Ramsden, the Dean of Arts, and Reader in twentieth-century British History, himself an Oxford man, believes that many of the faculty's undergraduates in English and history would cope with an Oxbridge education but is less sure of the others. The fact is that of the seventeen Arts professors at Queen Mary's, eight are Oxbridge, while thirty-one of the sixty-three other listed academics in the faculty are also Spires and Backs.

In the law faculty, one of the strongest outside Oxbridge, twelve of the 29-strong academic staff are Old Firm, including four of the seven professors. Mathematical sciences, which incorporates several branches of physics, is no different. Here, of the forty-two staff, twenty-six are Oxbridge. There are no fewer than thirteen professors, and nine of these are Oxbridge. Physics proper has a staff of thirty-six, fourteen of them Oxbridge. Professors of physics total thirteen; Oxbridge's total is ten. Only a handful of the engineering dons are of the company; the same is true of medicine and chemistry, but nowhere are the ancient universities not represented out of all proportion to their number.

Queen Mary's, a progressive, well-run college, is no more than typical in its staff recruitment policy. Any survey of English universities would confirm that the Oxbridge leaning at the upper end is almost a commonplace. An overwhelming majority of junior lecturers are metropolitan or 'provincial', but in the race for promotion in the higher grades it is Oxbridge products who have the edge until, at professorial level, a straight majority in many disciplines is from the Spires and Backs. This may explain why so many academics who have taken their primary degrees elsewhere go on to to research at Oxford and Cambridge. They know they will be offered the best facilities there and experience an incomparable life-style far removed from anything they have enjoyed before. But, crucially, they also know that it will give them (Oxon.) or (Cantab.) after their names – suffixes that are worth their specific gravity in gold. It could, of course, be argued that this enduring tendency merely reflects the gilded pair's 'added value' and is all to the good – spreading the Oxbridge bounty. Equally, it could be said to reflect an inbuilt bias and a remarkably effective academic imperialism. For Oxbridge has always cast a long shadow. The view of Robert Anderson, dealing with the nineteenth and twentieth centuries, is that 'the original dynamism and distinctiveness of the civic universities gave way to imitation', while K. H. Jarausch, writing in *The Transformation of Higher Learning, 1860–1930* (Chicago, 1983), believes that the English civics, under the spell of the ancient duo, 'altered their entire mission from higher technical training towards the traditional university function'. These are dire charges, but at least they are historical, since (happily) overtaken by events. The residual nod towards the Isis and the Cam represented by a preference for Oxbridge graduates among the staff of other universities needs still to be resisted. After all, if provincial degrees are not good enough for provincial academics, what hope is there for the rest of us?

CHAPTER EIGHT

MONSTROUS REGIMENTS

A woman is a creature that cannot reason and pokes the fire from the top.

(REV. RICHARD WHATELY, ORIEL COLLEGE DON, 1870)

OXFORD AND CAMBRIDGE HAVE ALWAYS BEEN exclusive, but never more so than in their deliberate exclusion until the latter stages of their history of half the human race. Women were not admitted to either university until around the time of the second Reform Act, and into our own period were tolerated only on sufferance. London University (established 1836) accepted women to read for degrees in 1878 and was quickly followed by the other Redbrick foundations. At Oxford, however, women undergraduates were not sanctioned until 1920, while at Cambridge, where the 'fair sex' had been permitted to sit for 'local' examinations as long ago as 1865, the wait did not come to an end until 1948. Irene Vaughan, a First World War ambulance driver who later set up the first overseas operational unit in the Women's Royal Naval Service, sat her finals at Oxford in 1911, accompanied by a chaperone, but was not awarded her degree until seventy-four years later, when she was 95. Around the turn of the century, one uncompromising don, observing that just one man and one woman had turned up for a lecture he was scheduled to give, closed the proceedings with the immortal ruling: 'Since there is only one person present, this lecture will be postponed until tomorrow.' Fifty years later, C. S. Lewis's literary friends at Oxford, the 'Inklings', were stunned by the arrival among them of Lewis's future wife, Joy Gresham, an outspoken American who dared to contradict their opinions and clearly thought of herself as their equal. They didn't know where to look to conceal their embarrassment and rage. Male undergraduates were often no better. 'There are three types of women at the university,' said one, languid opponent of the proposed admission of women as members of the Oxford Union in the 1950s: 'the beautiful, the clever and the vast majority.' His view prevailed, and the Union did not permit women to take part in debates until 1963.

Today, while some awkwardness persists, women are an integral part of the Oxbridge landscape. They are regularly presidents of the Union societies at both universities and are vital to the success of the Footlights. They play sport, win 'Blues' and stand successfully for election in JCRs, the Students' Union and political associations. Ironically, the one field in which they have yet to make the full contribution that their talent demands is in academic performance. But that, as we shall see, is an area clouded with misogyny, speculation and doubt.

No individual played a greater role in the advancement of women in higher education than Emily Davies, the Victorian proto-feminist. Without her, and others of her ilk, Oxbridge could well have remained monastic and enclosed right into the present century. Davies was a lobbyist of genius, passionately committed to her cause, and it was mainly due to her efforts that a pioneering women's college, based previously in Hitchin, was transferred to Girton, outside Cambridge, in 1873. The new college – the first, incidentally, to have corridors rather than the traditional 'staircases' for its undergraduates and their teachers – was deliberately sited out of town, 'near enough for male lecturers to visit but far enough away to discourage male students from doing the same'. Due to the fact that Girton had enjoyed a previous incarnation in Hertfordshire, Newnham, dating from 1871, is generally regarded as the second women's foundation. It was the brainchild of Anne Clough, an agnostic ally of Davies, and assisted by Henry Sidgwick, a Fellow of Trinity College, who, unusually for his sex, had long felt that women were being unreasonably denied a proper education. Oxford, meanwhile, though late into the women's game, soon caught up and passed its ancient rival. Lady Margaret Hall, named after Lady Margaret Beaufort, 'scholar, gentlewoman and saint', opened for business in 1878, and Somerville and St Anne's followed together just twelve months later. St Hugh's, dating from 1886, and St Hilda's, founded in 1893 by Dorothea Beale (of 'Miss Buss and Miss Beale, Cupid's darts do not feel'), completed Oxford's nineteenth-century total, and in fact it was not until the opening of New Hall,

Cambridge, in 1954, following a determined campaign by existing female graduates, that any further provision for women was made in either place. Finally, in the 1960s, arising from the activities of a women's dining club, Lucy Cavendish College, for mature women, was founded, also in Cambridge, admitting its first undergraduates in 1971 and achieving approved status in 1984. By then, the coeducation revolution had swept both universities so that, today, only Newnham, New Hall and Lucy Cavendish in Cambridge, and St Hilda's in Oxford remain women-only.

It may seem to some an odd kind of progress that there should now be fewer women's colleges at Oxbridge than there were in the 1950s, or even the 1930s. Sexual equality exacts its own price, however, and one of the most costly has been the virtual disappearance of a genuinely radical tradition. Juliet Campbell, the Mistress of Girton (who did not even know the college had gone mixed until she was invited to become head of house upon her retirement as British ambassador to Luxembourg), is aware of the need to preserve a valuable slice of university history and has organized an annual Emily Davies Forum in memory of the great reformer. But she is still glad that the college now admits men. 'It was absolutely right', she recalled, soon after her appointment. 'It is the real world, and I was happier to become Mistress of a mixed college.'

Not all women agree. Somerville, Alma Mater to Margaret Thatcher, whose female students fought a noisy campaign several years ago against a proposed switch to mixed status, is now, in 1994–5 admitting its first male freshers. The Principal, Mrs Catherine Hughes, another former diplomat, herself a graduate of St Hilda's, believed that the college had to appoint more male Fellows if it was to keep up standards and attract funding and argued that the only way to ensure this was to turn its back on 115 years of single-sex tradition. Those who disagreed, mainly girls of between 18 and 21, were passionate in their conviction that such an act was a betrayal of what the college stood for. More than two hundred women, bound and gagged as a symbol of their disaffection, stood outside the university offices as Lord Jenkins of Hillhead, the college Visitor, affected mediation, but all they got was a stay of execution. Women Together, it seemed, was a dead concept, and funding, as ever, was everything.

Somerville's submission to the unisex revolution was significant because of the extent of the opposition and the fact that it was so ruthlessly swept aside in deference to Mammon. The change mocked the precepts of the Victorian women's movement and embraced instead the notion that men and women must in future do everything together, regardless of such considerations as personal feeling, race, or culture. In time, the hurt will fade, and no doubt men and women Somervillians of the future will consider it strange that they should ever have been separated. What happened was, nevertheless, a sign of the times, and not necessarily a welcome one at that.

With hindsight, the arguments against female graduates are both quaint and preposterous, yet they reflected a view of women that was centuries old and seemingly immutable. In the early 1860s, one graduate of St John's, Cambridge set out his memories of college life.

In my day we were a society of bachelors. I do not remember during my career to have spoken to a single woman at Cambridge except my bedmaker and the wives of one or two of the heads of houses . . . We were beginning to propose some modification of the absurd system of celibacy . . . yet proposals to alter it caused horror.

(Leslie Stephen, *Some Early Impressions*)

No wonder homosexuality flourished. Women were thought to be inferior beings – decorative, and sometimes surprisingly sharp, but definitely not cut out for the intellectual cut and thrust of debate or for the equally vital business of sitting around common rooms, smoking a pipe and getting drunk on port. Fellows, bound by a medieval tradition of celibacy, were only given permission to marry in 1882, and the life they led, even decades later, was sexually as well as architecturally constricted, causing them to view academic pursuits as essentially masculine and women as extraordinary outsiders, good for child-bearing and little else. Breaking down the barriers took the best part of a hundred years. Even today, there are few women professors or heads of house and a dialogue continues on the supposed peculiarities of the female mind. W. W. Skeat, whose own endeavours in whatever field are long forgotten, wrote in 1887 to his friend Henry Sidgwick (the same Sidgwick who assisted in the foundation of Newnham), about an attempt that had just failed to admit women to degrees at Cambridge. He appears to see himself as 'concerned' for women's welfare and was probably typical of his time. Yet it is hard to imagine any man saying such things today.

If given the B.A., they must next have the M.A. and that would carry with it voting and perhaps a place in the Electoral Roll; a vote for the University Livings and all the rest. Even the B.A. degree would enable them to take 5 books at a time out of the University Library on a ticket countersigned by 'their tutor'. I am entirely opposed to the admission of women to 'privileges' of this character, and I honestly believe they are better off as they are.

(Quoted by Rita McWilliams-Tullberg, in *Women at Cambridge*, 1975)

Did I say it would be hard to imagine a modern man saying such things? Well, hearken now to Professor Norman Stone, current Professor of Modern History at Oxford. The Professor, a linguist and media don as well as an historian, is reflecting on the fact that fewer women than men, proportionately, are awarded Firsts at Oxford. He recalls that on a radio programme, hosted by David Mellor MP, he had 'joked' that it was 'a sign of the decline of civilization when women became more intelligent than men' and is outraged that Catherine Evans, Women's Officer at the university, has taken exception to his wit. His conclusion, following a peroration in which, *inter alia*, he lambasts mixed colleges for encouraging 'pestilential' relationships between the sexes, is, in its way, exemplary:

The 'Oxford University Students' Union' does absolutely nothing for anyone except its 'officers'. With its time-wasting, it probably accounts for quite a number of talentless females doing even worse than they might have done in examinations. The atmosphere that it, and its like, creates is only favourable to such episodes as . . . kangaroo-court rapes charges. For the general public, already not in love with students, these things must make the worst possible impression at a time when universities, not wrongly, complain they are badly served by the taxpayer. Must we go on stumping up money for these creatures?

(*Evening Standard*, London, 14 February 1994)

Unsurprisingly, the professor was pilloried by undergraduates for the views he expressed. The JCR at Merton urged the university authorities to give him a brain scan free of charge and to look into the possibility of a sex change that would allow him to deal with his 'obsession' with women from a fresh perspective. Stone, an essentially tolerant man, who thrives on combat and goes over the top mainly when called on to do so by Fleet Street, is far from alone in his belief that the advance of feminism throughout Oxford is not an unalloyed pleasure. The election of female Fellows of All Souls in the 1980s was traumatic for some of that college's existing members, and almost a decade on just a handful of women hold the fort for their sex. At the Chichele dinner which I attended in November 1992, Dr Margaret Bent, an eminent musicologist, who spent seventeen years teaching in the United States, looked around the walls of the college refectory at the solemn portraits of All Souls 'greats', and then at the ruddy faces of her colleagues down below passing port and Madeira at dinner. 'There are hardly any more women down here than there are up there', she remarked. Another woman Fellow remembered how one greybeard, now departed, would pass by on the other side if they met in the quad.

Generally speaking, the progress made by women at Oxbridge has matched that made in the outside world. It has, in other words, been painful and patchy, but ultimately irreversible. The ambience of the Spires and Backs remains characteristically masculine, but just as today's common rooms are less wreathed in smoke than they used to be, so have they had to adjust to the presence of clever women. Not all the men may like it, but there is little they can do. Undergraduates, too, are increasingly balanced between the sexes. At both universities – as in the student population at large – more than 40 per cent of those reading for first degrees are now female, and some further progress can be expected. The days when Oxford, in the words of Anne Scott-James, was like 'some wonderful party to which one had not been invited', are long gone. Only a handful of colleges remain single-sex (and those by the choice of women), and a gender-engendered atmosphere of normality – with all its inevitable tensions – is rapidly replacing eight hundred years of masculine malevolence.

In Oxford, ten years of women undergraduates at Magdalen were celebrated in a special Grace composed by the Rev. Dr Jeffrey John, a former Dean of Divinity. It was, naturally, in Latin, and according to Anthony Smith, the college President, is immaculately balanced between tradition and modernity. 'God is in the feminine throughout', he notes, 'but it is still orthodox.'

> Fons vitae benigna,
> Pariens et pascens prolem tuam,
> Qui hac in domo tantam et talem,
> munificentiam largita es nobis;
> Te magis hodie collaudamus,
> Iniustitiae claustris iamdudum diruptis,
> Adnumerasti nobis feminas consortes,
> Ut pariter omnes studiamus et collaboremus
> Ad beneficium universi populi tui
> et maiorem gloriam tuam.

> Kindly fount of life,
> bringing to birth and feeding your children,
> you have lavished such generosity upon us in this place;
> but today we praise you the more because [ten years ago]
> at last the gates of prejudice were broken down
> and women colleagues were added to our number
> so that together we might study and strive
> for the common good of all your people
> and for your greater glory.

It sounds better in Latin. William McGonagall appears to have had a hand in the translation. But at least the intent was there.

In 1993, controversy arose on two vital fronts: the promotion of women academics to top posts and the awarding (or not awarding) of Firsts to females. For a while, the debate was quite fierce. Women, having reached that crucial level of influence, from which there is no going back, appear to have decided spontaneously that the time had come for their next quantum leap. Elizabeth Llewellyn-Smith, Principal of St Hilda's, Oxford – a college which, in spite of everything, has remained defiantly single-sex – complained in a letter to the *Daily Telegraph* that the proportion of women to men in senior academic posts and fellowships at Oxford was 'disgracefully small'. She also rejected the suggestion, put forward by a male colleague, that women-only colleges were a threat to men's academic employment, arguing that many women positively selected single-sex institutions for religious or cultural, as well as personal, reasons. Twelve months later, little had changed, she said. 'I am not aware of any great breakthrough. In the latest readerships promotion exercise [the selection of senior staff as professors-in-waiting], just two of the nineteen readers appointed were women. I think that speaks for itself.'

Miss Llewellyn-Smith (one of a fabulous dynasty, the 'Llewellyn-Oxbridges', who have achieved academic distinction via the ancient duo), was at least pleased by the appointment in 1994 of three female heads of house at mixed colleges in Oxford. Dr Jessica Rawson (a graduate of New Hall, Cambridge), previously Keeper of Oriental Antiquities at the British Museum, is now Warden of lofty Merton, one of the oldest and grandest Oxford institutions, founded in 1264 by Walter de Merton, Bishop of Rochester and Chancellor of England. Marilyn Butler (St Hilda's), until recently King Edward VII Professor of English Literature at Cambridge, became Rector of Exeter College. Averil Cameron (Somerville), lately Director of the Centre for Hellenic Studies at King's College London, is the new Warden of Keble and a likely candidate for the vacant Wykeham professorship of Greek. If their appointment is seen as a catalyst for more female fellowships, then the example of St Anne's, which has had three women heads of house since going mixed in 1979, including the present Principal, Ruth Deech, is far from encouraging. Of the forty-two tutorial Fellows and lecturers listed for the academic year 1993–4, just eleven are female, and this in a college intimately bound up with the higher education of women since 1879.

Overall at Oxford, the position of women in senior positions has advanced only marginally in fifty years. Of 200 professors at the time of writing, 9 (4.5%) are women; of 126 Readers, 8 (6.5%) are women; of 934 lecturers, 164 (17.5%) are women. If it is hard to get started, the figures suggest, it is even harder to win promotion.

At Cambridge, progress has, if anything, been even more constipated. Gillian Beer, a Girton girl and former Booker prize judge, has recently taken on the presidency of Clare Hall, a mixed graduate college, founded in 1966, in addition to her role as Professor of English. Pat Easterling (Newnham), formerly head of the Department of Greek and Latin at University College London, is the

first-ever female Regius Professor of Greek – a considerable honour – while, just as significantly, Ann Dowling, an aeronautics
expert, has become the first of her sex to achieve a chair (albeit
ad hominem) in the hugely prestigious Faculty of Engineering. At
assistant lecturer level, the first rung on the academic ladder, the
news is better. Here, 29 per cent of the 1992–3 intake were women,
a fact which bodes well for the composition of senior jobs in the
new century, and 37.5 per cent of UK graduate researchers were
women. Yet for now, the position remains that of the 200 or so
Cambridge professorships, no more than 14 (7 per cent) are held by
women.

Nancy Lane, a cell biologist and Fellow of Girton, is author of
The Rising Tide a report on the role of women in science in Britain
commissioned by William Waldegrave, one-time Fellow of All Souls
and minister in charge of citizens' charters. Her research nationally
was not encouraging, but the two ancient universities were among
the worst offenders against the ideal of equality. 'The conspiracy
against women in science is even worse at Oxbridge than it is
elsewhere', she says. 'Hardly any women at either place win promotion to top positions, and in science if they do it is usually because
they have been elected to the Royal Society and so the men cannot
avoid it. It is absurd. Nearly 50 per cent of undergraduates in some
scientific areas at Cambridge are female, but there are just three
women professors, and that includes Ann Dowling. Women remain
what they have always been at Oxbridge – a wasted resource.'

Tess Adkins, Senior Tutor at King's, Cambridge, and Felicity
Hunt, head of Cambridge's Equal Opportunities Office, have argued
vigorously for measures to advance the cause of women in academe,
and partly as a result steps have at last been taken, including the
wider provision of crèches, improved maternity leave and the introduction of women's support groups. But there is still a long way to
go. In 1992, they point out, the percentage of women in academic
posts in British universities was 14.1 per cent, while at Cambridge it
was just 6.9 per cent.

Why is the proportion of women academics at Cambridge so much lower
than elsewhere [they ask]? Part of the explanation lies in the fact that
Cambridge is a self-regenerating community; at least two-thirds of its

senior members are recruited from Oxbridge graduates (in other universities the number of internal appointments is around a third). With only 34
per cent of the graduate students being women, the pool of graduate
students is not large enough.

(*Cam*, Michaelmas Term, 1992)

Oxford's situation has equally come under scrutiny. Writing in
the *Oxford Magazine* in the spring of 1993, Sandra Fredman and
John Gardner, Fellows in law at, respectively, Brasenose and Exeter,
warned that sexual discrimination in the allocation of top academic
posts was a subject that could no longer be ignored. 'Putting the
situation right', they said, 'is not merely a matter of moral urgency,
but also of legal obligation. Equal opportunities issues cannot be
dismissed as a distraction from more serious business without
running significant legal risks.' Twelve months on, Gardner claimed
to see a shift in the rules governing competition for posts but was
'disappointed' that only two out of nineteen Readers appointed in
February 1994, were women. 'It is a very unhappy situation. Part of
the problem is that academics tend to remain in their posts for a
very long time, and progress is correspondingly slow. One would
expect practices adopted generally in this field to have a much more
gradual application in universities than in other areas.' Some have
suggested the introduction of more fixed-term tenures as one way of
bringing in more women to the upper ranks. Gardner thinks not.
'These would be the very posts that women would tend to be
offered', he says.

Rebecca Nestor, Oxford's Equal Opportunities Officer, while
attempting to defend her university's record, comes to a similar
conclusion. 'We take equal opportunities pretty seriously', she told
the *Oxford Times*. 'But change doesn't happen as fast here as it
does at new universities, probably because the turnover is slower.
Once people come to Oxford, they never want to leave.'

It is true, but it is not enough to explain what is happening. The
real answer to the continuing discrimination against women is
much more deep-seated and almost certainly connects with the
innate conservatism of the common room culture still dominant at
Oxbridge. Oxbridge men are tweedy and, in the Pall Mall, St
James's sense, clubbable. 'Huffy-puffy pipes' is the phrase used by
Melvyn Bragg to describe their culture. Some of them openly dislike

women, others are 'charmed' by them, especially if they are pretty. But only a minority truthfully regards them as fully the equal of men, capable of the same logical dissection of the facts. And this in England's twin citadels of liberal humanism! 'Inferior to us God made you', intoned the Rev. John Burgon, Dean of Chichester, in a sermon addressed to women at New College, Oxford, in 1884, 'and inferior to the end of time you will remain.' Gardner has reflected long and hard on the plight of his female colleagues and raised it, with others, at the university's main discussion forum, the Congregation, in May 1993. The debate that followed was lively but largely inconclusive. The only advance made was a theoretical undertaking to create more female Readers – a commitment not since honoured – and Gardner emerged little the wiser for the experience. 'It is very hard to get people to expose their reasoning', he says. 'Existing practices become institutionalized, and it is extremely difficult to achieve the dynamics necessary for change.'

As Adkins and Hunt make clear in their article in *Cam*, one of the problems in pushing women academics forward at Oxbridge is the chronic shortage of top-rank female postgraduates, and this brings us on to the equally thorny problem of women and Firsts.

There is no getting round the fact that at Oxford and Cambridge women undergraduates are seriously underperforming. In 1993, at Oxford, 20.1 per cent of men were awarded Firsts, compared with just 11 per cent of women. The imbalance, in general terms, applied to nearly all disciplines, including English, and, to make things worse, the previous trend of women doing better in the 2:1 division was broken, so that 59.1 per cent of men scored Upper Seconds against 58.1 per cent of women. Twenty-five years earlier, when all women undergraduates at Oxford lived in single-sex colleges, the disparity in Firsts was much less: 11.2 against 9.7 per cent (although, significantly, neither figure was as high as today). Figures for Cambridge are available in considerably greater detail owing to an initiative by *Varsity*, the student paper, which took it upon itself in 1992 to revive gender comparisons, long dormant in deference to political correctness. *Varsity*'s findings – since taken up by the university proper – show an appalling imbalance. They also speak eloquently of the continuing disparity in subject selection between the sexes.

TABLE 8.1   FIRSTS AT CAMBRIDGE: MEN'S AND WOMEN'S
TOTALS

Subject	Men's Firsts 1993 (1992)	Total men	Women's Firsts 1993 (1992)	Total women
Economics Pt 1	10.7% (9.9%)	131	5.0% (12.8%)	60
Economics Pt 2	17.5% (16.8%)	120	7.0% (5.8%)	43
Engineering Pt 1A	22.1% (23.1%)	258	12.2% (8.0%)	49
Engineering Pt 1B	21.9% (22.3%)	237	8.3% (5.1%)	48
Engineering Pt 2	26.6% (18.8%)	139	3.7% (10.7%)	27
English Pt 1	13.9% (11.4%)	72	6.6% (4.0%)	121
English Pt 2	21.7% (23.1%)	83	15.8% (9.0%)	120
History Pt 1	15.9% (16.3%)	107	2.2% (0.0%)	93
History Pt 2	21.4% (18.3%)	131	7.4% (10.1%)	81
Law Pt 1A	16.8% (n.a.)	113	5.8% (n.a.)	104
Law Pt 1B	7.1%	156	3.0%	135
Law Pt 2	15.2%	145	9.8%	122
Maths Pt 1A	30.6%	216	10.8%	37
Maths Pt 1B	32.5%	157	15.7%	51
Maths Pt 2	35.5%	141	29.0%	31
Mod. Langs Pt 1	15.9%	107	15.1%	241
Mod. Langs Pt 2	18.9%	53	7.8%	116
Nat. Sciences Pt 1A	29.6%	392	18.5%	195
Nat. Sciences Pt 1B	20.4%	412	17.2%	180
Nat. Sciences Pt 2	24.4%	429	22.9%	235
Soc. Pol. Science Pt 1	14.0% (2.4%)	43	5.6% (7.1%)	54
Soc. Pol. Science Pt 2	17.3% (11.1%)	52	13.3% (23.8%)	75

What these incomplete statistics show is that in 1993 20.6 per cent of Cambridge men gained Firsts and only 12 per cent of women. Differences are particularly marked in engineering, a traditionally macho subject, in which, in the final, Part Two exams, 26.6 per cent of men gained class one degrees against a mere 3.7 per cent of women. It is difficult not to conclude that such a disparity owes more to the culture of the engineering department than to latent differences between the sexes. In the case of social and political science (SPS), a subject in which individual responses to society are encouraged and there are actually more women than men taking the

course, the discrepancy is less marked. Is it possible that preponderantly male examiners tend to set the sort of papers that appeal more
to men than to women? Equally, is a subject like SPS, which in the
1994–5 Cambridge prospectus is illustrated by pictures of a young
child wearing a variety of expressions, likely to be better suited to
the female mind? Such issues go beyond the scope of this book, but
they do show that Oxbridge, for all its scholastic endeavour, is no
better than anywhere else in encouraging women overall to perform
to their full potential.

Norman Stone, at Oxford, denies in his article in the *Evening
Standard* that there is any question of overt discrimination in the
allocation of degrees. Pointing out that in his history department
thirty-nine Firsts were awarded to men in 1993, compared with four
to women, he stresses the fact that candidates are marked by
numbers, not names. 'Yes', he adds, 'You *can* just about identify
sex through Standard Female Copperplate – green ink, vowels
shaped like handbags – but that happens, nowadays, very rarely.
One distinguishing mark of a certain kind of female brain, even
quite a well-educated one, used to be stream-of-consciousness un-
paragraphed gush, but we do not often see that nowadays. So,
discrimination by examiners it is not. What, then?' Professor Stone
does not know. He observes that part of the fault may lie with the
fact that 'bossy-boots' female dons tend to choose the wrong sort of
women in the first place and that mixed colleges are, by their
nature, an abomination, but other than that he is stumped.

Someone who feels she knows *exactly* why women are failing to
deliver their full consignment of goods is Allison Pearson, the
Cambridge-educated television critic of the *Independent on Sunday*.
Pearson, who had originally hoped to be a poet, not a journalist,
responded to Stone by calling for him to be flogged. If women were
underperforming at Oxbridge but holding their own at other universities, she said, it had nothing to do with colleges being co-residen-
tial. 'What makes Oxford and Cambridge different is a long and
distinguished tradition of misogyny.'

Charles Goodhart, a biologist and one-time Senior Tutor at
Gonville and Caius College, Cambridge, rather takes the Stone line,
arguing that women do better at single-sex colleges rather than in
mixed institutions where 'being in a minority they find the atmos-

phere hostile'. In so far as he and Stone are referring not to *all* women, but to *some* women, they are surely right. That said, it is worth bearing in mind that Barbara Castle, for one, who attended single-sex St Hugh's in the 1930s, only managed a Third in PPE but then went on to demonstrate a highly effective political mind in a glittering career spanning nearly fifty years. Women in the 1990s get fewer Firsts at Oxbridge, says Goodhart, 'because admissions standards for women have been relaxed over the last twenty years, but tightened for men'. This, too, has the ring of truth. Reform is a two-edged sword. He continues: 'You have to remember that there are 20 per cent fewer men now at Oxbridge, to make way for the women, and that men who would formerly have got Thirds are no longer getting in. Another problem is that women are not being tested in the areas in which they are strongest. Their positive skills are not emphasized. They are more aware of complexities and less inclined to pursue a single line of argument than men. They are less good at quick, half-hour summaries of information and they are not good at standing back and saying, 'This is what I think!' As a point of view, it is at least arguable. Many women, including Felicity Hunt, would agree. Another, ventured in a letter to *The Times*, is that 'some of the best women (often undervalued by their own families) do not even apply to Oxbridge'. But Goodhart – who has been known to deduce gender from the quality of hairs on a fruit-fly's bottom – also appears to believe, deep down, that, overall, women as a sex lack the capacity of men. 'Girls with first-class ability get Firsts', he says. 'But boys who are less able at seventeen or eighteen go on maturing and catch up and surpass most girls at twenty-one and after.' What *would* Emily Davies think? Another candidate for flogging, I fear.

One noticeable feature of Oxbridge women is the undeveloped nature of their networking. This, however, is changing as they become more established at the higher levels of their chosen careers. 'What is interesting today', says Felicity Hunt, 'is that women *are* now consciously networking – but on a different basis from men. They are not so much interested in the locus – which college, which year – as in the *quality* of the different contacts they have made in every area. We see it in business in such groups as 'Women in Management', and here at Cambridge we are encouraging women's networks because we think they are helpful and supportive. We hope our women students will carry on with their contacts after they have graduated and make use of them throughout their careers.' Have no fear, Felicity. They will. A survey in 1993 of the 'Top 50' women in the City of London showed nine Oxbridge graduates (all of them English) and seven from London, including the LSE. No other universities, save Bristol and Reading (twice each) appeared more than once on the list, and the great majority were entirely unrepresented. Major consultancy firms, like McKinsey's and Price Waterhouse, are beginning to tap Oxbridge women in a big way, seeing them as both clever and self-assured, and as these women rise the expectation is that they will extend a helping hand to their younger sisters. Certainly, they are as aware as their male counterparts of the privileged nature of their education, and though they are less tied to what Americans would call the 'frat culture' they are just as conscious of being part of an élite. They, too, wish to belong to clubs that treat them as a class apart, and, as a badge of their progress, are determined to force the United Oxford and Cambridge to live up to its name and admit women as full members. This, too, will happen. The reactionaries are merely covering their retreat. In responding positively to privilege, these modern women are no different from Virginia Woolf, who in *A Room of One's Own*, in 1928, declared that the only charge she could bring against the Fellows and Scholars of Oxbridge was that for centuries they had discriminated against her sex. 'If the spirit of peace dwells anywhere', she wrote, 'it is in the courts and quandrangles of Oxbridge on a fine October morning.'

Dame Edith Sitwell, another formidable post-Bloomsbury woman, was equally seduced. In *A Unicorn Among Lions* (Weidenfeld & Nicolson, 1981), Victoria Glendinning (Somerville) recalls how, in 1951, Sitwell received a letter from Maurice Bowra, then Vice-Chancellor of Oxford and Warden of Wadham, telling her that the universir had decided to award her an honorary doctorate of literature. She was thrilled. She replied at once that it would be 'the proudest and happiest moment of my life'.

Afterwards, she wrote again, thanking Bowra for his 'wonderful' hospitality. 'The day my ten-page book *The Mother* appeared seemed to me then the summit of happiness', she gushed. 'But it was the beginning of the journey. And this is the arrival at my destination.' Later still, when congratulating John Gielgud on a similar honour, she remained transfigured by the experience. 'Fools', she told him, 'are made doctors by other fools in other universities, but no fool has ever been given an Hon. D.Litt. by Oxford.'

If women have found it hard sometimes to travel the Oxbridge road, they have refused to give up. Rather, they have steeled themselves to the task and are queuing now to reap their rewards. The equality they seek, and will ultimately achieve, is equality within an élite. By the year 2010, or thereabouts, they will be like the pigs in *Animal Farm*. They will look at the men and the men will look at them and nobody will be able to tell the difference.

CHAPTER NINE

HIGH SOCIETY

AS WE ARE FOREVER BEING REMINDED, the flower of Oxbridge blooms not just in the tutorial room and the examination hall, but on the playing field, the stage, the front page, the platform – everywhere there is an audience and an opportunity. This is the most audacious group of young people in the country, sharp as a knife, hell-bent on worldly success. Oxbridge leisure is a deeply serious business – much more serious, for many, than dull old books and lectures – and a self-conscious preparation for later life. One joins the Union Society or the political clubs in order to enter Parliament or the Inns of Court. Student drama is intended to lead on to careers in television or the theatre. The editorships of *Isis*, *Cherwell*, *Oxford Student*, *Varsity* and *Granta*, or wickedly insightful contributions to the same, are followed by confident applications to Fleet Street. Prowess on the sports field gains its rewards not only in the adulation of the masses but later, in the High Court, the City and the Bank of England. The two universities are in a sense microcosms of London, with dual graduation, in academic discipline and high-profile leisure activity, the passport to greater pleasures.

Of the principal institutions, three stand out above the rest in a crowded field: the Oxford Union, sport, in all its traditional guises, and the Cambridge Footlights Society.

Union Dues

I first met the then president of the Oxford Union when I asked her for a table for one. It was early in the summer of 1993, during the Trinity term, and I was staying at the Randolph Hotel doing research on this book. Katherine Wade, the president (for it was she), was standing in a black, patterned dress by the head waiter's lectern, and I foolishly assumed it was her job to assign tables.

Ms Wade was scandalized. 'Do I *look* like a waitress?' she demanded. Apologizing, though secretly pleased by my error, I scuttled away. Minutes later, after I had been seated, Madam President entered the dining-room proper at the head of a small party made up of what turned out to be Union officers, in evening attire, and the stately, if slightly *distrait*, figure of John Mortimer. It transpired that the author, playwright and barrister was giving a little talk that night at the Union building and was to be offered dinner beforehand to break the ice, as it were. By great good fortune, the group was placed next to me and I was able to listen in on their conversation for the next hour or so while pretending to be engrossed in a book.

Mortimer was on his best, most disingenuous form. 'Now then, my dear,' he began, 'are you the president of the Union for the year or just the term?' (this from a man who had read for his degree at Brasenose and been back to Oxford many times since, not least to visit his daughter). His youthful companions let it pass. When their guest pointed out that the Union had been fun years ago under the 'charming' Benazir Bhutto, female officer number two, a whey-faced girl in black, pointed out that society dignitaries were all idealists now. Bhutto, she said, wanted the platform. The third member of this precious quartet, a young man earnest as a Nuremberg prosecutor, complained about a left-wing speaker who had turned up to a debate in a 7-series BMW. 'Yes,' one of his companions replied, 'but we got wonderful publicity.' Mortimer refused to express shock at any such example of compromised integrity. After all, he said, Peter Jay had worked for years for Robert Maxwell. Swiftly, the conversation moved on. The great man did not want to talk about politics. He wanted to talk about pornography. 'Do you read it? Don't you, really?' Between giggles and copious draughts of white wine, he told them tales about a play he had seen 'in which a lady has it off with her gardener' and about the missing bits of the 'Squidgy' tapes, involving a rude telephone call between the Princess of Wales and a (then) unknown male friend. His stories evoked only painful silence. The officers ate dutifully and essayed only the most perfunctory sips of wine, as though thinking of England. This was evidently not Mortimer's way at all. After a bit, still clinging to the wreckage of his conversation, he held up the bottle he had just emptied and waved it hopefully in the congealing air.

Mortimer: 'Another?'
Woman in black: 'Not for me.'
The President: 'Nor me.'
Young man: 'No, thank you.'
Mortimer (*aghast*): 'Well, perhaps coffee and a liqueur'
Woman in black: 'I don't drink coffee, or tea.'
President: 'Perhaps we should discuss our game plan for the evening.'
Mortimer (looking like Charles Laughton in *Spartacus*): 'Well, yes, of course, if that's what you want.'

Later, after his talk – a rambling affair about the act of writing – jolly John was at once questioned from the floor on the importance of Oxford to his career. No doubt his interlocutor wished to be reassured that without his three years 'neath the Spires, the creator of Rumpole would have had to be content with being a solicitor's clerk. If so, he was to be disappointed. The guest speaker's chief memories of his student days were of Lord Longford shooting a cook through the foot during the war and of the feverish efforts by heterosexuals, including, presumably, himself, to achieve romantic relief. Mortimer may have adapted *Brideshead Revisited* for television and introduced a whole new generation of non-readers to its peculiar mores, but the book's notion of a class-based superiority was, he said, 'a bit of a myth'.

This is not what the eager young Unionists wished to hear. They had joined for the advantage and the training. They didn't want to be told Oxford didn't *matter*. Talking to Sir Peregrine Worsthorne, the columnist and former editor of the *Sunday Telegraph*, after a debate in which he took part in 1993, the same Kate Wade said she was sure she would end up in politics, having first made a pile of money in the City. Perry naturally enquired in which party's interest she intended to stand and was nonplussed to be told that she would wait and see. Presumably that is what is meant by idealism in the 1990s.

Union debates are supposed to be parliamentary in character and incredibly witty. The reality is that the undergraduates ape the manners of MPs, with the audience baying like lunatics and raising whole series of points of order while the president sits aloft on his, or her, throne, flanked by other officers, for all the world as though in training for the despatch box or, just possibly, the Woolsack. Sometimes it all goes off swimmingly, and there will be a few lines in the serious papers next day about what the Chancellor or the Leader of the Opposition said in a wordy debate on the economy. Just as frequently, alas, the safety valve is blown from its mountings. In the Michaelmas term of 1992, a debate on sexual manners degenerated to such an extent that Marcelle d'Argy Smith, editor of *Cosmopolitan* magazine, the sponsor, walked out in disgust. The president, Chris Hall, was 'completely plastered', she said, 'and couldn't string a sentence together'. He wore a multi-coloured clown suit and drank freely while his guests were forced to listen to a stream of adolescent, sexist humour from the floor. Afterwards, Hall apologized, but the damage was done. To add insult to injury, the Union voted soon afterwards to hold pop concerts in the debating hall and to cost the idea of a second subsidized bar.

Sir Edward Heath, president in more decorous times, does not approve of such plans. 'The Union is an institution which does not require change', he told *The Times*. 'It was not intended to be a venue for pop concerts or excessive drinking. The job of the Union is to provide a debating society, a library and a meeting place where undergraduates dine and drink together in moderation. More drinking and partying will ruin it, just like they have spoiled the House of Commons.'

Several other 'showpiece' debates in 1993 were equally vapid. The motion 'That this house believes it is the duty of everyone to exploit their assets' was proposed by Jerry Hall, 'actress and super-model', supported by Miss World, from Moscow, and Melissa Bell, an actress from the Australian soap *Neighbours*. Opposing were David Thomas, last editor of the now-defunct humorous magazine *Punch* (an interloper fom King's, Cambridge), Louise Bradshaw, a feminist from Christ Church, and Mike Maloney, a celebrated photographer, fresh from the University of Life. There was no vomit this time and only sniggers in place of high-volume filth, but there was little that shone out either, nothing to linger in the mind beyond the three women's considerable physical charms.

Real debates, on issues of consequence, do continue, with speakers of national and international stature attracted by the venue. One at least is mandatory each term. Gradually, however, with shameless media support, it is the fun sessions that are taking over. The 'King and Country' debate of 1935, in which, amid considerable uproar and imperial chagrin, the student body pronounced that it was not prepared to take the king's shilling against Hitler, remains, after all these years, still the only time the Union actually influenced events. (They weren't even correct: when it came to it four years later, Oxonians flocked to the colours.) Since then, with decreasing seriousness, it has generally been about training ambitious would-be politicians (mainly Conservative) to become parliamentary hecklers and a secondary group to be television interviewers or barristers. Women were not permitted to take part as full members until 1963. Barbara Castle, the former Labour minister, recalls how she and her friends from St Hugh's were expected to sit in the public gallery 'cheering on the gladiators' and had boycotted debates as a result. But women have since made up for their long absence and today are at least as ambitious as the men. Modern debates, even when they are serious, are very much hit-and-miss affairs, full of clichés and windy rhetoric, and receive media attention purely because they involve visiting statesmen, show-business folk and government ministers defending their failed policies.

Perhaps it is the cynicism of a hard age that has determined the present mood. When Ronald Reagan spoke at the Union before Christmas 1992, he delivered what for him was a good speech, without fluffs or ideological excess. Some among the audience truly appreciated the effort the octogenarian former President had made on their behalf. Others were just along for the laugh. Tim Short, an engineering student, issued a verdict that will no doubt have reassured the White House: 'The reception', he said, 'was almost as good as we gave Eddie the Eagle [a failed ski jumper] and the game-show host Jim Bowen.'

Assessments of the worth of the Union itself tend to be pompous and self-serving. 'Again and again in its history, the young speakers who catch the president's eye have gone on to catch the eye of the country, even the eye of the world', is the somewhat unctuous view of David Walter, a journalist, in his book, *The Oxford Union*. There is some truth in this, but only occasionally is the interest shown objectively justified. The 'skills' used by MPs in the bear-pit of the Commons were, after all, in many instances honed in the Union, and it is no coincidence – as Sir Edward Heath has hinted – that standards have slipped noticeably in both chambers since the war and show few signs of recovery.

The Union Society building, a handsome construction, dating from 1857, is reached, amid a jingle of bicycles, via Frewin Court, off Cornmarket, in the very heart of Oxford. A cheerful student hubbub greets the visitor. Members are crowded in every corner, often with pints of beer in their hands, and there is an immediate feeling of clique-ridden camaraderie. To the left of the entrance, with its porter's desk, the Old Library houses a famous collection of nineteenth-century books and is overlooked by some of the finest pre-Raphaelite murals in the country. The debating chamber, with platform, oak panelling and lofty windows, is almost equally fine. Although it is open to all within the university, and at a recent count had 8,500 student members, it remains a private club, with a joining fee of close to £100, and has to pay its way. A retinue of thirty uniformed staff looks after the place as though it were a gentlemen's club in Pall Mall, providing a subsidized bar and restaurant, as well as a jazz club, and keeping order in the midst of chaos. Everyone defers to the president, who, though in office for a mere eight weeks, is expected not only to assemble teams of eminent speakers but also to ensure that the society is run as a proper business, with formal accounts and a programme of structural maintenance. When it became clear in the mid-1980s that the place was falling down, an appeal was launched, and such was Oxford's pulling power that a number of large corporations, including a Japanese bank, coughed up several million pounds towards the cost of restoration. That is how things are done at Oxbridge. The alarm is raised, and friends in high places come racing to the rescue.

Considering its reputation, the Union does not yield a steady stream of brilliant 'personalities'. It may well produce more political figures than any other single source – certainly any other university source – but its lists of obscure, once hungry functionaries and downright unknowns reads pleasingly like Beachcomber's List of Huntingdonshire Cabmen. The visitor can see them all – or most of them – in the photographs that cover the walls of the main lobby and the central stairwell. Ambitious faces, haughty stares, shining cheeks: where are they now? Running the City, arguing in the High Court, cutting costs at the BBC. But the pictures are never boring. They are fun. The 1973 gathering of living presidents, assembled for the society's 150th anniversary, was definitely one for the record. We had a bouffant-haired William Waldegrave, then recently elected a Fellow of All Souls, blissfully unaware that he would end up touting John Major's citizens' charters round a disbelieving public; we had Michael Heseltine, who had moved heaven and earth to become president nineteen years before and, having almost thrown his career away under Mrs Thatcher, moved them again in 1992 to become President of the Board of Trade; we had the lordly William Rees-Mogg, who announced in 1993 that his court challenge to the Maastricht Bill was the most important constitutional case for three hundred years, and promptly lost it; we had Jeremy Thorpe, whom everyone supposed a latter-day Edwardian but whose alleged peccadillo with Norman Scott evoked scenes from a suppressed Feydeau farce; we had Michael Stewart, amiable and bland, a permanent blank page in the history of the Labour Party; we had Dingle Foot (Paul obviously couldn't make it), Max Beloff, Tony Howard, Christopher Hollis, Chris Tookey, Richard Seligman, Alan Herbert and a load of other Herberts, all presided over for the evening by the then incumbent, M. Austerberry, yet to leave his mark on history.

Photographs of the Union Standing Committee down the years are similarly rich in humour. Lord Soper pops up again and again, looking increasingly cherubic, clearly a Union stalwart. Lord Hailsham gazes out like a brilliant pixie, with and without his sticks. So does Richard Crossman, taking a few hours away from his diary. We have George Woodcock, looking jowly and élitist, as a New College man should; Giles Brandreth, sans pullover, sans *gravitas*; Chris Hitchens, a self-conscious intellectual 'rebel', brazen in his open-necked shirt (actually he took a Third in PPE from Balliol); a variety of Indians, including several Sikhs in turbans and beards, displaying the sub-continent's almost touching veneration for a great English institution; Benazir Bhutto, first with flowing black hair, then with her fundamentalist-chic headscarf; little Colin Moynihan, stepping out with Douglas Hogg and 'Mrs Douglas Hogg'; John Smith and his good buddy, Teddy Taylor; the late Eric Heffer, scourge of the Establishment; and, from Trinity term 1982, no fewer than three directors of Lloyds Bank. We even have, from 1990, the Princess Royal, seated alongside one Melanie Johnson (pres.), Sir Ashley Ponsonby, the Lord Lieutenant of Oxfordshire (Balliol) and the incomparable 'Queenie' Hamilton, Lord Mayor of Oxford.

This is what the Oxford Union is *really* about (Cambridge, by the way, has much the same, but it means less). It is theatre. It is about presentation over performance – the triumph of the whim. It is about lobbying and backbiting and infighting and transient victories lovingly inscribed in the record, as though they mattered. It is about being seen with the right people. It is about artful talk and dressing up as a way of life. It is about inter-Union boat races, with both sides in dinner jackets. In essence, it ought to be harmless student posturing and nothing more. But there *is* more. There is the myth. If you become president of the Union, you must be special, it is said. You must be a cut above the rest, with a potential that is denied ordinary folk, and it is this that marks you down for a gilded future. Some 80,000 life members of the society are out there waiting, including more at Central Office, Whitehall and the Inns of Court than you could shake a stick at, and, by George, they are very much impressed that you got where you did. It is the prestidigitation of the pork barrel, and the crazy thing is, it works.

Play the Game

Sport is in one sense the antithesis of Oxbridge, which is supposed to be founded on love of learning. But of course, there is no contradiction at all. There is even an intellectual rationale for the obsession of so many of the dons and undergraduates with the success of their teams, especially against the old enemy. It is the rationale of the public schools and muscular Christianity: a healthy mind in a healthy body. The truth is not so much that they like sport (which is common enough and needs no defence) but that they think it is played by their chaps with particular distinction and in a unique spirit. Thus, the 'great' Oxbridge sporting occasions are presented as national spectacles, in which we are all supposed to become involved. It matters not that they are generally ordinary. What captures the imagination of the public – or is thought to – is that the muddied oafs and flannelled fools in question are no ordinary, common or garden practitioners, but Oxbridge's finest, and therefore 'the envy of the world'.

When either of the two Varsity eights takes to the water against top-class opposition, more often than not they come off second-best. The same applies to the college boats, which are often left trailing in the wake of those from London, Durham, Nottingham and elsewhere. It is not that they are bad crews. If the truth be known, they are better than many, with longer traditions and superior facilities and interest. But they are distinctly vincible, and at Henley and other open competitions have to row for their lives. The point is that you would never guess this from the veneration accorded them each March for the Big One. *The Times*, commenting on the 1993 Boat Race, won by Cambridge for the first time in eleven years, reflected that it dramatized 'a peculiarly English archetype of heroic and meaningless conflict' – this, be it realized, of a contest in which eight of the sixteen oarsmen were from overseas. 'Cambridge', the newspaper continued, 'have had little to cheer about for the past eighteen years, except for having dominated the Cabinet with their Cambridge mafia – if that is really something to boast about. Their victory this year is gratifying to the English love of eccentricity. Provided, say Oxford fans of the tribal rite [Nigel and Harriet Bonkers], that it is understood that next year the race reverts to its natural order.'

From the next warehouse along at Fortress Wapping, the *Sunday Times* took a rather different line, nevertheless according the race full coverage on both the news and the sports pages. 'On a near perfect spring day', its two-man Boat Race staff reported,

the 139th meeting between the two universities had all the ingredients for failure as a spectator sport and social event: it was Oxbridge in a society striving for classlessness, aggressive masculinity in the age of the new man. But a worldwide television audience of 150m and 35,000 people lining the four-and-a-quarter mile route on the Thames were testimony that the appeal of the race lives on. Peter Moore, London's town crier, said it was the least élitist of Britain's big sporting attractions. 'It is a free event for lords and ladies, dustmen, billionaires and roadsweepers', he said.

Rather more billionaires than roadsweepers, one imagines.

Rugby is equally inflated by the Oxbridge air line. Flat caps, tweed jackets and hampers are assembled in their thousands for the annual fixture between the light and dark blues at Twickenham, the game's HQ. The fact that in 1994, for instance, the semi-finalists in the Commercial Union universities championship were Sheffield Hallam and Northumbria universities (both former polytechnics), the West London Institute and Roehampton Institute of Higher Education cuts no ice with the rugby establishment. It has been known for years that neither Varsity side would make it into rugby's first division. But that is to miss the point. The fabled pre-Christmas encounter is presented as an advertisement, not as a serious contest. Celebrity players are slipped in 'for the experience', lengthy previews are provided in both the weekly and daily press, and radio and television pipe the spectacle directly into the nation's homes. Two colleges, Keble at Oxford and Hughs Hall at Cambridge (not, strictly, part of the university), can be viewed at one level as rugby factories, and regularly contribute more than half of their respective sides. Their *de facto* sports scholarships are a blatant challenge to the Corinthian ideal; the comparison with sports jocks at US colleges is all too obvious. A cartoon by Mahood in the *Daily Mail* after the 1992 match aptly sums up the position. Two boys are racing up a school pitch passing a ball while simultaneously reading history and maths primers. The teacher, standing on the touch-line, remarks to a smiling parent: 'We want them to play rugby at Oxbridge.'

Big business interests and lobbyists *adore* Twickenham, granting it the same kind of attention as Ascot or the golf Open Championship.

Who can blame them? 'What is so wonderful about the Varsity match', trilled a Radio Four commentator after the 111th Twickers thriller – won for the second year in succession by the light blues – 'is the glimpse it gives of the game's future.'

An even more special case is cricket. Here, the two university elevens are granted automatic first-class status, and each spring and early summer have four-day fixtures with half of the professional county sides. Oxford actually managed a win over Middlesex in 1992, following a too-generous declaration by Mike Gatting, while Cambridge's most recent taste of glory (at the time of writing) was its defeat of Kent at the start of the same season, when the professionals were just beginning to unwind from their winter sleep. In general, the Varsity sides are regarded as cannon fodder by the counties. 'We were always under the cosh', according to Graham Pointer, secretary of the Cambridge eleven in 1987–8. They serve a function of sorts, helping the counties limber up, but defeat, as often as not, is in sight even before the shine has gone off the ball. Yet who is the captain of England? Michael Atherton, of Downing College, Cambridge. Who was the chairman of selectors who put him there? Ted Dexter, of Jesus, Cambridge. Who is chief executive of the Test and County Cricket Board? Alan Smith, of Brasenose, Oxford. And who is the president of the MCC? Dennis Silk, of Sidney Sussex, Warden of Radley – another Cambridge man. Practice, it seems, takes place not so much in the nets as in the network. Christopher Martin-Jenkins (Fitzwilliam, Cambridge), editorial director of *The Cricketer* and a leading BBC commentator, when asked why, with such a dismal record, the Varsity sides should continue to enjoy privileged treatment, replied grandly that the two were 'a breeding receptacle for future England captains'. In support of this unabashed élitism, *Cam*, the Cambridge alumni magazine, last year described Atherton, Lancashire's enterprising vice-captain, as being 'groomed to lead England', and graduates from the Fens were no doubt delighted, towards the end of the national side's disastrous 1993 test series against Australia, with the selectors' confirmation of their man. The author of the *Cam* piece, BBC match commentator Tony Lewis, is, of course, himself a past England captain. More to the point, he was a double Blue, in both cricket and rugby, at Queens' College. Dexter, who resigned as cricket supremo in the autumn of 1993, following a miserable series against Australia, after he announced Atherton's promotion spoke of the young man's 'pedigree' for the task. The late, lamented Brian Johnston (Eton and New College), for years Radio Three's 'Voice of Cricket', was equally delighted, but, gleefully, so were Atherton's colleagues at Lancashire, who had carved the initials 'FEC' (Future England Captain) on his locker door. To cricket lovers everywhere, Athers's assumption of command was an entirely natural process. Among the sport's chattering classes, only Fred Trueman, Geoffrey Boycott and Ray Illingworth (Hon. BA, Hull), working-class York-shiremen, are likely to feel uneasy about the Varsity bias, but they were saying nowt, while the comments on the subject of I. T. Botham and Gatting – despite their long apprenticeship to Mike Brearley (St John's, Cambridge) – would almost certainly be unprint-able. Illingworth did, however, have personal cause for satisfaction. A players' revolt against the imposition as Dexter's successor of his old rival from Oxford, Mike Smith, led to a dramatic eleven to nine vote in favour of the Yorkshireman, who had actually *applied* for the job and campaigned hard. Smith, in charge of the side during the somewhat inglorious winter tour of the West Indies in 1994, was far from inconsolable when the news was broken. 'We are all on the same side, wanting a winning England team', he drawled. 'I was *sounded out* [my italics] about doing the job some time ago, and I would have been happy to do it. But you can't say it was a life's ambition.' No indeed. Perish the thought.

An indication of the importance attached to Oxbridge's unique university status within cricket came in 1993 with the first edition of *Wisden* under its new editor, Matthew Engel. Traditionalists were outraged when Engel – a political scientist from Manchester Univer-sity – left out the time-honoured list of Oxbridge 'Blues' from his authoritative volume, arguing that the two ancient rivals were 'clinging to the illusion that they are playing first-class cricket'. The new man, it was felt, had gone too far, and it was even argued that, without its 'Blues', *Wisden* would cease to have value as a 'serious' work of reference.

Association football, by far the most popular team game in the world, is also played at Oxbridge, but, significantly, is entirely without cachet. Enthusiasts, and there are many at both universities, can play away to their hearts' content, but they will not attract lasting publicity. The reason? Rugby is a game for thugs played by gentlemen, soccer is a game for gentlemen played by thugs. Half-Blues are awarded in soccer – as in boxing, hockey and tennis – and much enjoyment is derived from the taking part. The game itself, however, is without any meaningful imprimatur and continues to be regarded by college authorities and traditionalists as merely a pastime, not a rite.

One sportsman passing his time extremely profitably while at Varsity was Matthew Syed, reading PPE at Balliol. Alas, his sport, at which he excels, is table tennis, about as glamorous in the cloisters as tiddlywinks, and when Syed invited a friend from the game to dine, together with another Balliol man, at college, the result was embarrassment all round. According to *The Times*, 'Neither Old Etonian college man nor blunt-speaking northern international could understand the other, confirming Syed's view that, socially at least, his sport and his politics could not mix.'

Poor Syed. One sympathizes. But at least he recognizes what is going on. 'In Oxford, I feel I have to perform intellectually and talk in a particular way. To be honest, I find the place a bit pretentious at times. People want to appear to be intellectual. I was accused of being a "yob" the other day. The problem is that I'm switching lives so often, it's hard to make real friends in either place.'

Athletics has at least got real past glories to look back on. Harold Abrahams's intrepid run twice around the Great Court of Trinity College, Cambridge while the clock struck twelve would be remembered even if it had not featured in *Chariots of Fire*. His subsequent 100-metres triumph in the 1924 Olympics, alongside that of his friend, Eric Liddell, in the 400 metres, is the stuff of legend. But there were other Oxbridge victories, too. The Marquis of Exeter, no less, an Oxford man, won the 400-metre hurdles at the 1928 Games. The world's first sub-four-minute mile, achieved in 1954 by Roger Bannister (Exeter College, Oxford; now Master of Pembroke, Oxford) remains one of the greatest sporting moments of all time, and there were sterling achievements as well by Chris Brasher (St John's College, Cambridge; founder of the London Marathon) and Christopher Chataway (Magdalen, Oxford; later an MP, minister and banker). One might even recall the efforts of Jeffrey Archer (Brasenose), the unputdownable Tory apparatchik, who ran ('never fast enough') for Great Britain in the mid-1950s before going on to write a succession of bestselling popular novels. It all sounds good, and indeed is entirely laudable, even romantic. But British athletics

today have streaked away from Oxbridge. None of our top performers in the 1993 World Championships was a Blue. None of our
previous year's Olympians of track and field had trained beneath
the Spires or jogged along the Backs – although Sir Bob Scott,
chairman of Manchester's failed bid to hold the 2002 Games, is an
Oxford man. Effortless superiority has given way to superior effort,
and Oxbridge is stuck in the starting blocks.

Hey, Diddly-dee

The Cambridge Footlights Society, founded in 1883, is in several
ways Oxbridge incarnate. Clever, witty and windy; shrewd, self-
confident and sharp; inspired, entrepreneurial and empty: it is all of
these things, and more. Or is it less? Stephen Fry, Footlit while
reading English at Queens' College at the beginning of the '80s,
looks back fondly on what was a truly formative experience.

An endless and eternal cry has been circulating in Cambridge [he told
Varsity in 1993] that Footlights is really crap. They've been saying that
since 1439. The huge spectre of John Cleese was hanging over it. Griff
Rhys Jones had just started doing *Not the Nine O'Clock News* and we
thought that there would never be a famous Footlights person again. I
never had anything to do with Footlights at all for my first two years – I
just wasn't interested. I thought it was for people who wanted to be
professional singers and wacky pranksters . . . Then I wrote a play in the
second year, which went to Edinburgh, and because it was a comedy Hugh
Laurie was dragged off to see it. I hadn't met Hugh before, but I knew of
him – he was rather distinguished for having been in Footlights in his first
year and the Boat Race in his second. At the beginning of my last year,
after the Edinburgh production, Emma [Thompson] came round and said:
'Poor old Hugh has sort of inherited Footlights and he needs someone to
write with. Can you go round, to meet him?' So I went round to his room
in Selwyn and we started writing the panto for Michaelmas.

With luvvies like this, who needs friends? Small wonder that
more drama, and more comedy, is produced at Cambridge than at
any other university in the world. Later, when observing the impact
of Oxbridge on film and television, we shall see how Fry's band of

brothers (and one sister), including Martin Bergman and Tony Slattery, went on to take Broadcasting House and Hollywood by storm. For the moment, however, it is enough to recall how they stole the show at the 1981 Edinburgh Fringe, winning the inaugural Perrier trophy for best comedy routine with a revue (since described by fellow Footlers as as 'complete crap') that, in spirit at least, they were to echo in Kenneth Branagh's 1992 film *Peter's Friends*. They were fêted, they were courted. Agents couldn't get enough of them. A triumphal tour of Australia followed, and then the heady climb to real fame and fortune through writing and professional perform-ance. Only Slattery found the going a bit rough at first. He dropped out for a time and built his reputation slowly and painfully around London's comedy clubs. In the end, however, he was fully rehabili-tated and reincorporated into the mafia, and he is now a television regular, commanding high fees for making risqué remarks.

It is the sort of super, soaraway saga which has been associated with the Footlights Society for the last thirty-five years (what happened before then is lost in the mists of time). *Beyond the Fringe*, a late 1950s–early 1960s co-production by a group of Oxbridge graduates, starring, among others, Jonathan Miller (St John's, Cambridge), Alan Bennett (Exeter College, Oxford) and Peter Cook (Pembroke College, Cambridge), had changed the way in which intelligent English humour was perceived. Henceforth, it was to be less mannered, less static, less stuck in country-house drawing-rooms. Instead, it was to be satirical and well-informed, even esoteric, and decidedly anti-Establishment, with a strong meas-ure of social and political comment. Above all else, it was to be inventive and outrageous, with leanings towards the surreal, and in this department generations of the Footlights club were destined to be the brightest stars.

John Cleese – the Banquo at every Footlights feast – joined the society from Downing College in 1961, where he was introduced to the late Graham Chapman in time for the annual revue and subse-quently toured with the troupe in London, New Zealand and New York. Eric Idle, a Pembroke man, with whom Cleese was to link up in *Monty Python's Flying Circus*, appeared on the scene a year or so later and ended up as president of the society, a role later assumed by Clive James, his devoted disciple, also of Pembroke, whom he recruited at the 1963 Footlights 'squash'. The next president to leave his mark was probably Rhys Jones, in the early 1970s, following which – leaving aside the singular contribution of Jimmy Mulville, an impresario and gag-writer rather than a performer – there was a creative lull lasting several seasons. Frustration, alas, is rarely the midwife of talent. The next bombshell was not dropped, by Stephen Fry & Co., until the end of the 1970s, and succeeding generations have been climbing out of the crater ever since. David Baddiel, half of the now defunct Newman and Baddiel comedy duo, is the most recent 'big name' to have emerged from the process (Bob Newman, though also a Cambridge man, took to comedy only after going down), but strings of Footlers wait impatiently in the wings. Andy Parsons and Henry Naylor, recent graduates now treading the boards in London, are already being touted as the next Smith and Jones, and new attractions, like Steve Punt and Hugh Dennis, are rising rapidly to the fore, with the ardent support of their friends.

It is an impressive litany – all the more so since there are rarely more than twenty active members of Footlights at any one time, and each of these is likely to remain in for at least two of their three student years. Productivity is high. There is the Michaelmas pantomime, a spring review and then the summer tour, leading to top-billing at the Edinburgh Fringe. In between comes a series of 'smokers' – cabaret evenings held either in the Cambridge Union or at the Amateur Dramatic Society's theatre in Park Street – attended by audiences of 200 or more bright young things, desperate for levity. A lot of effort goes into preparing these varied comedic outings, more in some cases than goes into revision for exams. But all the time the minds of those taking part are fixed on Edinburgh and the opportunity it uniquely presents for fame and fortune. This is where the main London agents check out the talent. They may well have dropped in surreptitiously to lesser shows, or even smokers, but, for Footlers, the Fringe is centre-stage and the major focus of their entire undergraduate careers.

The conventional wisdom is that Footlights humour is much sharper and better-crafted than that from Oxford. It is also thought to be more cerebral. Oxonian humour is seen as rooted in English tradition, but with a darker, melancholy aspect. This may be accurate or it may not, but one cannot help suspecting that partisans simply draw on the differences eternally perceived between the two universities and then superimpose appropriate traits on their respective comic traditions. The truth is probably a great deal simpler. 'I was in a revue at Oxford', Mel Smith told the *Oxford Student* in 1992, 'and we thought we were the bees' knees. But the truth of the matter is that we weren't very funny. Footlights in those days were funnier, much, much funnier, much more out front and much more variety-based.'

This sounds more like it. Being funny, as is often remarked, is no laughing matter, and at Cambridge, even at the expense of their studies, they are ready to put in the hours.

Clive James, arguably a previous incarnation of Clive Anderson (yet another Footlights stalwart), recalls in *May Week Was in June*, volume three of his compulsively readable *Unreliable Memoirs*, that his first hit on the Footlights stage came with a sketch covering the forthcoming nuptials of President Johnson's daughter, Luci.

Cast in the form of a running commentary, as if the wedding were a football match, the piece went on and on like a novel by Thomas Wolfe before Maxwell Perkins had persuaded him to cut it down to merely mammoth proportions. [Later] I trimmed my masterpiece by several minutes before going public with it in the Pembroke smoker. At the cost of sacrificing some of the more obviously political content, the laugh lines were brought closer together. What I was then engaged in, I realized much later, was the first stage in a laborious process of learning to remove the connective tissue so that the argument could be unified by tone rather than logic.

Bare bones, indeed. But he was learning his trade.

The 1994 president of Footlights, Robert Thorogood, an historian from Downing who plans to be an actor and already gives interviews as though he were Donald Sinden, maintains that part of the reason for the club's success is its commitment and sheer work-rate. 'We produce twelve hours of material a year, and that's enough to fill an entire comedy series on the BBC. No one else does this.' But he admits that the deference of the outside world has a lot to do with the esteem in which they are held. 'We have a platform no one else enjoys. Television and the press are always ringing us up – especially the *Telegraph*. They seem interested in every detail of what we do.' As if to prove the point, he reveals that just hours before we spoke, he and his friends had appeared on *This Morning*, on ITV, with Richard Madeley and Judy Finnegan. 'They were sponsoring a competition for young comedy writers and they brought us on to show how it was done. But we weren't going to be allowed to compete, they told us, because we would "obviously win it".' This is the sort of veneration Footlights is used to. After the '81 Perrier award, it was allegedly made clear to the club that they wouldn't win again in '82, 'because that would look bad for the organizers'.

Thorogood accepts, reluctantly, that there is a Cambridge mafia in comedy but denies it is a network 'as such'. What it is, he says, splitting hairs like Edward Scissorhands on Speed, is 'a group of friends and acquaintances who grew up together and share the same interests'. The fact is, he has been able to discuss ideas with Griff Rhys Jones, David Baddiel and Rory McGrath while still an under-graduate and already has firmly established contacts in the BBC and Granada Television. If he had not decided to take up straight acting, there would have been lots of people in the business looking out for him, and he is confident he could have got a start as a 'runner' somewhere on the comedy scene.

Daniel Mazer, Thorogood's deputy in 1994, read law at Peter-house but lost all ambition to become a barrister the moment Footlights entered his soul. He claims that he put in five hours a day, five days a week, on society business most of the year and, in the lead-up to the summer tour, had virtually no time for academic work. The '94 revue, rejoicing in its title *The Barracuda Jazz Option*, was still formative as the build-up to finals began, but centred on five soldiers who disappeared at the end of a bloody war and later returned as a kind of satirical A-Team. It was due to be taken to a variety of venues, beginning, naturally, in Oxford, and was slotted in for the Pleasance Theatre, one of Edinburgh's biggest and best, for August.

Small, black-haired and angular, like a malevolent pixie, Mazer is well aware that he has turned his Cambridge career on its head by ignoring his studies to concentrate on comedy. But he sees no problem with the choice he has made. 'There was a lot of juggling at first, but the end result is that the law ball has been dropped. I wouldn't want to be a barrister now. If I hadn't got into Cambridge and had gone to Bristol, there's no way I would have ended up in comedy. There's no equivalent forum elsewhere. I want agents to come and see me. I want coverage from the national press. We're high profile here, and this is my moment.'

After Cambridge, he sees himself performing at the better London venues, avoiding the bear-pits and aiming for slots at Jongleurs and the Comedy Club. But long-term, it is film and television that most attract him.

There is no doubt that he has enjoyed every minute of his burgeoning career.

When I first joined, in my second year, I expected Footlights would be an impenetrable clique. In fact, it's very friendly. Generally, there's a three-year cycle. Third-years encourage freshers. They encourage them. They all love the club and want to keep it going. I don't expect to fail now.

People from the club leave every year and go into the business. This means I already know a six-year span of Footlights comics. It's a huge network. This leads to envy from outsiders, of course. I already know radio producers and people on the circuit. Footlights veterans can get over any gulf in ability through contacts. Some – and I won't mention any names – have succeeded who shouldn't. But we are all in it together and we help each other out. To be honest, if I wasn't part of it, I'd hate us.

It sounds like bliss. And it is. But a cloud, no bigger than a man's hand, appeared on the horizon in 1994 with the ending of a three-year sponsorship of the society by Holsten Beer. A subsidy of £15,000 a year is not easily forgone, and Mazer and his pals – most of them men – were having to pull back from their characteristic profligacy and dip deeply into club savings. But was he down-hearted? Not a bit of it.

Mazer believes that the reason so many Oxbridge comics make it big is that they believe in themselves and do not accept the possibility of failure. 'Oxbridge gives you an arrogance. You're pleased with yourself and have confidence in your ability. Footlights audiences are also phenomenally generous. You rarely come off badly. They know that we are going to go on and make it in a tough business and they bask in the reflected glory of seeing us at the dawn of our careers. It's something to tell their friends about. It's part of the Cambridge experience.'

And what about other audiences? Surely they are not all so welcoming. A pleasurable pause follows. 'Well, we did have a few problems with students at Durham once', he recalls. 'There were hecklers all over the place. We weren't put off though. We just stood there shouting back at them: "Three As! Three As! Three As!" That soon shut them up.'

CHAPTER TEN

RICHLY ENDOWED

NEW YEAR'S DAY 1994 BEGAN UNCOMFORTABLY for the Old Firm. Stephen Castle, the Cambridge-educated political editor of the *Independent on Sunday*, reported on his newspaper's front page that 'a special government subsidy for Oxford and Cambridge is to be cut to bring them more into line with other universities'. In future, apparently, the Treasury would require the duo to come up with substantially more of the cash needed to sustain their college network, and with it the unique system of tutorial instruction.

For years, there has been criticism of the fact that Oxbridge is awarded higher fees than its competitors simply because of the self-imposed demands of collegiate education. Other universities, hard-pressed by the Exchequer, are resentful of the fact that a coterie of élitist communities on the Isis and the Cam, many of them profiting from long centuries of endowment, should be subsidized at a level considerably above the going rate. The belief in many Redbrick departments is that, given the same resources, they could do as good a job as the favoured pair: in other words, that much of Oxbridge's 'effortless superiority' stems in fact from privilege and wealth. Such murmurings of discontent in provincial common rooms tended in the past to be dismissed as mere envy, but in more straitened times have begun to find powerful echoes in Whitehall. Determined to achieve 'value for money', and perhaps even embarrassed by the obvious inequity at the top of what are perceived to be public institutions, the present Conservative Government, most of whose members passed through the quads and courts on their way to high office, have had to consider a cutback in support for Oxbridge's gilded youth in excess of what they could expect on a per-capita basis elsewhere.

But the New Year's Day exclusive, though on the right track, turned out to be less dramatic than it sounded. For a start, the Treasury review to which it referred, though it had been recommended in the Croham Report on university funding as long ago as 1987, was incomplete. Second, according to officials, any cutbacks in the level of college revenues paid by local education authorities and the Higher Education Funding Council for England and Wales (HEFCE) would have to be compensated, at least in part, by a rise in the two central block grants. As things stand, grants paid to the two universities proper are reduced by approximately 42 per cent of what might otherwise be due to allow for the fact that some £2,800 per student *extra* is paid directly to the colleges. Reform of the existing arrangments along the lines suggested, even if it did mean an overall reduction in the rate of subsidy, would have to include an increase in central funding. The importance of the change would consist, therefore, not so much in its scale – requiring a net yearly increase in private funding per undergraduate of about £1,200 – as in the departure it would represent from established procedure. Oxford and Cambridge, less in some eyes than the sums of their parts, are well aware of the difficulties of defending privilege within a state system. They know that in consequence they will at some stage be required to step up even further the own-resources component of their funding. But such a development is not seen as the end of the world. Some colleges and departments even welcome the prospect, looking on it as an opportunity to put up further barriers against state intrusion and thus, if anything, to reinforce their separateness. The Campaign for Oxford, launched in 1988 under the patronage of the Queen Mother, and the Campaign for Cambridge University, which began a year after, with Prince Philip as patron, are the clearest evidence of the realism with which the *ancien régime* views its future. Oxford's original target of £250 million has long since been revised upwards and, though technically its life is finite, like a church spire appeal it looks like acquiring permanent status. At Cambridge, where the appeal is directed at more specific ends, fresh goals seem certain to emerge that will accord it a similar long-term character. The assumption is that the two universities will take advantage, albeit nervously, of government parsimony and cut still more of their ties to the state than is presently the case. Overseas funding, chiefly from America and

Japan, directed through research grants and the two standing appeals, should permit the duo to present themselves, at least aspirationally, as international institutions, having a physical location in the United Kingdom but without any pronounced local patriotism. They are not expected to go overboard on this. A majority of undergraduates will continue to be British. A rising percentage, however, is likely to come from overseas – from the United States, Japan, Germany and the Far East – and these will be charged the sort of rates that should help ensure institutional survival and growth. How welcome such a shift will be to the British people is a moot point. Many will feel that being British – more especially *English* – is a large part of Oxbridge's charm and that the Best of British is better than international anonymity within a medieval theme park.

It is an old story. Money buys resources, facilities and staff, which in turn ensure a high level of teaching and encourage research. It also keeps undergraduates and dons in the style to which they have become accustomed. As Ted Tapper and Brian Salter observe in their meticulously researched study, *Oxford, Cambridge and the Changing Idea of the University* (Open University Press, 1992): 'Integral to the image of the [two] is that they are wealthier institutions than other British universities.' Tapper, Reader in Politics at the University of Sussex, and Salter, Senior Research Fellow at the University of Kent at Canterbury, make clear that the tradition of Oxbridge funding sees the state as a minority shareholder, to be kept, as far as possible, at bay. Yet by 1970 the central grant element in funding of the two was more than 60 per cent of income, just 10 percentage points less than for UK universities as a whole, and the rate of increase is described by Tapper and Salter as 'remorseless'. They conclude: 'Should their appeals succeed even beyond their wildest dreams, Oxford and Cambridge will continue to remain for the foreseeable future essentially state-funded institutions.'

The Tapper and Salter analysis and a parallel critique, *The Decline of Donnish Dominion*, by A. H. Halsey (Clarendon Press, 1992), have been received almost as divine revelations by their subjects. Sir Richard Southwood, Oxford's Vice-Chancellor until 1993, told colleagues and friends in his final public oration that the two books set the context in which future developments must be discussed. Acknowledging Tapper and Salter's judgement – a judgement not shared by the author of the present volume – that neither of the ancient universities had so far managed to work out what role they should occupy in the years ahead, Sir Richard observed: 'In so far as we have freedom to influence the form or direction of Government proposals, we should do so against our own clear vision of the future, and not respond in a partial and grudging fashion. If the Government is determined to empty the bath, we must be sure we hang on to the baby.' There were five key issues.

First, the balance between undergraduate teaching and research was altering profoundly. In a series of moves, 'each small in itself, but slow and deliberate, like those of a good chess player', funding for research and funding for teaching had been separated. Dons could soon be required to account for time spent on each. The effect would be to tip the balance of money voted to the university increasingly heavily towards research, the quality of which was now subject to external assessment. Twice as much of Oxford's income now came from research funding and postgraduate fees as from funding for undergraduate teaching. Even if allowance was made for the college input from fees, the balance in public funds was still slightly in favour of research and postgraduate study.

Second, Sir Richard said, the tutorial system itself had come under threat. The only way that a university could now avoid losing funds earmarked for teaching was to take more students. Each year, it had to achieve the national level of 'efficiency gain', defined by increasing student numbers at minimum cost, in order not to lose out on funding. Protests that teaching quality would be impaired had been neatly turned on their head by the Department of Education's decision to assess teaching quality not in order to reward excellence but to guard against unacceptably low levels.

Oxford and Cambridge differed markedly from the national average level of student-teacher contact, Sir Richard – a distinguished zoologist – went on. More than half of Oxford students were regularly taught in groups of three or fewer, whereas in other universities no more than six in a hundred were taught in this way. 'We must defend this method. But we should ensure that the two halves of our teaching system, the college tutorials and the university lectures, seminars and practicals, are effectively co-ordinated.'

The former Vice-Chancellor's third point was that capital funds for building maintenance would henceforth be contingent on good estate management.

Fourth, he said, a joint working party of the Funding Council and representatives of the universities had been set up to consider restructuring the academic year into three semesters or four terms, 'with a view to optimizing efficient expansion'. In his view, shorter degree courses might be appropriate for mature students and for two-year vocational courses, but the agreed European minimum requirement for mutual recognition of qualifications was three years' full-time study. He quoted Sir Ralf Dahrendorf, the German-born Warden of St Antony's: 'University education is like wine-making – a maturing process which takes time. You can speed it up, but the end result will be of inferior quality.'

Sir Richard's oration, considered unusually hard-hitting, sums up many of the fears which Oxbridge dons have concerning the future of their time-honoured way of life. There is a recognition that change is under way and cannot be stopped. At the same time, they are desperate that it should be sympathetically managed and should not detract from the unique nature of Oxbridge traditions. The tutorial system, a previous Vice-Chancellor had insisted, was 'the best method ever devised for training minds and exposing fallacies ... generations of Oxford graduates owe their subsequent success in life to their tutors.' Few, including opponents of the system, would disagree. Dons are anxious above all else that teaching and university administration should remain a matter for them, with the state kept firmly in the margins. Sir Richard's view was that reforms were not necessarily detrimental to Oxford, nor inevitably a threat to academic freedom:

But they are being imposed on us from outside. When they are fully implemented, this University will find that it has to operate in a manner very different from that of the past. The choice we face is between determining what is vital for Oxford and adapting in the way that will preserve those essentials, or blindly resisting every aspect of change. The latter course, I believe, would ensure that much that is valuable would be swept away, like King Canute before the incoming tide.

Listening dons knew only too well that their solemn-faced orator was, for the most part, speaking no less than the truth, and both Sir Richard's successor, Dr Peter North, a jurist and past Principal of Jesus, and Sir David Williams, Vice-Chancellor of Cambridge, are now actively engaged in damage limitation exercises and the discreet restraint of government impulses.

Sir David is the first Cambridge Vice-Chancellor to serve under the new seven-year rule, and will continue in office until the summer of 1996. His 341 predecessors, dating back to 1412, each served only two years in the job and, until fairly recent times, regarded it as more ceremonial than administrative in character. That attitude is now dead. Formerly a law professor at Cambridge and President of Wolfson College, Sir David read for his own first degree at Emmanuel and thus knows his university at every level, from the bottom up. What impresses him most, he says, speaking from his spacious office in the University's Old Schools, is its 'comprehensive, and inevitably élitist, spread of subjects', particularly in the sciences. 'Most other universities specialize or go for a niche to secure their reputations. Warwick, for example, concentrates on engineering, economics and maths. We do the lot.' Some London colleges, he concedes, are 'outstanding' – King's, UCL, Imperial – but still lack the 'historical perspective' of Cambridge. 'Some may argue that we are accorded a special place that we do not merit, but I have to say that other universities are not pressing the issue. There is a feeling that we must have flagships.' On the extra cash that is required from the Government and local authorities to sustain the colleges and maintain supervisions (tutorials), Sir David is equally sanguine: 'I acknowledge it is an anomaly. But it is an acceptable one which helps shore up a vital reserve that has proved its worth.'

Such relaxed confidence, combined with a kind of serene practicality, is entirely typical of Oxbridge top brass. They address problems and look for solutions; they find it difficult to believe that the system they represent could in some way be fundamentally flawed. Thus, Sir David, in remarking that rivals such as Harvard, Stanford and Yale are much richer than Cambridge, also observes 'that some of the great American universities envy our combination of research and teaching'. The Vice-Chancellor, a tireless fund-raiser, spends

many weeks each year touring the world in search of major contributions, and is rarely disappointed. He takes a keen interest in the
Campaign for Cambridge and maintains the closest possible contacts
with the USA and Japan while at the same time nurturing the
university's 'very warm relationship' with India and with continental
Europe.

The Vice-Chancellor is aware of the growing importance of
foreign students to Cambridge and of the pressure to move ideologic-
ally 'offshore' as a global institute. But he worries that too much
might happen too fast that could change the university's character
for ever. 'We must not go too far. We must retain our UK base and
bias. The US and the Pacific ring cannot provide us with all our
growth and we must not expect them to. There are other ways in
which we can exploit our foreign connections without giving up
our identity.' One example cited by the Vice-Chancellor is the
Cambridge Examining Board, a syndicate of dons which runs
examinations in more than a hundred countries. The board, like the
Cambridge University Press, has won the Queen's Award for export
achievement and is a substantial contributor of funds. There is, in
addition, the Cambridge Commonwealth Trust and the equivalent
Overseas Trust, both of which helped deflect the damage done by
the overseas fees rises imposed under Thatcher. All three are important factors in Cambridge's recent development and are one reason
why its formal campaign didn't have to start earlier.

Sir David is obviously well aware of the need to maintain close
links with former students round the world. Friends of Cambridge
University, an association of former students, has branches throughout North America and the Commonwealth and is experiencing
rapid growth now both in Japan and continental Europe. *Cam*, the
alumni magazine, is sent out three times a year to 136,000 graduates,
detailing every aspect of the university's needs for the future while
carefully evoking nostalgia for a golden past. The American branch
of the Friends, run until recently by Stephen Bragg, whose father
and grandfather jointly won the 1915 Nobel Prize for physics, has
more than 8,000 members, and the Vice-Chancellor spends part of
each year addressing groups of these, and others, at campus
gatherings.

Capital, on an industrial scale, is vital for the continued prosperity of Cambridge. The Glaxo Institute for Pharmacology would never have been possible out of public money. The Judge Institute of Management Studies followed a donation in 1991 of £8 million by Paul Judge, a Cambridge alumnus who made his fortune from the buy-out of Cadbury Schweppes, to which was then added £5 million from Simon Sainsbury, of the Sainsbury retailing family. Citibank and National Westminster Bank between them helped solve an acute accommodation crisis at the Department of Economics and Politics. The Global Security Programme ('working where the North-South, East-West axes intersect') was made possible primarily by grants from the MacArthur Foundation. Outside funding, much of it from abroad, also assisted in the creation of the Isaac Newton Institute for Mathematical Sciences, the Interdisciplinary Research Centre for High-Temperature Superconductivity ('an extremely important development for this country and for other countries', according to the Vice-Chancellor) and the Centre for Protein Engineering. Going back a little further, Robinson College was the result of a gift of £17 million from the Cambridge-born television rentals tycoon Sir David Robinson, who threw in a further £1 million, as a surprise, on the day 'his' college was opened by the Queen in 1981. Sponsored professorships have meanwhile become a commonplace. While the prestigious Regius chairs continue to enjoy appropriately regal respect, it is more usual these days for professors to be paid by the likes of Montagu Burton, Kraft Foods, or Guinness.

Unsurprisingly, Oxford has evolved a similar tradition. The Squibb Corporation of America provided £20 million for a pharmacology unit. The Nissan Institute of Japanese Studies was a gift from the Tokyo-based car giant. Four institutes, for American Studies, Management Studies, European Studies, and Socio-Legal Studies, are either planned or already under way as the result of endowments, and others are under discussion. Rolls-Royce helped fund research that produced the exotically named Isentropic Light Piston Tunnel. A total of seventy-two new and existing academic posts, including the Fiat-endowed Chair in Italian Studies, inaugurated by President Francesco Cossiga of Italy, are sustained by funds raised through the Campaign for Oxford, which by February 1994 had yielded £284 million via 17,000 donors.

This is generosity on a scale made possible only by power-projection and the presentation of Oxford and Cambridge as major players on the international academic stage. At Manchester, by contrast, founded in 1851, with more than 15,000 full-time students, the first development officer (from Oxford) was appointed only in the summer of 1994. 'We don't even try', a spokesman said prior to the new man's arrival. 'We don't do any fund-raising as such. In the north, we expect to work for our money, we don't just ask for it.' Fifteen miles to the west, in Liverpool, a similar policy vacuum obtained.'We did have a development officer', a spokesman confided, 'but he left some time ago and the post has not been filled.' So did this mean that there was no external funding directed at Merseyside's oldest university, with its 12,000 undergraduates? 'Far from it. We recently opened a new horse hospital at the veterinary school at a cost of £1 million – and a lot of that came from donations.' What, though, of the future? Surely some action had to be taken if Oxford and Cambridge were not to walk away with the lion's share of everything. The spokesman considered this before replying. 'Mr Ellis, you may not realize it but there is now a national body which brings donors and alumni together with fund-raisers – the last meeting was held at Cambridge as a matter of fact – and there is at least one representative on this body from each of the universities, including ourselves. So you see, development is alive and well in Liverpool. How successful it is, I don't know.'

Such negative attitudes are widespread in provincial England, and one can only be thankful that Liverpool's academics are considerably more dynamic than its managers. The university in 1993 attracted a research income of £30 million, and in the same year Liverpool's Interdisciplinary Centre for Surface Science (shared with Manchester) was confirmed by the Science and Engineering Research Council as a 'centre of excellence', on a par with Cambridge's renowned institute for superconductivity. Any development officer worth his salt would have been organizing fund-raising on a grand scale on the strength of these achievements – or at least dying in the attempt. In Liverpool, as generally up and down the country, the tradition simply isn't there and the argument is lost by default.

Praise, though, where praise is due. When it comes to income support, the performance of Oxbridge has a bravura quality to it that leaves the others standing. The pairing's confidence, bordering on arrogance, carries all before it, bolstered by centuries of certainty. Advantages are exploited shamelessly. The arrival in Dallas or Tokyo or Frankfurt of Sir David Williams or Dr Peter North is like that of a medieval potentate. They are invited to the finest salons and the grandest board rooms. The rich and famous are theirs to command. To shake their hands and to offer them mere money is for bedazzled donors to enter into a covenant with history.

Yet for all their pulling power and impressive entrepreneurial pazzazz, the Old Firm faces a long-term struggle based on a factor over which it has no control: undergraduate demography. Relative to the general advance in student numbers, Oxbridge is falling further and further behind. The ancient universities in the 1930s had more than 10 per cent of the nation's undergraduates. Today, that figure has shrunk below 2 per cent, and is still falling. That is why, in spite of an intensified and revamped policy of élitism, they cannot hope endlessly to sustain their existing level of dominance. In a world in which most of the country's graduates are produced elsewhere, reform has to be combined with realism. Vocational universities, like Bradford and John Moores, have joined London and Durham, the older civics and a handful of later creations, such as Essex and Warwick, as popular alternatives, often offering top-notch courses tailored to industrial and professional requirements. The government service is at the same time being obliged to spread its net wider than the Isis and the Cam in the annual trawl for recruits, while such institutions as the law and the City are under mounting pressure, however gradual, to reflect more faithfully the society in which they earn their profits.

What is noticeable is that Oxbridge's retreat from cosy, old-, style privilege in the face of these changes has not been a rout, but rather an orderly withdrawal. It has even done them good. It is probably true to say that the two have changed more in the last ten years than in the previous hundred. They have realized, in a more egalitarian, meritocratic age, that privilege is no longer a right – it has to be *earned* – and the lasting impact of this discovery has been a long-overdue retreat into excellence. Standards for undergraduate entry are at an all-time high. Firsts, not Seconds, are being presented as a realizable goal for everyone, and those held not to have the potential to perform at the highest level are accordingly being denied entry. Just as ruthlessly, if infinitely less creditably, dons and college administrators have dug deep into their storied past as a gilt-edged investment in the future. History as an asset – especially to the Americans and Japanese – has become a vital weapon in a fight in which the central maxim appears to be 'Winner takes all'. It seems cruel, but who can blame them? As others have raised their game, Oxford and Cambridge have raised theirs higher. Far beyond the stuttering efforts of all but a handful of their rivals, they have adjusted with ease to the new international order, cleaving firmly to their self-belief while slowly switching allegiance from the old British to the new global Establishment. Such flexibility is a tribute to their intelligence and guile. Machiavelli would have been lost in admiration. It is, though, much more than niche marketing, however inspired. It is something else, too. It is a measure of how much the world in general wishes them to succeed.

This brings us to another central point. The dark side of Oxbridge can never entirely be obscured from view. The more dubious, élitist values which the two represent in terms of Britain's social and economic development this century, altered somewhat to take account of the new meritocracy, go increasingly unchallenged. They also leave their imprint on the university system as a whole. Tapper and Salter see Oxbridge – or people's perceptions of Oxbridge – as a principal reason for the failure of their competitors to develop along more rational lines.

It is our contention that Oxford and Cambridge represent the most complete examples of what we have termed the traditional ideal of the English university. Although as a consequence of this they must be considered exceptional institutions, they have had a profound influence upon the character of British higher education in general. They have been crucial in forming the values of the English model of university to which much of the rest of the system of higher education has aspired and, even more certainly, against which it has been judged. The form that the model has taken at Oxford and Cambridge may be unique, but the values on which the two universities are founded have echoed loudly and persistently throughout the twentieth-century history of higher education in Britain.

Halsey documents this same pattern, even to the extent of reminding us that Sussex University, using Oxford as its model, was once known as 'Balliol on Sea'. Oxbridge graduates, he relates, who go out from the cloisters to embark on Redbrick careers, do so in the hope of one day returning 'home'. Tapper and Salter, equally cynical, observe that on the ideological front, UK universities, steeped in the Oxbridge ideal of donnish sovereignty, were 'arguably one of the critical reasons for the failure of Britain to match its societal needs – especially the needs of the economy – to the performance of its educational system'. Strong words. But all is not lost. Turning to the future roles of the legendary pair, they remark:

Although their influence may be more restricted in the future, the prestige of Oxford and Cambridge will remain as high as ever. Within a system whose component parts perform different functions, the idea of a status hierarchy based on common criteria should be irrelevant, but the old values die slowly, and if Oxford and Cambridge can retain their commitment to small-group teaching centred in the colleges, and maintain their first-rate research records, they will continue to be seen as Britain's premier universities.

Later, they add:

whether they are 'world class' or not is an entirely different matter. Perhaps in the past we have judged their academic pre-eminence rather too easily, measuring it against a British standard of variable quality rather than the leading universities worldwide.

In Cambridge's campaign prospectus, the dilemma facing the dons is clearly laid out:

Government spending, though now substantial, can no longer support the ongoing improvements that allow Cambridge to maintain pre-eminent quality across proliferating disciplines, continue to have international impact in science and scholarship, remain unshakeable in its commitment to teaching and student life or continue to protect its cultural legacy. The time has come again to enlist the kind of private benefaction that, for its first 700 years, enabled Cambridge to travel its road to eminence.

Oxford's introductory peroration on the same theme is adroitly entrusted to Seamus Heaney, the recently retired Professor of Poetry, whose humble origins in the boglands of Mid-Ulster seem forgotten as he expounds on the higher values of an Isis education.

Every contribution to university funds, large or small, personal or corporate, becomes a contributory element in the project of defining and fortifying a civilized life for the whole of our species. This may sound like exaggeration but a moment's reflection will prove that it is not. Those who have been commemorated as benefactors of Oxford University today, and in all the previous years of our history, and those who will be so commemorated in the years ahead – all of them have distinguished themselves by acts of magnificence, by inscribing their names in the university's grateful memory, in a context where indeed every art and every enquiry, every action and choice, seems to aim at some good.

There's no doubting whose side he's on. Heaney has come a long way from the days when he wanted to be a farmer like his father, 'his shoulders globed like a full sail strung between the shafts and the furrow'. Today, it is 'acts of magnificence' he's after, helping to define 'a civilized life for the whole of our species'.

What is undeniable is that both Oxford and Cambridge, at faculty and departmental level, languish far behind their great American rivals in terms of wealth. Cambridge, in its campaign prospectus, discloses that it had just $339 million in accumulated central endowments in 1989, compared with $1.6 *billion* at MIT, $3 billion at Princeton and $5 billion at Harvard – the last founded as a Cambridge satellite. The Cambridge figure is for endowments only and does not take into account the immense contribution to funding made by the state. Even so, the income gap it reveals is real. What needs to be borne in mind is the difference between Oxbridge benefactions and the rest in this country. In Merseyside, John Moores University, with 21,000 registered students (7,000 more than either of the dynamic duo), is seeking to raise just £6 million in its appeal and expects to take years to achieve its goal.

Both prospectuses go out of their way to emphasize the 'world-class' natures of the institutions they represent. Oxford boasts of its '800-year tradition as a centre of international scholarship'. It quotes John Brademas, President of New York University, as saying,

'Oxford does not just need America, America needs Oxford', and cites the facts that not only were four of the original thirteen states founded by Oxonians, but that today, in addition to President Clinton, five Senators, two Governors and two Supreme Court Justices are Oxford products. Nor does it end there. A dozen US universities and colleges are evidently headed by Oxonians, while, as we have seen, great American foundations, like Mellon, Kellogg, Rockefeller and Ford, felt sufficiently in the university's debt to make handsome past donations. Currently, we are told, more than 16 per cent of Oxford's students come from outside Britain, while a total of 25,000 Oxford graduates live overseas. Commonwealth ties are also stressed, particularly with Canada, Australia, New Zealand and the sub-continent. Germany's long connection – cemented by the recently restored Rhodes Scholarships from that country – is marked today by the German Friends of Oxford University. The campaign in France was launched in the British embassy in Paris by no less a person than François-Xavier Ortoli, former President of the European Commission and a friend of Lord Jenkins of Hillhead. Other European committees have been established in Spain, Portugal, Italy and Greece. More important, however, is the role played by former students in Japan, Singapore, Hong Kong, South Korea and Taiwan. Undergraduates from Japan have been attending Oxford since 1868, 'immeasurably strengthened by the presence of members of the Imperial family'. Japanese corporations have made significant financial contributions. The Nissan Institute was opened at St Antony's College in 1981, and this was followed by a 'major benefaction' in 1990 for a second, purpose-built institute and two new academic posts. Many scholarships have been established for Japanese students, with funding coming from the Mitsubishi Trust, the Industrial Bank of Japan, Nippon Life Insurance and Sumitomo Bank. Singaporean students are multiplying at Oxford, while in Hong Kong – another fertile source of undergraduates – Sir Run Run Shaw has donated £10 million to fund the Institute of Modern Chinese Studies that will bear his name. No potential source of revenue is left unexplored. Oxford is cashing in its chips. One of the most enduring benefits of the Campaign for Oxford is the opportunity it provides to link foreign alumni and interests into a world-wide network of steering committees. Operating through the continuing support of the Oxford Society, and in some countries the joint Oxford and Cambridge Society, these successful and influential groupings are said to have led the way in 'keeping old friendships alive and making new ones'. President Cossiga of Italy, speaking in the Sheldonian Theatre on the occasion of the inaugural lecture by the first Fiat-Serena-endowed Professor of Italian Studies, showed that he had grasped the message and was ready to play his part. 'I wish every success for your work in the universal republic of arts, letters and sciences of which Oxford, our Oxford, the Oxford which is both English and European, has for centuries been one of the most prestigious capitals.' Jan Morris could hardly have put it better.

Not to be outdone, Cambridge wheeled out its seventeen living Nobel laureates (the most recent César Milstein FRS, who won the prize in 1984 for his work in immunology) to help ensure that the university in the Fens 'continues as a world centre of learning for the benefit of future generations'. Hamish Maxwell, chairman of the American Friends of Cambridge, also pitched in. 'Whether we attended Cambridge as undergraduates or graduate students, as faculty or as visiting scholars or lecturers, I am convinced that the experience made a special and sometimes unique contribution to our educations, our intellectual curiosity and our abilities to lead fulfilling lives.' Maxwell, presumably, would not have been fully able to lead a fulfilling life if he had not spent time in Cambridge, and out of gratitude he is now seeking to put something back. Other alumni are equally gushing. Miriam Margolyes, the actress, can scarcely contain her enthusiasm (or her punctuation). 'To be in a beautiful place, learning your chosen subject from some of the best people in the world, sharing intellectual, sexual and emotional discoveries with bright colleagues from all over the world – is it a dream? No – just Cambridge, whose benefits and joys, and – above all – whose people, resonate in my life even now, thirty years after I graduated from Newnham.' Miriam, darling, you have said it all.

It is all truly extraordinary. Lance Liebman, Dean of the Columbia University School of Law, informs us that 'there is never a week when I do not think of my experiences at Cambridge, now thirty years ago'. Bill Rogers, the former US Undersecretary of State for Economic Affairs, refers to his time by the Cam as 'one of the

towering intellectual experiences of my life'. Ray Dolby, the chairman of Dolby Labs Inc. which revolutionized recorded sound quality, speaks of Cambridge providing him with a 'wide, wonderful
window on the world'. Perhaps they are all right. Perhaps Cambridge is indeed an intellectual Camelot, led by the Knights of the
High Table, on whose magnificent countenance the rest of us can
only gaze in wonder. But then again, perhaps it's just a bloody good
university that has been well provided for over the centuries by the
British Establishment but now thinks the *world* owes it a living.

At college level, removed, for the most part, from grand strategies
and geopolitics, things are very different. Here, endowment income
is vital and liberating. 'We wretched and needy men', runs the
Grace of Magdalen, presumably as a joke. For the twenty Oxford
colleges and seventeen Cambridge colleges for which figures are
continuously available, gross annual endowment incomes calculated
at 10-year intervals between 1950 and 1990 were as follows:

TABLE 10.1 GROSS ANNUAL ENDOWMENT INCOMES OF
COLLEGES

| | Number of Colleges | | | | |
	1950	1960	1970	1980	1990
Under £10,000	3	1	0	0	0
£10,000–£25,000	13	6	0	0	0
£26,000–£50,000	9	12	4	0	0
£51,000–£75,000	4	4	5	0	0
£76,000–£150,000	6	8	13	0	0
£151,000–£250,000	2	5	7	6	0
£251,000–£500,000	0	1	7	10	1
£500,000–£1 million	0	0	1	14	9
£1–2 million	0	0	0	6	16
£2–5 million	0	0	0	1	10
Over £5 million	0	0	0	0	1

Source: Oxford and Cambridge universities (quoted by Tapper and Salter)

From the above, it can be seen that the thirty-seven Oxbridge
colleges covered by the survey enjoy private incomes similar to

successful small or medium-sized companies. Trinity College, Cambridge, the overall top earner, has an endowment income of well over £5 million a year, and rising, while St John's, King's and Caius, Cambridge, and Christ Church, St John's, All Souls, Merton, Queen's and Nuffield, Oxford, are not all that far behind. Those colleges which by accident of history are not particularly well endowed or which do not yet *have* a history are assisted by some – but not all – of their luckier confederates. At Oxford, the eight colleges with the lowest net statutory endowment incomes are given help each year by the big earners via the College Contributions Committee and are thus able to provide their undergraduates and Fellows with the basic facilities and comforts for which the dreaming spires are renowned. The problem with the begging bowl approach is that it is good for topping up, less good at transforming paupers into princes. St Edmund's Hall is one of the oldest and prettiest, but also one of the poorest, colleges in Oxford, with a long tradition of turning out teachers and clergymen. Its bursar, Geoffrey Bourne-Taylor, complains that he cannot call on armies of rich alumni to bale him out and has to go cap in hand to the Contributions Committee each year just to make ends meet. An experienced don at neighbouring Magdalen, where £10 million is being spent on new student accommodation, sympathizes and wonders which of the poorer colleges will be the first to go belly up. 'I have heard some sorry tales', he reveals. 'There is terror behind the façade of confidence.'

Magdalen is one of a number of Oxford colleges which have started officially recognized business expansion schemes designed to raise a total of £30 million. Graduates and others have been invited to purchase shares in companies which offer either a fixed return or, more daringly, growth in line with the performance of the FTSE 100 index. One scheme, run jointly by Magdalen and Balliol, is being managed by Sir Bruce MacPhail, a former merchant banker and managing director of P&O, who read of the idea in the *Sunday Telegraph*. Sir Bruce, an alumnus of Balliol and Harvard and a member of the council of Templeton College, simply wanted to help and hopes to raise £20 million.

Serendipity is a regular phenomenon at Oxford. In the early summer of 1993, Takeshi Funahashi, a Japanese golf-course developer, with no known spirene connections, wrote out a cheque for £1.5 million to help build a new quad at Merton, one of the wealthiest colleges. Funahashi was somehow persuaded to part with his cash by Sir Peter Tapsell, the Tory MP for East Lindsey, a Merton man who a year earlier had secured Japanese backing for the Oxford Union.

Despite the immense wealth of Trinity (one estimate values its endowments at £500 million), the incomes graph at Cambridge is somewhat steadier and the standard of living there is more uniform than is the case with its great rival. It has, however, been going equally long. At Gonville and Caius, a plaque to the college benefactors stretches back through the centuries. In 1518, John le Strange 'gave a thousand sheep'; in 1896, Edward Sladen 'gave the Burmese gong'; more recently, Martin Davy, a physician and ex-Master, was 'the donor of his library and a country house'. To give an idea of the largesse involved in Cambridge life, consider the following. Jesus College has asked its alumni for £11 million, no less, for a new court and library, while Churchill is spending £7.2 million on a continuing education centre and Downing has spent £2 million on a classical-revival library extension. Money for this growth comes partly from donations and partly from expansion schemes similar to those at Oxford. The Cambridge College Consortium aims to raise nearly £20 million for Churchill, Pembroke and Trinity Hall, offering 13 per cent a year over five years for higher-rate taxpayers.

Colleges remain the essence of Oxbridge life. Science and technology eat up more and more funds in centralized locations, adding urgency to the need for fund-raising at home and abroad. Yet it is around the quads and courts, where books are read, essays are written and the dons conduct their exhaustive tutorials and supervisions, that the soul of the institution continues to repose. As communities (typically) of between 200 and 300 scholars, comprising dons, researchers and undergraduates, they obviously have to husband their resources with care, yet as Dr Jonathan Steinberg, Vice-Master of Trinity Hall, Cambridge, confirms, even 'modest' colleges, with no great background of wealth, are from time to time the beneficiaries of unexpected bounty.

'We have never been thought of as one of the richer colleges – not like Trinity or St John's, just across the road. But Cambridge in general and Trinity Hall in particular is getting richer. Endowments are still coming in. Two years ago, an old member died and left us £3 million.'

But, for all its manifold frustrations, there is no other place in the world most dons would rather be. 'Nowhere else has this kind of ambience, says Jonathan Steinberg. There is nowhere else where I could know all my students by their first names or follow their careers from admission right through to graduation and beyond. Today, Oxbridge is ahead of the rest in endowments and standards of living. Our physical circumstances here are better than anywhere else in the world. We can entertain better and cheaper than anyone in Harvard or Yale, and it is all to do with endowments.'

Hopelessly in love with both location and vocation, he says he has never seen a more beautiful place than Cambridge and is willing to administer its patrimony for nothing. At the same time, he is conscious of its shortfalls:

We run our own investment portfolios and finances. One of my colleagues even looks after the drains. We work very hard – seven days a week, from 7.30 to midnight. I have worked flat out for the last eighteen months. We work three times as hard as any provincial dons. We do all our own administration, own letters, own interviewing. I haven't had a Sunday off for months, and I've only recently been assigned a secretary. And it's all unpaid. We have recently opened up a European masters' course, and a variety of other courses, too. And we've got 180 graduate students. I'm tired. There's so much to do. We have an intrusive, populist government, and a lot of uncertainty. We have to safeguard the future. I decided to generate a better alumni society. I also have to think of our 650th birthday, in the year 2000. At the same time, all of us have to consider the private agenda to privatize Cambridge – to float us off as separate colleges and charge higher fees. This would mean we would have to double the size of our endowments and provide more scholarships for those who couldn't afford the fees. Privatization would be hard work for us, but we could do it. The way things are now, fees make up just 37 per cent of college income. It may not happen. The Government may chicken out. But we have got to be ready.

It sounds exhausting. And it is. But, as Steinberg points out, after twenty-seven years he is still there, defying the odds in the name of privilege. He is an instantly recognizable Oxbridge type – an awe-somely articulate professional historian moonlighting in administra-tion as a 'gifted amateur'. Ironically, neither of his sons went to Oxbridge. One went to Manchester, where the fees are £2,000 less per annum than at Cambridge (but where he had to share a room with three other students), and the other to Liverpool.

Much of the dirty work in college administration is carried out by the bursars, often ex-military figures who like to view dons and students as regiments and themselves as adjutants to the colonel. One well-known Oxford bursar, who prefers to remain anonymous, says he has to negotiate everything, from loo rolls to butcher's meat, and at the same time chase up recalcitrant undergraduates trying to avoid paying their battels bills. Other duties are even more wearying. 'I have to wet-nurse the dons. These people are very sharp, very clever, but they've been cocooned for years from the real world. They put on an act. If they can pretend to be helpless and get some other sucker to do things for them, they will.' Discussions on policy matters raised before the college governing body (the head of house and elected Fellows) go 'on and on at prodigious length', he complains. 'It can be interesting, but frustrat-ing too. It's so democratic, it can drive you mad.' So what sorts of things do they discuss? 'Their "appalling" pay rises; the problems of research money and how to get it; the cost of university fees from non-EC foreign students; SRGs [scientific research grants] – they're a recurring nightmare; LEA [Local Education Authority] grants, which are often insufficient for students properly to survive, so that sometimes we have to subsidize them ourselves; everything from Rhodes Scholars to the cost of wine and access to the Fellows' Garden.'

If it is not a particularly elevating picture, it is at least a human one. One of the redeeming features of Oxbridge life, from the point of view of the social leveller, is the fact that it is conducted largely in village communities, where everyone knows everyone else and each person, from masters and dons through to the porter, 'scout', 'gyp', bedder and chef, has a recognized status. What *might* be thought unjust about this otherwise agreeable set of circumstances is the fact that it is subsidized heavily by the state while available to only 2 per cent or so of students, plus staff and postgraduates, who are admitted into its golden circle. That two ancient, self-governing institutions should offer so much on a plate to a lucky, largely self-selected élite, and then offer them the world as well (without even ensuring that they will know what to do with it), is at the heart of what is wrong with the present system. Privatization, so beloved of the dons, is seen as a means of reinforcing the academic apartheid that has been created over the centuries. Internationalization has the same end in view. What Oxbridge wants is to be left alone to pick and choose what it wants to do, and the question is: should we be paying them quite so handsomely for excluding the rest of us from the debate?

CHAPTER ELEVEN

GETTING ON (1)

The Greasy Pole

WE SAW EARLIER HOW THE OXBRIDGE PHENOMENON starts at the top, even if not, for now, at the very pinnacle of power. John Major's Cabinet – ostensibly directed towards the creation of a 'classless society' – is steeped in Oxbridge. Douglas Hurd, Kenneth Clarke, Lord Mackay, Michael Howard, Peter Lilley, John Patten, Michael Portillo, Ian Lang and John Gummer all studied at Cambridge. Oxford, traditionally more dominant, is represented by Michael Heseltine, Sir Patrick Mayhew, Tony Newton, Gillian Shephard, Ann Widdecombe, John Redwood and William Waldegrave – the last two being Fellows of All Souls. If this is the 'level playing field' of contemporary Tory ideology, it is clearly Fenners or Iffley Road that they have in mind. Even the exceptions are instructive: John MacGregor, a Scot, took first-class honours at St Andrews, and by virtue of his race is only an *ex officio* member of the political Establishment. Malcolm Rifkind, another Scot, chose the Edinburgh route and remains vocally indebted to Morningside. David Hunt studied abroad, at Montpellier, as well as at Bristol; Virginia Bottomley opted for Essex and the London School of Economics (one of the dolorous duo's few rivals with the stomach for a fight). John Wakeham, elevated to the leadership of the House of Lords, did not continue his formal education beyond Charterhouse.

Most obviously missing from the alumnar roll-call from the cloisters is, of course, John Major himself. Those who know the Prime Minister say that he is painfully aware of his lack of a university education. His old school, Rutlish Grammar, in south London, guards his O-level results as though they were a state secret, but Varsity, it seems certain, was never on the cards. Fellow ministers know this, and his advisers in Downing Street are careful not to parade their cleverness in too obvious a manner. There is no doubt, though, that Major is utterly saturated in Oxbridge. Sarah Hogg, head of the Policy Unit, took a First in PPE from Oxford's Lady Margaret Hall. Of other courtiers at the time of writing, Alexander Allan, the Prime Minister's principal private secretary, went to Clare College, Cambridge, Jonathan Hill, the political secretary, to Trinity College, Cambridge, and Sir Roderic Braithwaite, a foreign affairs adviser, to nearby Christ's College. Gus O'Donnell, Major's press secretary for his first three years, took his first degree from the University of Warwick but then switched to Oxford, where he took an M.Phil. from Nuffield and achieved a Blue in soccer. His replacement, Christopher Meyer, formerly number two in the Washington embassy, went from Lancing to Peterhouse and then to Bologna, where he completed his academic career at the Institute for International Studies. In February 1993, John Holroyd, of Worcester College, Oxford, previously First Civil Service Commissioner, joined the team as appointments secretary and (oddly enough) ecclesiastical secretary to the Lord Chancellor, keeping an eye on episcopal movements. The fact is that it is just about an Oxbridge clean sweep, and for a leader who once failed to get a job as a bus conductor both humiliating and daunting. Though party colleagues during 1993's fitful economic recovery were on occasions scornful of their boss's non-graduate status – so much so that Lord Archer (an Oxford 'Blue') was wheeled out on Radio Four to point to the precedent of Jim Callaghan, an elementary schoolboy – there is no doubt that the Prime Minister's 'common man' status had been useful as a marketing device. This was why he chose the soap box over the computerized console when campaigning in the 1992 general election. This was why he appealed so much to the ordinary voter. He had not reinvented himself. He had remained obstinately 'nice'. Oxbridge, one cannot help thinking, would have taught him to smile and smile and be a villain still. At the same time, it would have taken from him his invaluable sincerity.

Academic achievement, as distinct from attendance, is not, in any case, the key feature of most politicians' time at Oxbridge. Some of our leaders – as will be shown later – worked extremely hard and came away with Firsts; others, though, barely scraped through, so intense was their interest in other aspects of undergraduate life. According to *Varsity*, the Cambridge student newspaper, Norman Lamont, John Major's accident-prone first Chancellor of the Exchequer, scored a lowly Third in English Part I at Cambridge and a scarcely better 2:2 in Economics. His right honourable friend Sir Norman Fowler, who abandoned the Thatcher Cabinet in 1990 to spend more time with his family, only to scuttle back upon Major's arrival at Number 10, was another Third-rater at Cambridge. Both of Major's Environment Secretaries, Michael Heseltine (Oxford) and Michael Howard (Cambridge), had to be content with Seconds, as had John Patten, the Education Secretary, who, despite all manner of reforms aimed at improving 'parental choice', has failed dismally to earn the respect of teachers. Sir Patrick Mayhew, the Ulster Secretary, charged with helping chart a new course for Ireland, went one step further and managed only a Third in Jurisprudence at Balliol. Surely, such modest achievement tells us something – for example, that the ministers concerned are not necessarily front-rank intellectuals. Possibly. If so, the lesson goes unheeded, and the question of what they were doing at Oxbridge in the first place is not even asked. What matters, even today, is not *what* you did but *where* you did it, which societies you joined and who you met along the way.

In the case of Michael Portillo, who was appointed Chief Secretary to the Treasury in Major's 1992 re-shuffle, the who and the where were almost inseparable. Maurice Cowling, a leading history don at Peterhouse, was a big influence on Portillo's thinking, particularly around the time of the 1974 miners' strike, which brought down the government of Edward Heath. After graduating in 1975, the future minister was at a loose end in the private sector, working for an air-freight business at Heathrow. He was bored out of his mind (Tories prefer extolling private enterprise to practising it) and rang Cowling for advice. His former tutor mused for a moment, then said: 'Well, if you'd been interested in politics, I would have suggested that you go to Conservative Central Office.'

'But I *am* interested in politics', Portillo replied. Cowling was delighted. He rang Chris Patten, then working for the chairman of the Conservative Party, now Governor of Hong Kong, and put in the word that helped secure his young protégé the job that was to speed his rise to power.

Regard can sometimes even cross the party divide. When Bryan Gould, the left-wing former Labour MP, since returned to his native New Zealand to be Vice-Chancellor of the University of Waikato, was reminded that he had taught Stephen Dorrell, the Conservative Treasury minister, while a don at Worcester College, Oxford, in the 1970s, he was quite unabashed. 'I must admit, I had forgotten about Stephen', he laughed, when asked if Dorrell might make it to the top. 'But it's a lack-lustre Cabinet and he would certainly adorn it.'

An incredible, if all-too-believable, 154 Tory MPs are Oxbridge-educated out of a parliamentary total of 335, and the higher a member rises in the party hierarchy the more likely he is to be from one or other of the ancient universities. At cabinet level, as we have seen, the proportion reaches 77 per cent, and can go higher. The link between Varsity and influence could scarcely be stronger.

That is in the world of men. The female line is very different – or at least it used to be. Only a minority of Conservative women MPs bothered with Oxbridge, or indeed with university at all. Partly, this dearth reflects the fact that until the 1960s women undergraduates were something of a rarity, confined to a handful of 'bluestocking' halls. It also suggests, however, that women, at least until recent times, have been less willing to exploit privilege than most men. Women's pedigrees illustrate a significantly more pronounced, and democratic, independence of mind, plus the fact that, unlike their male counterparts, they seem to value themselves beyond narrow academic geography. Among those of the established generation who do possess degrees, Edwina Currie and Dame Elaine Kellet-Bowman each had the foresight to attend St Anne's College, Oxford, but Lynda Chalker, after a promising start at Roedean, found herself seduced by the Teutonic delights of Heidelberg, and the estimable Teresa Gorman, scourge of the misogynist faction in her party, scored a First from London. Other Tory women are either Redbrick or else embarked on a political career only after raising a family. True, of the Major Cabinet's female trio, Gillian

Shephard selected St Hilda's College, Oxford, and Ann Widdecombe Lady Margaret Hall as their first steps on the road to glory. Thus far, however, they have been outshone by Essex girl Virginia Bottomley, whose main contact with Old Learning is through her eccentric husband, Peter, a graduate of Trinity College, Cambridge. Women's distinctive, and more personal, approach to career advancement suggests that networking (the Kit-Kat Club aside) is a predominantly male phenomenen, and one for which women have in the past shown little aptitude or sympathy. No doubt, as they move into the second and third generations of influence, and as more doors – including those of the London clubs – are thrown open to them, this will change. Indeed, it is changing already. And then equality of inequality can be theirs, too.

Across the floor of the Commons, Labour's connections with Oxbridge underwent a profound change during the Kinnock years. Gone are the days when Harold Wilson, himself a New College don, could look across the cabinet table to a 'privilege' of well-scrubbed Oxford faces, including not merely that irrepressible *enfant terrible* of the right, Denis Healey, and the biographically incontinent Richard Crossman, but Tony Benn, the millionaire doyen of the left. The Oxford mafia seated smugly around him in Number 10 used to infuriate George Brown, Wilson's ebullient Foreign Secretary, who had not benefited from a university education at all, let alone one that mattered. His biographer, Peter Paterson, recalls that Brown used to rage over the way in which he was patronized by his better-bred socialist colleagues, most of whom spoke 'properly' and tended to regard him as an auto-didactic upstart. Things are different today – albeit less different than they were before the 1992 election. Under Neil Kinnock, only about one in six Labour MPs had been to Oxbridge, but of the sixty-five first-time Labour members in the present House, no fewer than fourteen were Spires or Backs – all in England – representing more than one-fifth of the intake and a New Age swing to Oxbridge south and east of the borders of 21.5 per cent. A total of fifty-one members of the current Parliamentary Labour Party went to Oxford or Cambridge, providing 20 per cent of the People's Party, against 33 per cent for the House as a whole, and if we remove Scotland, with its separate system, from the total, the percentage of Oxbridge socialists from

England and Wales rises close to a third. It affects all classes and all groups. Labour's first black woman MP, Diane Abbot, is a graduate of Newnham College, Cambridge, while its first Asian member of the Commons was Keith Vaz, from Gonville and Caius. Kinnock himself, having contrived to pluck defeat from the jaws of victory in his fight with John Major, had acquired his degree, with difficulty, at Cardiff, and was never accorded intellectual respect. His successor, the late John Smith, who, to judge from his speeches, wished to storm the citadels of privilege only so that the suited men from Walworth Road could occupy them, took the low road to Edinburgh that is the mark of the true Scot. While Tony Blair, elected to the job of Prime-Minister-in-Waiting following Smith's untimely death, is, of course, a product of Fettes School and St John's College, Oxford. Should he take his party into government at the next election, he will be the first Oxbridge man to do so since Harold Wilson, and it was noticeable during his campaign for the leadership that he captured the support of practically the entire Tory press.

Roy Hattersley, a Yorkshireman, who wished desperately that he had gone to Oxford, endured three years at Hull; Robin Cook, like his new master, chose Edinburgh; Margaret Beckett, Manchester, and Harriet Harman (curiously for a St Paul's girl, more than one in three of whom are Oxbridge), York. Among the ranks of the first Smithsonian Shadow Cabinet, Tony Blair, still young and thrusting, read law at St John's, Oxford, before heading briefly to Lincoln's Inn, but only Bryan Gould, as a New Zealander, chipped on both shoulders, went so far as to collect a BLC at Balliol and then – such audacity! – take up residence as a Fellow and tutor at Worcester. Small wonder he felt constrained to resign. How the Redbrick element of the current meritocratic team, re-created as social democrats, not 'gentlemen', would have survived their inevitable brushes with the Oxbridge mandarins can now be only a matter for conjecture. At least Kinnock would have had the advantage of native guides. Larry Whitty, general secretary of the Labour Party, studied economics at St John's, Cambridge, before going into trade unionism and politics. Charles Clarke, Kinnock's chief of staff, is not only a Cambridge man: famously, and disruptively, he was also president of the university Students' Union in the 1960s. Peter Mandelson, his mercurial predecessor, now MP for Hartlepool, was another insider, from St Catherine's, Oxford, and is widely credited with making Labour both double-breasted and (almost) electable.

Those Labour and trade union leaders who did not make it to university proper are not excluded for ever from exposure to academe's most potent charms. Ruskin College, founded in 1899 by two rich Americans, Charles Beard and Walter Vrooman, in memory of England's greatest art historian, allows working men and women to spend two years in full-time study, usually for a diploma in politics and economics, while soaking up the ambience of privilege. Five present-day Labour MPs, including the proudly proletarian Dennis Skinner, the 'Beast of Bolsover', and John Prescott, the 'Mouth of the Humber', jumped at the option, as did any number of trade unionists, and each proclaims his achievement in the pages of *Who's Who*. One can well appreciate why Beard and Vrooman (who sound like an American law firm) chose Oxford. They wanted 'ordinary' people to have a chance in life that circumstances had hitherto denied them. But don't the modern socialists, obsessed with how the electorate perceives them, *love* it? Bernard Shaw's dictum that 'a workman ought to have a vulgar prejudice against Oxford' cuts no ice with such as these.

With the Liberal Democrats, the rough edges were fewer to begin with. The SDP's original Gang of Four had impeccable university credentials. Roy Jenkins (Balliol, past president of the Oxford Union, currently Chancellor of the university), David Owen (Sidney Sussex, clearly in line for an Oxbridge mastership), Shirley Williams (Somerville, ditto), and Bill Rogers (Magdalen) had each taken advantage of the English Establishment's supreme self-improvement facility. David Steel, as a Scot, was given the customary Celtic Waiver and went to Edinburgh, while Paddy Ashdown took the action-man alternative of the Royal Marines, subsequently learning Mandarin in what might be characterized as a belated bid to understand the ways of Whitehall. Alan Beith, the Liberal Democrats' cool and highly respected Treasury spokesman, turns out, meanwhile, to have been a belt-and-braces man. He attended both Balliol *and* Nuffield, recognizing, one imagines, that all potential hitches are to be avoided in the complicated *dressage* of power. Young Matthew Taylor, successor to the late David Penhaligon in

Truro, was less greedy and contented himself with three coeducational years at Lady Margaret Hall – though he took care to be president of the Union. Simon Hughes, the MP for Southwark and Bermondsey, was similarly abstemious: Selwyn College, Cambridge, bastion of Low Church ethics, was his choice.

The political reality in the 1990s in respect of Oxford and Cambridge is that the House of Commons is little different today from what it was in the 1890s. Then, with the landed gentry jostling with the new professionals and self-made industrialists for parliamentary ascendancy, a considerable proportion of MPs was not Varsity-educated. Yet, on the front benches, the tone was definitely set by the men from the Isis and the Cam. Today, this is, if anything, more the case with the Tories than it was then, while Labour and the Liberals continue to show that the tradition is alive and kicking in opposition politics as well. It would be an exaggeration to say that the ancient universities control the politics of the United Kingdom as we approach the year 2000. But they still count in a way that would surely have surprised the 1960s radicals who promised us a new dawn and the Age of the Common Man. We still have a long way to go.

Yes, Minister

There is a scene in *Yes, Prime Minister*, the award-winning BBC comedy series, in which Sir Humphrey, the Secretary to the Cabinet and head of the Home Civil Service, is seated at high table with the Master of 'Bailey College' and his colleague, the bursar. The three are surrounded by the detritus of a fine dinner, and among the discarded napkins, overturned wineglasses and guttering candles they enjoy a post-prandial port and cigars. Finally, the Master leans across conspiratorially and takes Humphrey into his confidence.

The Master: I'll be retiring in three or four years. Isn't that when you retire from the Civil Service?
Humphrey [*interested*]: Yes.
Master: Hmm. The Bursar and I think you could be the chap to

succeed me as Master of Bailey. [*Humphrey's eyes light up*] But
... [*he looks away*]
Bursar: ... but the Dean is paranoid that we're intriguing in this
matter behind his back.
Master: That is why we decided to discuss it with you while he's
away.
Humphrey: Oh yes. Quite.
Bursar: So the only way you can become Master is if we can dump
the Dean.
Humphrey [*nodding*]: But how?
Bursar: It isn't easy. He's a lazy devil. Only has to do four hours'
work a week. Give one lecture and a couple of tutorials and he's
got tenure for life. He's only got two interests – cricket and steam
engines.
Master: Never reads a new book, never thinks a new thought.
Humphrey: I see. So being an Oxford don is the perfect job for him.
(Antony Jay and Jonathan Lynn, *The Bishop's Gambit*, BBC Books)

In the end, the Dean – who does not believe in God – is made a
bishop ('Anything I should know about him?' the Prime Minister
asks. 'Only that he went to Winchester and New College, Oxford.'),
and the way is cleared for Humphrey to slip into the Master's
Lodge just as soon as he leaves Downing Street. The Prime Minister,
though not entirely convinced that his Cabinet Secretary isn't pulling
a fast one, is soon persuaded that it is all for the best. Everyone is
satisfied, and the credits roll.

Power-lobbying in real life is less amusing, though just as deadly,
but what the above extract does in fact illustrate quite accurately is
the intimate bond, made up of loyalty and affection, between
Oxbridge and Whitehall. The Civil Service, at its upper end, is
fundamentally an Oxbridge creation, and its leading lights, as well
as wining and dining regularly at their old colleges, often return
there as administrators for what is probably the most agreeable five
or ten years of their lives. Between the mandarins and the dons,
relationships are close and enduring – and mutually productive.

Sir Humphrey is, of course, a first division man. The 'First
Division' of the Civil Service is among the most fabled of British
institutions. If it is ridiculed for its love of obfuscation (in triplicate)

and its supposed dress code (pin-striped suit, club tie, bowler hat, furled umbrella), it is also respected for the stability and integrity it brings to the troublesome business of government. Some may feel that the service's high flyers might be better occupied in industry or research, where the end product of their labours would be more obvious to the nation. Yet at the end of the day (5 p.m., where possible), even their critics are forced to concede that the job of administration and bureaucratic supervision has to be done and that this stiff-backed brotherhood, circling the instruments of power like pilgrims round the Ka'aba in Mecca, is an essential component of public life.

Whether so many of them need come from the same two universities is another matter. Most of the present generation of top Civil Servants, and their deputies, suffered a cloistered education, as did a majority of the middle-ranking departmental heads and around half of the 30-somethings currently jostling for position.

We have already noted that the Home Civil Service is headed by Sir Robin Butler KCV, CVO, late of Harrow School and University College, Oxford, where he took a First in *Litterae Humaniores* (Mods and Greats) in 1961. There is little doubt that Sir Robin will in due course be offered an honorary fellowship at his old college, and it is also possible he will end up a head of house. It is already the case that he is a member of the United Oxford and Cambridge Club, as well as of the Athenaeum, Brooks and the Anglo-Belgian, and he is a governor of his old school. Such a man is not a revolutionary. It is simply not in his nature. When he joined the Treasury in 1961, direct from Oxford, Butler was a fast-stream intellectual and looked ahead confidently to the realization of his Establishment dream. He was not to be disappointed. Everything that was promised came to pass, and having reached his goal, he is not likely to tear down the system that put him there.

Reform is another matter. With the publication in November 1993 of a report on Civil Service career management and succession planning, commissioned by Sir Robin, steps have at last been taken to dilute the impact of the administrative fast stream, and with it the influence of Oxbridge. Under the proposals it contains, the 620 top jobs in Whitehall, at grades 1, 1a, 2 and 3, should in future be filled by open competition. Insiders will naturally be considered, and can be expected to perform well – after all, they know the ground. Crucially, however, specialists from outside will also be encouraged to apply and will be hired should they impress the Civil Service Commissioners as the right candidates for the job. Senior positions, including those within the mandarinate, will be advertised in the press, and the requirement will be to 'strike a balance' between ensuring that external talent is recruited where required and reassuring those on the inside that they still have the prospect of promotion to the inner councils.

It is a brave initiative, long overdue, for which Butler deserves credit. The extent, however, to which it might reduce Varsity dominance remains to be seen. Whitehall has a way of dealing with undesirable measures; effectively it buries them. Previous reports have come and gone, and who remembers them? There was the Fulton Report in 1968, which called for a refining of management skills and the opening up of the service to experts from outside Whitehall. There was the 'Next Steps' initiative in 1988, which set up a large number of administrative quangos but left the core of the profession untouched, like a giant redwood merely singed by a forest conflagration destroying all else in its path. Resistance to change is endemic. Existing fast-stream bureaucrats will not easily give up what they regard as their inheritance. There may also be a tendency by some recruiters to admit mainly those outsiders who already appear familiar. An unknown number of outsiders having the necessary qualifications and seniority in their own professions to qualify will themselves be Oxbridge, with a sympathetic ethos, while applicants from within could expect, in many cases, to enjoy the favour of their bosses. That said, the long-term effect could be considerable and represents the biggest squall to threaten the furled umbrellas for a generation.

At the time of writing, however, an alphabetical search of the ministries reveals few surprises. Richard Packer, permanent secretary at Agriculture, Fisheries and Food, is one. The head of possibly the least glamorous department (known universally as Ag and Fish), Packer did A-levels at the City of London School and took both his B.Sc. and his Master's at the University of Manchester. Sir Christopher France, top man at Defence, began his education at humble

East Ham Grammar School, but subsequently won a place to New College, Oxford. Sir Geoffrey Holland, at Education and Science, went to Merchant Taylors' and St John's, Oxford, while at the Department of Employment, Eton and King's, Cambridge was the well-worn route chosen by Nicholas Monck. The Environment Department is headed by Richard Wilson, late of Radley and Clare College, Cambridge, at which he was an Exhibitioner. Health is in the care of Graham Hart, of Brentwood School and Pembroke College, Oxford, and the Home Office has as its permanent secretary Sir Clive Whitmore, ex-Sutton Grammar and Christ's College, Cambridge. Hayden Phillips, curator of our National Heritage department, moved from Cambridgeshire High School down the road to Clare College, Cambridge (where he coincided with Richard Wilson). At the Northern Ireland Office, there are two permanent secretaries, one based mainly in London, the other in Stormont. John Chilcot, the London man, went from Brighton College to Pembroke College, Cambridge (where he was an Open Scholar), but David Fell, exercising what might be termed Paddy's Pardon, opted for Queen's University, Belfast, and took a First in Mathematics. The combination of street cred with Establishment cred is thought to be particularly efficacious. Slightly removed from the hurly-burly of Whitehall, the Lord Chancellor's office has as its permanent secretary Sir Thomas Legg, who studied at St John's College, Cambridge, Alma Mater of his political master, Lord Mackay of Clashfern. Sir Russell Hillhouse, brandishing Jock's Waiver, took his 'highers' at Hutcheson's Grammar School and an MA at the University of Glasgow. The Social Security Department is in the hands of Sir Michael Partridge, another Merchant Taylors' man, who, like his boss, Sir Robin, took a First in Mods and Greats, in his case at St John's. Patrick Brown, a polyglot late entrant to the service, is another distinguished Redbrick product. From the Royal Grammar School in Newcastle, he won a place at the School of Slavonic and East European Studies, in London, and now heads the Department of Transport – in which his knowledge of command economies is no doubt much appreciated. Trade and Industry, once the ministerial bailiwick of the 'Chingford Skinhead', Norman Tebbit, has as its permanent secretary Sir Peter Gregson, who, from Nottingham High School (where he overlapped with Kenneth

Clarke) went on to Balliol and yet another First in Mods and Greats. The Treasury, supreme powerhouse of government, with its veto over ministerial spending, is, perhaps surprisingly, the most open of departments. Sir Terry Burns, the permanent secretary, went from Houghton-le-Willow Grammar School to Manchester University and the London Business School. The chief economic adviser, Sir Alan Budd, took his Ph.D. at Churchill College, Cambridge, but from Oundle School had gone initially to the LSE. Andrew Turnbull and Sir Nigel Wicks, the Treasury's two other under-secretaries, went respectively to Enfield Grammar and Christ's College, Cambridge, and to Beckenham and Penge Grammar, then Cambridge and London. Finally, Michael Scholar, the aptly named head of the Welsh Office, having taken A-levels at St Olave's in Bermondsey, south London, went on to St John's, Cambridge (where he is now a Fellow) and to Berkeley.

What is most interesting about this cavalcade of learning, much of it steeped in the languages of ancient Greece and Rome, is the relative absence of public schools. True, Eton, Harrow, Merchant Taylors' and Radley are represented, but so are Beckenham and Penge Grammar School and similarly modest establishments in Bermondsey, Surrey, Essex and East Ham. The Civil Service, it would seem, is already rid of its traditional Great School ethos and is the product of every kind of secondary education. Yet, at university level, the Oxbridge binary culture, while shaken, has not been broken and is likely to persist, more or less intact, for decades to come. A Varsity view of the world even today is the highest common factor at the most senior ministerial briefings, and Redbrick exceptions to the rule, when not Celtic by origin, remain few and far between.

Oxbridge networking remains ruthlessly efficient, and in Whitehall's upper echelons it carries all before it. When Sir Peter Kemp, second permanent secretary at the Cabinet Office, with special responsibility for the Civil Service, lost his job in 1991, amid considerable controversy, Liz Symons, general secretary of the prestigious First Division Association, herself a graduate of Girton, commented on *Newsnight* on BBC2 that he hadn't fitted in and had failed to establish a proper rapport with his colleagues. 'He didn't go to Oxford', she added. Later, however, she denied such sentiments, averring instead that it was Kemp's *feeling* that he hadn't gone to Oxford that was the trouble. Either way, Butlerism, clearly, had some distance to go.

Towards the end of 1993, Kemp – a high-minded product of Millfield School and the Royal Naval College, Dartmouth – illustrated the apparent contempt he felt for his former colleagues' values in a report, *Beyond Next Steps: a Civil Service for the 21st Century*, published by the right-wing Social Market Foundation. He pointed out that the modern service, with some half a million employees, was 10 times bigger than that required to run the empire at the turn of the century and, with an annual running cost of £20 thousand million needed to shed at least 125,000 jobs if it was to provide value for money.

'The world of Whitehall and Westminster can be an extraordinarily cloistered place', he wrote. 'Ministers, especially those who have been in government for a long time, risk losing all contact with the real world. The same goes for many of the senior civil servants, of whom Sir Humphrey is barely a parody ... while there have been many welcome breakthroughs, at the centre old attitudes and the old guard prevail.'

Robin Butler, as we have already observed, does not come from the School of Hard Knocks and could hardly be expected to adopt a policy of slash and burn. But he is, as we have seen, a genuine reformer. Indeed, being the kind of fair-minded intellectual he is, the fact that he personally has profited so comprehensively from the existing system may well have impelled him partially to redress its core injustice – the fact that, like the central lanes in the old Soviet city streets, reserved for party bigwigs, the Oxbridge route through Whitehall is generally free of all encumbrance. Sir Robin, as urbane as a Nash terrace, has said publicly on several occasions since taking over at the Cabinet Office in 1988 that he wants the 'net cast wider', so that talent, wherever it comes from, is rewarded in the service. He is not, though, going to bust a gut to achieve his end. 'If you look at the fast stream', he told *The Times* in 1993, 'about 40 per cent come from Oxbridge, whereas at the time I entered [1961] it was about 75 per cent. I do not regard reducing the number of Oxbridge entrants as a good thing in itself. What is important is to get people trying from the widest possible field, and not being put off because they think the Civil Service is an Oxbridge preserve.'

Logically, Sir Robin's stand, supported by the Prime Minister, means nothing less than giving the other 121 universities a chance to compete on a genuinely equal footing. It means, for one thing, competition papers that are not most easily answered by graduates of a tutorial system, confident and expansive in their approach. It means accepting that those lacking the 'effortless superiority' and 'side' of a Varsity product are not necessarily the worse for it, merely different. The appointment in 1992 of Stella Rimington as director-general of MI5 – the first-ever head of security to be photographed shopping – showed what could be done. Mrs Rimington, married to John Rimington, a graduate of Jesus College, Cambridge, now head of the Health and Safety Executive, is an alumnus of Edinburgh and achieved her present office in spite both of being a woman and of having the audacity to present non-Oxbridge credentials. MI6, however, remains in the circle. In March 1994, it was announced that espionage overseas would be controlled by David Spedding, a former diplomat and graduate of Hertford College, Oxford. Spedding, who managed only a Third in history (demonstrating once again that it is not what but *where* that counts), took over from Sir Colin McColl, a former diplomat and a graduate of Queen's College, Oxford. So not much change there. Any genuine reform of Whitehall's corridors of influence has to mean graduates from outside the magic circle being positively enjoined to apply for the Administrative fast stream and, once their names are entered for competition, being recruited in sufficient numbers, on merit, to shatter the patrician ethos of Whitehall and encourage new voices to be heard in the corridors of power. Such change might be thought a tall order. And it is. But if Butler does not put it into effect, the Cabinet Secretary's meritocratic talk will in the end be dismissed as mere window-dressing designed to look good to passers-by. The Graduate Recruitment Group of the Civil Service Commissioners, responsible for liaison with the universities, tended in the past to devote much of its time to Oxford and Cambridge and to give only sporadic attention elsewhere. Officials would visit London, Bristol and Manchester almost every year, but smaller and more out-of-the-way locations received pastoral care on what was at best an occasional basis.

Accordingly, not only most recruits, but most applicants, were Oxbridge, with only a handful of determined suitors taking up the challenge from beyond the Pale. Today, the group works equally with every university, or tries to. Visits are made on a regular basis to each institution, and, vitally, careers services are kept fully informed of changes in procedure and the requirements of the jobs in question. Students, even from the former polytechnics, are assured that if they do well in their examinations and impress the recruitment assessors, they stand the same chance as anyone else of being accepted into a programme of accelerated promotion that could, in theory, end with their becoming permanent secretaries, or even successors to Sir Robin.

A personal initiative by the Cabinet Secretary, consistent with his expressed wish for a more widespread trawl, is the 'Links' scheme, under which permanent secretaries volunteer to monitor the performance of target universities. So does this mean that Loughborough, say, or Aston, or Lampeter is now safe in the concerned embrace of a top mandarin, whose earnest wish it is that 'his' adopted boys and girls should do better each year in the competition for places? If so, with no acceptances between them from 171 applications in 1992–3, the trio still have a lot of ground to make up, and there is little evidence so far that they are even at the same starting gate as Oxbridge. One recent factor operating in favour of the Redbrick sector is the presence as second permanent secretary of the Office of Public Service and Science of Richard Mottram, who took a First in International Relations from the University of Keele in 1967 and describes himself in his entry in *Who's Who* as having entered the fast stream of the Department of Defence 'by open competition'. Mr Mottram is seen as a coming man and owes nothing to Oxbridge. Perhaps he will be the one to see to it that others like him, with provincially refined talent, build up their Whitehall representation at an appropriate rate.

Progress has not, therefore, been entirely absent. It is more that it is slow and painful. In the 1993–4 competition year, 13,898 graduates, all with Firsts or Upper Seconds, entered the lists for the Civil Service fast-stream. A miserly 362 jobs were on offer, yielding a success rate of just 2.6 per cent. Oxford produced 714 of the applicants, Cambridge 599, and the two were rewarded, respectively,

76 places and 70 places. Thus, in return for 9.4 per cent of the applications, Oxbridge picked up 40 per cent of the jobs.

The ratio of success to failure for Oxbridge in 1993–4 was 11.2 per cent. For Bristol, it was 4.5 per cent; for King's London, 1.5 per cent; for Edinburgh 6.4 per cent, and for Hull a depressing 0.5 per cent. Many universities, like Loughborough (with 99 applicants) and Oxford Brookes (with 64), were awarded no places at all, and the average success rate was 2.6 per cent. It was therefore more than four times likelier an Oxbridge candidate would succeed in 'fair and open competition' than an applicant from anywhere else.

But even the 40 per cent figure, though already disproportionately high, does not reflect the stubborn nature of the Oxbridge bias within the core of the Service. Graduates from the Spires and Backs who won admission to the key administrative fast stream rose from the 1992–3 figure of 54 per cent to 58 per cent in 1993–4, while at the level of Administrative Trainee/Higher Executive Officer (Development), the year-on-year increase was even more startling – from 48 per cent to 59 per cent.

What remains, in spite of this remarkable inequity, is the fact that four out of ten of the new generation of apprentice mandarins are already Redbrick. They may have had to beat the doors down to get in, but they have made it just the same. The result, logically, should be that by the year 2015, or thereabouts – and perhaps earlier – we should have our first Redbrick Cabinet Secretary (the name of Richard Mottram springs to mind), and the first of his kind not eligible for membership of the United Oxford and Cambridge Club. Experience, however, shows that high flyers from outside the established axis rarely fly quite so high as those from within, and it cannot entirely be ruled out that ranks will close ruthlessly in future to ensure a controlling majority of Oxbridge permanent secretaries well beyond the millennium.

'It is impossible to say where the present Civil Service reforms might end', Sir Robin told the Political Studies Association at Leicester University in 1993. 'The idea of the Civil Service as a comfortable and secure sinecure has gone ... but it would be a travesty were that replaced by the image of a service in which only the bottom line mattered.'

Diplomacy

Since 1973, there have been six heads of service in the Foreign and Commonwealth Office. All have been Oxbridge. The present incumbent, Sir John Coles, formerly High Commissioner to Australia, is a Magdalen man and a member of the United Oxford and Cambridge University Club. His predecessor, Sir David Gillmore, was a graduate of king's College, Cambridge. Most – though not all – of the FCO's political bosses have the same stamp. Douglas Hurd, Foreign Secretary since 1989, and himself a former diplomat, moved seamlessly from Eton to Trinity College, Cambridge, where he was a Major Scholar and served a term as president of the Union. The deputy under-secretary and political director of the service at the time of writing is Leonard Appleyard, of Queens' College, Cambridge. The four other deputy under-secretaries are alumni of, respectively, Magdalen (in two cases) and New College, Oxford, and St Catharine's, Cambridge. Of the fifteen assistant under-secretaries, nine went to Oxford and three to Cambridge. Bristol, London and Reading were the student destinations of the remaining trio.

An A–Z of the overseas staff reveals little different. From Algeria (New College) to Zimbabwe (St Catharine's), the men – and, occasionally, women – we send out to represent British interests are Oxbridge to their deep heart's core. Examination of the academic provenance of ambassadors and their deputies in our top sixteen foreign missions in 1993 (Washington, the United Nations, the European Community, Nato, Moscow, Bonn, Paris, Rome, Madrid, New Delhi, the Holy See, Beijing, Pretoria, Cairo, Tel Aviv and Canberra) breaks down as follows: Oxford seventeen, Cambridge eleven, others one, don't knows or none, three. The same, or nearly, would be true of any other sixteen top overseas posts.

When questioned about this rather startling bias, the FCO, like a crippled battleship on the run from pursuers, instinctively makes smoke. The assurance is given that all will be different in twenty or thirty years' time, when the latest recruits from today's meritocracy have risen to the top of their profession. It is hard, however, to see how this could possibly be so. Not only have diplomatic apologists been saying as much for generations, while Oxbridge continues to rule, but the latest graduate entry into the fast stream is 73 per cent from the old duopoly. The 1993–4 Administrative intake (those expected to rise to counsellor at least) was small, in keeping with Treasury-imposed cutbacks. But of the twenty-two who succeeded in winning a place out of the thousands of applicants from all over the country, sixteen were from the ancient universities, just six from the rest. In 1992–3, when even fewer – just fourteen – Administrative grade diplomats were taken on, eleven (79 per cent) were Oxbridge. Exeter, Manchester and the former South-West Polytechnic, managed one each, while other institutions had to be content with successes in the lower-level, Executive grade of the service, which pushes paper, issues passports and deals with matters of commerce (trade!). The fast stream, according to a spokesman, concentrates on policy and intellectual problems and is offered accelerated promotion to the top jobs as well as privileged access to politicians and the most senior mandarins. The Executive, or 'main stream' wallahs, by contrast, deal with the public and are likened more to senior clerks and middle managers. 'They are two distinct and distinctive career options', the spokesman says. Unsurprisingly, candidates from Oxford and Cambridge are rarely chosen for this essential but unglamorous second division work, which has become the principal Foreign Office base not only for Redbrick applicants, but for ethnic minorities and women. Just two out of the twenty-seven trainees from 1992/3 who approached their calling by the tradesmen's entrance had Oxon. or Cantab. after their names.

The same provenance principle applies to the British Council, not actually part of the Foreign Office but a kind of cultural annexe to our embassies round the world, running offices, libraries and language schools in ninety-eight countries. One-third of the council's grant-in-aid comes from the FCO, and Sir David Gillmore sits on the board. Sir Martin Jacomb (Worcester College) is chairman; his deputy is Lord Chorley (Caius); the director-general is John Hanson (Wadham). 'We work extremely closely with the Foreign Office', a spokeswoman says. 'We share the same objectives and apply similar ground-rules.' Evidently.

It would be wrong to suggest that there has been no change whatever in recruitment trends. There are many more diplomats today from ordinary middle-class backgrounds than would have been the case when John Sparrow, a celebrated Warden of All

Souls, sat regularly on the selection board, and there are even occasional specimens from the working class. Yet, for the most part, such *arrivistes* have already had their rough edges knocked off them at Oxbridge, and, since the service pays for its officers' children to go through private schools – often boarding schools – both they and their families have been granted automatic social transference to the Establishment. Without Oxbridge, such candidates would have little chance. It was college life, to observe Foreign Office parlance, that produced a 'level playing field'.

Lord Plowden (Pembroke, Cambridge, Honorary Fellow 1958), criticizing the Oxbridge domination of Britain's representational services overseas in a report in 1964, concluded that 'We cannot regard the present situation as satisfactory either to the Foreign and Commonwealth Services or to the universities.' Michael Stewart, Labour's Foreign Secretary four years later, tried, somewhat feebly, to respond and called in a group of vice-chancellors from around the country to advise him on what should be done to broaden selection. Their somewhat doleful conclusion, actually proposed by a Redbrick representative (himself no doubt from academe's inside track), was that the 'best brains' went to Oxbridge and things were pretty much all right as they were. Stewart (St John's College, Oxford; president of the Union 1929), was obviously relieved and decided to leave well alone. Recalling this episode in *The Diplomats*, an acclaimed study of the Foreign Office published by Jonathan Cape in 1977, Geoffrey Moorhouse acknowledged the widespread view that diplomats continued to be recruited 'from too small a circle, educated in the public schools and at the universities of Oxford and Cambridge'. He then produced a list of the 1976 hierarchy which showed that of the twenty-six top men (no women) in the service at that time, only five had not been to public school and just three had not attended Oxbridge. Seventeen years later, little has changed.

In 1950, 90 per cent of fast-stream entrants were Oxbridge. By 1965, the figure had fallen to 74 per cent, and seventeen years later, in 1982, had slipped a further fraction, to 72 per cent. The absolute nadir for privilege came in 1991, when just ten out of nineteen fast-stream recruits, or 52 per cent of the total, came from the duopoly. But the reaction was swift. In 1992, as we have seen, Oxbridge struck back, to 79 per cent, and in 1993–4 held firm, at 73 per cent.

Set against the enormity of the conformity, it hardly seems to matter what the top men have to say from their ornate offices in King Charles Street, overlooking St James's Park. The statistics shout for themselves. Yet Peter Carter, the FCO's head of recruitment, himself an Oxford man, is emphatic that there is no institutionalized bias in favour of Oxbridge and has not been one for many years. He does not excuse the complete lack of correlation between Oxbridge's 7 per cent share of the UK graduate total and its 75 per cent proportion of fast-stream recruits to the Foreign Office. Instead, he points to 'a culture at Oxbridge of applications to the diplomatic service' and to the 'impression' he has formed over the years that 'the negative factor of our being associated in the public mind with élitism in a perverse way actually appeals to a certain kind of Oxbridge undergraduate'. Yes indeed. No quarrel there. 'It is a truism', Carter goes on, 'for which we make no apology, that we are looking for the brightest and the best, not only in terms of academic achievement but in social and interpersonal terms. Oxford and Cambridge self-evidently select the most accomplished candidates among applicants from the schools, then provide them with the intimate and demanding tutorial system, unique in this country, which induces confidence and refines their analytical skills.' Graduates taught in large numbers in seminars, he adds, can hardly be be expected to compete on equal terms. But there is more. It is not just that Oxford and Cambridge confer advantage through their exclusive, and expensive, teaching system. The lesser orders don't apply because they don't think they are in with a chance.

We run up against prejudice – really quite ingrained prejudice – when we visit other universities. I have had students come up to me at jobs fairs and say, 'You don't really want to give me a job, you want to give it to someone from Oxbridge'. And there are still some non-Oxbridge careers advisers who tell their students not to apply to us because they will only be wasting their time.

Peter Carter is evidently appalled.

We are determined to consider everyone, regardless of their background. We visit other universities, at their request, even though it is frequently expensive to do so, and we never turn down an invitation from any institution which wishes to see us. We make a point of making the same presentation wherever we go, with only slight adjustments for particular circumstances, and even if the chances of success, at a former polytechnic, say, are minimal, I still insist on going and encouraging them to apply.

Although governed by its own Order in Council, the diplomatic service is provided with its fast-stream recruits by the same agency, Recruitment and Assessment Services (RAS), as the rest of the Civil Service. Thus, it is not directly involved in the initial 'fair and open' competition for places, and all graduates are considered, from whatever university or college they come. Carter says: 'We obviously want to ensure that we get the best kind of candidates that suit our needs, but in my own case, though I am a selector with RAS, I only ever see a few of the candidates each year who are seeking to join the service, and we are bound in the end to take the names which are afterwards put before us.'

It all sounds extremely fair and aboveboard. And in a way, it is. The fact remains that even if the Foreign Office is not itself loading the dice in favour of Oxbridge, most of the double sixes still come down firmly in their favour, while the Redbricks, and even Scottish universities, continue to score a dismal two each. Carter, reasonable but realistic within the Establishment's narrow parameters, sees only a 'slow and slight' decline in this dual dominance. In ten years' time, he jokes, the proportion of Oxbridge entrants will have dropped from 1993's 73 per cent to ... 71 per cent. 'But I doubt it will go much lower than that.'

Elitism is built into the fabric of the Foreign Office, which, famously, was constructed to a classical design by Gilbert Scott after Palmerston had shunted off his original Gothic model to St Pancras Station as insufficiently grandiose. Arrogance springs naturally from King Charles Street. When Sir Kenneth Berrill, himself from Trinity College, Cambridge and successively Fellow and bursar at St Catharine's and King's, was asked to enquire into the running of the department in 1975, he concluded that it was out of touch with British life and dismissive of the Home Civil Service. His report created a considerable stink within the Establishment, including a flurry of angry letters to The Times, and was largely ignored. Such reform as there has been has come largely from within, and, today, the service sees itself as one of Britain's last class acts, able to draft codicils and protocols at the drop of a bowler hat that will let Britain off the hook on Maastricht, keep us on-side with the Serbian mainstream while publicly condemning their extremists, and work 'loyally' to hand over the Hong Kong Chinese to Beijing while appearing to be concerned solely with the establishment of post-colonial democracy. Arguably, of course, it is the politicians who pull the strings. But even if most ministers were not themselves products of the same group of colleges and the same university societies – and thus of like mind – they would prefer anyway to be seduced by the do-nothing, say-nothing school of Whitehall diplomacy. Britain's diplomats, smooth as silk, somehow supercilious though their policies are more often supine, seem actually to *want* to run British foreign policy down, as though it were a factory that is bound to close and might as well do so in an orderly fashion. 'Our task now is the orderly managment of decline', a senior FCO man told Margaret Thatcher. For this sad purpose they remain admirably equipped. They are professional and skilled, and superbly trained, not least in 'hard' languages.

What is lacking, crucially, is any persistent identity with the central core of national thinking. Public opinion to these Alpha administrators is not a factor. They leave that to the politicians, who in turn dismiss it as unsophisticated fol-de-rol and turn back to their advisers and their whispered solicitations. What Britain's diplomats offer the public in the post-colonial, post-independence age is a nation put into administration (*their* administration), and the conviction that they, with their polyglot patriotism and arcane traditions, know better than anyone they 'serve' what needs to be done in difficult days. It is a simple policy, and a ruthless one, and it is conducted in secret. As we decline into being an offshore province of Europe plc, rather than even *trying* to be leaders within a family of nations, the Oxbridge-run Foreign Office regards it as its final service to the country to hand it over, with its 'vital' institutions purring like pussy cats, to the super state where its true ambitions now lie.

And let no one doubt that British foreign and foreign trade personnel are rapidly going *communautaire*. One need only look for confirmation of this to the growing Oxbridge migration to Brussels and Strasbourg since the 1973 Treaty of Accession.

Dod's *European Companion* for 1992 provides a comprehensive list of the senior administrators and advisers who fill the upper echelons of the EC Civil Service. Each member of the Twelve has a staff allocation, based on population, as part of the total establishment, and at the time of writing Dod's had the details of 116 Britons from the Commission, the Council of Ministers, the European Parliament, the European Investment Bank, the Economic and Social Committee, the Court of Justice, the Court of Auditors and the European Political Co-operation Secretariat. These are the 'faceless' men and women who actually keep Europe going, supported by a small army of lesser beings, such as statisticians, technicians, secretaries and security guards. They range downwards from the twelve-strong Commission itself, and its advisers, through directors-general and permanent representatives to directors, heads of unit and press officers. Not included are the slightly more junior figures, usually recent recruits, who must wait a few years for the necessary seniority. But the list does provide a faithful Who's Who of Britain in Europe and indicates clearly where they came from and the talents they bring to bear.

- Sir Leon Brittan, our senior commissioner, and a vice-president under Jacques Delors, responsible for Competition Policy and Financial Institutions, gained an MA from Trinity College, Cambridge, before going on to Yale. As well as being a QC, and a long-time Tory minister, he speaks French, German and Italian.
- Bruce Millan, Labour's appointee, is a Scot, and, using his Celtic Waiver to its fullest extent, avoided higher education entirely until he was able to pick up a brace of honorary doctorates from Dundee and Heriot-Watt universities and a fellowship from Paisley College. He is a chartered accountant and a former Secretary of State for Scotland, and speaks French, the language of the Auld Alliance.
- David Williamson, Britain's highest-ranked *fonctionnaire* in Brussels in the 1992 Dod's, is a classicist, who read Mods and Greats at Exeter College, Oxford, in the 1950s. He moved from Whitehall, where he was a high flyer in agriculture, and speaks French as well as ancient Greek and Latin. He also *reads* Italian.
- Peter Wilmott, director-general of Customs and Indirect Taxation, studied modern and medieval languages at Trinity College,

Cambridge, before embarking on a career with HM Customs and Excise. He speaks French, but can also recognize Anything To Declare (or not, these days) in Dutch, German and Italian.

- Geoffrey Fitchew, director-general of DGXV (Financial Institutions and Company Law), took his first degree at Magdalen College, Oxford, and then read economics at the LSE. French is his second language, too (why is it always assumed in Britain that foreigners speak French?), but in addition he can read a balance sheet in German, Italian and Russian.

- Sir John Kerr, the UK member of the Committee of Permanent Representatives (Community ambassadors), is another Scot, but, as an intending diplomat, wisely opted for the University of Oxford after his years at Glasgow Academy. He converses freely in French and Russian.

So far, the scoreline reads: Oxford 3, Cambridge 2, University of (Scottish) Life 1, Others nil. In the list overall, with its 116 names, the tally is: Oxford 36, Cambridge 27, English Redbrick (including London) 30, Scottish Universities 10, Irish 5, Welsh 2, French 2, Art School 1, 'Life' 3. Thus, Oxbridge, which at the time most of the above officials were of student age was producing less than 10 per cent of all British graduates, has secured 55 per cent of the Euro-total, including all but one of the top posts. Stripping out the Scots, Irish and Welsh contingents boosts the already impressive total to a daunting 66 per cent (two-thirds) for England, with only the federation of London, by far the largest university in the country, even approaching double figures.

To assist in the selection of UK graduates for the various Community institutions, the Civil Service Commissioners, through the RAS, have since 1990 organized yet another 'free and open competition'. The resulting scheme, according to the Commissioners' Report for 1990–91, is aimed at increasing the number of UK nationals in fast-stream positions in Europe working as administrators, lawyers and economists. Recruits are employed by the Cabinet Office but are loaned to other government departments for relevant European work experience prior to sitting the relevant EC competitions. In 1991, the first year of the new programme, forty-five appointments were made, and of these thirteen came from Cambridge and twelve from Oxford, with the remaining twenty divided among the ninety-five other universities and (then) polytechnics. The Oxbridge proportion was 56 per cent, just above the penetration rate for already established high flyers. A year later, the Oxbridge share had risen to 66 per cent, or two-thirds, indicating, if anything, a future UK Eurocracy more duopolistic than ever. All of those who sat the exams, including those from former polys, possessed either first-class degrees or Upper Seconds. At interview, however, at which the academic origins of each candidate are known, those possessing the unique 'interpersonal' skills of Oxbridge, inculcated through college life, continue to press home their advantage.

Nor does it end there. New graduates from the twin peaks are pouring into Brussels in ever greater numbers each autumn to take up one-year work-experience posts as *stagiaires*. Oxbridge has flocked to the *stage* in a big way, seeing it not only as an excellent means of expanding networking into Europe but also as an amusing and sophisticated finishing school, replete with champagne and sex, that looks better on the CV than a year as an aid worker and can, in some cases, be as vocationally useful as an MBA. Researchers and graduate assistants, usually on a one- or two-year attachment, also have a mainly Oxbridge flavour. Among the 1993 Brussels intake in this area was Stephen Kinnock, son of the former Labour leader, who, after Cambridge and a year at the College of Europe, in Bruges, became a research assistant to Gary Titley, Labour's MEP for Greater Manchester West. Interestingly, Kinnock the Younger did not choose Cardiff, or Liverpool, or the LSE to establish his credentials. He mainlined, just as Margaret Jay, daughter of James Callaghan, did – in her case, at Somerville – and from his office off the rue Belliard will be looking to a prosperous future for himself and his family in the new, egalitarian Europe. Neil will be proud of him. Other universities try to compete, and there are small cadres from London and Manchester and from Edinburgh, Bristol and York in the community's colour-coded *coulisses de la politique*. But the fact remains that Brussels, which knows an élite when it sees one, has already been charmed, impressed and bowled over by the existing mafia and extends its hand uncomplainingly to the Chosen.

The converse of this convenient co-operation (based ostensibly on open competition, but clearly affected by provenance) is Oxbridge's steady build-up of continental undergraduates – a process that is growing apace. In 1993, Oxford held a conference, organized by Lord Weidenfeld, vice-president of the Campaign for Oxford, and Sir Ronald Grierson (Balliol), chairman of General Electric, and chaired by Prince Hans Adam von Liechtenstein, to introduce a new movement, the Europaeum, 'motivated by a desire to place Oxford and the United Kingdom in the vanguard of moves to educate the next generation of leaders in Europe'. Typically, the venture, which is being launched at a cost of £15 million, entails a link-up between Oxford and a group of other élite universities, including Bologna (the oldest in Europe), Leiden, the French Sciences Po and the Catholic University of Louvain. Cambridge, assuredly, will not be far behind. It may even, typically, attempt to pass its rival on the inside track. For Brussels wants more British administrators. There are new worlds to conquer and the game's afoot. The enduring duo will follow power or influence wherever it leads, and once they have got a grip they do not easily let go.

The Best Men

Cecil Rhodes (1853–1902) had expected his monument would be Africa. One of the empire's great adventurers, his error on the durability of Britain's place in the world was no greater than that of Sir Winston Churchill – a seer without benefit of an Oxbridge education – who, even after the Second World War, dreamed of a continuing *Pax Britannica* on which the sun never set. Rhodes was wrong about Africa – miserably so. The country that once bore his name has since been reborn as Zimbabwe, and his grave, high on a hill, looks over a continent tested almost to destruction by poverty, tribalism and chaos. For his more permanent legacy, we must turn north and west, to Oxford.

It was a bequest that nearly did not happen. Rhodes was already a successful financier in southern Africa when he found the time to come up to Oxford in 1873, and over the eight years it took him to scrape a degree he was constantly distracted by the need to manage his considerable investments and to make regular visits home.

Moreover, he had been turned down by his first choice, University College, whose tutors felt he was not honours material and eschewed 'pass men', and was lucky to be taken in by Oriel, in mark of which favour he was to leave them £100,000 in his will – a sum worth several millions today. Having got in, what is perhaps strange is that, although he mixed very little with his fellow undergraduates and did not live in college, preferring lodgings in the city, he fell utterly in love with the place and remained besotted for the rest of his life. Even when he lay dying, his thoughts turned back to the dreaming spires – in his case, literally, as a friend quoted to him from Matthew Arnold, (author of that well-worn phrase, as well as of 'city of lost causes'), the lines beginning: 'Beautiful city, so venerable, so lovely . . .'

The reason for this enduring affair was simple, but deep-seated. Rhodes had had a *dream*, and came closer to realizing it than almost anyone of his day. He dreamed of the British Empire stretching from Cairo to the Cape and from Arabia to the Pacific, and of the mother country, in concert with the United States, spreading civilization to every corner of the earth. Central to his vision was the idea of Oxford – the Oxford of Benjamin Jowett – as an institute for the instruction in civilized values of young men; men who, as secular missionaries, would then spread learning and good government to the heathen. Like Jowett, Master of Balliol for most of the last quarter of the nineteenth century, he believed passionately in a patrician class, and it was in perpetuation of this warped ideal, as well as of himself, that he endowed his famous scholarships bringing to Oxford students from America, the colonies and (in response to what he saw of its growing strength in Europe and Africa) imperial Germany. To put it bluntly, as he would himself, Rhodes wanted Oxford men ('the best men to fight the world's battles') in key positions of power around the world, and he was prepared to invest heavily to achieve his end.

Nearly 6,000 Scholars have so far had their names entered in the register at Rhodes House, Oxford. At first, they were all white and all males, but 'new' Commonwealth candidates were eventually admitted, and even women were granted entry in 1976. The German quota, filled originally by imperial whim, was suspended with the outbreak of the Second World War and not reactivated for many years. Despite the fact that Scholars from Germany were renowned for their resistance to Hitler (Adam von Trott zu Solz, a pre-war stipendiary, was tortured and executed for his part in the 1944 bomb plot), it was thought politic to leave the Kaiser's list in abeyance. More recently, eight new Scholars from Europe have been added to the total, joining Canadians, Australians, South Africans and New Zealanders, as well as a growing contingent from the sub-continent and beyond, in reinterpreting Rhodes's concept of a global bureaucracy. Many past Scholars, assisted by Oxford's boost to their C.V.s have graduated to top positions in public life, especially in law and administration, and several have even gone on to lead their countries, including, Bob Hawke, the former Prime Minister of Australia.

There is no doubt, however, that it is the US Rhodes Scholars who are best known and exhibit the highest profile. A number have achieved high public office in America, including Senator J. William Fulbright (later to found his own scholarships) and Dean Rusk, Secretary of State under Kennedy, and two rose to be justices of the Supreme Court. Yet another, rather less bureaucratically inclined, was the singer and film actor Kris Kristofferson. Kennedy, an anglophile in spite of his Irish roots, whose closest confidant outside the family was probably Harold Macmillan, later Chancellor of Oxford, offered places in his administration to no fewer than sixteen former Scholars in the early 1960s. A second peak is, of course, that brought about by Bill Clinton, the forty-second and current President, who came to University College in 1968 for a two-year stay after graduating from Georgetown University.

Clinton's elevation to the most important job on earth was a cause for almost unparalleled celebration in his Alma Mater. The Campaign for Oxford, seeking £340 million for a host of projects, was in full swing, and the impetus given by an old boy in the White House was incalculable. The President's honorary doctorate, granted at a milestone Encaenia in the summer of 1994, was inevitable from the word go, and even the fact that it was delivered substantially in Latin did not obscure its primary purpose of joining Oxford once more to the temple of the gods.

In the context of such adulation, it is an irony that Clinton does not appear to have enjoyed himself beneath the Spires. R. Emmett

Tyrrell, editor-in-chief of the *American Spectator*, recalls that Clinton, rather than dine with his fellow students in college, ate in the town market-place almost every day and was bothered by the class orientation of what he saw around him. Perhaps it was just the climate of the times. It was 1968, after all, and the future politician, then long-haired, with a beard, was preoccupied with such matters as the Vietnam War, against which he demonstrated in London, and marijuana, which allegedly he did not inhale. It is a fact, moreover, that he has regularly turned to fellow Rhodes Scholars for advice throughout his presidency, retaining at least, ten as consultants, fund-raisers and organizers. He may not have liked England, or even Oxford, all that much, but he was still mindful of the honour and remains conspicuously faithful to the network.

What, though, does Oxford remember of young Bill? According to *Oxford's Famous Faces*, by John Dougill (Oxface Publications, 1993), the then dean of graduates at University College is taking no hostages to fortune: 'Mr Clinton was an amiable person whose record at the college was impeccable. [He] did not strike me as some hairy horror or he certainly would not have been a member of my dining-club.'

Indeed not, Dean. Not only dining-clubs, but Encaeniae for 'hairy horrors' are not what Oxford is about. Were standards to slip that far, even for a President of the United States, Cecil Rhodes would be turning in his grave.

The G&G

Politicians govern, Civil Servants administer, the Foreign Office represents us abroad and the Eurocrats ensure that fog no longer cuts off the Continent. But who recommends? Who issues strictures? Who analyses and reviews what is going on and points a finger at the guilty? Why, the G&G, of course. The Great and Good, those stalwarts of royal commissions, of inquiries, of 101 councils and agencies, are with us today as never before. The new democracy our weakened flesh is heir to requires ombudspersons and committee members by the hundredweight, or, more probably today, by the metric tonne. Fair administration of the people seems to require that an unelected élite should be set in judgement over the various institutions that govern our lives.

The G&G, that extraordinary collection of conservative high achievers relied on by the Cabinet Office to adjudicate on the nation's failings and, where necessary, to prescribe a better future, is by common consent almost a definition of the Establishment. It is a complete list, so far as can be worked out, of the safest pairs of hands in the country – those who can be relied upon to monitor unrest, smother excess and apprehend wrongdoers. Their number is thought currently to approach 5,000, having been updated with the fall of Margaret Thatcher, and is listed on a computer somewhere in the bowels of Downing Street. Sir Frank Cooper (Pembroke College, Oxford, Honorary Fellow 1976), a former permanent secretary at both the Northern Ireland Office and the Defence Ministry, said in a 1986 lecture at the London School of Economics: 'All organizations and institutions, whether public or private, commercial or charitable, business or academic, paid or voluntary, have an establishment. It consists of those who, within that organization or institution, are the group which exercise power or influence and, particularly when applied to the public sector, are generally regarded as seeking to resist change.' He was not talking specifically about the G&G. He meant the class of men and, increasingly, women, who seek to ensure that progress conforms to reasonable expectations but does not, in any serious regard, damage the status quo. Within companies, specific regions, or local government, such moral guardians and experts can be drawn from any number or combination of people and forces. At national level, invariably, they are the best-known, most 'responsible' elements in the key sectors of society, and a majority are from Oxbridge.

It is not a universal rule. Not everyone on the G&G is from the Isis or the Cam. To take one example, the Broadcasting Standards Council, adjudicating on matters of taste and decency on radio and television, is chaired by Lady Howe, wife of Sir Geoffrey, the former Foreign Secretary. Lady Howe, unlike her husband (and, indeed, her predecessor, Lord Rees Mogg), is not an Oxbridge product, having taken a B.Sc. from the LSE as recently as 1985. She is, however, with all her outspokenness, something of a rare bird on the quangos front. Strictures from the Broadcasting Complaints

Commission are put by Canon Peter Pilkington (Jesus College, Cambridge); Sir Cecil Clothier (Lincoln College, Oxford) is chairman of the Police Complaints Committee; Andrew Britton (Oriel) is director of the National Institute of Economic and Social Research; the president of the Policy Studies Institute is Sir Charles Carter (St John's, Cambridge); Sir John Banham (Queens' College, Cambridge) looks after the Local Government Commission. Inquiries, another duopolistic bastion, can also be infiltrated. Sir Patrick Sheehy, whose 1993 report on the future of the police caused widespread dismay within the constabulary, made his way in the world entirely without benefit of a university education. All he had to commend him was Ampleforth and the Guards – and his chairmanship of BAT Industries. His report ran into early flak from Paul Condon, commissioner of the Metropolitan Police (St Peter's, Oxford), and other senior officers, and was effectively shelved. The influential Calcutt Inquiry into privacy, intrusion and the press was headed by Sir David Calcutt QC, Master of Magdalene College, Cambridge (and Chancellor of the Church of England's diocese of Gibraltar), who scored a Third in his law tripos while at King's in the early 1950s. The arms to Iraq scandal, involving underhand machinations at both Westminster and Whitehall, was placed firmly – and fatally – in the hands of Lord Justice Scott, who came to England from South Africa to read law at Trinity College, Cambridge, and went on to become a rugby Blue. Sir John May, a Balliol Scholar, was charged with enquiring into the circumstances surrounding the conviction of the Guildford Four. The commission that examined the future of the criminal justice system – and proposed restrictions on our historic right to trial by jury – was led by Lord Runciman of Doxford, the geographical suffix of whose title ought really to have been Doxbridge, since as well as being a Fellow of Trinity College, next the Fens, he is a past Fellow of Nuffield College, 'neath the Spires. Less awesomely, Sir Michael Connell QC, an alumnus of Brasenose, who lists his recreations as steeplechasing, cricket and foxhunting, headed the Jockey Club inquiry into the 1993 Grand National fiasco, in which a number of horses were all but strangled by the starting tape, and placed most of the blame on a junior official. It may not seem entirely fair to the average punter, but Oxford had spoken, and, as always, that was an end to the matter.

The ultimate G&G 'professional' was unquestionably Lord Franks of Headington, whose entire life, crammed with responsibility, centred on Oxford and the world it commanded. Franks ('my life is my university') was variously an undergraduate, Fellow, Praelector and Provost of Queen's College, Provost of Worcester College, an Honorary Fellow of six other colleges (including St Catharine's, Cambridge, and the London Business School), Chancellor of the University of East Anglia and a member of Oxford's Rhodes Trust. In the mid-1960s, he led a famous commission of inquiry into Oxford itself, centred on the need to increase efficiency and democratize intake, and later went on to head a committee reviewing British policy in the lead-up to the Falklands War. Franks was at different times British ambassador to Washington, a director of Lloyds Bank and other finance houses and a leading member of committees scrutinizing official secrets, political memoirs and political honours. He was a trustee of the Pilgrim Trust, the Rockefeller Foundation and the President Kennedy Memorial Committee. He was even for six years chairman of the board of governors of the United Oxford Hospitals. If anyone in Britain could be held to have personified the Establishment, it was Oliver Franks – and the imprint of Oxford ran through him like the name of the town through Blackpool rock.

An Epilogue for Power

Government, the Civil Service, the Foreign Office: these three comprise the executive of the state and its principle agents. Democracy and order depend on how they function. During the Scott Inquiry into the sale of arms-making equipment to Iraq by the Matrix Churchill company prior to the Gulf War, the way in which Britain is routinely deceived by its public servants at the highest level was stripped bare. Ministers and officials were shown again and again to have lied or evaded their responsibilities, putting their own convenience before the truth even at the potential cost of innocent businessmen going to jail.

In outline, the directors of Matrix Churchill, a Coventry engineering firm, had been given permission by the Department of Trade and Industry to export machine tools to Iraq which they knew would be used by Saddam Hussein to make arms and ammunition. A ban on such sales was in force at the time, but the DTI, in concert with the Foreign Office and the Ministry of Defence, secretly amended the terms of the ban so that Matrix Churchill could proceed with what were lucrative orders. When HM Customs, who were not in on the deal, rumbled the sale and prosecuted the company's directors, ministers and senior officials, under the guidance of the Attorney-General, arranged for a series of public immunity certificates (PIIs) to be issued concealing the Government's role in the affair under the guise of national security. Had it not been for a ruling by Mr Justice Smedley (University College London) requiring that the relevant facts be presented to the defence, jail sentences for the directors would almost certainly have followed. As it was, they went free.

Nearly everyone involved in the case, apart from the company directors, is an Oxford graduate. There was William Waldegrave, a former Fellow of All Souls, who while at the Foreign Office agreed that the secret change in the rules should not be disclosed to Parliament. There was Sir Nicholas Lyall (Christ Church), the Attorney-General, who 'instructed' his colleagues to sign the PIIs. There was Douglas Hogg (also a Christ Church product), a second Foreign Office minister, concerned that the matter should not become public lest it cause a 'stink'. There was Sir Robin Butler (University College), the Cabinet Secretary, who told Lord Justice Scott that half-truths were sometimes acceptable in government. There was Alan Clark, yet another Christ Church man, who as minister of state at the DTI first sought the necessary change in government guidelines. Cambridge, very much the minority partner, was represented by Douglas Hurd (Trinity College), the Foreign Secretary, and Kenneth Clarke (Gonville and Caius), Home Secretary at the time, who each went along with the cover-up and, in the case of Clarke, uncomplainingly signed PIIs. And then there were the legions of officials and departmental solicitors, normally 'faceless' but forced on this occasion to reveal how they had conspired to present a united case that would cause the least embarrassment to ministers and Whitehall. They, too, practically to a man, were Oxbridge. The only key government witness not to have attended the Spires and Backs (or indeed any university) was Tristan Garel-Jones, an ex-Foreign Office minister, now retired from politics, who was pressed by officials to sign certificates while his master was out of the country and then was left to carry the can.

What would Benjamin Jowett have thought of these fine, upstanding members of the Oxbridge community? Would he not have been ashamed – and relieved that at least no Balliol men were among them? Fortunately, not all honour was lost. Michael Heseltine, the President of the Board of Trade, often denounced as an unscrupulous opportunist, signed his PIIs only under written protest and noted to the judge that the issue of disclosing or withholding documents vital to the defence was, in his view, entirely a matter for the courts.

Sir Richard Scott, raised in South Africa and sceptical of English Establishment values, is, of course, himself one of the anointed. He is a graduate of Trinity College, Cambridge, while his counsel, Presiley Baxendale QC, entered chambers by way of St Anne's, Oxford. Scott is an outsider; Baxendale is a woman. Neither is typical of their calling. They are, however, along with Heseltine, the only individuals bound up in the Matrix Churchill affair of whom Britain's primary temples of learning can be proud. The story of how the law, too, is an Oxbridge preserve is the next chapter in our roll-call of privilege.

CHAPTER TWELVE

GETTING ON (2)

Inner Temple

IT HAS OFTEN BEEN REMARKED that lawyers move seamlessly from public school to Oxbridge to the Inns of Court. Their lives are passed shuffling from one collection of medieval buildings to the next, bundles of paper under their arms, arguing in public with mirror images of themselves. Their knowledge of lives outside the courtroom is necessarily considerable, but is gained vicariously, as a result of their calling. In the nature of things, most non-legal personnel they come across in the course of their work are either law-breakers or persons *accused* of law-breaking, and the effect, as with journalists, is to turn lawyers in on themselves, trusting mainly each other. Background and familiarity are what count, and the Isis and the Cam provide an abundance of both.

At the very top, the Lord Chancellor is almost *de jure* Oxbridge. F. E. Smith, the first Lord Birkenhead, a famous holder of the office in the inter-war period, was so obsessed with Oxford that in retirement he had his country home remodelled to resemble Wadham, his old college. Others are less extreme. Lord Hailsham, who served for twelve years under Sir Edward Heath and Margaret Thatcher, was a Scholar at Christ Church and president of the Union and is now a distinguished Fellow of All Souls. The present incumbent, Lord Mackay of Clashfern, was, as a Scot, permitted to read for his primary degree at Edinburgh, but quickly took out the necessary insurance for England by becoming a Major Scholar and Senior Scholar in mathematics at Trinity College, Cambridge. It was a period in his life that has stayed with him, and it has done much to open for him the doors of the English Establishment. The

Judicial Appointments Group at the Lord Chancellor's Office, having responsibility for the vetting of future judges and preparing them for office, is (at the time of writing) headed by Robin Holmes, a graduate of Clare College, Cambridge. Of his principal deputies, only Richard Grobler, from Umtali, Zimbabwe, exercising a Colonial Pardon, studied outside the cloisters – at the University of Cape Town.

The two most senior judges in the country are the Lord Chief Justice, Lord Taylor and the Master of the Rolls, Sir Thomas Bingham. Lord Taylor, supreme in the criminal law division, won an exhibition from the Royal Grammar School, Newcastle, to Pembroke College, Cambridge. Sir Thomas went from Sedbergh to Balliol and is now his old college's official Visitor, reponsible, among other things, for the confirmation of its Master. Both his sons also grew up to go to Balliol.

Sir Stephen Brown, president of the Family Division of the Court of Appeal, attended Malvern, then Queens' College, Cambridge. The Vice-Chancellor, Sir Donald Nicholls, moved from Birkenhead School to Liverpool University, but then swiftly secured a Foundation scholarship to Trinity Hall, Cambridge, where he won first-class honours, with distinction, and has since been elected an Honorary Fellow.

The eleven Law Lords, who form what is in effect Britain's Supreme Court, were educated as follows:

Lord Keith of Kinkel: Edinburgh Academy; Magdalen College, Oxford

Lord Templeman: Southall Grammar School; St John's College, Cambridge

Lord Griffiths MC: Charterhouse; St John's College, Cambridge

Lord Ackner: Highgate School, London; Clare College, Cambridge

Lord Goff of Chieveley: Eton; New College, Oxford

Lord Jauncey of Tullichettle (Scot.): Radley; Christ Church, Oxford; University of Glasgow

Lord Lowry (N. I.): Royal Belfast Academical Institution; Jesus College, Cambridge

Lord Browne-Wilkinson: Lancing; Magdalen College, Oxford

Lord Mustill: Oundle; St John's College, Cambridge
Lord Slynn of Hadley: Sandbach School; Goldsmith's College
  London; Trinity College, Cambridge
Lord Woolf: Fettes; University College London

Lord Woolf, out of the eleven, is the only one of the Law Lords
who did not attend an Oxbridge college. At this august level, even
the Scots and Irish fall into line. Almost all are in addition Honorary
Fellows of their old colleges.

The places of education of the twenty-seven Lord Justices of the
Court of Appeal (those contained in the 1993 Bar List) make similar
reading. They are:

Sir Tasker Watkins VC: Pontypridd Grammar School; Welsh
  Regiment RA, Second World War
Sir Francis Purchas: Marlborough; Trinity College, Cambridge
Sir Brian Dillon: Winchester; New College, Oxford
Sir Anthony Lloyd: Eton; Trinity College, Cambridge
Sir Brian Neill: Highgate School, London; Corpus Christi College,
  Oxford
Sir Martin Nourse: Winchester; Corpus Christi College, Cambridge
Sir Iain Glidewell: Bromsgrove School, London; Worcester College,
  Oxford
Sir John Balcombe: Winchester; New College, Oxford
Sir Ralph Gibson: Charterhouse; Brasenose College, Oxford
Sir Patrick Russell: Urmston Grammar School; University of
  Manchester
Dame Elizabeth Butler-Sloss: Wycombe Abbey School; Bar School
Sir Murray Stuart-Smith: Radley; Corpus Christi College,
  Cambridge
Sir Christopher Staughton: Eton; Magdalene College, Cambridge
Sir Michael Mann: Whitgift; King's College London
Sir Donald Farquharson: Royal Commercial Travellers School;
  Keble College, Oxford
Sir Anthony McCowan: Epsom; Brasenose College, Oxford
Sir Roy Beldam: Oundle; Brasenose College, Oxford
Sir Andrew Leggatt: Eton; King's College, Cambridge
Sir Michael Nolan: Ampleforth; Wadham College, Oxford

Sir Richard Scott: Michaelhouse College, Natal; University of Cape Town; Trinity College, Cambridge

Sir John Steyn: Jan van Riebeeck School, Cape Town; University of Stellenbosch; University College, Oxford

Sir Paul Kennedy: Ampleforth; Gonville and Caius College, Cambridge

Sir David Hirst: Eton; Trinity College, Cambridge

Sir Simon Brown: Stowe; Worcester College, Oxford

Sir Anthony Evans RD: Shrewsbury; St John's College, Cambridge

Sir Christopher Rose: Repton; University of Leeds; Wadham College, Oxford

Sir Leonard Hoffman: South African College School, Cape Town; University of Cape Town; Queen's College, Oxford

The gallant Sir Tasker Watkins, a genuine hero from the Second World War, and Dame Elizabeth Butler-Sloss, the solitary woman on the list, are the only two Appeal Court judges not to have read for a degree – though Dame Elizabeth has since managed to become an Honorary Fellow of St Hilda's College, Oxford. Sir Michael Mann is the single representative of capital learning, having studied at King's, London, while batting for the north is Sir Patrick Russell, a graduate of Manchester. Redbricks, it seems, are not the best materials for building a career on the bench. Of the remaining judges on our second list, ten are Cambridge men and thirteen are from Oxford – an Oxbridge total of twenty-three, or 85 per cent. If we add the fact that the current president of the International Court of Justice in The Hague is Sir Robert Jennings, a former law professor at Cambridge, and that two out of the last three UK judges of the court were Cambridge men, we can see how deep, and how wide, the influence runs. Many judges retain links with their old colleges and are not infrequent attenders at dinner. One, Sir Christopher Rose, was even briefly a don. A familiar feature in this context is the recurrence of honorary Oxbridge fellowships. So close is the connection between the judiciary and the ancient universities that the most senior judges are elected Fellows almost as a matter of routine. Many of the Law Lords and Appeal Court judges went to public school, with Eton, Winchester and Radley scoring highly. A surprising number, however, did not, some even going up to Varsity from inner-city grammar schools. The truly surprising feature is probably the strength of the South African connection, based in the main on Rhodes Scholars but also including Sir Richard Scott, a Cambridge man, whose inquiry into the Matrix Churchill affair did so much to destabilize the government of John Major. The lesson here is: if you want to interpret the laws of England at the highest level, the Veldt is as good a place as any from which to start. But do, please, finish on Christ Church Meadow or Parker's Piece.

Lord Taylor, delivering the Dimbleby Lecture in November 1992, showed that he was aware of the need for at least some reform of the Bench:

It is true that, until recently, the Bar and therefore the Bench tended to be drawn from the middle class upwards and may not always have related easily to the problems of the less fortunate. But in the last twenty-five years, our society has become more homogeneous. The legal profession increasingly reflects that trend. I believe judges now do understand the problems of the poor, of the homeless and of the handicapped. More judges now are drawn from modest backgrounds. No longer is the public school-Oxford route *de rigueur*. I am proud to have been a local grammar school boy. But we ought not to overdo this approach to the point of making it a campaign against excellence. We surely want intelligent, well-educated judges. So let us have bright candidates from whatever stratum of society, from good schools of whatever kind and from universities whether they be Oxbridge, Redbrick or what were latterly polytechnics. But it would be foolish slavery to the idea that judges should be representative to draw them otherwise than from those trained in the law, experienced in the courts and best suited for the job.

It is an interesting sequence of points. Lord Taylor boasts of his 'local grammar school' education (without mentioning that it was at one of the best schools in the country), but chooses not to allude to his Cambridge exhibition. Subsequently, while endorsing the call for a wider trawl of academe in the search for a more balanced judiciary, he cautions against going over the top ('we ought not to overdo this approach'). The nation's top law officer is in favour, at best, of incremental reform. He is not ready to rock the boat.

Nor, one suspects, are most of his senior colleagues. The Lord

Chancellor, Lord Mackay, in overall charge of the system, has several times referred to the need to bring more women and ethnic minority candidates into the profession but has not, so far as can be traced, made any specific mention of educational background. He is 'firmly against proposals for a judicial appointments commission' and believes that, in terms of selecting judges, the interests of justice can best be served by the 'progressive introduction of open advertisements for some judicial vacancies', coupled with 'specific competitions' and a review of application forms. So where else can one turn for change? The present chairman of the Law Commission, Mr Justice Brooke QC, charged with keeping our legal system up to date, turns out to be a Balliol classicist, with a double First in Mods and Greats. His predecessor, Mr Justice Gibson, was a Scholar at Worcester College, Oxford. And who is the Director of Public Prosecutions, who took over in 1992 from the disgraced Sir Allan Greene (St Catharine's, Cambridge)? It is, of course, Mrs Barbara Mills QC, a former Crown Court Recorder, one-time Gibbs Scholar at Oxford's Lady Margaret Hall.

Barristers, unsurprisingly, sport pedigrees similar to those of judges. The four Inns of Court in which they function (Inner Temple, Middle Temple, Lincoln's Inn and Gray's Inn) are often compared to Oxbridge colleges, with formal 'hall', libraries, large medieval endowments and government by 'benchers', the equivalent of Fellows, who sit at high table and make the rules. But if there is an undeniable bias towards the Spires and Backs, reform is beginning to make itself felt. The current chairman of the Bar Council (1994) is Robert Seabrook QC, a Zimbabwean, who read for his LL B at University College London. Seabrook may, however, be the exception that proves the rule. A Tory, considered on the reforming right of his profession, he told *The Times* immediately after taking office: 'I love the traditions of the Bar. It is a wonderful profession. It offers a marvellous quality of life in the most agreeable circumstances.' A classics don at Christ Church could not have put it better. Seabrook's predecessor as leader of England's 7,700 barristers – 5,000 more than in 1960 – was John Rowe QC, a Brasenose man and member of the United Oxford and Cambridge University Club. As chief executive, the council chose not a Varsity product, but a leading member of the alternative, military Establishment,

Major-General John Mottram, a one-time member of the Special Boat Squadron, mentioned in despatches, and a former ADC to the Queen. Nothing too daring there: the Services have always been close to Varsity affections, and several retired officers are in fact college bursars, including Lieutenant-Colonel Mike Campbell-Lamerton, the former rugby international, at Balliol, and Commander S. H. Stone, at Exeter, who, having recently changed sex, now prefers to be known as Susan. More significant was the appointment, in March 1993, of Heather Hallett QC to be the Bar's first woman director of public affairs. Everyone, rightly, approved of such a 'progressive' move. But how many will have noted the other crucial fact on Ms Hallett's C.V. beyond her gender – three years at St Hugh's, Oxford?

The old edifice of the law, centred on school, university and chambers, is far from shattered, but is starting to crack. Advocacy in the 1990s is more than ever a target profession for the economically ambitious, and the volume of Redbrick and other lawyers is growing remorselessly. They have much ground to make up. In the 1993 edition of *Hazell's Guide*, nearly three-quarters of the 745 Queen's Counsel still practising at the Bar were from one or other of the ancient universities, with the majority of the rest coming from London or from City law schools. The 1992 intake showed little change on recent past profiles. The Lord Chancellor in that year admitted a total of sixty-nine barristers to the inner circle – a procedure which virtually guarantees successful applicants a lucrative career for the rest of their lives. Of the new Silks, twenty-two came from Oxford – including, as we have seen, the exemplary Ms Presiley Lamorna Baxendale, counsel to the Scott inquiry – and fourteen from Cambridge, giving a total for the Spires and Backs of 52 per cent. A further ten came from the London federation, twelve from provincial universities, including the former polytechnics, three from overseas and two from Scotland. The balance of six qualified at Bar School.

A year later, in 1993, Oxbridge did somewhat less well. Of the seventy QCs gazetted, thirty-one were Oxbridge – sixteen from Oxford and fifteen from Cambridge – giving a Varsity penetration of 45 per cent. London, as ever, came third, with eight appointees, but no fewer than nineteen hailed from provincial universities and the remaining twelve from Bar Schools.

Dr John Baker, Professor of English Legal History at Cambridge since 1988, is not surprised that his former charges do so well. 'I wouldn't like to claim that our system is best. One-to-one supervision, for example, is largely gone now. But what we do have is superb teachers – more than half of them from Cambridge – and extremely good facilities. Still only 50, Baker is a former head of the entire law faculty and its one-time director of studies. Such responsibility, however, could never have been more than temporary. The Cambridge law faculty is Britain's largest – larger even than that of Oxford – having more than 800 undergraduates, 150 graduates studying for an LLM and upwards of 100 engaged in doctoral research. Baker points out that there are some seventy academic members of staff, many of these internationally renowned. 'It is quite common for advocates to the International Court of Justice in The Hague to come back to Cambridge to lecture students on their experience. Judges and leading barristers from London are a commonplace. The quality of teaching really is exceptionally high, and the faculty is thriving. I would expect to see my first Silks within five years.'

Both Oxford and Cambridge, like their main rival, London, are refusing to rest on their legal laurels. Nor are they confining themselves to the traditional studies of Roman and common law. Oxford – whose final year examinations are still known as the Final Honour School of Jurisprudence – has just begun a four-year course in Law with Law Studies in Europe, the third year of which is spent following a prescribed course at an institute in an EC member-state. Cambridge is to expand its existing Centre for European Law, which has links with the University of Poitiers, and offers selected undergraduates the chance to spend an academic year in France. Thus, the two are following a strong modern trend, with a slight divestment in Britain being balanced by acquisitions in the new Europe.

Many Oxford law graduates go on to shine brightly in the legal firmament, as QCs, top solicitors, or judges. Just as many end up as accountants, and a fair proportion as actuaries, politicians, or entertainers. Logical minds, combined with wit and style, are the most portable of all qualifications. Clive Anderson aside, there is less drift in the Other Place. Most Cambridge law graduates, according to Baker, go straight into the profession, where they are often joined by graduates of other faculties who have taken a conversion course. Nine out of ten become solicitors, and the remaining thirty or so each year study for the Bar. 'They nearly all go to London chambers', he says, 'against my advice. They feel it's the right thing to do to be trained by the big City firms.'

Expectations of success are felt equally at Oxford. John Jones, Dean of Balliol, himself a chemist, remarks with evident pride on his college's legal ascendancy. 'Most of the law students I was at Balliol with are now QCs. But you don't even have to have read law to achieve distinction. Sir Thomas Bingham, our college Visitor, studied history [gaining a First in 1957], and look at him now – Master of the Rolls. What is really vital is getting into the right chambers early on and knowing the right people. That is where Balliol men have an obvious advantage.'

Roger Henderson QC, a Recorder of the Crown Court since 1983 and a leading member of the Bar Council, heads a leading set of such London chambers. His own route to the top was classical. He secured a major scholarship from Radley to St Catharine's College, Cambridge, in 1962, and there won first-class honours in law as well as the faculty's Adderley Prize. In 1980, he took silk, and for more than a decade has been a leading counsel and a member of the Senate of the Inns of Court. He is aware of the traditional Oxbridge domination of the Bar but believes it is lessening rapidly. There are currently thirty-seven lawyers in his chambers, including six QCs, and of these nineteen are Oxbridge – fractionally above 50 per cent. However, of the twenty-one juniors taken into pupillage since 1975, only eight are Old Firm (a mere 38.5 per cent), including the three most recent appointees. The University of Buckingham, Britain's first privately funded degree-awarding institute, associated with free market principles, has contributed three of the team in recent years, and two more came from the University of East Anglia. London, surprisingly, scored just one.

This trend, says Henderson, is significant:

We had 400 applicants this year [1993] for three places and shortlisted 40. Of those who were not shortlisted, a dozen had Firsts. They were a mix. We draw no distinction between Oxford and Cambridge and anywhere

else. I don't devalue a provincial degree. I assume that no one is going to
be brighter than an Oxbridge First with a stunning reference from his
tutor. But if a Liverpool graduate applies with a First and his professor
tells me that in his twenty-eight years, or whatever, in the job he has never
come across so brilliant a student, then as far as I am concerned his choice
enters the room as an equal.

It would be unrealistic to assume that an Oxbridge First can easily be
bettered. Oxbridge retains its pre-eminence, with London next, and other
Firsts may not have the same quality. But in the end we select from the
best people, regardless of provenance. What we are looking for is academic
excellence, general clubbability and strong outside interests.

Henderson and his colleagues are in the vanguard of change. Not
every leading Silk will share his admirable sense of equity. That
said, an actual majority of those called to the Bar as juniors in 1993
did not, it is thought, have the prized Oxon. or Cantab. tags to their
degrees, and, logically, this should mean that the QC list for 2012
will prove substantially more varied than the class of '92. By then,
perhaps, just half of the country's Silks will be Oxbridge, a mere
two-thirds of the judiciary and three-quarters of the law lords. We
may even have a Lord Chancellor and a Lord Chief Justice who
studied together at the University of Central Lancashire, in Preston.
Somewhow, though, I doubt it. The base may be narrowing, but it
still rises to a point, and the point is, Oxbridge looks after its own.
As the *Oxford Alternative Handbook*, published by the Students'
Union, puts it: 'Solicitors' firms, in particular, never tire of plying
undergraduates with drinks parties and telling them how wonderful
they are ... Contacts can be made, facilitating any future career in
the subject.'

In fact, solicitors, save for those at the very top, are less dominated
by ancestral voices. Barristers bleat and strut, as though scoring
debating points; solicitors, despite winning the right to appear for
their clients in the Crown and High Courts, mainly advise and
prepare the ground – more counsellors than counsel. Many are
Varsity types, especially in the more prestigious London practices,
but many more are not. Peter Carter-Ruck, for example, possibly
the best-known solicitor in England, now aged 80, went to school in
Oxford, but then took his law exams through the Law Society. The
current (1994) president of the Society, Roger Pannone, is a

product of both the Manchester and London colleges of law; his predecessor, Charles Elly, is a graduate of Hertford College, Oxford; the man before that was Mark Sheldon, an alumnus of Corpus Christi. Over the years, the balance of Oxbridge to Redbrick at the top of the governing body has been about 60/40.

Walter Merrick (Trinity College, Oxford), assistant secretary-general of the Law Society, has no doubt that the English legal profession has long been governed by Oxbridge:

The Bar was always seen as something of a continuation of Oxbridge, with cloisters, libraries and candle-lit dinners. This was its strength. It was also its weakness. From our point of view at the Law Society, it was part of our sense of inferiority that barristers treated solicitors as outsiders. That sense of inferiority has been around a long time. Often, junior barristers would act as tutors at their old colleges, while seniors would pay regular visits, to lecture and attend functions. Most of us were made to feel excluded.

But then, in the 1970s and 1980s, solicitors struck back. The bigger firms, usually in London, began to organize Oxbridge milk rounds, looking for the brighter graduates. Promising young undergraduates were invited to special dinners in Oxford and Cambridge, where they were told of the changing role of the solicitor by young people who had already made a success of it. And it worked. By 1987, there had been a complete turnabout. Now *we* were getting the best people – attracted by glossy promotional material, high starting salaries and, very often, their fees and loans written off. Big firms, like Linklaters & Paines, Slaughter & May and Clifford Chance [the largest of all, with more than 160 partners] offered not just the stability of regular earnings, but full-time training officers. They were hungry for the best talent.

But are Oxbridge people necessarily the best? Not always, it seems. Merrick believes that the wheel of fortune has since turned again.

There has been a tremendous explosion of lawyers over the last ten years [there are now 60,000 solicitors, compared with 40,000 in 1970], and Oxbridge could not possibly provide all the candidates necessary. Increased government spending on legal aid, the need to make sense of EC legislation and GATT regulations, business expansions and bankruptcies, takeovers, mergers, fraud, the housing boom and its aftermath, the general increase in crime: these are all areas in which solicitors are intimately involved. But they often entail specialist skills, and these are what are being encouraged more and more.

In the 1990s, firms are looking for qualities that Oxbridge has not traditionally produced. When I was reading law at Oxford in the 1960s, I was trained to be a High Court judge, but not much else. Today, we are looking for relaxed, computer-literate polyglots, familiar with business and able to communicate easily. We want people who can listen to clients, not just tell them what to do. This has been a big boost for the provincial universities.

Graduates today who enter solicitors' firms as articled clerks will as often as not be specialists in another field entirely, who have then taken a one-year conversion course offered through the College of Law. Oxford and Cambridge, with their vast undergraduate law faculties, do not benefit from this tendency and are in a quandary as a result. 'We are not in the business of conversion courses', one Oxford spokeswoman said. 'Our law undergraduates follow a three-year course designed to give them a deep understanding of the philosophy as well as the practice of law. It is not seen as a vocational qualification.'

This, no doubt, will change. It cannot be long before the existing order gives way to one which, in part at least, offers legal studies in combination with, say, modern languages, business administration, or computer studies. Just as many of the better Oxbridge law graduates are now going into solicitors' firms, including those who hope to end up as advocates, so the ancient universities will have to respond to the fact that in the market-place the law is there to solve problems, not debate them.

This fact noted, and remembering that the ancient universities between them turn out little more than 500 law graduates each year, the fact remains that whole swathes of the present legal Establishment, and their principal assistants, were at university together. As Walter Merrick puts it: 'Oxbridge continues to enjoy a certain cachet, and there will continue to be a large Oxbridge cadre in both branches of the profession for the foreseeable future. Their existing influence will dilute only slowly, and should be clearly visible well into next century.' This seems right. The Redbrick wall is taking shape and should prove sturdy and impressive, but it will never quite eclipse the old grey stones. There are, were and ever shall be, wheels within wheels, Amen.

Next case!

City Slickers

We saw in Chapter 2 how, according to *Graduate Varsity*, the Cambridge newspaper for research students, 48 per cent of graduate recruits to the major City firms are Oxbridge. This high-density absorption starts in the innermost sanctum. Lord Leigh-Pemberton, the embattled former governor of the Bank of England, who achieved his barony soon after presiding over the collapse of sterling in 1992, studied at Trinity College, Oxford, becoming an Honorary Fellow in 1984, and thirteen of his seventeen fellow directors were Oxbridge. His replacement is Eddie George, described in the press as 'underprivileged' but in fact a product of Dulwich College and Emmanuel, Cambridge, and a key mover and shaker for at least a decade in the City. Number two at the Bank is Rupert Pennant-Rea, an Afro-Irish graduate of Peterhouse (Zimbabwe) and Trinity College (Dublin), who while in this country has married into three good English families and is an Oxbridge man in all but fact. The big four clearing banks are run largely by men with Oxon. or Cantab. prominent on their C.V.s (Jeremy Morse, the chairman of Lloyds, even lending his name to television's most celebrated chief inspector), as are the merchant sector and the brokerage houses, in which so much of the prevailing ambience comes, fully formed, from Varsity days. At NatWest, the chairman is Lord Alexander of Weedon, who read English at King's, Cambridge. His chief executive is Derek Wanless, a graduate in law from . . . King's, Cambridge. The Barclays top man is Martin Taylor, who took a Second in Oriental Studies at Balliol and then went on to star as an analyst at the *Financial Times* before joining Courtaulds, where he ended up as chief executive of the demerged Courtaulds Textiles. One of Taylor's last acts at Courtaulds was to appoint Pippa Wicks, aged 30, to be finance director. Ms Wicks has a degree in zoology from Oxford but says she is not afraid to ask 'silly' questions of the financial fauna among whom she now moves. Her pedigree will not have harmed her chances.

The *Sunday Times*, in its 1993 City Top 100, found that forty-one of the leading jobs in the Square Mile were held by Oxbridge graduates, against ten from all other UK universities combined. A top City figure was quoted as saying: 'Recruitment costs money and effort. That is why the "milk round" gets done in Oxford and Cambridge and we all fish in the same pond.' In a single issue of *Varsity* in the autumn of 1993, there were display ads for the following firms, inviting attendance at recruitment drives in Cambridge's major hotels: Union Bank of Switzerland, Banker's Trust, S. G. Warburg, LEK Partnership, Citibank, Coopers & Lybrand, Monitor Company, Unilever, Morgan Stanley and Booze, Allen & Hamilton. In succeeding issues of the paper, Oliver, Wyman & Co., C. S. First Boston, Gemini Consulting, Boston Consulting Group, Smith System Engineering, Ernst & Young, Barclays Bank, the British Merchant Banking Association, L'Oréal, Bain & Co., A. T. Kearney, Proctor & Gamble and Mckinsey were added to the list. Arthur Andersen, one of the world's largest consultancy firms, was meanwhile seeking ten 'outstanding graduates' and seemed to have a shrewd idea where to look for them.

A letter to *The Times* in 1993 dealing with industry's views on the Maastricht treaty was signed by twenty-seven key figures from the world of business. A total of thirteen were Oxbridge – 47 per cent – and the lead signatory, Sir Michael Angus, then president of the Confederation of British Industry, was (like John Birt of the BBC and Charles Pollard, chief constable of Thames Valley Constabulary) a Visiting Fellow of Nuffield. Wherever business turns to conversation and debate, Oxbridge rises like a gasometer from the surrounding landscape. The chairman of the Audit Commission is David Cooksey, late of St Edmund's Hall. The Banking Ombudsman, Laurence Shurman, took his degree just next door, at Magdalen. David Coleridge, the former chairman of Lloyd's of London, the crisis-hit insurance market, was something of an exception, having neglected entirely to continue his education beyond Eton. But his heir, Nicholas, went to Cambridge and Trinity College and was appointed editorial director of Condé Nast in 1989 at the age of just 32. Coleridge's second son, Christopher, opted for

Oxford, where he produced a magazine that briefly attracted the attention of the diarists before disappearing after just one issue. Lloyd's itself meanwhile played safe next time round and placed its future in the hands of David Rowland, another Trinity alumnus, and Robert Hiscox, of nearby Corpus Christi, both of them determined reformers.

In at the Sharp End

Few middle managers are Oxbridge and only a tiny minority of 'sharp end' operators and innovators. For the most part the moving parts of British industry are fashioned not in the cloisters but in the provinces, in Bradford, Newcastle and Manchester, and, even yet, in the University of Life. Here, more rugged types, reminiscent of British inventors and entrepreneurs of past centuries, still survive, even if under constant pressure from banks and overseas competitors. It is the same with new businesses. Factory start-ups are mostly by self-made men (and sometimes women), either with no third-level education or with technical degrees from unfashionable universities like Hull, Loughborough and Stirling. Management buy-outs are similarly the preserve of pushy executives with big ideas – ideas only rarely fashioned on the Isis or the Cam. What happens, however, when small companies become large companies and are then passed on to the next generation is frequently that dynamism is replaced by breeding. Thus, the Pilkingtons, of Pilkington Glass, have become mainstays of Cambridge, usually Trinity or Magdalene, with a subset which prefers Oxford. The Sainsburys reverse this bias: most of the second and third generation of this great retailing family are Oxford products, with a minority that favours Cambridge. The Moores – heirs to the football pools and retailing empire – and the Tetleys play the Oxford card, as did Rocco Forte, chairman of the hotel chain that bears his father's name, while the Cadburys are Cambridge through and through, dividing their allegiance between King's and Trinity. The families concerned are frequently generous benefactors, but the trend itself is of long standing. Brunel, the great engineer, was a classic self-made man, of formidable energy and genius. But once he had established his name, it seemed appropriate that it should be perpetuated at Oxford, which is where his son went, to read classics. It is not a path calculated to breed initiative and hunger. As the late Sir John Moores put it, somewhat ruefully, when considering his progeny's patchy performance in the family business: 'My sons had the disadvantage of a good education.' Few are immune. The English – including assimilated outsiders – consider culture and breeding to be the natural accompaniment to wealth and are embarrassed should they appear *nouveau* in the company of 'old money'. Public school, followed by three years at a decent Oxbridge college, is what is needed, providing heirs to newly established fortunes with the polish and social entrée their rougher-hewn fathers did not have the opportunity to acquire.

Enterprise is not, of course, entirely dead in the Britain of the 1990s. There are still innovators and go-getters, like Richard Branson, owner of the Virgin empire; Alastair Morton, co-chairman of Eurotunnel; Lord Hanson, of Hanson plc; Lord King, president of British Airways; and Sir Clive Sinclair, the inventor and president of British Mensa. Few, however, are from Oxbridge. Of those listed above, only Morton, a graduate of Worcester College, Oxford, had the benefit of a cloistered education, and his bold initiative, the Channel Tunnel, has been dogged by bad luck and broken promises since its inception.

There is a reason for this. The climate of Oxbridge is overwhelmingly reflective and conservative. The ambience has been created, layer upon layer, over the generations. Initiative is, by contrast, dynamic and forward-looking. It is also innate. At our ancient universities, the emphasis is more on the abstract and the pure than on the inspired, and the trained mind – a mind that functions at a high level but along orthodox channels – is seen as Varsity's finest product. To dons, originality is virtually synonymous with wit, and wit is seen as integral to wisdom. Lateral thinking, outside of the science laboratories, is viewed primarily as a useful skill when tackling *The Times* crossword puzzle or a re-draft of, say, the Maastricht Treaty on European Union. The effect of such conditioning is stifling. Look to Oxbridge for gifted advocates, astrophysicists, surgeons and administrators, but do not expect to find many who are willing to risk everything for a new idea. They will battle in the lab or in the courtroom, not in the marketplace. If Branson had gone to a decent college after Stowe, he would probably be a Lloyd's broker by now, or an accountant with Goldman Sachs. But Virgin Airways would probably never have got off the ground.

Median Position

Yes, I admit it. This is personal. It was in 1979, while being interviewed for a job on the international edition of the *Financial Times* by the avuncular, but formidable, J. D. F. Jones, that I first came across the Oxbridge mafia. An Ulsterman, who had not only dropped out of school but also out of two universities, I was bemused not merely to be asked when I had gone up to Oxford but, more importantly, which college I had attended. Other would-be recruits to the Pink'n had the same experience. One applicant, now deputy editor of *Scotland on Sunday*, was greeted with a cheery 'Ah, the Balliol poet!' – a statement based on some amateurish efforts in his college magazine – but the rest faced routine interrogation. Fortunately for them, most were able to come up with the desired response. Others, alas, were not. Of the few (including me) who slipped the net, one, after prodigious effort, went on to be a celebrated media correspondent; another, from Florida, eventually became deputy head of news; a third, educated at the Sorbonne, has ended up as number two to the managing editor. Each has enormous resilience and drive. Others of my intake who *had* gone to Oxbridge went on to prosper on an unexceptional, but effortless, upwards curve. One, after six years abroad, became political correspondent (and is now foreign editor of the *Sunday Telegraph*); a second, returned from Buenos Aires, was appointed labour correspondent; a third was posted to Mexico, then Brussels. These were the exceptions. Most of the Redbrick Reserves survived as office juniors or else found new employment, having been largely ignored. I resigned in 1986 after being denied an interview for a vacancy overseas for which I was particularly suited. The then editor, Sir Geoffrey Owen (Rugby and Balliol), assured me in writing that he looked forward to discussing my application with me but then gave the job directly to a keen young Cambridge Blue without seeing me.

It was not, as we have seen, that *everyone* at the *FT* had been to Oxford or Cambridge. Significantly, many of the sub-editors – troglodytes, unlikely to meet the public – had not. Yet at the executive level, all but a handful were alumni, and so were nearly all of the senior writers. It was something of which I was increasingly aware and which I firmly believe counted against me and my kind. Later, while a feature writer with the *Sunday Telegraph* – a job given to me by the then editor, Peregrine Worsthorne (Peterhouse), effectively out of embarrassment that his deputy, Alexander Chancellor (Trinity Hall), had *twice* failed to show up for lunch with me – I learned from Michael Hart, a Fellow of Exeter College, Oxford, that it was an annual routine for the *FT* to write to Oxbridge tutors asking them to recommend promising undergraduates for jobs at Bracken House. I was to discover, later still, that this was also the practice at *The Times*, whose senior staff see themselves as very much an Oxbridge fellowship and where selected undergraduates are invited to London for the summer vacation to gain 'work experience'. At the *Independent*, the link has been formalized through bursaries – internships – which are offered overwhelmingly to Oxbridge, while on the *Guardian* it is considered virtually *de rigueur* to have been to a decent college. On and on it goes. A friend, who is a senior executive at *The Times* and distressingly Magdalen, at one point seriously explored the possibility of a quarterly dinner at the college for journalistic old boys, from which I would be pointedly excluded. 'Hee, hee', he says. 'It's your own fault for not going to a proper university.' At the *Telegraph*, too, everyone who is anyone is an Oxford or Cambridge man – or woman. Older, non-Oxbridge people are being phased out through compulsory redundancy and 'natural wastage', their shorthand and reporting skills replaced by the diaphanous, if well-bred, talents of the diarist. At the time of writing, only one member of the staff of 'Peterborough', the *Daily Telegraph* gossip column and the paper's habitual means of apprenticing young recruits to the trade, is not Oxbridge, and he is a veteran of many years' experience. Peterborough's editor, the urbane Quentin Letts, though a graduate of Trinity College, Dublin, was up at Cambridge for a year before crossing the pond and, as an Old Etonian, doubtless felt he had little left to prove. When asked once by a journalist with a degree from Newcastle University (ironically the husband of Valerie Elson, admissions officer of Christ Church) if he might work some shifts on the column, Letts's reply was brutally honest: 'I'm afraid', he told the hapless Geordie, 'our preference here is for graduates of Oxbridge' – a judgement subsequently confirmed by Max Hastings, editor of the *Daily Telegraph*.

All the editors of the 'quality' press, save two, are members of this most exclusive brotherhood. From Oxford, we have Peter Stothard of *The Times* (Trinity); Hastings, the *Daily Telegraph* (University); Richard Lambert, the *Financial Times* (Balliol); Peter Preston, *the Guardian* (St John's); Andreas Whittam-Smith, the *Independent* (Keble); and Jonathan Fenby, *the Observer* (New College). With the departure of Donald Trelford (Selwyn) after eighteen years in charge at *the Observer*, Charles Moore, of the *Sunday Telegraph*, a graduate of Trinity College, Cambridge, is the sole extant Cantabrigian. But an army of his fellows is waiting in the wings, and in ten years' time the élitist balance may have been restored. The leading magazines are little different. Bill Emmott, editor of *The Economist*, and Ian Hislop, of *Private Eye*, each passed three years at Magdalen; Dominic Lawson, of *The Spectator*, an ex-*FT* man, followed his father, Nigel, to Christ Church. In the tabloid sector, the influence is understandably less. Nicholas Lloyd, of the *Daily Express* (Teddy Hall), is the only Oxbridge man to edit a so-called 'popular' newspaper, most of his rivals being either Redbrick or academically untutored. Even here, however, there are significant exceptions. What is the first thing that Paul Foot, far-left commentator for many years of the *Daily Mirror*, now back with his cronies on *Private Eye*, tells us in his entry in *Who's Who*, beyond that he was born, is married and has three *s*? Why, that he was editor of *Isis*, 1961, and president of the Oxford Union in the same year. The doughty defender of the downtrodden and one-time editor of the *Socialist Worker* remains distinctly proud of his Varsity achievements. While he may not be representative of his tabloid colleagues, he is far from alone. Every year, trainees and other new staff taken on at the *Sun*, the *Mirror*, the *Daily Star* and the *Express*, include strategically chosen Oxbridge alumni, to be used as social bridges to the Establishment. Within the genuine heavyweights, only Andrew Neil, the outgoing editor of the *Sunday*

Times, and Ian Jack, of the *Independent on Sunday*, come from outside the magic circle, and both, significantly, are Scots. Jack, a gifted writer and commentator, is unique in not having been to university at all (though, tellingly, he can reel off the precise Oxbridge pedigrees of most of his staff), while Neil, now seconded to Fox TV in New York, is a product of the University of Glasgow, a foundation vying in antiquity with both Oxford and Cambridge but regarded by England's snobocracy as provincial and 'Redbrick'. An aggressive meritocrat, who led the Wapping revolution, Neil has refused, famously, to allow his lack of the customary provenance to hinder him and employs journalists of every background, and none. His boss, Rupert Murdoch, known as 'Red' Rupert while at Oxford in the 1950s, has, conversely, seen fit to endow an Oxford professorship in his own name (located at his old college, Worcester) and has even been seen 'feasting' at All Souls.

Another high table trencherman was the late fraudster and newspaper magnate Robert Maxwell, whose clutch of honorary doctorates included awards from the Universities of Moscow, New York and Aberdeen. The Bouncing Ruthenian loved being taken for an intellectual, and it is odd to discover that his most lasting link with domestic academe was the enforced sale of his lease on Headington Hall, his council-owned stately home, to the new Oxford Brooks University, a one-time polytechnic. Somehow, Maxwell, even in the depths of his infamy, neglected to fund an Oxford chair. His preference was for a Balliol fellowship – no doubt using money that was hard-earned in the market-place – and the honour of being the Maxwell Fellow persists to this day. Adam Swift, son of the novelist Margaret Drabble, is the current holder but, understandably, prefers to discuss other matters. The one surprise is that it was never held by any of Maxwell's Oxon. children, each of whom (by coincidence, surely) was admitted to Balliol, a college which prides itself on its high academic standards. Philip, the eldest, opted for physics, in which he secured a second-class degree. His siblings each read history and modern languages, Kevin taking a Second, Ian and Ghislaine mere Thirds. No inherited genius there, then – but no problems getting into Oxford either.

Significantly, the élitist approach to news and comment of the broadsheet press is worse in the 1990s than it was before the coming to power of Margaret Thatcher. Her egalitarianism – such as it was – may have been intended to transform British society and place the emphasis on native talent. In the fourth estate, the response was to ditch meritocracy and fall back on breeding. True, it was mainly the *brighter* specimens who were encouraged, but from the narrowest and most traditional base. Even the *Sunday Times* is now affected and draws most of its graduate trainees from the Spires and Backs. It is as though the destruction of tradition represented by the flight from Fleet Street and the subsequent docklands diaspora had to be compensated for by an atavistic retreat into privilege. As we approach the millennium, Oxbridge, and all it stands for, is as entrenched as ever.

My point, in listing these melancholy developments, is not to dwell on the Oxbridge domination of the press (and me) but to show that my general thesis is borne out by practical observation and experience. Critics of the idea of a 'conspiracy' to preserve Oxbridge's special position need only be referred each day to the contents of our serious newspapers – obsessed as most of them are with what is happening by the Spires and Backs – and to the provenance of those who select what appears in their pages. Editors and leader-writers may rail against the closed shop; in their own lives they wouldn't have it any other way.

So much for the influence of Oxbridge on the press. Let us now retune to radio and television. State broadcasting caught the virus early. This was in spite of the example of Lord Reith, a puritan Scot to the hypocritical core of his being, having no hint of the tyrannical twins in his background. Michael Checkland, the former director-general of the BBC, first learned to push paper at Wadham College, Oxford. His successor, the controversial John Birt, blossomed at nearby St Catherine's and is currently a Visiting Fellow at Nuffield. His director of programmes, Liz Forgan – poached from Channel 4 – took a Second in modern languages at St Hugh's, Oxford. Marmaduke Hussey, the corporation's patrician chairman, began his rise to influence at Trinity College, Oxford, while most of Auntie's senior news and current affairs specialists, like Sir Robin Day (Teddy Hall, Oxford); John Simpson (Magdalene, Cambridge); Jeremy Paxman (St Catharine's Cambridge); Peter Jay (Christ Church, Oxford); Martin Bell (King's, Cambridge); David Dimbleby

(Christ Church, Oxford); Libby Purves (St Anne's, Oxford); Mark 'Sahib' Tully (Trinity Hall, Cambridge); even the late Brian Redhead (Downing, Cambridge) learned their easy familiarity with the corridors of power via the flagstones of the quads and courts. Frank Bough, too, the intermittently disgraced devotee of bondage and illegal substances, is a dyed-in-the-woolly-jumper Merton man, and an Oxford Blue to boot. Robert Harris, the political commentator and author, recalls that in his year as a BBC graduate trainee, fourteen out of fifteen of his colleagues, himself included, were Oxbridge. A graduate of Selwyn College, Cambridge, and a former president of the Cambridge Union, he says he deplored such obvious bias, yet when he held his reception for his book *Fatherland*, it was at the United Oxford and Cambridge Club.

Oxbridge unites the world of politics, public policy and state broadcasting. Marina Warner, the 1994 Reith lecturer on Radio Four, author of a host of respected tomes, mostly of a feminist bent, was one of two girls selected in her final year at St Mary's Convent, Ascot, to apply for Oxford. The other was Sarah Hogg (née Boyd-Carpenter), the Prime Minister's top policy adviser, and wife of Douglas Hogg, the Foreign Office minister. Both were awarded Firsts – Warner in French and Italian, Hogg in PPE. They do not move in the same circles, but, vitally, their circles intersect. Power and influence, the indivisibles of Oxbridge, having once been granted are removed only by scandal.

Over at ITV, the picture is less cosy. Many of the better-known independent broadcasters and producers are certainly from the famous floodplains, but rather more are not, and there is not, yet, any feeling of a Varsity mafia running the show. The reason for this is almost certainly that the independent sector has not so far been institutionalized. It remains fragmented, competitive and dynamic, and many of its top executives came from industry, not programme-making or administration. At network level, Oxbridge begins to emerge. Dawn Airey, for example, a Girton Girl, is Network head of children's and daytime programmes. Companies are merging, and as their powerful bosses enter the rarefied world of the Establishment so, within senior management and to an extent also in the creative sector, the ranks of the Chosen are slowly increasing. Christopher Bland, the multi-millionaire head of LWT until its takeover by Granada, was 'Hastings Exhibitioner' at Queen's College, Oxford, and Melvyn Bragg, one of his leading programme-makers and a major shareholder (as well as being chairman of Border TV), was at Wadham. Other 'insiders' include Alexander Bernstein, chairman of the Granada group, late of St John's, Cambridge, and Ian Ritchie, managing director of Tyne Tees, from Trinity College, Oxford. Against that, Sir Michael Bishop, the chairman of Channel 4, went no further than Mill Hill school, and Greg Dyke, chairman of the ITV Council, is a graduate of York. The latter pair represent a type that, though threatened, remains robust and almost violently competitive. In news, diversity is already under pressure. The chief executive of ITN, recruited from *The Economist* (virtually an Oxford college in absentia) is David Gordon, a PPE graduate from Balliol. Many of ITN's best-known names, including Michael Brunson, Glyn Mathias, Zeinab Badawi and Rob Moore, are Oxbridge mainstream, and there is a growing feeling among reporters in ITN's Gray's Inn Road headquarters that, if you want to get to the top, theirs is the example to follow.

Happily, for the moment, sufficient exceptions remain to suggest that the summit can still be approached from other directions without lethal hazard. Independent radio is similarly open-minded. Richard Eyre, managing director of Capital Radio, read PPE at Brasenose, and after an early start with key Oxbridge employers Proctor & Gamble, and a period in advertising, succeeded his fellow Brasenose graduate, Nigel Walmsley, as the boss of Britain's biggest independent radio station. Walmsley then had other fish to fry, going on triumphantly to take charge of Carlton Television, Capital's TV *alter ego*, and win for it the lucrative franchise formerly held by Thames. On the other hand, Michael Green, Carlton's founding chairman and chief executive (not to be confused with the other Michael Green, controller of Radio Four, late of New College, Oxford), ceased his formal education after Haberdashers' Aske's. The only link here is that Green's wife, the Hon. Janet, is the daughter of Lord Wolfson, who has lent his name to not one but *two* Oxbridge colleges, one in either place. This, though, is to stretch a point. As has been said, the story is far from one-sided. There are many self-made men, and women, in the independent sector, from all universities and none. Even in the key area of regulation (normally an Oxbridge preserve), the Cantabrigian Joce-lyn Stevens may be deputy head of the Independent Television Commission, but in practice much of his time is taken up with running English Heritage and the real power at the ITC lies with its chairman, Sir George Russell, a graduate of Durham and a profes-sional northerner of the best kind. Moral supervision is similarly split. Colin Shaw, late of St Peter's College, Oxford, is director (though not chairman) of the Broadcasting Standards Council, and the Rev. Canon Peter Pilkington, of Jesus, Cambridge, heads the Broadcasting Complaints Commission, but the Radio Authority is in the safe hands of Major-General Peter Baldwin, who began his army career as an enlisted man with the Royal Signals.

The influence of the ancient universities in administration, news-gathering and policy-making at the BBC is well known. What is more surprising, perhaps, is the fact that college tentacles extend even into the nominally more proletarian world of keeping people amused.

BBC light entertainment was not always dominated by Oxbridge. *Round the Horne*, for example, with the likes of Kenneth Horne, Kenneth Williams and Bill Pertwee, was clever, but connected easily with the masses. Ray Galton and Alan Simpson, the most famous comedy writers in the corporation's history, who scripted *Hancock's Half-Hour* and *Steptoe and Son*, left school at 15. But with the coming of 1960s, everything changed. John Cleese, David Frost, Graham Chapman, Eric Idle, Michael Palin, Tim Brooke-Taylor, Bill Oddie and Graeme Garden were Oxbridge to the core. Later versions – Griff Rhys Jones, Mel Smith, Rowan Atkinson, Stephen Fry and Hugh Laurie – were no different, and an entire host of 1990s newcomers has continued the trend without interruption. Their takeover of the laughter business has been startling. Angus Deayton, clever-clogs host of *Have I Got News for You*, a celebrity news quiz on BBC2, is one of the most recent wits from the cloisters to make the big time. A graduate of New College, Oxford, he has Ian Hislop, the editor of *Private Eye*, as one of his two team captains, while a frequent guest is Tony Slattery. Both are fellow Oxonians. Deayton, an ardent linguistics student at university, lists among his Oxford friends, Richard Curtis (*Blackadder, Mr Bean*) Helen Atkinson Wood (*KYTV, Style Trial*), Philip Pope (*Who*

Dares Wins, Spitting Image) and the prolific Geoffrey Perkins. Friends he had yet to make included Rory McGrath, Rhys Jones, Fry and Clive Anderson – all from Cambridge, and Jimmy Mulville, the television impresario, a former president of Footlights. As far as one can tell, about the only comics he knows who don't come from the twin citadels are Paul Merton and Alexei Sayle, each relentlessly clever zealots of the working class. Sayle makes no bones about his early reaction to the Oxbridge network: 'I was twisted with hatred and rage for those people', he recalls, with a smile. Merton, whose Equity name, entertainingly is that of one of Oxford's most ancient colleges, is fully aware of the social forces operating against him and his ilk and once even thought of applying to Cambridge as a mature student. 'It would take three years out of my life', he reckoned, 'but accelerate my career by ten. Today, having at last made it to the top in spite of his integral disadvantage, he has come to accept that he will always be the one on *HIGNFY* asked to make sense of conundrums put to him in Latin or French, while the other side watches, benignly, as he wriggles on the élitist hook they have cast him. 'I don't see myself as any kind of class warrior', he told the *Sunday Times Magazine* in the summer of 1993. 'Of course there is an old boys' network in comedy, like everywhere else. It's no accident that the Oxbridge/Hampstead set get straight into television while performers without those kind of connections are still slogging round the cabaret circuit. But that [the bias] is the only difference.'

The *only* difference! The fact that most of those who achieve early recognition are Oxbridge and most of those who have to work the clubs for years are not! Merton's artfully contrived insouciance is an example either of the built-in cringe of the British working man or else, more probably, of the relief felt by the brighter among them that they have been permitted – against all their expectations – to break wind with their betters.

Rik Mayall, another outsider, told Melvyn Bragg once on *The South Bank Show* that the only way to cope with the Oxbridge crowd was to go for their jugular. 'They feel they don't know about real life.' He arranged a sketch in *The Young Ones* where Scumbag College played Footlights College in *University Challenge*. Stephen Fry and Emma Thompson, as part of the Cambridge side, were assisted shamelessly by the inquisitor, who had been to Cambridge with one of their fathers, while the Scumbags, overcome with frustration, were reduced to physical violence.

What is noticeable is that nearly all of the best-remembered dead comics of television – Marty Feldman, Tony Hancock, Dick Emery, Tommy Cooper, Eric Morecambe, Les Dawson, Benny Hill, Frankie Howerd – received no formal education at all after the age of 15, let alone three years at Oxford or Cambridge. It is also noticeable that the present comedic caperers divide neatly into Varsity chaps, with Oxon. and Cantab. after their names, and blokes who never made it beyond O-levels or GCSE. Hale and Pace, Billy Connolly, Lenny Henry, Vic Reeves, Bob Mortimer: like Merton, Sayle and Mayall, they eschewed university entirely. About the only funny Redbrick comics are Jasper Carrot (Birmingham) and Harry Enfield (York). The rule, which they break, is the same as for class in general: come from the top or the bottom – getting stuck in the middle simply isn't funny.

Female comics, as with female politicians, don't appear to have learned the rules. But there are very few of them, and, with the exception of 15-stone Jo Brand, a former psychiatric nurse, they seem unlikely to tip the balance. Dawn French and Jennifer Saunders are certainly not Oxbridge. Ruby Wax is an American. Although Victoria Wood went to Birmingham, her sometime partner, Julie Walters, never got closer to university than playing the eponymous mature student (the one who noticed that assonance didn't rhyme) in *Educating Rita*.

Oxbridge's triumph is an absurd comic masterpiece. As if to rub it in, even Ben Elton, though without an Oxbridge degree himself, turns out to be the nephew of a former Regius Professor of English Constitutional History at Cambridge. In a profile of two hugely popular neo-punk comics, Rob Newman and David Baddiel, in the 'Night and Day' section of the *Mail on Sunday*, one of the first pieces of information we are given, in a pre-text standfirst, is that the pair – now embarked on solo careers – are 'Cambridge-educated'. Newman did not join Footlights, but wishes he had, the article tells us. Baddiel, having discovered his gift for comedy while still at school, was more clear-sighted: 'the route was clear – Cambridge, Footlights, stand-up comedy.' He got a double first in

English. The routines the two perform on stage are essentially scatological and pornographic (in the nicest possible way) and are unsuitable for television much before midnight. This has not stopped producers from trying to project them, suitably sanitized, into our living-rooms. They may be rude boys, but, by golly, they're clever.

Novel Approach

In the beginning was the word, and the word was culture. Culture is what Oxbridge is supposed to be about. By culture, of course, is meant that broad sweep of artistic and intellectual achievement, and manners, by which each civilization is remembered – and in England there is no doubting the most fecund recorded source.

Chaucer managed to make himself known in the England – indeed, the Europe – of his day without spending three years at either of the two infant universities. Shakespeare, a grammar school boy, preferred the box office to the porter's lodge. (Had he taken a degree the loss to literature might have been considerable: he could have become Lord Chamberlain to Elizabeth, deciding on which plays to put before Her Majesty and which young hopeful should receive the royal favour; he was, after all, a sucker for money and position.) Dickens was another to have missed out, thank God, preferring the Medway and the Swale to the Isis and the Cam, while George Eliot, Jane Austen and the Brontës were simply the wrong sex to apply. In modern times, with the middle classes, and women, having the easy option of Oxbridge to kick-start their careers, few have chosen any other course. Among contemporaries, as far as those who win the major prizes go (e.g. Kingsley and Martin Amis, A. S. Byatt, Brigid Brophy, Craig Raine, V. S. Naipaul, Julian Barnes, Claire Tomalin, Ted Hughes, Margaret Drabble, Frederic Raphael, John Fowles, Anita Brookner, Will Self, Peter Ackroyd, Victoria Glendinning, Richard Adams, James Fenton, Joanna Trollope, John le Carré, Iris Murdoch, Ben Okri), Oxbridge is almost always the connecting thread. One towering aberrant was the late Anthony Burgess, a polyglot novelist and visionary with a gift for music, who read for a degree in his native Manchester and later taught at Birmingham. Though showered with doctorates and decorations at home and abroad, he was not honoured by either of the ancient duo. Seamus Heaney ('Famous Seamus' to his Irish confrères) both studied and taught at Queen's University, Belfast, exercising his Celtic Waiver, but then dramatically entered the mainstream by becoming Professor of Poetry at Oxford and, almost immediately, publishing his own selection of poets from the Spires and Backs. Playwrights, though fractionally less prone to the disease, are far from immune. Dennis Potter, iconoclastic scourge of the Establishment, not only served his time at New College, Oxford; while there he was editor of *Isis* (and *Idol*-ized in its pages) and in 1987 was pleased to accept an honorary fellowship. 'I went to Oxford in a slightly terrorized state', he recalled several years ago. 'It seemed like a gulf, a world apart. I thought it would be full of intellectual giants, and it was fully of sick pygmies.' Exceptions do, of course, exist. Tony Harrison, who went from Leeds Grammar School to Leeds University and later became both a distinguished classicist and an award-winning poet and dramatist, is one, but is so rare as almost to be in need of state protection. Another, Alan Ayckbourn, who did not go to university at all, has ended up, like Heaney, an Oxford professor (this time of contemporary drama), learning at last how to put on an Act. His chief rival for audiences, John Godber, prefers to seethe with resentment at his exclusion. Despite having studied drama at doctoral level for five years at Leeds, he believes that his lack of a 'proper' education is still holding him back. *Teechers*, the second most performed play in Britain in 1991, has never been filmed, and Godber thinks he knows the reason why. 'I'm not in the Oxbridge mafia', he told the *Independent*. 'I didn't go to the right parties . . . I'm not in with the set who decide which films and TV programmes will be made. There's clearly a theatre scene – people who network – and I'm not very good at that.' Different opportunities produce different responses. John Arden – author of *The Business of Good Government*, *Island of the Mighty* and *Whose is the Kingdom?* – wound up at the Edinburgh College of Art, but, prior to his career diagnosing Britain's ills, had taken care to pass three years at King's College, Cambridge. Alan Bennett bumbled brilliantly through an undergraduate career at Exeter College, Oxford, learning most of what he knows about the English class system along the way. (He was to recall years later that when his parents came to visit him from Yorkshire during his first term and he took them for dinner at the Randolph Hotel, he was horrified when his mother turned to the waiter and asked if she could just have a poached egg on toast.) David Hare, an associate director of the National Theatre and one-time resident dramatist at the Royal Court, was a disciple of Jesus, Cambridge, while Michael Robson, an alumnus of Teddy Hall, Oxford, whose TV credits include *Hannay* and *The House of Eliot*, even went so far as to call his daughter Zuleika (Zuleika *Robson* – geddit?). Another Cambridge man, this time from Trinity Hall, is Nicholas Hytner, director, among other memorable productions, of *Miss Saigon, The Madness of George III, Carousel* and *Xerxes* (winner of the *Evening Standard* opera award, 1985). Hytner's dad, the barrister Benet Hytner QC, a former member of the Bar Council, is also a graduate of Trinity Hall. Others have succeeded without help from precedence. David Storey studied art at the Slade, the Oxford of the plastic arts, and the intellectually complex Tom Stoppard and Sir Andrew Lloyd-Webber, the most successful composer of musicals since the genre's American heyday, dispensed altogether with higher education. Stoppard, born of a Czech father, became a journalist at the age of 16 and wrote *Rosencrantz and Guildenstern are Dead* while still in his twenties. He has been awarded seven honorary doctorates, none of them from Oxford or Cambridge. Lloyd-Webber, a product of Westminster School, hit the keys and the boards running, and has never had to look over his shoulder at anyone. Such are the doers.

Among the critics and reviewers, the nonconformist tendency is rare. Scholarly opinions in England only truly count when they are acquired in a decent set of rooms or over a malmsey at High Table. Professor Terry Eagleton, the dissident poststructuralist, with a soft spot for dead ideology, prefers to launch his salvoes against the Establishment from the comfort of St Catherine's College, Oxford. His Marxism, formed under Raymond Williams at Cambridge, is in its detached didacticism no less subversive of the old order than the Stalinism of Anthony Blunt and the rest in the 1930s. Happily, it is equally tolerated, and indeed must be owned as evidence that lost causes, of a kind, will always have a home beneath the Spires. Another doughty opponent of conventional thinking – this time from the right – is Roger Scruton, Professor of Aesthetics at Birkbeck College London, and visiting Professor of Philosophy at Boston. Scruton's acute intellectualism seems to cover the entire field of philosophy and the arts; he is a keen believer in scholastic diversity and sceptical of the Oxbridge duopoly. Nevertheless, it was at Jesus College, Cambridge, that he took his first degree and at austere Peterhouse, where he was a resident Fellow, that he completed his doctorate. Another leading London academic followed a similar path. Karl Miller, Lord Northcliffe Professor of Modern English at UCL and co-editor of the influential *London Review of Books*, read English at Downing College, next the Fens (where he overlapped with Brian Redhead), and began his editing career with a series of *Poetry from Cambridge* in the 1950s. The careers of these dedicated metropolitans also point up another key tendency in academe – the ubiquity of Oxbridge men (rarely women) in Redbrick chairs. Pick up *Who's Who* and leaf through it for as many professors as you can find, and the majority will have taken their own degrees at one or other – sometimes both – of the ancient universities. They may support provincial excellence. One cannot help feeling that they are just waiting for the call to come 'home'. Back among the literati, Auberon Waugh, founder of *The Literary Review*, is a Christ Church man, though not in fact a graduate, and chooses most of his contributors from the quadrangles. The Hon. Toby Young, son of a Labour peer and now chief bottle-washer at the *Modern Review*, took no chances and managed to pack in Brasenose, Oxford, Trinity College, Cambridge *and* Harvard before taking up his pen. Clive James, as prolix a literary commentator as he is a television presenter, graduated originally from Sydney University but, like his illustrious compatriot Germaine Greer, did not feel he had truly arrived until he had taken up his place at Cambridge. At Pembroke, he was to encounter that sternest of critics, F. R. Leavis, who had become 'like an old volcano that goes dead in its central crater but unpredictably blows hot holes through its own sides and obliterates villages which thought themselves safe'. James has not quite followed the Master's lead in this regard. The hot air content of his prose remains, however, decidedly uplifting. Malcolm Bradbury, author of *The History Man* and adapter for television of Tom Sharpe's *Porterhouse Blue* – a flawed comic masterpiece of

Cambridge life – is a notable exception to the rule. He took his first degree at Leicester and now teaches with distinction at the University of East Anglia. If he has had a more profound influence on recent generations of young English writers than almost anyone, it is despite, not because of, the location of his platform. Asked last year to comment on the impressive publishing power of his alumni, Bradbury was entirely unabashed: he was competing, he said, with an already established mafia – 'the Oxbridge mafia'.

This is the point. Alternatives can be found. They are, indeed, readily available. But literature and learning have in this country become so inextricably bound to an Oxbridge education that the obvious danger – of a moribund, tunnel-visioned culture – is visible only to the few. Oxbridge 'usually' produces clever, civilized people, but they have an imprimatur on them. They are monocultural. They speak with the same voice. Even when they have different views of the world – as, for example, with Martin Amis and Salman Rushdie – one knows instinctively that, where possible, they go to the same parties, have the same range of publishers and editors and regard each other as a mutually intelligible fraternity.

Publishing, in general, reinforces the stereotype. Efforts have been made in recent years to free up the rusty bolts securing the world of books to the ivory towers, and many executives, particularly in companies set up in the Thatcherite '80s, are from other universities or none. Yet the bolts do not give easily. Not only do the two universities run their own, immensely successful, publishing houses (the Oxford University Press, in particular, being one of the great imprints of the world), they provide the opposition with an influential minority of their senior staff. Harriet Spicer, managing director of Virago, was introduced into publishing by Carmen Callil, who had first met her through Graham Wimeru – later of Quartet Books – a mutual friend from Oxford. 'Does anybody want to go and see this girl from St Anne's?' another undergraduate had asked, and Wimeru (with Spicer subsequently in tow) had said, 'All right.' At first it was straight boy meets girl. Only later did it become networking. 'It always struck me as ironic', Spicer was later to recall, 'that my career as a feminist publisher should have started with a blind date.' Oxford, as we have seen, impels its children forward with greater force than anywhere else – save, naturally,

Cambridge. In a letter to *The Times* in the autumn of 1993, lamenting the continuing *fatwah* on Salman Rushdie, seven of the sixteen signatories were Oxbridge, two were from the services, one from London, one from Bristol and one, Paul Scherer, of Transworld Publishers, abandoned his education after Stonyhurst. If we assume that just two of the five unknowns – i.e. those not listed in either *Who's Who* or *Debrett's People of Today* – i.e. were Oxbridge, then an actual majority of those expressing their public concern for a Cambridge man in trouble were from the ancient duo, much as they would have been thirty or even fifty, years ago. Today, élitism persists in publishing, but is being challenged by technocrats, like Michael O'Mara and Eddie Bell. The catchment area is broadening. Refuseniks from Bristol and York are insisting that their birthing places on the Severn and the Ouse be added swiftly to those of the Isis and the Cam, and others from Essex and Exeter are queuing for recognition. Change, though, has been neither swift nor, thus far, wholly convincing. The president of the Publishers Association is Sir Roger Elliott, Wykeham Professor of Physics at Oxford (club: United Oxford and Cambridge); the chief executive is Clive Bradley, late of Clare College, Cambridge.

Acting is slightly different. Thespians are frequently uneducated, save at drama school, where they are taught to understand texts, pull faces and breathe properly. Sir Ian McKellen (St Catharine's, Cambridge, Honorary Fellow 1982) is something of an exception, as was Richard Burton before him. Others are Nigel Davenport (Trinity College, Oxford), the president – what else? – of British Actors Equity, Davenport's ex-wife, Maria Aitken (St Anne's), and Miriam Margolyes (Newnham).

An Oxford actor with a steady reputation these days for playing 'typical' Englishmen is Hugh Grant, star of *Four Weddings and a Funeral*, who began his career with *Privilege*, an undergraduate squib, about a group of Oxonian toffs, and then went on, via *Oxford Blues*, to star in *Maurice*, a version of E. M. Forster's celebrated drama of homosexuality at Cambridge. By the time he got to play a repressed upper-class cuckold in Roman Polanski's erotic thriller *Bitter Moon*, Oxbridge was no longer up there in the credits, but the message had surely come through loud and clear.

Contemporary Oxbridge drama, unlike student theatre elsewhere, has always been treated seriously by the media. Oxford and Cambridge troupes expect to go on tour and to pick up awards at festivals. Directors and others from London attend their principal productions, which are often highlighted in the press, and are entertained afterwards to champagne and heady parades of youthful ambition. In 1994, when *Accidental Colour*, an amateur effort on the theme (appropriately enough) of incest, was staged by Varsity players in the Old Fire Station theatre in Oxford, *The Times*, among others, noted that the author was Rowlan Joffé, a second-year undergraduate and son of the film director, Roland Joffé, and that its co-star was Brasenose girl Claudia Solti, daughter of Sir Georg, the eminent conductor. Oxford (like Cambridge) remains what it has always been – not just an exceptional university, but a natural home for the children of those who have established national reputations, and a launch-pad for their careers.

Though only a minority of famous actors were formally schooled beyond the age of 18, the most cursory examination of directors' backgrounds usually reveals an Oxbridge umbilical. Jonathan Miller, former artistic director of the Old Vic, before that associate director of the National, now a tireless international producer-director, first trod the boards from his base at St John's, Cambridge, where he helped inspire *Beyond the Fringe*. Ned Sherrin, author of innumerable stage reviews and one of London's most enthusiastic producer-directors, first rehearsed his gay abandon at Exeter College, Oxford. Asked about the recent restoration in *Isis* of the Oxford 'Idol' – axed in 1961 by David Dimbleby – Sherrin was, as ever, found for words. 'I think it is a very good idea that they are bringing it back. After all, if you can't have a bit of élitism at Oxford, where can you?' Sir Peter Hall, English drama's grand panjandrum, with an entry in *Who's Who* only marginally shorter than Barbara Cartland's, read English at St Catharine's, Cambridge at the end of the 1940s (to be followed there in due course by his son) and remembers how he was expected to conform to established norms of behaviour. Trevor Nunn, freewheeling director emeritus of the RSC, studied just down the road at Downing a decade later, and now lives with the actress Imogen Stubbs, a former Scholar and graduate first-class of Exeter College, Oxford. Miss Stubbs, who trained as a classical actress, was not too proud to wear a revealing micro-skirt for the first episode of ITV's detective series *Anna Lee*, but covered up thereafter. When the ratings did not improve, one admiring critic was moved to comment that she was clearly 'too intelligent' to do justice to a bad script. Three years after Nunn went up to Peterhouse, Richard Eyre, destined to be artistic director at the National, chose the same austere college. Hall, Nunn and Eyre will have been inspirations to that extraordinary Cambridge set of the late 1970s, centred on Martin Bergman, Stephen Fry and Emma Thompson, which has done so much to reintroduce the cult of the British screen act-or. This undeniably talented group, which has been contemplating its collective navel ever since graduation while simultaneously winning awards and banking huge wads of cash, is best seen in *Peter's Friends*, the Kenneth Branagh movie from 1992 about a Cambridge coterie that meets up again after ten years and bursts into tears in consideration of its genius. All the cast had to do, one imagines, was replay conversations from one of their regular weekends at the Fry house in Norfolk, then add a bit of sexual spice, with just the merest hint of personal failure and *Angst* for the sake of artistic integrity. Theirs is self-indulgence on a scale that only genuine 'luvvies' could properly appreciate.

Other stage-struck Cantabrigians include Declan Donnellan, an associate director at the National and winner of several major awards, including the Olivier Prize, and his companion, theatre designer Nick Ormerod, both of Queens' College. Donnellan takes up the story in an interview in the *Independent on Sunday*. 'It was 1972. I had just gone up to Cambridge and wanted to do lots of theatre. Nick and I were introduced at a rehearsal for a European tour of *Macbeth*. Britain was going into the Common Market, and so all these anorak'd, long-haired students were going to be wined and dined by European ambassadors. I found the whole thing unbearably glamorous.'

Would it have been the same if they had gone to Bradford? One thinks not. No matter. Lodged together at Queens', ignoring what Ormerod describes as the 'incestuous, bitchy, highly competitive nature of college theatre', the two quickly became inseparable. It took a while for them to achieve the success they now enjoy. They had wanted to be lawyers at first and only discovered their true vocation later. But Cambridge, without their realizing it, had already established the connections and pointed the way.

One of the latest exponents of the Oxbridge ethic in the theatre is Sam Mendes, artistic director of the fashionable Donmar Warehouse Theatre, in London. Still only 28, Mendes went straight from Peterhouse, Cambridge, where he was a scholar, to be assistant director of the Chichester Festival Theatre, and soon after began directing for, among others, the National and the RSC. He won the Most Promising Newcomer award in 1989 and has been hailed, inevitably, as the new Peter Hall. His talent speaks for itself. One wonders, however, how much more difficult he would have found it to make his mark if Cambridge had not given him an early lift-off. His career, if not his personality and character, is reminiscent of that of Mike Clode, from the pages of Frederic Raphael's 1976 novel, *The Glittering Prizes*. Clode is the massively ambitious senior producer of the Cambridge Amateur Dramatic Club, whose 'golden age' in charge of student theatre comes to an end with a triumphant *Much Ado About Nothing* before Clode himself moves on, seamlessly, to stake his claim in London's West End, and thence to Hollywood. Whether Mendes will end up in Los Angeles, staging musicals, remains to be seen – his recent revival of *Cabaret* certainly suggests interest in the genre – but back at Varsity his wide-eyed successors must sense a bright new star in the firmament. Later ADC luminaries, Linnet Taylor, a fellow Peterhouse undergraduate, and Stephen Brown, from Jesus, display no signs of doubt in respect of their calling. 'We're always looking for new people keen to try any aspect of theatre work – directing, producing, writing, acting, lighting, sound and design', they reveal in the 1994 student handbook. 'And don't worry if you're not experienced. We run workshops in all aspects of the theatre.'

Film is seen as *the* art form of the twentieth century, and the most democratic. In Britain, élitism still manages to make its mark on the celluloid. Michael Winner, auteur behind the tasteful *Death Wish* series and *Dirty Weekend*, as vulgar as a boxful of monkeys, attended Downing College, Cambridge; Ken Loach, ascetic darling of the left, steeped in muck and brass bands, imbued his radicalism at St Peter's, Oxford; Lindsay Anderson, director, among other films, of *This Sporting Life* and *O Lucky Man*, is a Wadham man. Peter Greenaway, on the other hand, outwardly more Oxbridge than either of them, was originally a painter, trained at Walthamstow College of Art. Lord Attenborough is an exception. After grammar school in Leicester, young Dickie won a place at RADA, where he was the Leverhulme Scholar and Bancroft medallist. He was thus, in his choice of finishing school, quite unlike his brother, David, of *Life on Earth* fame, who opted for Clare College, Cambridge, and has been an Honorary Fellow since 1980. Alan Parker, director of *Midnight Express* and *Mississippi Burning*, switched to film from advertising, where he was a copywriter, and is entirely his own creation. Richard Eyre, the theatre director, equally at home in film, with successes like *The Ploughman's Lunch* and *Loose Connections* to his credit, is, however, as we have seen, a Cambridge man, as is Stephen Abbot, of Corpus Christi, one of the original driving forces behind Hand Made Films and later executive producer of *A Fish Called Wanda*. The best-known critics are divided almost equally. Derek Malcolm, of *The Guardian*, and Sheridan Morley, of everywhere else, both went to Merton College, Oxford, but the *Daily Telegraph* man, Hugo Davenport (son of Nigel), took the then trendy option of the University of Sussex ('Balliol on Sea'), while Alexander Walker, of *the Standard*, a heavily disguised Ulsterman, exercised his Prod's Pardon and went to Queen's University, Belfast. Dilys Powell, the profession's unquestioned doyenne, is, naturally, a Somerville girl, and a bluestocking to boot. By contrast, Barry Norman, the BBC's resident guru, rose to celebrity via a redundancy notice from the entertainments editor of the *Daily Mail*.

Arts administration – the apotheosis of the theory that those who can, do and those who can't, leach – is largely an Oxbridge preserve. Lord Gowrie, who took a Second in English at Balliol in 1962, is now chairman of the Arts Council, having previously been both Arts Minister and chairman of Sotheby's. Lord Palumbo, his predecessor, seemingly determined to rip the heart out of the City of London and replace it with the Towering Infernal, learned the art of shifting his ground at Worcester College, Oxford. All but a tiny few of his sixteen fellow councillors, who include one professor emeritus and one former president of the Oxford Union, were similarly privileged, and of those who were not, two were Scots and one has since become a member of the University of Cambridge Careers Syndicate.

Other arts bodies follow the same pattern. At the Royal Opera, Jeremy Isaacs (Merton College, Oxford) is general director and Angus Stirling (Trinity College, Cambridge) is chairman of the board. Neil MacGregor (New College, Oxford) is director of the National Gallery, under the chairmanship of Lord Rothschild (Trinity College, Cambridge). The director of the Tate is Nicholas Serota (Christ's, Cambridge). *His* chairman is Dennis Stevenson (King's, Cambridge). William Oddy, of New College, is Keeper of Conservation at the British Museum. The pattern, though not entirely unbroken, continues through the ranks. At the English National Opera, there was a slight frisson of controversy in 1993 when David Mellor, a genuine opera lover as well as an adulterer, was asked to join the board. But it is difficult to see why. Mellor, as we know, is a Cambridge man, from Christ's, and of his seventeen new colleagues five are fellow Cantabrigians and five, at least, are from Oxford. The chairman, the Earl of Harewood, was up at King's, Cambridge after the war and became an Honorary Fellow in 1984.

English letters, English literature, English learning: without Oxbridge, where would they be? One answer is, surely, a little less well bred, but none the worse for it. If Shakespeare could hack it without a proper college background, if Wordsworth preferred the Lakes to Parker's Piece, if Dickens could highlight injustice without benefit of Mods and Greats, and if George Eliot and the Brontës could summon up genius from their imagination alone, then so can anyone with talent and resolve. The ancient universities, which can so readily appear as temples of thought, can also be viewed in another light – as preservation halls. Literary and philosophical enquiry in this country, if it remains trapped in these twilit cloisters, could end up the Dixieland jazz of world culture.

CHAPTER THIRTEEN

GETTING ON (3)

Holy Trinity

IT IS SMALL WONDER THAT a majority of colleges at Oxford and Cambridge are named after major biblical personalities. All the older foundations were specifically religious in character and function, and even after the Enlightenment retained something of the atmosphere of the seminary. Bishops and other church leaders are generated here as though by immaculate conception, with dons as the subsequent midwives of the Faith. Oxbridge is where the English Church acquires its peculiar ambience, linked closely to the panoply of the state, and where it learns to associate Christianity with good table manners and the exercise of power.

Moses would have made a first-class Dean of Christ Church; Luke could have tried for a medical fellowship at Caius; Job might have wrestled with fund-raising at Wolfson, Churchill, or New Hall, which need money as much as anywhere else but can gain cult status only with age. Both Herod and Pilate, for very different reasons, would have been Oxbridge men, as would Paul. The great apostle's proud declaration of his Roman citizenship when up against it with hostile forces compares well with the often heard, 'Actually, I was at Balliol.' Peter would have been a grammar school rugger Blue, with a respectable second in land husbandry from Selwyn or Teddy Hall, ripe for estate management or mass salvation. Christ, however, would have had problems. He comes across much more as a typical Redbrick scholar – well-intentioned, meritocratic, lacking in 'side' – and could well have found the innate snobbery intolerable. In his favour, from an Oxbridge perspective, is his impeccable, *sui generis* pedigree, and this, coupled with a suitable Exhibition, possibly at one of the less fashionable colleges, like Keble or Homerton, might just have tipped the balance.

The sad – one might say, the *pathetic* – fallacy about this cosy association between the secular and academic cloisters is that Oxbridge this century has failed utterly to deliver the goods. Once the bedrock of national stability and self-esteem, a convenient bridge between the gentry and the rest, the modern C. of E. is in unstoppable decline, desperate for consensus, robbed of its authority and passion. Bishops and other leading clerics, self-obsessed to their mitre-tips, bicker endlessly about everything. The chronic rancour over women's ordination; the quasi-humanist revelations of the former Bishop of Durham; the unholy wrangle between Lord Runcie and Terry Waite over who was responsible for the hostages fiasco; the sadly gay pursuit of a novice monk by the ex-Bishop of Gloucester, Peter Ball (ironically from Queens' College, Cambridge); the running feud over power and money between dean and canons that turned Lincoln Cathedral into a Trollopian farce: these are what the Church of England has become in the public mind. Radicals, meanwhile, are heavily engaged in a febrile attempt at liberation theology – the notion that if you can demonstrate your ideological *Angst* in a 'caring and practical' way, the punters will think it has something to do with God.

In all this, Oxbridge is mightily engaged. Bishops, deans and other senior clergy are recruited practically to a man (no women thus far) from the ranks of the Oxbridge elect. Very few are state school and Redbrick. It may be thought significant that the current Archbishop of Canterbury, Dr George Carey, is not Oxbridge, having obtained his first and subsequent degrees in London. But it is also significant that, in spite of his position, he is not universally regarded as part of the Church's inner council. Rather, he is seen by many as a simple-minded evangelical, more drawn to the tambourine than the Prayer Book – a product of the Low Church tradition, whose practices are anathema to the rival Anglo-Catholic Establishment. His principal opponent, Dr John Habgood, the Archbishop of York, was at Eton and King's, Cambridge, and is much more typical, as was Carey's predecessor, Dr Robert Runcie (Brasenose), and the Archbishop before that, Dr Donald Coggan (St John's, Cambridge). Habgood is already regarded by many as the true leader of responsible Church opinion. With women's ordination now a reality, alternative leaders will be available in dioceses up and down the land. The new Bishop of London, Dr David Hope, is a principal focus for this parallel hierarchy. Though absent-minded enough to obtain his primary degree at Nottingham, he soon made up for the lapse by taking a D.Phil. at Oxford's Linacre College and going on to be principal of St Stephen's House, reaction's inner sanctum. The recently retired Bishop of Durham, Dr David Jenkins, for many years number four in the hierarchy, followed a less circuitous route. Yet another alternative pole – this time for the agnostic tendency – Jenkins may have had doubts about some of the more traditional tenets of the faith but had no qualms whatever about which route to choose in the profession of his career. He took his first degree at Queen's College, Oxford, and remained to become first a lecturer, then a Fellow, chaplain and Praelector in Theology. This is more like it. The Church incarnate. You don't get many Oxford praelectors to the pound, not even in the rarefied cloisters of St Cuthbert's Cathedral.

Many other bishops follow the same pattern – almost as if it were *de rigueur* for intending prelates to be exposed to Oxbridge for as many years as possible as an act of purification. Look, for example, at the career of Eric Kemp, the Lord Bishop of Chichester. Having won his way from Brigg Grammar School, Lincolnshire, to Exeter College, Oxford, he took orders at nearby St Stephen's House and then spent just two years as a curate in Southampton before becoming librarian of Pusey House, chaplain of Christ Church, acting Fellow at St John's, Fellow, chaplain and lecturer back at Exeter, Dean of Worcester, examining chaplain to various dioceses, Proctor in Convocation to the University of Oxford, the Bishop of Oxford's Commissary for Religious Communities, chaplain to the Queen, etc., etc., until, finally, he was elevated to the purple in Chichester. An orthodox Anglo-Catholic academic, who, unusually for a practical prelate, prefers that his priests should believe in the divinity of Christ, he sounds more like a communist apparatchik or a minor character from *The Canterbury Tales* than a functioning modern pastor. What were those titles again? Bishop's Commissary. Shades of the Inquisition! Proctor in Convocation. For God's sake! And then they wonder why the pews are emptying.

The Church, for its sins, is one of the purest exponents of the Oxbridge ethic: of the two archbishops and 40 diocesan bishops currently serving in England, 36 took their first degrees at Oxford or Cambridge. Only Robert Williamson, the highly articulate Bishop of Southwark, born in Belfast, did not attend university. Barry Rogerson the Bishop of Bristol, with a BA in theology from Leeds, is the purest Redbrick representative. William Bentley, Bishop of Gloucester, was another Leeds man, but went on to take holy orders at Westcott House, Cambridge, while John Waine, Bishop of Chelmsford, followed his time at Manchester, with a period at Cambridge's Ridley Hall.

Right and left, high and low, rich and 'comfortable', the men in the back-to-front collars are united in their devotion to the Spires and Backs. William Westwood, the Bishop of Peterborough (in the Lords since 1984) may think of himself as a champion of Thatcherite meritocracy, housed in a medieval palace because he, unlike his rivals, had shown he had the Right Stuff; educationally he is as orthodox as they come. He read for his first degree at Emmanuel, Cambridge (becoming an Honorary Fellow in 1989) and took orders at nearby Westcott House, reserved exclusively for Oxbridge ordinands. Next in line for the Lords, once a vacancy falls due, is the Rt Rev. Peter John Nott, Bishop of Norwich, another Cambridge man and former chaplain of both Fitzwilliam and New Hall. Even the 'radicals' are, to misquote Sam Goldwyn, excluded in: last summer, Lord and Lady Longford travelled to Oxford to attend an Encaenia for, among others, Archbishop Trevor Huddleston, the veteran anti-apartheid campaigner and an alumnus of Christ Church. Lady Longford recalled afterwards how Huddleston had received his honorary doctorate of divinity from the Chancellor, Lord Jenkins, 'who looked like an infinitely benign Buddha', before giving a clenched fist salute. Clearly, she ventured, Oxford was no longer a 'home for lost causes'.

Roman Catholicism has had a chequered history in its ancient bastions. 'There is something in the Oxford air', wrote J. A. Froude in 1870, 'mysteriously conducive to Popish error.' Cardinal Newman and the Oxford Movement saw things rather differently, putting paid to centuries of prejudice, and with the subsequent abolition of the religious test, in 1871, a major comeback was staged. Generally speaking, candidates for mainline positions within the revived hierarchy joined their Anglican brethren in attendance at secular colleges. Specialists, however, looked to their own institutions. St Benet's Hall, tucked in behind St Giles, at the junction with Woodstock Road, was constructed in 1897 and has since become Britain's élite Benedictine college. Its greatest alumnus to date is His Eminence Cardinal Basil Hume, a former Abbot of Ampleforth who, despite his French blood, is the first truly English Prince of the Church for a century. Dom Henry Wansbrough, the present Master of St Benet's, says the college, with around forty undergraduates, was set up because Ampleforth towards the end of the Victorian age had few teachers with degrees and needed a place in which monks could matriculate and pursue their studies in a properly religious environment. Oxford, we are assured, was simply the starting point – as distinct from, say, Walsall – and Dom Henry is insistent that there is no question of genuflecting before the altar of English privilege. 'In fact', he says, apparently dealing with an alternative church leadership to which only he is privy, 'bishops with Oxbridge degrees are pretty rare, and it is not a normal practice for seminarians to be directed towards either of the two universities. Our religious orders, with their educational role, have, it is true, a greater bias in this direction – the Master-General of the Dominicans, Timothy Radcliffe, for example, is an Oxford man and taught at Blackfriars [College] – but overall the English College in Rome still has a greater sway.' Father Henry, a diminutive figure in black, very gentle and quiet-spoken, who has been known to mow the college lawns himself as he contemplates God's grace, or grass, teaches New Testament studies in the theology faculty and is on the university panel for select preachers.

He is not, let it be said, by any means an isolated figure. There are homes in Oxford for the Franciscans and the Dominicans, and the Society of Jesus is ensconced in Campion Hall, designed for the purpose by Sir Edwin Lutyens and opened in 1896, the year before St Benet's. At Cambridge, too, there is growing representation. St Edmund's College, founded in 1896 by Henry FitzAlan-Howard, fifteenth Duke of Norfolk, is a leading seminary, which also takes in a limited number of laypeople. Originally situated in the Catholic Presbytery in Hills Road but long since transferred to its present site on Mount Pleasant, it became a graduate college in 1965, and ten years later was accepted as a full constituent college of the university. It had arrived. Integration between Catholics and the rest is now generally complete in both universities, and with it has come an inevitable subscription to the principles of Oxbridgean supremacy. The former headmaster of Downside and national chaplain to the Catholic Students Council (author of *Dear Church. What's the Point?*), Dom Raphael Appleby, read for his MA at Christ's College, Cambridge. Though Derek Warlock, the Archbishop of Liverpool, managed to summon up his reverence without benefit of a Varsity connection, both Cardinal Hume's deputy, Maurice Noël Léon Couve de Murville, Archbishop of Birmingham, and Michael Bowen, the Metropolitan and Archbishop of Southwark, took the cloth after Downside and Trinity College, Cambridge, with the former even co-authoring a book, *Catholic Cambridge*, highlighting the university's distinguished Roman past. Among existing prelates, a majority are either Irish or graduates of Rome, but the innermost clique is pre-eminently Oxbridge. Gerald Thomas, one of several auxiliary bishops of Westminster, entrusted with the pastoral care of West London, graduated from Christ's College, Cambridge. A fellow student there was David Konstant, now the Bishop of Leeds. One of the English hierarchy's key media figures is surely a classic case. Crispian Hollis, the Bishop of Portsmouth, went straight from Stonyhurst to Balliol (and later to the English College in Rome and national service in the Somerset Light Infantry). For eleven years, he was Roman Catholic chaplain to Oxford and then went on to be deputy head of religious broadcasting at the BBC. Is he the one to watch when Basil Hume finally hangs up his red hat? Watch this space – or, more probably, the purple prose of the *Catholic Herald*, whose editor, Christina Odone, a graduate of Worcester College, Oxford, is an ex-Cathedra model of new Catholic orthodoxy.

It may be thought significant that in a review in *Oxford Today* of Walter Drumm's book *The Old Palace: The Catholic Chaplaincy at Oxford* (Veritas Publications, Dublin) Charis Gray observes that 'this history of "chaplaincraft" in Oxford is also the history of Catholicism in Britain since the emancipation'. There is some truth in the claim. It is a bold one, even so.

Most of the century's lay Catholic luminaries are unmistakably of the company. Theirs is a drum-roll of academic privilege: not only Lord St John of Fawsley, but Evelyn Waugh (Hertford College), his son, Auberon (Christ Church), Graham Greene (Balliol), Lord Longford (New College), Lord Rees-Mogg (Balliol), the Duke of Norfolk (Christ Church), David Bell, chief executive of the *Financial Times* (Trinity Hall), Chris Patten, governor of Hong Kong (Balliol), Paul Johnson, historian and journalist (Magdalen). If this is diversity, what could the Catholics do with unity?

Not for nothing are true Nonconformists felt by their betters to belong to lower orders. Many, if not most, Bible-thumpers positively eschew the Oxbridge mafia. Yet it was at Oxford that John Wesley and his brother Charles developed Methodism, which for some years after was to remain a despised sect in the city, openly derided by dons and others of higher degree. Dr Johnson, massively pompous about his university status, was among those who, upon hearing that six Wesleyans had been sent down from Oxford in 1768, prounounced it entirely fitting. 'A cow is a very good animal in a field', he wrote, 'but we turn her out of a garden.' Well, for Wesleyans at Oxford, as for opponents of women's ordination, times change. Oxbridge Methodists abound in the 1990s. Manchester College, Oxford, established as early as 1786 and exclusively for mature students, has as its Principal the Rev. Dr Ralph Waller, a leading Methodist theologian. Also in Oxford, and affiliated to the university, is Westminster College, a lay-training institute, the communications unit of which is headed by the Rev. Dr Colin Morris, an Oxford graduate who was once Select Preacher at Cambridge and went on to be head of Religious Programmes at the BBC and controller of BBC Northern Ireland. In the Other Place, Wesley House, probably the Methodists' leading theological foundation, is part of the Cambridge University Federation, and its students are members of the university and read for a degree. Like Westminster College and Cheshunt College, its Presbyterian and Congregational equivalents, Wesley, founded in 1921, has proved a fecund source of leadership, producing, among others, the 1993 president of the Methodist Conference, the Rev. Catherine Richardson – the first woman to hold the office in more than two hundred years – and her successor, the Rev. Brian Beck.

Who today is Britain's best-known, and best-loved, Methodist?

Why, Lord Soper, of St Catharine's, Cambridge. Lord Soper is a radical and a pacifist, still preaching to the unconverted each Sunday from Speakers' Corner, in Hyde Park. Yet in 1966 he became a Fellow of his old college, and later he accepted an honorary Cambridge DD. He, too, regardless of his protestations, is an Oxbridge freemason.

Jewish Britons are no different. If anything, they are the most élitist of all. Sir Isaac Wolfson, the life president of Great Universal Stores, though not a graduate himself, was so impressed with the ancient universities that he founded his own college, Wolfson College, in Oxford, for graduate scientists and, later, endowed the former University College, Cambridge, to such an extent that in 1973 it, too, took his name. Sir Raymond Hoffenberg, the eminent endocrinologist, has been President of the Oxford Wolfson since 1985. Dr Jonathan Sacks, the Chief Rabbi, took time off after his studies at Caius, Cambridge, in the 1960s to find out if it was really possible to be religious and think at the same time. Having satisfied himself that it was, he now considers his years at Cambridge to have been 'the most influential time of my life'. Rabbi Julia Neuberger, the best-known figure in the Liberal branch of her faith, took an MA at Newnham (Fellow). Hugo Gryn, from Radio Four's *Moral Maze*, senior rabbi of the West London Synagogue, is another Cambridge alumnus, while Rabbi Lionel Blue, a former convener of the ecclesiastical court of the Reform synagogues of Great Britain, known for his gentle homilies in *Thought for the Day*, read history at Balliol. Lord Weidenfeld, the publisher, and Sir Isaiah Berlin, the philosopher, have each been elected fellows of All Souls; Lord Sieff, the elder statesman of Marks & Spencer, is an Honorary Fellow of his old college, Corpus Christi, Cambridge, and the Master of Balliol, no less, is the American geneticist and Nobel laureate, Professor Baruch Blumberg. Oy Vay! This is cultural assimilation of the highest order. To complete the picture, the Oxford Centre for Postgraduate Studies, the largest of its kind in Europe, has been established in a manor house just outside Oxford, with a faculty drawn mostly from college Fellows. The centre has a formidable board of governors and hopes to attract equally formidable endowments. It could have been sited in Walsall or Rochester, but the governors thought not. Oxford, they felt, had the right ring to it.

Islamic Britain has not so far come under the institutional sway of Oxbridge, but the chances are that this is simply because it is too recently established. According to Jan Morris, 'the saddest and loneliest grave in Oxford' is that of Abdulillah Azzam Abdullah Saleh al Mohdar, who died in 1963, aged 15. 'He is buried high in the cemetery at Headington, overlooking the towers of this Christian city, with his feet pointing to the east indeed, and the epitaph "God Bless Him", but 3,000 miles between him and Mecca.' In time, no doubt, he will be less lonely. *Living Islam*, an historical survey of the Muslim presence in England, appeared in 1993 from BBC Publications, written by Akbar Ahmed, a Cambridge academic, and Oxford equivalents are surely in preparation. Even so, it is likely to be some years before Islamic values hold a significant place at high table. Most British imams are first- or second-generation immigrants and have as a key concern the control of education by the mullahs, not the dons. Islamic fundamentalists will in the meantime have done nothing to endear themselves to the ancient universities by their treatment of Salman Rushdie (King's College) following the publication in 1988 of *The Satanic Verses*. The death sentence passed by the late Ayatollah Khomeini (an alumnus of Qom) on the hapless author of this supposedly blasphemous work was probably the first on a Varsity man, for reasons of heresy, since the heroic days of Latimer and Ridley and their close friend, Thomas Cranmer (Cambridge men, burned in Oxford). Fellow authors, and liberals of every persuasion, many of them from the Spires and Backs, have since rallied to Rushdie's cause, among them Tariq Ali, one of the first wave of British radicals of Islamic origin. Ali, naturally, is a fellow member of the Brotherhood, a former stalwart of the Oxford Union who, like Rushdie, looks and sounds the part. He has proved, if proof were needed, that revolutionary socialism, even if it is unwelcome at the mosque, continues to have a ready home in the cloisters.

Religious disputes have long punctuated academic life. Both Oxford and Cambridge have, after all, been governed by the Church for most of their history, and only last century did it become possible, by Act of Parliament, for dons to be lay persons or to marry. But though the Church and the universities were perforce close, relations were frequently strained. John Wycliffe, Oxford's leading scholar in medieval times – who named his city 'the vineyard of the Lord' – was driven out, along with his followers, for seeking to uphold the university's independence against a corrupt Church and State. A later generation of Oxford reformers conducted a famous debate on religious reform with the great Erasmus (also a frequent visitor to Cambridge), and it was Cranmer, Latimer, Tyndale and Coverdale, from the Other Place, who laid the foundations of true Anglicanism in response to the revolution ushered in by Luther. The tradition of disputation continued right through the Civil War. William Laud, Archbishop of Canterbury under Charles I, a High Church administrator so stern that he ended up losing his head to vengeful parliamentarians, had spent years as a don, first as President of St John's, then as Chancellor of the university. G. M. Trevelyan, in his *Shortened History of England*, is in no doubt that Laud's difficulties as Primate stemmed from his academic background. 'He treated broad England as he had been permitted to treat Oxford, but it is easier to trim a University to pattern than a nation of grown men.' Certainly, the Archbishop appears to have learned his intolerance while at Oxford. He once told the dramatist John Shirley that he could not allow him to become a priest because he had a mole on the side of his face. Shirley, while no doubt wishing he had a barefaced cheek himself, liked it less in Laud and took holy orders instead at Cambridge.

In the eighteenth century, with Oxford and Cambridge at their most decadent, it was Wesley who provided fresh impetus, and in the Victorian age, as an aesthetic and intellectual reaction to the increased influence of nonconformity and Low Church practices, came the Oxford Movement. Few English clerics, with the exception of Becket and the Tudor martyrs, have made as much impact as Newman. The vicar of St Mary's church, Oxford, he was a spellbinding orator, whose congregation regularly included the pick of the university, both undergraduates and dons. He felt that Anglicanism was in danger of severing its Catholic roots and, with his friends, John Keble, a priest and poet, and Edward Pusey, the Regius Professor of Hebrew, founded first the Anglo-Catholic Movement and then the Oxford Movement, aimed at re-establishing the paramountcy of ritual worship and practice and the pre-eminence of theology in Oxford's increasingly secular curriculum. Their *Tracts for the Times* were variously held to be visionary or scurrilous and had enormous importance for the development of the Church, in all its forms, in modern England.

The Oxford phenomenon, from small beginnings in the senior common room of Oriel College, quickly spread, culminating in Newman's reception into the Church of Rome in 1845 and, ultimately, his election as Cardinal in 1879. Many Anglicans were shocked by Newman's defection. Others were thrilled, including his friend, Henry Manning, of Balliol, who followed suit in 1851 and actually beat him to a red hat by four years. Not only did Newman's example hasten the demise of the regulations preventing Catholics and Jews from attending Oxbridge – and requiring all dons to be priests – but the blow he struck for High Church values is felt to this day, so that Pusey House and St Stephen's House are strongholds of Anglo-Catholicism, or 'bells and smells', and principal bulwarks against the acceptance of female ordination.

The presence of the Established Church is everywhere on view. Christ Church Cathedral is integral to the Oxford college that bears its name, and its Dean, appointed by the Crown, is also head of college. Magdalen maintains a celebrated choir and a Dean of Divinity, and all but a brace of the newest colleges have their own chapels, with appointed clergy.

The story at Cambridge, at any rate after the death of the Tudor martyrs, was less dramatic, but almost as integral to the life of the Church, whose worthies dominated its curriculum. In the seventeenth century, the Cambridge Platonists, definitive Fensmen, for some years enlivened, or rather mortified, the scene with their appeals for an end to materialism and a return to the stern moralism of Plato and Erasmus. They were not men to be trifled with. Their leader, Ralph Cudworth, Master successively of Clare College and Christ's College, published in 1678 what is surely the quintessential Cambridge opus, *The True Intellectual System of the Universe*, and there can be little doubt that he would expect it to be taken just as seriously today as he himself took it at the time.

Emmanuel College, a Platonist stronghold, built on the site of a thirteenth-century Dominican friary, was founded in 1583 by Sir Walter Mildmay, at the time Chancellor of the Exchequer to Queen Elizabeth I. His intention was clear-cut and impeccably

Cantabrigian: 'that it should be a seed-plot of learned men for the supply of the Church, and for the sending forth of as large a number as possible of those who shall instruct the people in the Christian faith.' For the next fifty years or so, the college was an exemplar of Low Church practices, and it suffered for this under Charles I, subsequently becoming Laudean in emphasis, with its chapel once more centred on the altar, not the pulpit. The modern college, with several exquisite buildings off St Andrew's Street and some of the prettiest gardens in Cambridge, is a gentle, tolerant kind of place – so tolerant, in fact, that its best known theologian, and Dean, the Rev. Don Cupitt, famously does not believe in God. Its Master, Lord St John of Fawsley (a graduate of Fitzwilliam, as well as of Christ Church and Yale), is meanwhile a patrician papist, who could never have shared so much as a tailor with Cromwell, and the chapel, rebuilt by Wren in 1668, is an exemplar of High Church orthodoxy.

The Rev. Brendan Clover, Emmanuel's chaplain, rejects the notion that Oxbridge has an iron grip on UK Anglicanism. 'It might look that way if you were to leaf through Crockford's, but I doubt very much it will be the same in twenty-five years' time.' He has faced difficulty, he says, in having some of his intending ordinands accepted by the Church selectors, and he suspects that the trend has begun to move against Oxbridge and away from intellectual Christianity. He acknowledges, however, that the pendulum has a long way to go. No fewer than three current diocesan bishops are Emmanuel men, and he himself passed his undergraduate years at nearby Gonville and Caius before taking holy orders at Cuddesdon College, Oxford.

Evolution, action and reaction continue. The mistaken belief following the abolition of the religious test that Church influence at Cambridge would soon diminish was countered by the foundation of Selwyn College in 1882. Named after George Selwyn, an early Anglican bishop in New Zealand, it was modelled on Keble, at Oxford, and still requires its Master to have taken holy orders. It was aimed at the rising middle class and has maintained, in the proper sense, a kind of classless appeal – though whether its undergraduates can best be characterized as 'combining sober living and high culture of the mind ... with Christian training', as the statutes lay down, is surely to be wondered at.

Show, in fact, as much as learning, is built into the fabric of Cambridge. King's College Chapel, Henry VI's elegantly vainglorious indulgence, with its exquisite fan-vaulted ceiling, rood screen and pencil-thin perpendicular windows, is the English Church at its most sublime. The enduring brilliance of the college choir, internationally renowned for its Christmas and Easter broadcasts but on song virtually every day during term time, adds immeasurably to the appeal, while Rubens's *Adoration of the Magi*, one of the artist's finest religious works, draws the eyes of worshippers inexorably to the high altar.

The Church is well aware of its debt to the two universities. In cathedrals from Durham to Wells, tombs and plaques proclaim the links. Bishops right up until the Stuarts used to move almost seamlessly from Oxford or Cambridge to the great offices of state, and the three-way spread of power, with the sovereign as head of the Church, seemed to them as natural as breathing. Lincoln Cathedral is typical. Its chapel of SS Peter and Paul is ostensibly dedicated to students everywhere. In practice, so far as English institutions of higher education are concerned, it is undergraduates from Merton, Exeter, Queen's, New, Christ Church and All Souls colleges at Oxford, and King's, St John's, Trinity and Sidney Sussex, Cambridge who are most remembered in prayers. Oh yes, and also the nearby Scunthorpe Technical College. (Presumably if that had not been included, the diocese would have been accused of élitism.)

Much that is wrong with the present state of the Faith in England does not, needless to say, derive from the Church's Oxbridge powerbase. The de-mythification of England is probably inexorable, and structural, and a tragedy in any case only to those who care about such things. Yet, as with the government of the country at large and its professions, the administration of the Church remains overwhelmingly in the hands of an Oxbridge mafia. They talk well and sonorously and, on great state occasions, play their assigned parts with distinction, as though minor players in a grand opera. Yet the fact remains that, between them, they have detonated an ecclesiastical neutron bomb, in which the churches have been left standing but the congregations have vanished. This does not please them, but they ignore it. In an age when anything goes has taken over from belief among the educated middle classes and R.E. has been replaced by pluralist studies, Church leaders, engaged, like the

Foreign Office, in administering decline, have covered their embarrassment at the loss each week of 1,500 of their flock with fine words that merely serve to confuse. There is hardly any divine observance left in the population. Most ordinary people regard vicars as bit-players at weddings and funerals and see bishops as bores in drag, cut off from real life by their ritual obscurantism. If the present hierarchy – a few notable exceptions aside – is still perceived to represent another world, that world is Oxbridge and flannel, not God and His revealed word. Such is the sum of the Church's latter-days' achievement as we approach the millennium.

One man who saw clearly, if archly, the way in which Anglicanism was tearing itself apart was Canon Gareth Bennett, an eminent Oxford theologian, who contributed an anonymous preface to Crockford's *Clerical Directory*, in 1987, heavily critical of the then Archbishop of Canterbury, Dr Robert Runcie, and was subsequently hounded to his death. Bennett, steeped in Oxford like a pickled egg in vinegar, had been embittered by his lack of preferment, and in his contribution to Crockford's recklessly offended against the first rule of Oxbridgean orthodoxy: don't mess in your own backyard.

The truth is [he wrote] that Anglicans have never been happy with questions which require them to set out a coherent doctrine . . . the various traditions or parties in the Church of England have always lived in a quite remarkable intellectual isolation from each other, and it is on the doctrine of the church that there has been the least meeting of minds . . . the liberal ascendancy has transformed the younger clergy. The number of ordinands from the Catholic and Evangelical traditions of Anglicanism has diminished and been replaced by men and women of a remarkable uniformity of outlook.

Bennett complained that too much of modern Anglican thinking was formed at Westcott House and Cuddesdon, and would obviously have preferred such a weight of influence to have been wielded instead by Pusey House and St Stephen's. Either way, however, the focus remains at Oxbridge, where undergraduates learn to talk, almost literally, with one voice and absorb a cultural ethic more unifying than mere belief, centred on 'decency', clubbability and keeping the show on the road. To the modern Anglican prelate, beset as he is by such vexed questions as paganism, poverty, divorce, abortion, women priests and overt homosexuality, what truly matters is holding fast to the central tenets of belief: croquet, Earl Grey, a good malt, Eights Week, civilized reticence and the knowledge that, surely, God is none other than the Master of Celestial College. Top-level debate within the Church, whether behind closed doors or in Synod, remains even more than at Westminster an extension of the Oxford and Cambridge Unions, faithfully reported each week in the *Church Times* (editor, Bernard Palmer, King's, Cambridge). It is clever and refined, occasionally sharp, but above all it is rooted in earthly concerns. The factions may draw apart, as with the women's issue, or they may unite, as on the need to pour further resources into the inner cities, but the terrestrial thread that joins the key players never quite breaks. It is an object lesson in class survival, and one in which the women, when they have completed their breakthrough, will no doubt play their part. Once the Church of England was said to be the Tory Party at prayer. It would be more accurate today to describe it as Oxbridge on its knees.

What makes the above critique personally awkward to advance, if not to sustain, is the fact that many of those in charge in the Church are self-evidently civilized and 'nice'. I have yet to meet a bishop or other leading clergyman I didn't like. Had I spoken with Tony Harvey, sub-dean of Westminster, or Harold Goodrich, Bishop of Worcester, I would almost certainly have been bowled over by their tolerance and impressed by their scholarship. The same, as it happens, goes for dons. They are not only clever, which is to be expected, but (usually) reasonable and unassuming, and invariably good-mannered.

One such is Jeremy Begby, Vice-Principal of Ridley Hall, Cambridge, which for many years after its foundation in 1881 was associated with evangelical Protestantism but now organizes 85 per cent of its teaching within the ecumenical framework of the Cambridge Federation of Theological Colleges. Begley, who also teaches undergraduates, agrees the the proximity and facilities of the university proper are undoubtedly an attraction to intending ordinands, just as Wycliffe College, Ridley's counterpart 'neath the Spires, is boosted by its links to Oxford. While valuing the work carried out within other academic institutions, he still accords a special place to the ancient pioneers. 'We are not saying that this approach is the only way, but it is true that we take our links with the university extremely seriously. They are of immense importance to us. The connection helps us to make sure that what we teach has intellectual integrity, and we also believe it important for ministerial formation.'

The most uncompromising defender of Oxbridgean values – and the most entertaining – is Father Philip Ursell, the Principal of Pusey House, Anglo-Catholicism's unofficial Central Office. Although standing four-square with the High Church traditionalists, who would rather go down clutching their incense than give in to a coeducational clergy and evangelical simplicities, he remains an individual of enormous charm and compassion, with a wicked sense of humour. What is slightly odd about his position is that he is not, strictly speaking, an Oxbridge man at all. He took his first degree at University College, Cardiff, and only won his Varsity spurs by becoming chaplain of Emmanuel, Cambridge (where he was Brendan Clover's predecessor). 'A Welshman coming to Oxford on the make, I suppose you'd call me.'

On issues of Church leadership, he does not mince his words. Seated in his office in St Giles, just up the road from where the Oxford Martyrs met their grisly end, he is uncompromising in his beliefs. He regards the longstanding clerical drift in Anglicanism as a disaster, and blames what he sees as the provincial character of the current leadership, personified by Dr Carey, for creating a situation in which the Church has lost all authority and sense of direction. 'Carey is an aberration – an experiment that hasn't worked', he declares. Then, employing the motto of Pusey House, he continues: 'The Lord is a God of knowledge, and Oxbridge has always given class to young people without background. It is a stimulating, privileged environment, in which those who have already arrived look after their own. This is not unusual. It works. The two universities have a unique concentration on religious administration and deliberately target Church organizations. The result is that decisions on Church appointments are often made here in the corridors – and the poor bastards from Hull don't get a look in.' He smiles to indicate the joke, but he's not finished yet. Instead, unabashed to the end, he goes on to quote a colleague, the Rev. Peter Southwell, chaplain of Queen's College, as confiding in him that it was important for an Archbishop of Canterbury to have been to the right school and Oxbridge, 'so that he can eat and talk properly at high table without feeling self-conscious'. He adds, unsurprisingly: 'I would support that.'

The good Father, for whom meritocracy is but the vestibule of privilege, approves heartily of what he claims to have been the decision of the Roman hierarchy to emulate the old Anglican Establishment by anchoring English Catholicism firmly to the ancient universities. 'Archbishop Cardinale, the former Apostolic delegate, was behind this move', he reveals. 'Ampleforth or Downside, then Oxbridge, has become an approved Establishment route, and Basil Hume's appointment as Cardinal was its central achievement, a great coup. St John Stevas [Lord St John of Fawsley] said that Hume was the epitome of an English archbishop, whereas Carey seemed like an old-fashioned Catholic – ignorant and a bully. And he was right.' There is a pause. 'Are you religious yourself? Or do you have doubts? You do? Well, you must learn to embrace doubt and still get down on your knees and pray. That's what is needed today. Scholarship and worship are complementary. They go hand in hand. If we forget that, we are lost.'

Such calisthenic Anglo-Catholicism is entirely absent from the mind of the very Rev. John Drury, the Dean (and head of house) of Christ Church, Oxford's grandest college. Drury is more discreet, less outspoken, than Ursell, more obviously emollient, yet the distance between them, on the university question at least, is slight. The Dean, now 57, began his higher education at Trinity Hall, Cambridge, where, according to his *Who's Who* entry, he achieved a First in his history tripos and then a 2:1 in theology. After ordination via Westcott House, Cambridge, he became a curate for three years, but immediately after that reverted to his true vocation by becoming chaplain of Downing College and then moving to Oxford to take up the chaplaincy and a fellowship at Exeter. Later still, having dallied with diocesan administration in Norwich and university teaching in America and the University of Sussex, he became the Dean of King's, Cambridge, and then, the ultimate accolade, Dean of Christ Church. What was it, I wondered, that had attracted him to the Church?

'I became a clergyman because I very much admired Robert Runcie, who was at that time Dean of Trinity Hall, and Owen Chadwick, the college chaplain [later Master of Selwyn and

Vice-Chancellor of Cambridge]. Dr Runcie was very influential. He was always organizing talks and was something of a whizz in ancient history.' And was this the reason for his enduring connection with the ancient universities? 'Well, of course, I did teach in Sussex for some time. I suppose, though, the answer is that in the Oxbridge context you get a Christian Church that is open to people and to ideas. It represents the true liberalism and pragmatism of the Church of England. It would be wrong to push it or exploit it – as sometimes happens with ambitious curates – but the fact is that the Church debates the faith in an Oxbridge kind of way. What is important is that you treat this fact as though it doesn't matter and just get on with the job.' And that job is? 'I take the sacraments. I preach. I keep to old-fashioned rituals. The cathedral, after all, is always there. Mainly, though, I am caught up in administration. Realistically, this is what takes up most of my time.'

Administration is not, alas, always as easy as it sounds. One of the more serious scandals within the Church in recent times has been the disastrous performance of its investment portfolio. During the property slump of the late 1980s and early '90s, the Church Commissioners managed to wipe £500 million off the value of assets. As it happens, only around half of the hapless men were Oxbridge, including Michael Alison MP (Wadham) and James Shelley (University College), but this gilded tendency, like its counterparts in Lloyd's, does not appear to have read the writing on the wall and lacked a Delphic touch at a difficult time. The bishops, meanwhile – Blessed are the pure in background for they shall see Sees – scarcely knew what was going on and, with the exception of the former Bishop of London, Dr Graham Leonard (Balliol; later Select Preacher to the University of Oxford and Honorary Fellow of Gonville and Caius), no more gave a lead on the cash front than on matters of the spirit.

Those seeking to divine an end to duopolistic preferment will take little heart from the intrigue surrounding the appointment of a new Bishop of Durham, to succeed David Jenkins. The next man in, we were quickly told, was 'almost certain to have a distinguished academic record' (code for you-know-where). Front runners were listed in *The Times* as Canon Geoffrey Rowell, chaplain of Keble College, Oxford (for the Anglo-Catholics); Stephen Sykes (St John's,

Cambridge), Bishop of Ely and one-time Regius Professor of Divinity at Cambridge (for the evangelicals); and John Polkinghorne (Trinity College, Cambridge), President of Queens' College, Cambridge and a former Cambridge Professor of Mathematical Physics (the 'imaginative' outsider). In the event, the successful candidate, confirmed by the Queen, acting on the advice of the Prime Minister, acting on the advice of the Crown Appointments Commission and the Secretary for Ecclesiastical Patronage, turned out to be Michael Turnbull, previously the Bishop of Rochester. Turnbull is an evangelical and a former chief secretary of the Church Army, and is known to believe in God. He is also an MA of Keble College, Oxford. George Carey's reign at Canterbury does not mean an end to the Oxbridge domination of the House of Bishops any more than John Major's arrival in Downing Street heralded a Redbrick era in government. The Archbishop, born in the East End of London, is more densely surrounded by natives of Oxbridge than Custer was by Indians at the Little Big Horn. His chief of staff, John Yates, known as the Bishop of Lambeth, is a Jesus man, from Cambridge. Andrew Purkis, his secretary for public affairs, holds an Oxford D. Phil. Hector McLean, secretary of the C. of E. Crown Appointments Commission and appointments secretary to both Canterbury and York, is a graduate of Pembroke, Cambridge, and a member of the United Oxford and Cambridge University Club. Finally, Carey's own suffragan in Canterbury, the Bishop of Dover, Richard Llewellin, is a Fitzwilliamite and was ordained at Westcott House, the very seminary where Robert Runcie and John Habgood were once principals.

The parallel with Major is almost too strong. Writing in *The Church of England – A Portrait* (Simon & Schuster, 1993), Michael De-La-Noy, a former Lambeth press secretary, reflects on the difference between the present Archbishop of Canterbury and his immediate predecessors. 'Michael Ramsey', he observes, had 'an instantly recognizable donnish humour'; Donald Coggan 'had two first-class degrees' (both Oxbridge); Runcie had 'wit' and 'basic profundity'. And the current man? 'Perhaps Dr Carey finds difficulty expressing, either in writing or verbally, the beliefs he holds.' He 'will always conscientiously do the very best he can, but ... his best may not prove good enough.' Was ever a servant of God more damned with faint praise? The runes have been cast. When the grander prince-bishops have resolved their present quarrels, or grown weary of them, poor George Carey will leave to make way for his 'betters'. Indeed, he has already announced that he is to take early retirement. Anglicanism may, famously, be a broad church; it still rests firmly on two pillars.

CHAPTER FOURTEEN

JAM TOMORROW

CRITICIZING OXFORD AND CAMBRIDGE IS like coming up with a new slant on Shakespeare. Those who attempt it are walking on eggs. So deeply ingrained is the pair's academic tyranny on our national psyche that, in a curious way, it has become invisible. Everyone knows that the two enjoy an unjustified level of dominion; few discuss the fact. It is as though there is nothing to be done and we may as well get on with clearing the debris from more deprived areas of Britain's slum economy. Why fix something that isn't broken? people ask. The conventional view, as put, for example, by Jan Morris, is to say that the twin universities, for all their foibles, are an inestimable part of our shared heritage and we should be damned grateful they are there at all. More objective commentators, like Anthony Sampson and Jeremy Paxman, authors respectively of *The Anatomy of Britain* and *Friends in High Places*, shake their locks and express the hope that the dual dominance might somehow be diluted in the future. But there is little obvious conviction behind their words. In the latest, revised edition of his classic work, published in 1992, Sampson (Christ Church, Oxford, lest it be forgotten) concludes that 'the more the old universities are opened up to comprehensives and day schools, the more they cultivate their privilege'. Later, while suggesting that Varsity influence in industry and finance might actually be fading, he observes: 'The faster the majority of universities expand, the more they contrast with the two ancient cities, which stand like enchanted islands in the midst of storms.' Paxman, with seeming approval, quotes the director-general of the Institute of Directors, Peter Morgan (Trinity College, Cambridge), lambasting 'dons caught in a timewarp', and tries conscientiously to be critical of Oxbridge. Alas, he undoes his efforts with a last, Freudian slip. 'Increasingly', he observes, 'the difference between the two universities are less significant than the similarities, and the distinctions are more between Oxbridge and the rest of higher education:

Both have had to work hard to combat the image of braying frivolity beloved not only by the popular press but by the small, most privileged sector of the undergraduate body. Precisely because they appear to belong to a gilded world in which youth is put on first-name terms with influence, they are consciously avoided by many who might easily pass the entrance requirements. But once inside, the cosiness, the seriousness with which frivolous pursuits are taken, the brittle common room manner, provide the ideal orientation for Westminster or Whitehall.

Paxman (an Exhibitioner at St Catharine's, Cambridge, at the end of the 1960s) predicts a gradual decline in Oxbridge influence beyond the millennium. Nevertheless, a natural oligarch, from his arched eyebrows to his infinitely expressive fingertips, he cannot help feeling that his own peer group from the quads and courts may have something special about it after all. Writing of the fact that the fast stream of the Civil Service is still more than half occupied by Oxbridge products, he reflects: 'It is . . . a disproportionately large number, but when the two universities are attracting a disproportionate number of the best students, it would be perverse to try to manipulate the selection process against them.' So much for his view, quoted earlier, that 'many' outsiders 'might easily pass the entrance requirements.'

Other social pundits seem blithely unaware of the institutional imbalance and perceive criticism of the Oxbridge model as mere jealousy and ignorance. Lord Annan, living, like Lord Franks before him, in a rarefied world of *grands décisionaires, bien pensants* and *mentalités*, is, for all his manifest wisdom and decency, hopelessly captivated. He shows, according to Robert Anderson, in *Universities and Elites* (Macmillan, 1992), 'how the academic dynasties of re-formed Oxbridge, linked by marriage and kinship, integrated the university world into other parts of the political and public service élite'. But Franks and Annan grew up in a different age. Others have no such excuse. In *Whitehall* (Secker & Warburg, 1989), an exhaustive study of the modern Civil Service, Peter Hennessy, a product of St John's, Cambridge and still just forty-seven, shows

that Annan's patrician attitudes have been passed on safely to the
next generation. He joins Paxman (forty-three) in seeing the twin
universities' grasp on government as not something to be 'unduly'
worried about. Yet, this is strange. For in an article for the spring,
1992 issue of *Cam*, the Cambridge alumni magazine, he demon-
strates that he understands only too well what is really going on
behind the glamour:

Each time we create a new set of institutions intended (rightly) to be
different from Oxford and Cambridge, with sometimes more prosaic but
equally vital purposes – whether they be the post-Robbins universities in
the 1960s or the polytechnics of the 1970s – a slow, unacknowledged
process of status creep gets underway. It is almost as if the original DNA
of the British university system – monasteries with a library attached, i.e.
Oxford and Cambridge – remains so potent a genetic code that all
successor institutions are marked by its characteristics. Could it be that
this powerful atavism explains why it is so much easier for colleges to
touch their alumni for funds for a new library than for any other kind of
capital development? It is a painful, almost heretical thing to say for
someone like me who adores the place in general and his old college in
particular, but national higher education policy can only succeed if policy-
makers, funders and course designers alike cast from their minds the
memory of those shimmering success stories on the banks of the Cam or
the Cherwell.

Quite so – and well expressed. Where once there was Oxford and
Cambridge and then the rest, now we have Oxbridge, the established
Redbricks, led by Bristol and Durham, and, last, and very much
bringing up the rear, the former polys. It is an irony that the system
should now be complete in English eyes: upper class, middle class
and working class ('I know my place'). Hennessy, however, for all
his insight, is not always blessed with the ruthless objectivity he
seems to require of others. As far as the Establishment is concerned,
in *The Great and The Good*, published in 1986 by the Policy Studies
Institute, he makes not one single mention of Oxbridge, even
though at least two out of every three of those whose contributions
he discusses in its pages went to one or other of the two universities,
and sometimes both. The preface to his slim volume acknowledges
the help given to him by twenty-four professionals while carrying

out his researches or in having them broadcast on Radio Three. Of these (excepting two whose education is not recorded), no fewer than sixteen were Oxbridge – a hit rate of 70 per cent – including one former Vice Chancellor and two heads of house. We should not be surprised, therefore, when Hennessy tells us that he enjoyed, 'even relished' his own time at Cambridge, in the late 1960s. He has profited from it to this day.

A more dispassionate point of view is advanced by Anderson, a specialist in education and opportunity. Anderson's comprehensive critique of Britain's university system looks back on the Oxbridge model and sets it against successive creations, including the civics, the Scottish universities and others, up to the 1960s. Dealing with the nineteenth century, he concludes that 'behind the stubborn defence of the privileges of Oxford and Cambridge lay the persisting ideal of a national élite with common values and experience'. An Oxford degree during this long period 'had well-understood social advantage, but otherwise formal graduation had little career value, and university education remained ill-defined and not clearly distinguished from secondary schooling.' The great public schools were for many years dominated by the opinions of Thomas Arnold, as prescriptive in his way as St Benedict in the religious life of the Middle Ages. Oxbridge, at the same time, was under the sway of Benjamin Jowett, the archetypal Master of Balliol. Between them, these two established the model that was to take Britain into the twentieth century, and, so long as the path they chose was the Appian Way, no one dared to cross them. 'Only when British history ceased to be regarded as a success story', writes Anderson, 'was a hostile spotlight turned on the phenomenon.'

That spotlight has been trained now for fifty years. Between 1900 and 1950, the great civics grew in size and complexity. They went through their period of Oxbridgean deification and slowly came out the other side. In the 1960s, they were joined by the 'new' universities, which were held, wrongly, to constitute a complete break with the past, and then, over the next thirty years, by the polytechnics and institutes of higher education. Along the road, the emphasis has shifted, gradually but inexorably, away from philosophical inquiry and towards such practical pursuits as applied science and technology, modern languages and business studies. The original duo, in their ivory towers, responded to the changes afoot at varying speed. Cambridge, by application of its collective mind, rapidly became one of the greatest scientific powerhouses of the world, particularly in physics, but made little money out of its genius owing to a fatal lack of commitment to market economics that is only now being addressed. Oxford, meanwhile, preferring the limelight to the spotlight, continued for years to concentrate on the humanities, especially history, philosophy, law and the classics, and its current high reputation in science has been hard-won and made possible mainly by the generosity of alumni and huge industrial corporations. Medicine has, of course, been studied at both places for many centuries, and there is no doubting the quality of the research or of the graduates produced. Yet London (so long as the effects of government cuts can be resisted), Edinburgh, and even Belfast, have equivalent status in the field. Here, too, the market made a late appearance. (Oxford, it should be remembered, was the university in which penicillin was discovered and then sold off to America for next-to-nothing as of no obvious value. Engineering, a series of disciplines in which both now excel, alongside Imperial College, Warwick and Leeds, was, by contrast, a latecomer. Pioneers, like Professor Alec Broers at Cambridge, would have been looked down upon as dull plodders a generation ago. In languages, other than Latin and Greek, the two are probably above average, no more, in a crowded market, and appear to find it difficult not to surround the study of how, say, German or Russian are written and spoken with philosophy, phonetics and ancient history. Business management, as a cerebral, yet practical pursuit, has arrived in Oxbridge last of all, and only now are the pair coming to terms with the lucrative world of the MBA. No one should be surprised by this. Dons have run Oxford and Cambridge for centuries and have always seen decision-making as an essentially amateur activity, to be fitted in between tutorials. Only now is reality impinging.

What is clear is that all too often the Old Firm have been dragged into the modern world by developments elsewhere. If they have responded effectively, indeed impressively, to the need for change, only rarely have they been pacemakers. And always, when investment has been required to make change possible or to enable them to catch up and surpass their rivals, they have paraded themselves as exceptional, glamorous and uniquely deserving. Oxford and Cambridge prey shamelessly on the public's perception of them as something apart, in a world of their own. Simultaneously, their networks, as intricate as a spider's web, ensure that they are taken at their own estimation. The result, in the dawn of the millennium, is that the duo, though reduced in their overall impact on affairs, are as tightly knit and self-regarding as ever, and as cosily assured of their success.

Ever since the Beveridge Report, successive British governments have promised greater equality of opportunity and an end to privilege as the prerogative of the ruling class. The only thing is, it doesn't happen. Jam tomorrow has been the conservative assurance of the Establishment for generations. In the 1960s, we were told that Britain was undergoing fundamental change that would result in a more just and equable society – and in a way it was. Labour's Oxbridge Government, under Harold Wilson – a man so steeped in Varsity life that he even got married wearing his academic robes – abolished the grammar schools at a stroke, and replaced them with the flawed and chronically underfunded comprehensives that have done more to promote private education among the middle classes than any other piece of legislation in history. Out with the old and in with the new was the slogan for a generation. The new universities, presented by staff and students alike as liberal wonderlands, in which drugs were tolerated and received wisdom was turned on its head, began to take a hold on popular imagination. Oxford and Cambridge, inviolate for centuries, found that, for the first time, they had a fight on their hands for the cream of the nation's youth. It was a phenomenon, and like most phenomena it didn't last. By the end of the seventies, the concrete had begun to rot in the various National Theatre look-alike campuses, and the vogue they had enjoyed began similarly to crumble. The ancient duo, drawing on their considerable reserves of experience and self-esteem, reasserted themselves in revised form, introducing the more meritocratic entrance procedures that, with alterations, persist to this day. It was a shrewd response, assisted by the inadequacies of their rivals, and quickly restored them to their accustomed dominance. Today, with occasional nods in the direction of London and elsewhere, the Establishment is once more substantially reliant on Oxford and

Cambridge as the twin founts of power and influence, and the concentration of effort by the duo's administrators has been on making their élitist construct more accessible, rather than allying it to the mainstream. The resultant vehicle is, it is true, less of an exclusive landau, more an elegantly appointed omnibus, with leather trimming and polished wooden facia. But its direction remains unchanged: Whitehall, Westminster and the Law Courts, via Bedford Square, Fleet Street and Broadcasting House. It is not *admission* to Oxbridge that lies at the heart of the problem. That issue has long since been addressed. What remains to be tackled is the easy passage to power and influence of Oxbridge graduates. They are offered five-star treatment while most of their rivals have to make do with bed and breakfast. Even where they *are* good, they are no better than the best of the rest, only better treated. It is the public perception of the *other* universities that, above all else, has to be altered, so that their top graduates can have equal status with those from the Isis and the Cam. This should not be impossible. It is, after all, already a reality within the natural meritocracy of science and engineering. To achieve a First in a provincial university that has too few teachers, and perhaps conducts its business from run-down, over-subscribed facilities, situated behind an abandoned factory, must be at least as good as doing the same at Oxbridge, where the best of everything is laid on with a trowel and the servants call you 'sir'.

Of the many mistakes and misjudgements that can be laid at the feet of Britain's governing class in the course of this century, one of the most serious is that 'clever' people should, in the main, be trained as administrators, not doers. Oxbridge has played a major part in this. The belief is that intelligence corresponds to the suave and confident use of language. A 'bright' young man or woman is reckoned to be able to talk in a loud voice in the right accent and to be able, effortlessly, to instil respect on the part of inferiors. A general education, strong on logic and reasoning, is given to such as these while they are up at Oxford or Cambridge. They become classicists, or PPE-ists or historians, and then, with their minds linked in sequence and their initiative all-but extinguished, they are handed over to the professions, in which they then rise quickly to the top.

Scientists, engineers, medics and linguists are an obvious exception to this, but, as we have seen, Oxbridge scientists are known more for their application of pure thought than for their contribution to the national economy. There is no harm in this. Pure science is vital and needs to be encouraged. Yet it is noticeable that while 'vocational' universities, like John Moores, Brunel or Bournemouth, are patronized as mere providers of technologists, the Cavendish at Cambridge and the Clarendon at Oxford are revered as though they were the cathedrals of British scientific thought. The fact is that both approaches have their merits and are equally deserving of respect. There is no doubt, however, that, with the Pacific Rim nations rising rapidly in the firmament and the United States, Germany and France fighting hard to retain their share of technological supremacy, it is a more practical, down-to-earth approach to science that is required in our universities, breeding the kind of specialists who can work with distinction for Rolls-Royce, British Aerospace, Pilkingtons, Westland and other leading-edge producers.

There are at Oxford and Cambridge teams of world-beating scientists who, with help from industry, apply themselves on a full-time basis to problem-solving. These are the dons and their most-favoured postgraduate researchers. Many undergraduates, however, take their degrees and then look for soft jobs in the civil service, the City, accountancy or the law. Only a minority actually spend their careers in industrial laboratories or among machinery. This 'lesser' role is left to the 'lesser' universities. Thus, while the boardrooms and capital investment houses are stuffed with well-paid Oxbridge alumni, the factory floors are kept running by the Redbrick reserves, who may not speak in appropriate tones to impress their betters but at least know a thing or two about widgets.

It is the mono-culture at work: the concept of an in-bred intelligentsia, essentially conservative and self-regarding, having dominion over a beta class of technocrats and clerics who, in turn, lord it over the sweating masses. One does not have to be a socialist for this interpetation of our recent history to make sense. One has only to look at the Georgian and Early Victorian homes of the governing class (Oxbridge), the suburban semis of the line-managers (Redbrick) and the tower blocks and little boxes of the workers (comprehensively ill-educated).

In theory, there is considerable respect for the sort of social and educational flexibility that alone can maximize our nation's potential. In practice, at least as far as the ancient universities are concerned, the main flexibility shown is in the area of admissions.

What is most difficult of all to eradicate is the feeling that all this is part of the natural order of things. Tony Smith, president of Magdalen College, Oxford, believes that the only areas of British life that continue to work well are those – the BBC, the City, Parliament, Whitehall – controlled by Oxbridge. 'When you look at the industries that have declined, you feel that if they had been in the hands of Oxbridge graduates they might have rescued them.' So why weren't they? 'Ah, this is a real problem. Society continues to be prejudiced against business and commerce.' And who controls society? 'Well, Oxbridge, I suppose . . .'

So where do we go from here? I have stressed again and again my admiration for the academic achievements of Oxford and Cambridge. The two universities have long and remarkable histories and a unique architecture and ambience that inspire both reverence and affection in those lucky enough to study there or who remain as dons. The quality of teaching is frequently high, provided by two of the most distinguished groups of thinkers and researchers in the country, and the intimacy of the tutorial and supervision systems in which this teaching is chiefly delivered is widely admired. Yet it cannot continue to be the case that, having gained once, by the fact of admission, graduates of Oxbridge should go on gaining in perpetuity, as though the porter's lodge leading into the splendid intimacy of college life on a fresher's first day is, on another level, the grand entrance to professional preferment and the marbled portico of the Establishment. For too long, the easy assumption has been that the 'best people' go to the dynamic duo. More than that, there is an unspoken conspiracy between those who are both bright and conventionally ambitious (with an implicit belief in networks and establishments), who hope to congregate with others of their kind, and dons from the ancient universities, who wish to preserve their funding, status and way of life for ever. The shared objective is to concentrate a self-selected group of the brightest and the best at Oxbridge and then to send them out as emissaries of their generation. Alumni benefit from the lifestyle and mores of Oxbridge.

They acquire important contacts throughout an entire range of English – and European – society. The universities benefit from being seen as unique and essential institutions of learning, without which this country would be intellectually impoverished. The compact is a constant, underlying refrain among staff and students, echoed in large areas of English society, and, when projected into the future, has the hallmark of a self-fulfilling prophecy. To reject this stance is not to reject excellence. High standards ought always to be encouraged. To object to donnish dominion is not to deny the ancient universities their natural academic pre-eminence. They have that anyway. Rather, the nation as a whole, including its employers, must learn to cherish virtue, dedication and ability as rare qualities, *wherever they are found*, and not go on for ever placing one pre-destined group on a pedestal, leaving the rest either to stare upwards at them in a mixture of wonder, frustration and rage or else, worse, unaware that anything untoward has happened.

The present system is not just unfair, it is almost criminally wasteful. We now have 123 universities in Britain, including the separate colleges of London and Wales and the former polytechnics. Some are struggling. Some may never quite make it. Others, though, are splendid institutions, which have kept the light of learning aflame often in the most difficult of circumstances but which in socio-political terms are still not accorded the recognition they deserve. Employers, seeking the leaders of tomorrow, have for years short-circuited the weary business of selection by placing too much reliance on the Oxbridge gene pool. Today, with more graduates than ever jostling for position, it would be impossible for Oxbridge to cream off all the best jobs, even in its traditional core professions. Yet, perversely, the proud pair, and all they stand for, have in our 'meritocratic' age come to be valued even more than before, so that the modern 'Milk Round' frequently excludes many universities altogether, concentrating instead on its traditional favourites. Such generic nepotism is as contemptible as it is lazy. By all means, let young people continue to look to the dreaming spires. And if they get there, good luck to them. They have probably worked hard and are clever and deserve their three years in the sun. But the same sun should shine just as warmly on Manchester, Newcastle, Southampton, Canterbury and all the other towns and cities where scholarship has put down roots. There are, as we have seen, departments beyond Oxbridge providing first-class teaching in every conceivable area, where postgraduate research traditions are frequently second to none. Industry and academia have been forced to accept this. It must now be embraced actively by government and the Establishment. Britain in future should be guided, regulated and encouraged by a true cross-section of its people, not by a self-perpetuating élite, however open their competitions for admission. Graduates from the 121 deserve to be taken on trust, not just as technicians and middle managers, but as potential leaders of society, as good as anyone. It should not be one in a hundred of them who rises to the top of the professional ladder. It should be as many as have the qualifications, and the nerve, to justify their place. They have proved themselves over and over again. They deserve, as a result, equal treatment and public respect – and the sooner our professional masters, and their many allies operating the deference syndrome, acknowledge the fact, the sooner this country can begin to reassert itself both economically and in the councils of the world. It is equally, of course, incumbent upon the 'lesser' universities to give up the sense of inferiority with which so many of them are stamped. They must begin to demand, not simply apply for, their fair share of top posts, so that new generations of QCs, editors, judges, bishops and the rest are not confined to just two places of origin, however glorious, but are divided among the nation. Be assured, if they don't act on their own behalf, no one else will. They must, like the inner core of the London federation – a grouping which shows all the signs of wishing to establish a new triopoly of privilege – stand up for themselves more and proclaim their civic virtues from the rooftops. It was the Bard from Stratford Grammar who, as ever, got it right. 'It is not in our stars, dear Brutus, but in ourselves that we are underlings.' Oxford and Cambridge form a valued part of Britain's heritage which is not going to disappear overnight, or even over the centuries. Nor should it. But they do not any longer comprise, or define, our national intellectual achievement. It is time for Middle England to move at last to centre-stage.

INDEX

Friends of Cambridge University 210
funding 209–11, 215–24
law faculty 267
C19th attitudes to women 171–2
overseas students 12–14, 205–6, 210
proportion of women's Firsts 178–80
ratio of applications to places 161
tourist trade 57–8
underperformance of women 178–83
women in senior posts 175–6
women's colleges 169–70
Cambridge Union 99, 108, 142
Cambridge Commonwealth Trust 210
Cambridge Examining Board 210
Cambridge Footlights Society, see Foot-
lights Society
Cambridge Overseas Trust 210
Cambridge Platonists 307
Cameron, Averil 175
Campaign for Cambridge University
205, 215, 218
Campaign for Oxford 205, 211, 216–18,
253
Campbell, Juliet 170
Campbell-Lamerton, Lt. Col. Mike 266
Campion Hall 301
Carey, Dr George, Archbishop of
Canterbury 298, 312, 313, 315–16
Carrot, Jasper 285
Carter, Sir Charles 255
Carter, Peter 244–6
Carter-Ruck, Peter 269
Casey, John 131
Castle, Barbara 181, 188
Cavendish Laboratory 109, 130, 324
Centre for Protein Engineering, Cam-
bridge 211
Chadwick, Sir James 124
Chalker, Lynda 228
Chapman, Graham 198, 283
Chariots of Fire 196
Chataway, Christopher 196
Checkland, Michael 280
Cheshunt College 303
Chilcot, John 236
Chorley, Lord 243

Christ Church 159–60, 307
Church of England, Oxbridge and 43,
298–300, 305–16
malaise in 309–16
Churchill College 128–31, 221
civil service, Oxbridge graduates in
37–9, 232–41, 241–50
reform of recruitment policy 234–5,
238–41
Foreign and Commonwealth Office
241–50
Clark, Alan 258
Clark, Christopher 137
Clark, Jonathan 141
Clarke, Charles 230
Clarke, John 130
Clarke, Kenneth 15–16, 258
class system, Oxbridge and 48–52
Cleese, John 198, 283
Clinton, Bill 12, 253
Clothier, Sir Cecil 255
Clough, Anne 169
Clover, Rev. Brendan 308
Coggan, Dr Donald 298
Coleridge, David 273
Coles, Sir John 241
college finances 219–24
college structure and politics 7, 123–41,
221–4
comedy 44, 197–203, 283–6
comprehensive schools, jaundiced view
of 51, 322
Condon, Paul 255
Connell, Sir Michael 256
Conservative Party, Oxbridge graduates
in 36–7, 255–9
Conway, Martin 128
Cook, Peter 198
Cook, Robin 230
Cooksey, David 273
Cooper, Sir Frank 254
Corby, Ian 145–6
Couve de Murville, Maurice, Arch-
bishop of Birmingham 302
Cowling, Maurice 227
Crick, Francis 108–9, 111